W9-CQC-859

Grassland, Forest, and Historical Settlement

Frontier history usually focuses on personalities and events; the shaping forces of geography, climate and culture too often get short shrift. This inaugural volume in the Studies in North American Archaeology series demonstrates the immense contribution anthropologists can make to our understanding of frontier settlement.

The authors present the results of an analysis of the development of the central Salt River valley in northeast Missouri between 1818 and 1850. Undertaken as part of the Cannon Reservoir Human Ecology Project, the archaeological-geographical work covered 65,000 acres that will be inundated on completion of Cannon Dam and was coordinated with archival and documentary research covering an area of over 440 square miles.

Taking account of the myriad processes that led to specific adaptations, the authors examine—at the levels of region, community, farmstead, and household—the influence of physical and cultural factors on changing patterns of settlement. Of particular interest are such features as household composition, subsistence strategies, formal and functional aspects of residence, material goods, and the development of trade and service centers. In addition, the study employs a three-stage model of rural settlement to explore how a frontier population is affected by colonization, spread, and competition, and how each of these processes yields a predictable response in spatial organization.

Michael J. O'Brien is an assistant professor of anthropology at the University of Missouri-Columbia. His collaborators are Jacqueline A. Ferguson and William M. Selby, graduate students in the Department of Anthropology, University of Missouri-Columbia; Dennis E. Lewarch, a graduate student at the University of Washington; Chad K. McDaniel, an assistant professor of anthropology at the University of New Mexico; Robert E. Warren, a research archaeologist in the Department of Anthropology, University of Missouri-Columbia; and Lynn M. Snyder, a research archaeologist in the Department of Anthropology, University of Nebraska-Lincoln.

Studies in North American Archaeology
General Editor
W. Raymond Wood

GRASSLAND, FOREST, AND HISTORICAL SETTLEMENT

**An Analysis
of Dynamics
in Northeast
Missouri**

Michael J. O'Brien

With contributions by
Jacqueline A. Ferguson
Dennis E. Lewarch
Chad K. McDaniel
William M. Selby
Lynn M. Snyder
Robert E. Warren

*University of
Nebraska Press
Lincoln
and London*

Copyright 1984 by the University of Nebraska Press
All rights reserved
Manufactured in the United States of America

The paper in this book meets the guidelines for permanence and durability of
the Committee on Production Guidelines for Book Longevity of the Council
on Library Resources.

Library of Congress Cataloging in Publication Data
O'Brien, Michael J. (Michael John), 1950–
  Grassland, forest, and historical settlement.
  (North American archaeology series)
  Includes bibliographical references and index.
  1. Human ecology—Missouri—Salt River Valley—History.
2. Land settlement patterns—Missouri—Salt River Valley
—History. 3. Frontier and pioneer life—Missouri—
Salt River Valley. 4. Salt River Valley (Mo.)—Antiquities.
5. Missouri—Antiquities. 6. Clarence Cannon
Reservoir (Mo.) I. Title. II. Series
GF504.M8Q27   1984   304.2'09778   84–3660
ISBN 0-8032-3551-8 (alk. paper)

Contents

Figures

Tables

Preface

To the small band of families arriving in 1819, the Salt River valley of northeast Missouri must have appeared similar to the Bluegrass region of Kentucky they had recently left. In the uplands were large expanses of prairie grass dotted with islands of hardwood forests. Nearer the river and its tributaries the prairie abutted moderate to dense stands of timber that in most places continued unabated downslope to permanent sources of water. Game was bountiful, and the timber would provide ample building material for temporary housing until more time could be expended on permanent structures. Land was plentiful and fairly inexpensive relative to the rising prices back in Kentucky. Given a good year, the parcels of land recently purchased would supply the basic subsistence needs of the group. If these initial colonists could gain a foothold in this new land, they could soon send for relatives and friends back East.

As we show in the pages that follow, these pioneer settlers did establish themselves in this new but not totally unfamiliar environment, and within a short time relatives, friends, and others from the Bluegrass and surrounding regions of Kentucky and Tennessee began immigrating to the area in increasing numbers. Their success in colonizing the region was remarkable, and by the end of the 1820s established communities dotted the landscape. Within a few more years, commercial centers sprang up in several areas, and the inhabitants no longer were completely dependent on centers several days' journey to the east. During this early period, local governing bodies were formed, political subdivisions were created to assist internal government, and improved roads were constructed to link the widely scattered communities. By 1840 the region had ceased to be a frontier.

The frontier development of the central Salt River valley is the subject of this book. Research on Euro-American settlement of the region was conducted as part of the Cannon Reservoir Human Ecology Project, sponsored by the St. Louis District of the United States Corps of Engineers. Research centered on that portion of the Salt River valley to be inundated by the Clarence Cannon Dam and Mark Twain Lake. The project, parts of which are ongoing, is an interdisciplinary research program investigating interactions between man and environment on the southern fringes of the midcontinental Prairie Peninsula, a region characterized as a complex mosaic of grassland and forest biomes. The project focuses on both prehistoric and historical time frames and employs complementary techniques to understand how cultures changed through time across the region. On a broader scale, the results of the Cannon Project are important for maintaining a balanced view of cultural trends across the greater midwestern United States.

It is important to point out that the trends in frontier settlement and regional development documented here have not been analyzed from a strictly historical point of view. While portions of the volume necessarily deal with the development of the region from a historical perspective, the emphasis is on understanding various processes that shaped the region during the frontier period. In other words, our interest is not simply in documenting that culture change took place, but rather in investigating the processes behind the change. Our general approach to the analysis of frontier settlement of the central Salt River valley is derived from anthropology, settlement geography, and historical analysis. Contributors to the volume are anthropologists by profession, and we naturally bring with us the predilections attendant on the discipline. However, these predilections have been tempered by advances in method and theory made by settlement geographers and historians involved in frontier settlement analysis.

We believe that the work presented here—especially the formulation of a synthetic model of frontier settlement and the testing of its implications— represents a significant advance in the study of the American frontier. This book should be of interest not only to anthropologists, but to geographers, historians, and ecologists as well. Since the project grew out of an attempt to provide a theoretical grounding for the archaeological examination of early-nineteenth-century farmsteads, it should also interest archaeologists concerned with the Euro-American period.

The volume is organized around four levels of analysis: the region, the community, the farmstead, and the household. Cutting across each level is our assessment of the effect that physical and cultural dimensions had on frontier settlement. Chapter 1, Background and Approach, is an introduction to the Cannon Project. It defines the objectives and goals of the project, describes the project area, presents a brief history of work in the area, and discusses the synthetic approach used to generate and organize the data.

Chapter 2, A Model of Frontier Settlement, presents a theory of rural settlement location and attendant spatial correlates, discusses various cultural and physical factors that can influence settlement within, and expansion of, the biotope, and integrates these topics into a model of frontier settlement.

Chapter 3, The Roots of Frontier Expansion, examines frontier settlement in several areas of the trans-Appalachian West, with particular attention given to the Bluegrass region of Kentucky and the Boonslick region of central Missouri. Topics discussed relative to each area include the physical environment, land selection relative to environmental variables, the cultural environment, the development of regional centers, and the economic growth of the region.

Chapter 4, The Physical Environment: A Context for Frontier Settlement, describes the physical setting of the project area, emphasizing dimensions of the physical environment that may have been of particular importance to locational and land-use decisions of early-nineteenth-century Euro-American agriculturists. These dimensions are components of a model of the regional environment used in later chapters as a background for assessing changing physical dimensions of the human niche during the period of frontier settlement.

Chapter 5, General Patterns of Settlement and Growth in the Central Salt River Valley, discusses patterns of frontier settlement and expansion that occurred during six periods between 1818 and 1858. Within this context the chapter focuses on the founding of early settlement clusters across the region, the origins of commercial centers, and the development of transportation networks. Also examined are patterns in land entry exhibited by three classes of entrants: residents, nonresidents, and eastern speculators.

Chapter 6, Environmental Dimensions of Settlement, examines in detail patterns of land entry in a 56 square mile portion of the project area. A multivariate approach is used to isolate physical and cultural variables that correlate highly with tracts of land entered during four periods between 1818 and 1855.

Chapter 7, Social Dimensions of Settlement, focuses specifically on the social dimensions of settlement in an attempt to understand the processes that brought about aggregated settlement. Three dimensions are examined, including kinship and intermarriage, commonality of origin, and religious affiliation. These dimensions are analyzed from the point of view of relationships established in various source areas before immigration and after settlement in the project area.

Chapter 8, The Built Environment, examines farmsteads and their component parts from the standpoint of composition, spatial organization, and growth. Discussed in considerable detail are residential structures, especially one- and two-room log houses.

Chapter 9, The Frontier Household, analyzes various aspects of the rural household and farmstead to determine how closely the cultural and agricultural patterns observed among households in the project area correlate with the panregional tradition known as upper South culture. Topics covered include the upper South cultural system, household composition and size, wealth and status, agricultural production, material remains, and subsistence practices.

Chapter 10, Concluding Remarks, presents a set of conclusions regarding cultural development in the project area during the frontier period, based on the results of testing certain implications of the settlement model.

The Cannon Reservoir Human Ecology Project was funded by the St. Louis District of the United States Army Corps of Engineers, under contract with the Board of Regents, University of Nebraska–Lincoln. We acknowledge the assistance of persons connected with the Corps of Engineers who helped us through the bureaucratic hurdles connected with a large-scale project the size of Cannon. At one time (about 1977), the Cannon Project was the largest program in the United States sponsored by the Corps of Engineers in terms of money allocated for cultural resource studies. The responsibilities connected with such a project are enormous, requiring constant communication between agency and archaeologists.

A few of those who aided us include Richard Leverty, outdoor recreation planner, Washington, D.C., and Col. Leon E. McKinney, Col. Robert J. Dacey, Jack R. Niemi, Jack F. Rasmussen, John Clark, and John B. Hallquist III of the St. Louis District. Our liaisons with the Corps of Engineers were Owen D. Dutt, chief of the Environmental Studies Section, and Terry Norris, archaeologist in that branch. Owen and Terry continually offered us many kinds of assistance and showed intense interest through all phases of the project. As I have stated many times before, the success of the project was as much a result of their efforts as of ours.

I also thank a number of people at the University of Nebraska–Lincoln, including Max Larsen, then dean of the College of Arts and Sciences, and Francis Schmehl and Carl Mueller of the Office of Grants and Contracts. Carl R. Falk, then director of the Division of Archaeological Research, provided administrative support and guided the analysis of faunal material from historical period sites. Robert Pepperl, interim director of that office, also provided administrative assistance. Laurie Soward, administrative assistant in the division, provided bookkeeping and other services vital to the success of the project.

At the University of Missouri, I thank Don H. Blount, dean of the Graduate School, and Robert A. Killoren, director of the Office of Research Grants and Contracts. I also thank Peggy Loy, who provided bookkeeping and offered advice on clearing hurdles in hiring personnel and purchasing equipment. W. Raymond Wood, general editor of the series in which this book appears, deserves sincere thanks for urging us to finish the volume when our spirits were flagging. His editorial advice has added greatly to the final product.

Other persons deserve special mention. Clayton B. Fraser directed the Historic American Buildings Survey (HABS), which recorded a number of early structures declared eligible for inclusion on the National Register of Historic Places. Michael S. Weichman and James Denny of the Missouri Historic Preservation Program and HABS architect Kenneth Anderson offered advice on the eligibility of several structures and supported us through several bureaucratic headaches connected with obtaining determinations of eligibility.

I gratefully acknowledge the work of two of my colleagues on the project, Roger D. Mason and Jacquelyn E. Saunders. Mason's responsibility was to gather a variety of archival information regarding the frontier cultural system. Although his final manuscript has been published in a separate monograph series, some of his findings have been included here. Saunders was responsible for the archaeological excavation of seven rural farmsteads and the processing of recovered materials. Being a lifelong resident of the area, she showed enthusiasm for the project and attention to detail second to none.

I also acknowledge the assistance of many helpful and friendly officials and staffs of several county and state offices. In Missouri, Frances Ross, recorder for Ralls County, and Oscar Tawney, recorder for Monroe County, assisted Mason in compiling land transaction data. Lisa Griffin, manuscript specialist for the Western Historical Manuscript Collection of the State Historical Society of Missouri, provided valuable assistance in the search for documents pertaining to the project area. In Kentucky, I sincerely appreciate the help of Lewis J. Bellardo, Jr., state archivist and director of the Public Records Division, Department for Libraries and Archives, and Richard N. Belding, deputy state archivist and deputy director of the Public Records Division, for placing their research staff at my disposal and offering considerable assistance in tracing a never-ending number of leads into the backgrounds of project area residents. I also thank Edna Milliken, manager of the Archives Branch, and Frances Coleman and Jean Rudloff, research archivists, for their help in locating several documents and maps.

Most of the cartography and illustration was done by Thomas D. Holland and Susan J. Vale. Their drawings have added significantly to the volume. The manuscript was typed by Michelle Dietrich, Ramona Bradley, and Betty Dudley. Research assistants who contributed to the project included Thomas Myers, Judy Sawyer, Thomas D. Holland, and Forrest Frost.

I personally offer my sincere thanks to my wife, Nancy O'Brien, for her unfailing support of the project and her understanding of the many months of late hours it took to complete this book. I am indebted to Dale R. Henning, who has served as principal investigator of the Cannon Project since its inception. He has allowed me unlimited latitude in developing the scope of the project. I can think of no one for whom I would rather have worked.

Finally, I extend my sincere appreciation to the people of the Cannon region, particularly those in and around Perry, Missouri, for their support of the project. They constantly provided us with data on early residents that we never would have been able to gather otherwise. One person in particular deserves special mention. Eugene A. Henning, who at present resides in Lakeland, Florida, but who grew up in the Paris, Missouri, area, has spent much of his life compiling genealogies of his ancestors and working through the complex relationships that tied many early project area families together. He graciously lent me all his notes and manuscripts. Without his help the analysis of the role of kinship in the frontier settlement of the region—a significant part of our research—would have been impossible. It is really the story of his and other area residents' ancestors that is presented here. I hope we have done the story justice.

Background and Approach

Michael J. O'Brien

Research into early Euro-American frontier settlement of the central Salt River valley of northeast Missouri was conducted as part of the Cannon Reservoir Human Ecology project, established to investigate interactions between man and the environment on the southern fringes of the Prairie Peninsula.[1] Because this region is a mosaic of grassland and forest biomes, it is an excellent laboratory in which to test several assumptions concerning frontier settlement, including those that address the characteristics of land preferred by frontier agriculturists—a topic of much recent concern to American settlement geographers.

The project area, a region of approximately 444 square miles, centers on the Clarence Cannon Dam and Mark Twain Lake,[2] situated about 60 river miles above the confluence of the Salt and Mississippi rivers (fig. 1.1). Although archaeological excavations were restricted to the 65,000 acres of federal land in and around the proposed pool area, the Corps of Engineers granted permission to include a larger area for archival and documentary research. By extending coverage into upland areas, we were able to obtain a more representative picture of frontier settlement across the region, since we could investigate both the oak-hickory and tall-grass prairie biomes.

Frontier settlement potentially includes myriad topics, and because of this diversity in subject matter it is important to point out the focus of this study, along with its biases and limits of analysis. To that end, this chapter discusses the approach used to generate, order, and analyze the data relative to settlement within the region. As a preface to this discussion we present a summary of work carried out by the project during the course of investigations. Since the Cannon Project was a federally funded cultural resource

1. See O'Brien, Warren, and Lewarch (1982) for an extended discussion of the prehistoric archaeology of the region.

2. Completed in September 1983.

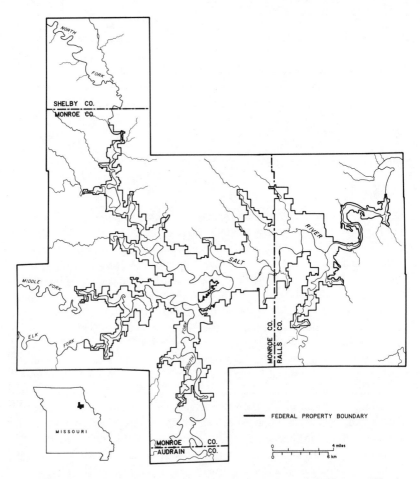

1.1. Location of the Cannon Reservoir Human Ecology Project area (after O'Brien and Henning 1982).

management program and this book serves as the final report of the project to the agency, we also briefly mention some of the steps taken to assess the resource base and to mitigate the damage to it. It may also be of interest to the reader to see how various research strategies and questions were used to formulate the overall research design, especially those questions whose answers came from analysis of the archaeological record.

Although one major goal of the project was to excavate several nineteenth-century farmsteads (O'Brien, Mason, and Saunders 1982), the archaeological data resulting from analysis of these materials in some respects played only an auxiliary role in the overall analysis of frontier settlement in the region. From the inception of the project it was deemed necessary to place the historical archaeological record within a broad-based research framework that addressed as many dimensions as possible of frontier settlement of the region. Historical archaeologists often either do not have access to extensive archival materials (which in some instances do not exist) or do not have the time to thoroughly investigate pertinent material. Hence they must rely solely on archaeological data. The problems under investigation frequently are of such magnitude that the archaeological data are not sufficient to address them adequately. In the present case, however, given the enormous amount of archival data available for reconstructing patterns of frontier settlement as well as for formulating a basis for understanding the processes that created the patterns, the archaeological data need not be put to such tasks. Rather, they can be used to test assumptions about household organization, subsistence, and the flow of goods through a frontier society. Some archaeologists may find such an approach rather limited, but given the other kinds of data available, the conservative approach seems justifiable.

Project Background

Historical-period research included three major areas of investigation: assessment of primary and secondary documentary sources; in-field survey for, and assessment of, historical sites and extant structures; and archaeological excavation of selected sites. Because of activities related to reservoir construction, these steps could not always be completed in that order. Hence fieldwork, which ideally would have been initiated after the completion of archival research, often was performed concurrently with it. As is explained in chapter 9, early in 1978 we decided to concentrate archaeological efforts in one 7 by 8 mile locale of the project area. Thus we decided to bypass the excavation of a regional sample of early farmsteads and to concentrate resources in an area over which we had reasonably good control of chronology and archival data.

Detailed archival work began in 1975 with a compilation of land purchase data and a brief historical overview of the region (Bremer 1975). The report contains geographical and geological descriptions of the area relative to agricultural potential and summarizes major historical developments in the area, noting the discovery of the Salt River by eighteenth-century French trappers and tracing the immigration of settlers from Kentucky and Virginia. It also examines settlement of the region in the context of rates and general patterns of land acquisition by individuals from 1818 through 1850.

During the next two years, workers carried out a field survey of historical structures using locational information derived from archival records, county atlases, and various maps. By using county atlases, we could ascertain relative dates of some structures, since if a structure appeared on one atlas but not on an earlier one it probably was built between publication dates (Saunders and Mason 1979).

Early in 1976 the Corps of Engineers issued a scope of work requiring that the historical site inventory be continued and an assessment be made of the significance of the sites. The resulting inventory included all known structures in the project area constructed or believed to have been constructed before 1920, as well as sites of razed structures. These included residences and farmstead structures, manufacturing sites such as mills and pottery kilns, and commercial buildings such as stores and inns. By December 1977, 337 sites and structures were recorded and assessed for eligibility for inclusion on the National Register of Historic Places. Subsequently, thirty-four site forms were submitted to the Missouri Office of Historic Preservation and then forwarded to the National Advisory Council on Historic Preservation for determinations of eligibility. These thirty-four sites were considered a representative sample of both rural architectural style and function in the project area. A representative of the Historic American Buildings Survey arrived in March 1978 to examine the structures and determine if any merited detailed architectural analysis. Based on his recommendation, fourteen structures plus one other that was not nominated were studied and drawn during the summer of 1978. A report describing these structures and others in the project area subsequently was published (O'Brien et al. 1980).

A research design organizing historical period research was compiled early in 1978 and submitted to the Corps of Engineers (O'Brien et al. 1978). As stated in the research design, immediate objectives of the proposed project were to:

1. Locate, map, and date as accurately as possible all traces of historical (pre-1920) occupation within the project area;
2. Identify the range of functional variability observable within and among the traces of occupation;
3. Formulate a model of the early historical (Neo-Boreal) environment of the region;
4. Delineate changing configurations of settlement systems and demography from 1800 to 1920; and
5. Compare the findings with previously defined patterns in the midwestern and eastern United States in order to clarify problems related to the analysis of:
   a. subsistence and exploitative patterns during the historical period;
   b. the extent of extraregional contacts (trade, commerce) through time; and
   c. the role of suprafamilial units in the development of community structure.

Research Questions

Based on these objectives, we selected a number of topics for investigation and formulated basic research questions. These questions fell into three groups: those that dealt with patterns and processes of settlement across the landscape; those that dealt with community structure and organization; and those that dealt with regional social and political organization.

Under the topic of *regional settlement,* we considered the following questions:

Settlement location. Why were certain areas of the biotope settled before others? What social institutions governed or conditioned where families settled? How much of a factor were a person's ties to his/her nuclear family in the decision where to settle?

Patterns and rates of land acquisition. What were the temporal trends in regional land acquisition? What role did national events like periodic depressions and bank collapses have on these patterns and rates?

Land use. How and why were different types of land used across the region through time? What economic or environmental factors influenced decisions regarding what types of agricultural production to undertake?

Land productivity. How different was the productivity of land in various parts of the project area? What are the variables that condition soil fertility, and were these known to early Euro-American settlers?

Under the topic of *community structure,* research questions included:

Family organization. Were nuclear families the rule rather than the exception in frontier colonization? How much of a role did extended families play in community development? What was the age/sex structure of immigrant families?

Household organization. What was the range in household size and in size of residential structures? Can the remains of specific household activities be found in situ? Can the location and composition of these activity remnants be used to infer specifics about the behavior of members of a household?

Social hierarchy. Are there differences in material goods from house to house within a community that are adequate measures of prosperity? Do these mirror data obtained from documentary sources such as probate and tax records?

Questions related to *regional organization* included:

Ideological forces. Did religion play a role in community development?

Commerce versus home production. How did the rise of commercial centers in the 1830s affect the economy and local production of agricultural as well as nonagricultural goods?

A recent report to the Corps of Engineers (Mason 1983) summarizes the methods and techniques of dealing with archival material that the project used to answer many of the questions posed in the research design. Since Mason treats in considerable detail the demographic characteristics of the frontier population and gives a thorough history of the region, these subjects are not discussed at length here. To order his analysis, Mason formulated twelve propositions, then tested their implications against data then available. The propositions were divided into three broad categories—locational decisions, economic development, and social stratification and wealth. Although subsequent research has allowed us to go beyond the limits of Mason's analysis of locational decisions, many of his conclusions are still significant, and where pertinent they are included here.

Thus this book is really a synthesis of eight years' effort to investigate and understand changes in the Euro-American settlement of the central Salt River valley. While several aspects of the investigation have been treated in varying degrees of detail elsewhere, there is no single overall summary of either the approach or the results of analysis. This volume serves that purpose. For the most part, the date 1850 is used as an end point of discussion. By 1850 most of the federal land in the project area had been purchased, and the frontier had long since passed to areas farther north and west. Although later periods were important to the overall development of the region and as such represent significant fields of research, we concentrate mainly on the frontier period.

The Approach

The Cannon Project is regional in its approach to Euro-American frontier settlement and deals with the interplay of the social and environmental dimensions that conditioned settlement. Regional studies are of growing importance in anthropology and geography as investigators have begun to see a continuing need to expand temporal and spatial frameworks for the study of human behavior (Johnson 1977:479). Regional analysis is the study of a specific unit of geographic space in which attention is focused on a specific population. Instead of focusing broadly on a topic or problem, such as the role of the speculator in the development of the frontier, regional analysis concentrates on a particular geographic area in which particular problems (e.g., the rate at which the availability of inexpensive land in northeastern Missouri attracted eastern speculators) can be isolated and studied.

The main benefit of regional analysis is that it allows one to develop a systematic approach in which the elements of form, function, and process can be examined in depth. A regional approach does not negate the potential for broadening the scope to include data from other geographic areas as needed. To the contrary, it lets one structure research so that the types of data incorporated can be carefully selected. Because of this structured approach, regional analysis also provides a framework for including results of more localized projects.

The general approach the project adopted contains elements of both ecology and spatial analysis. By definition, the relations between groups of humans, such as frontier agriculturists, and their physical and cultural environment are ecological. The processes that are shaped in part by these relations leave patterns upon the landscape, and many can be analyzed in a spatial sense. However, a hybrid ecological-spatial approach, or any approach, does not ensure that the processes that effect the pattern will be understood. Explanation of any phenomenon can come about only through reasoned inference stemming from a body of well-developed theory.

To explain the rationale behind using an ecological-spatial approach to the study of frontier dynamics in the central Salt River valley, the following section examines several approaches common in anthropology and geography and highlights specific problems inherent in them. These approaches are characteristic of the unidimensional paradigms that have plagued the analysis of man-land and man-man relations during the past several decades.

The discussion also points out the personal biases inherent in our approach, which is decidedly adaptationist oriented as opposed to mentalist oriented. Despite considerable recent work in geography and anthropology that employs behavioral and perceptual paradigms (e.g., Bunting and Guelke 1979; Rowntree and Conkey 1980), we are uncomfortable with these approaches. One reason for this discomfort is that implications of propositions formed during perceptual studies are often difficult if not impossible to test. Although later discussion in this volume does focus on early colonial-period perception of land, our assessment of preferred environmental dimensions is based on empirically derived observations, not on cognitive models.

General Approaches to the Study of Man-Environment Relations

More than any other discipline, anthropology and geography historically have emphasized the relations between man and environment. The field of study that ultimately arose as a result of an emphasis on understanding these relations—cultural ecology—was a direct outgrowth of the inadequacy of more deterministic models of how man was controlled or influenced by an inflexible physical environment. Before the development of cultural ecology, the deterministic models of the nineteenth and early twentieth centuries were replaced in anthropology by more possibilistic models, which viewed environmental factors not as causative but rather as setting limits for cultural developments (Grossman 1977:127). Guided by large bodies of newly acquired ethnographic data, possibilists attempted to minimize the influence of environment on culture. Similar trends occurred in geography during the 1920s and 1930s, owing in part to the collaboration between landscape geographers and anthropologists.

In an excellent article that contrasts historically the views and objectives of Americanist anthropology and geography, Grossman (1977) points out that between 1920 and 1950 both disciplines tended to emphasize the inductive approach over the deductive and specific statements over broad generalities. Because of the cross-disciplinary collaboration of persons like Sauer and Kroeber at Berkeley, both disciplines used the concept of culture area and looked to diffusion as a mechanism for the movement of cultural traits. This preoccupation with culture areas discouraged the advancement of useful generalities about man-environment relations, in part because of the size of the areas involved (Brookfield 1964), but also because of the lack of any explanatory power.

This inability to formulate even preliminary explanations for the patterns evident across the landscape was a direct result of an investigative emphasis on form rather than on process. Preoccupation with the form of the visible landscape "led to an unfortunate neglect of the less obvious, invisible forces which in some cases form cornerstones in the explanation of spatial patterns of human behavior" (English and Mayfield 1972:6). The advances of processual studies in anthropology were not felt until the 1950s, when the materialist paradigm gained acceptance over the mentalist approach (Harris 1968) and dissatisfaction with studies of social structure reached such a level that new avenues of inquiry were sought (Netting 1969).

The replacement for these avenues was cultural ecology, an approach championed by Steward (1955), who proposed that under certain environmental conditions the use of certain forms of exploitative technology and organization gives rise to certain patterns of social organization. Although Steward has been criticized for several methodological weaknesses in his approach (e.g., Vayda and Rappaport 1968), his work did emphasize that the sociocultural organization of a group is a mechanism (Grossman 1977:131) for adapting to a physical as well as a cultural environment.

Methodological refinements since Steward's pioneering efforts have led to a broadening of the scope of cultural ecology as studied by anthropologists and geographers (Morgan and Moss 1965; Stottard 1967). With this broadening, however, there has arisen considerable debate over what actually is being studied in a cultural-ecologically oriented investigation. In geography, for example, there is a decided emphasis on the study of land use (e.g., Simmons 1966, 1970), which often is viewed as a problem of spatial analysis. Indeed, as Grossman (1977:134) notes, some geographers view ecology and spatial analysis as separate, albeit related, forms of inquiry. In this perceived dichotomy, spatial analysis is viewed as being "concerned with factors affecting the location of specific activities. . . . Ecologic analysis is concerned with the interaction of the factors which define the activity itself, rather than with how the factors affect the location of the activity" (Clarkson

1970:706). A similar position is inherent, though often unstated, in much of the anthropological literature of the recent decades, especially that of settlement pattern analysis. Perhaps, as Clarkson (1970) states, this is due to the use of different theory, methods, research design, and techniques by those adopting each approach. Fortunately, it is not impossible to integrate the two approaches into a single framework. As Taaffe (1974:16) notes, "The spatial view can coexist with the ecological view and, in many instances, reinforce it."

One critical question that must be addressed in assessing the applicability of any approach is: Does it allow the identification of *pattern*? Can the approach be used to identify variability, isolate points or segments within this range, predict in a spatial and temporal sense where these points or segments will recur, and test these predictions? In short, a unified spatial-ecological approach must be able to identify patterns in the ways peoples adapted to and modified their environments.

One key aspect of a study of the adaptations of early-nineteenth-century Euro-American agriculturists to a midwestern river valley—such as that presented here—is *settlement*. A thorough analysis of human settlement of a region should address both the patterns that resulted from settlement, that is, the settlement configuration, and the processes that led to that pattern. Because of the rich diversity of topics included under settlement analysis—especially rural settlement analysis—it appears that such an analysis would present an ideal situation for an ecological-spatial approach. Despite the attractiveness of such an approach, it is apparent that the approaches and methods used in the analysis of settlement—both in a spatial and an ecological (processual) context—are as disparate as the definitions used to define settlement. While there is some overlap among the methods employed by anthropologists and geographers, the differences in the way settlement is viewed to a large extent condition the results of analysis.

Although "human settlements as the basic human phenomena in the cultural landscape form the subject matter of many social sciences" (Singh and Singh 1975:29), even within a single discipline the ways settlement is viewed are disparate. For example, the International Geographical Union's Commission on Rural Settlements in Monsoon Lands (1975) listed seven major and fifty minor research themes upon which the analysis of rural settlement could focus. Major research topics adopted by the congress include approaches to rural settlement geography; histogenesis of rural settlements and settlement patterns (including settlement archaeology); types, patterns, and classification of rural settlements; functional and spatial organization of rural settlements; rural buildings and house types; village studies; and planning and rationalization of rural settlements.

In a seminal article on the need to develop a focus for settlement geography, Stone (1965:346) states that "More than most present-day divisions of geography that of settlement needs defining." He recognizes that in this subfield the objectives are varied, developments have not kept pace with advances in other areas of geography, methods and classification are incomplete, terminology is indistinct, and textbooks and courses are limited. One immediate problem to which he calls attention is defining rural settlement and delimiting at what scale the analysis of such a settlement is to be conducted. Despite a rich and varied literature on the subject (which he cites at length), definitions and limits of analysis remain unclear. Although his assessment of the field was published in 1965, several points Stone raises are still valid criticisms.

From an ecological-spatial perspective Stone's (1965:347) definition of settlement as "the description and analysis of the distribution of buildings by which people attach themselves to the land" is not particularly useful because it ignores the entire social process that creates many end products, only one of which is the "built environment" he maintains should be the central focus of study. Jordan (1966:27) directed a similar criticism: "Not only does Dr. Stone attempt to draw too short a circumference around settlement geography, but also he tries to mark its borders too sharply." Stone is not alone in restricting settlement geography to structures, as can be noted in a discussion of the field by Singh (1975:4), who states that analysis should be limited to "(i) the facilities built in the process of human occupance of the land and (ii) their grouping."

One bias that is apparent in many geographical studies of rural settlement is the exclusion of *function* from general discussion and a greater implied or stated emphasis on *form*. One proponent of the importance of form is Jordan, who defines settlement geography as "the study of the form of the cultural landscape, involving its orderly description and attempted explanation" (1966:27). He sees the role of the cultural geographer as searching for factors that shape the cultural landscape: "It is the emphasis on *form* which distinguishes settlement geography (1) from economic, agricultural, and urban geography, all of which are primarily interested in *function* and (2) from population geography, which is concerned with the distribution and characteristics of human beings rather than with the form of the cultural landscapes created by these people" (Jordan 1966:28, emphasis in original).

To Jordan (1966:28), explanation is the end point of the scientific method. He also believes that description should come before explanation so that there is a clear conception of *what* is being explained. However, the description of the form of a cultural landscape will not lead to a useful explanation either of how a cultural system came into being or of how it changed over time once it was in place. Without an analysis of form, function, *and* process, there can be no in-depth understanding of a settlement system. More important, without some body of theory upon which to base the analysis, any attempts to *explain* the dynamics of the settlement process will be fruitless. The lack of such a scientific method led to Hudson's (1969:365) statement that "it appears that rural settlement location, unlike urban settlement, is a subject on which little theoretical work has been done."

Hudson's work in developing a theory for locational analysis of rural settlement is of particular interest here and forms the basis of a three-stage model of frontier settlement in the project area (chap. 2). His treatment of niche (theoretical) versus biotope (real) space represents a significant step beyond the simple characterization of settlement configuration (Mason, Warren, and O'Brien 1982:369). Hudson's work typifies a growing sentiment among some settlement geographers (e.g., Bylund 1960; Conzen 1971) that theory is needed to explain the processes that result in the varied patterns observed in the settlement record. Unfortunately, as has been pointed out, many analyses of settlement geography have been concerned simply with describing the built environment. Others have focused on describing the distribution of settlement types (farmsteads, hamlets, towns) by terms such as *random, regular* or *clustered*. In other words, research has concentrated on deriving mathematical expressions for these distributions instead of striving for explanations of the *processes* that created them (Mason, Warren, and O'Brien 1982:369). As Hudson (1969:366) states, "statistical technique is no substitute for theory."

In many respects, settlement studies in anthropology, especially in the subdiscipline of archaeology, have emphasized the same topics as those in geography, especially with respect to settlement form. Perhaps because of the "newness" of settlement archaeology, archaeologists have borrowed, whole-sale, concepts from settlement geography without realizing some of the pitfalls involved. Trigger (1967:151) defines *settlement archaeology* as "the study of social relationships using archaeological data," involving the explanaton of "functioning systems of economic, political and effective relationships within social groupings of people." He defines three successive levels of analysis for archaeological studies of settlement: the individual structure, community layout, and "the manner in which communities belonging to a culture or society distribute themselves over the landscape" (Trigger 1968:73). Trigger's definition of settlement archaeology in terms of studying social relations is by no means widely held in archaeology, possibly because archaeologists are inherently biased in favor of the importance of environmental variables in determining human settlement and because archaeology necessarily deals with an incomplete record, thereby making the study of social dimensions somewhat tenuous.

Central to the theme of settlement archaeology is the settlement itself and the pattern it assumes over the land. Most archaeologists would agree with

Chang's (1968:3) definition of an archaeological settlement as "the physical locale or cluster of locales where the members of a community lived, ensured their subsistence, and pursued their social functions in a delineable time period." *Settlement pattern* has been defined variously as "the way in which man disposed himself over the landscape on which he lived" (Willey 1953:1) and as "the manner in which a people's cultural activities and social institutions are distributed over the landscape" (Rouse 1972:96).

In the past twenty years *settlement pattern analysis* as one approach to generating archaeological data on a regional scale has gained wide acceptance in American archaeology. This can be viewed as at least tacit approval of the success of the methods and techniques of archaeological site survey in generating and ordering data useful in solving problems of general archaeological interest (cf. Schiffer, Sullivan, and Klinger 1978). The analysis of settlement patterns is termed by Willey (1953:1) a "strategic starting point for the functional interpretation of archaeological cultures" that reflect "the natural environment, the level of technology on which the builders operated, and various institutions of social interaction and control which the culture maintained." Sanders (1971*a*) defines settlement pattern studies as those dealing with the distribution of population in a given region and the analysis of factors responsible for the distribution. He later refined this definition to delimit the factors responsible for the distribution of settlement. Sanders (1971*b*:545) suggests that the existence of subtle systemic interrelations between the availability of natural resources and the development of social institutions serves to pattern both settlement and community configurations within a region.

Despite a healthy emphasis on the variety in forms of settlement patterns and on the range of uses of settlement pattern data, a major dichotomy in approach has dominated settlement archaeology. Trigger (1968:54) describes the *ecological* approach and the *social* approach. The first approach is based primarily on the assumption that patterns of settlement are products of the interaction of two dimensions—technology and environment; that is, they study how a society uses its technology to adapt to its environment. In stressing only two dimensions, the term "ecological" obviously is a misnomer for this approach. The second approach uses settlement pattern data to make inferences about the "social, political, and religious organization of prehistoric cultures" (Trigger 1968:54).

It is fair to say that most settlement pattern studies conducted to date have been heavily environmentally oriented. This slighting of social dimensions in favor of environmental and technological ones has tended to make many descriptions and models of settlement unidimensional. That is, when one dimension or class of dimensions is used as a structuring principle, important questions are overlooked—such as how settlement strategies reflect selective pressures or how the rise of certain social institutions is connected to selective pressure.

The uniting of the two approaches into a coherent whole has been slow in developing, partially owing to the biases discussed earlier: archaeologists' favoring of the environmental-technological approach and the related bias that, since archaeologists are faced with only remnants of past society (Rouse 1972), the safest level on which to operate is the technomic, that is relating to those things "having their primary functional context in coping directly with the physical environment" (Binford 1962:219). Thus, though there have been attempts (and some successes) to integrate analyses of settlement form with analyses of function and process, processual studies usually are limited to one particular aspect of culture.

The Study of Frontier Settlement

A topic that has long concerned not only anthropologists and geographers but historians as well is the settlement of frontier areas. As Davis (1977), Mason (1983), and others have pointed out, the significance of the concept *frontier* has long been a point of contention. In fact the very term *frontier* is difficult to define (Hudson 1977:13). As Lewis (1977:153) notes in his summary of differing views on the frontier, interpretations of the term vary considerably from user to user, but most share several conclusions. First, the frontier is an area in which the edge of an expanding society "adapts to the conditions of attenuated contact with the homeland and the physical conditions of a new environment" (ibid.). Second, the frontier is impermanent both temporally and spatially. Third, because of the repetitive nature of colonization, "it is also evolutionary in the sense that the sequential pattern of change that once occurred in the center of a newly settled frontier region tends to be repeated along its periphery as settlement within the region expands" (ibid.). Thus the frontier is both a process of change and the area within which it occurs. These points are summed up in Leyburn's (1935:1) definition of a frontier as "that region on the outer edge of settlement where pioneers are forced, for the sake of survival, to make new adjustments to a raw environment. It is a process, it is even a state of mind."

While historians have been in the forefront in the study of frontiers and frontier settlement and have made important contributions (e.g., Curti 1959; Davis 1977; Horsman 1970; Rohrbough 1978), the point can be made that the types of data historians employ often are qualitative rather than quantitative—a fact that heavily biases most attempts to form testable implications from available information. For example, after decades of argument over the validity of Turner's (1893) notions concerning the American frontier, historians appear to be no closer to a solution (cf. Elkins and McKitrick 1954) than they were in the 1930s, since the data needed to support or negate Turner's notion are difficult, if not impossible, to quantify. Although some historians (e.g., Curti 1959) argue to the contrary, historical analysis has been slow to prove them correct. The difficulty with such tests, as Hudson (1977:11) points out, is that Turner did not form a theory capable of being tested.

Alternatively, several pleas for objectivity in historical research dealing with the frontier have been made. For example, Horsman (1978:80) realizes a need for "in depth studies of limited areas across economic, social, and political concerns," and Swierenga (1973:111–12) calls for a "new rural history" that integrates ecological, demographic, behavioral, economic, and institutional approaches into a "framework for an overall history of rural development." Despite these pleas, there have been few attempts to construct an overall quantified approach to frontier analysis or to develop a theoretical framework within which such an approach would operate. In a provocative article dealing with social theory and the frontier, Bogue (1960) states that social scientists generally have taken the work of historians at face value rather than trying to explain the frontier process in terms of their own theory: "I would not argue that any frontier historian will find magic formulas in the work of the social scientists. Their research may, however, help us to slip the leash of tradition and consider the old frontier sources in a new dimension" (Bogue 1960:23). He ends his discussion of social theory and the frontier by stating: "There are challenges here. There is an additional challenge in the fact that history is a literary art and that many of those who generate social theory are hardly literary artists. The historian who consorts with behavioral theorists, who rides the wind of social theory, may indeed reap the whirlwind" (Bogue 1960:34).

It is, however, social scientists that have made the most significant advances in formulating a fairly concise understanding of the frontier and the processes that shaped it. While considerable emphasis is still placed on comparative studies of the frontier, these studies "have proven little but they have contributed much to our general knowledge of pioneer settlements around the world" (Hudson 1977:11). On the other hand, it is just what Bogue is arguing against—formulations of theory and explicit models to explain the frontier settlement process—that are the significant contributions being made by social scientists interested in the frontier. It was with this realization that frontier-period research in the central Salt River valley was planned and carried out.

The Integration of Approaches

It is evident from the preceding discussion that historical analysis, settlement geography, and anthropology all contribute concepts, methods, and techniques useful for analyzing frontier settlement. Historians have dealt with the problem of defining the frontier in geographical, sociological, and political terms and have compiled enormous amounts of data on the western movement of the American frontier. Geographers and anthropologists have treated settlement mainly in terms of form, compiling data on the distribution of communities across the landscape and, in some instances, on the description and distribution of elements within communities. With some exceptions, the functional and processual aspects of settlement have been either ignored or downplayed, so that any analysis of process—how settlements came into being or how they changed—is limited at best. Where function and process have been treated, analysis often has been unidimensional, with only certain sets of dimensions considered. By employing an ecological approach, which emphasizes social as well as physical environmental dimensions of settlement, we can reduce the effects of this bias.

Ideally, one would like to construct a model of frontier settlement and development that would include all the dimensions that led to the emigration of a population from a source area; caused them to immigrate to a certain target area; effected the distribution of settlement across the landscape; and led to the social, economic, and political development of the frontier region. Realistically, such a model is impossible to construct. While one may reasonably predict which factors were important to frontier migration, colonization, and spread and may even be able to measure the importance of several factors, developing a "complete" model is beyond current methodological limits. Similarly, it is impossible to generate a complete set of data relative to the importance of any single factor in determining or conditioning frontier settlement. For instance, the model presented in chapter 2 assumes that intermarriage and kinship bonds established in trans-Appalachian source areas conditioned to a large extent the spacing of farmsteads in the Salt Valley. While for some families there exist excellent genealogical data that can be used to construct case examples, it would be impossible to generate data for all families that ever resided in the project area. Additionally, for a complete analysis of settlement dynamics we would need the location of every farmstead in Kentucky between 1750 and 1830 to determine if the settlement patterns seen in the Salt Valley were transplanted from that particular source area.

To carry this one step further, the model assumes that soil quality, kind of biome, and timber density were important considerations in deciding which tracts of federal land to enter. In the project area, these environmental dimensions can be mapped spatially and compared with settlement locations. Since it is difficult if not impossible to pinpoint the precise locations of farms owned in Kentucky by later immigrants to the Salt Valley, and since there do not exist the kinds of eighteenth- and nineteenth-century environmental data for that region that exist for the project area, we cannot compare land-selection decisions in the two areas to any depth. This is unfortunate, since we would like to examine any changes in land selection criteria by early-nineteenth-century agriculturists who moved west. Thus, while some of the bias inherent in analyzing the frontier, especially its settlement, can be reduced by considering sociocultural as well as environmental dimensions, there are still large gaps in our knowledge of frontier settlement dynamics.

As noted earlier, one problem that has hampered analyses of settlement is the inconsistency in terminology for the components of settlement. The problem transcends semantics and proceeds directly to the questions of what settlement is and what its components are. In the mid-1960s American archaeologists began to realize some of the methodological and analytical limitations of settlement pattern analysis, especially in its heavy emphasis on form and usual consideration of only environmental factors. Parsons (1972) states that one of the more significant outcomes of this reassessment was the concept of the *settlement system* (Winters 1967; cf. Chang 1962). Winters (1969:110) distinguishes between settlement pattern and settlement system, defining the former as "the geographic and physiographic relationships of a contemporaneous group of sites within a single culture" and the latter as "the functional relationships among the sites contained within the settlement pattern . . . [and] . . . the functional relationship among a contemporaneous group of sites within a single culture."

An important outcome of the emphasis on the systemic nature of settlement has been a clearer definition of the components of a settlement system. One such component is the *community,* a term that is somewhat difficult to define (cf. Arensberg 1961). In one sense it can be viewed as "a social unit occupying a space in which its members interact" (Gjerde 1979:405), which can be expanded "to incorporate common goals and institutions that enable the members to identify with the sense of community" (O'Brien, Mason, and Saunders 1982:302). In another sense, a community can refer to the way remnants of a particular social unit are distributed within a single site (O'Brien and Warren 1982:22). In either case one can think of a community as a microcosm of a region.

In one of the more rigorous attempts to integrate the notion of community and settlement pattern into the concept of a settlement system, Trigger, in a synthesis of the determinants of settlement pattern, employed Murdock's (1949:79) definition of community as "the maximal group of persons who normally reside in face-to-face association" (Trigger 1968:60). One aspect of Murdock's synthesis is the often-overlooked fact that: "Whereas community size and location are influenced to a large extent by ecological factors, the layout of communities appears to be strongly influenced by family and kinship organization. . . . These relationships are not necessarily totally independent factors, since kinship relations are at least partly determined by ecological factors that operate through the medium of production" (Trigger 1968:62).

I previously introduced three levels of analysis for settlement: the individual structure, the layout of a community, and the distribution of communities over the landscape. Trigger (1968:73–74) states that the "patterns displayed at each of these levels can be viewed as being functionally related in some way to all aspects of a culture and therefore able to shed light on a variety of problems." Each level also is appropriate to the analysis of particular aspects of society: individual structures provide data on family organization and the relative importance of aspects of the social structure, community plans yield useful information about the community's adaptation to cultural and physical environments, and the distribution of communities reflects the overall social and political development of the region. Problem-oriented approaches that exploit the potential of each level simultaneously seem highly desirable (cf. Trigger 1968:74). In the following section these levels provide the nucleus around which are organized the four research topics we have used to organize discussion of Euro-American settlement in the central Salt River valley.

The Organization of Research Topics

The four general topics that form the nucleus of investigation of Euro-American settlement in the project area are the household, farmstead, community, and settlement. These topics subsume those briefly discussed in the opening section relative to the research design, with each topic building toward the level above and toward the analysis of the composite picture of settlement dynamics in the Salt Valley.

The Household

The most basic level of analysis is the *household*, defined as a group of related people living in the same residence who cooperate in performing a wide range of domestic activities (Winter 1974:981). One underlying assumption in the analysis of rural frontier households is that there were differences in wealth among them that are reflected in documentary sources, residence size, and amount of land owned as well as in the archaeological record. Concomitantly, status distinctions and social stratification are corollaries of an increasing economic complexity (Mason 1983) as a region moves beyond being a frontier. Since status is directly related to landownership (Berkhofer 1964:27; Lemon 1980:122; Mitchell 1977:238), the availability of large amounts of inexpensive frontier land tended to create a large middle class (Berkhofer 1964:27; Mason 1983). Mason (1983) notes that rates of development of status differentiation varied from area to area on the frontier (cf. Curti

1959; Lemon 1980), and he suggests that definite social stratification occurs as population increases and available land decreases, resulting in greater competition for remaining land (cf. Billington 1966; Mitchell 1977).

Tax and probate records, when they exist, are excellent sources of data concerning wealth. Despite some biases in these records, they present an adequate picture of both income and personal property. The archaeological record is also of some help in assessing relative wealth, but it can be used more readily to investigate other aspects of the household such as where various activities took place and patterns of discarding refuse. Certain biases are inherent in any attempt to use archaeological data to infer social behavior, and these biases must be assessed before the data can be employed. As with most archaeological sites, the length of occupation of residential structures in the project area has led to the mixing of archaeological deposits to the point that any attempts to delineate synchronous deposits are futile. In some instances, where additions to standing structures have sealed earlier deposits and the dates of the additions are known, archaeological materials can be dated to a relatively short time span. Thus, while archaeological excavation was able in some instances to fill gaps in our knowledge of frontier households, many excavated items simply were not up to the task.

Analysis of residential structures, in both a formal and a functional sense, has broad anthropological and geographical implications for understanding rural households. Factors that affect the built environment include variation in the physical environment as well as technological advances. Residential structures are defined as domestically oriented constructs that protect the occupants from the environment while allowing them to move within the structure and in relation to one another (Hunter-Anderson 1977:301–3). This definition, while realizing the importance of form, emphasizes the functional aspects of residential structures, that is, "the set of domestic activities composed of living . . . and role . . . elements" (O'Brien et al. 1980:20). Such an approach emphasizes the kinds of activities carried out within a residential structure in terms of the range of activities, their scheduling, group size associated with each activity, spatial requirements, and so forth (O'Brien et al. 1980:21). Although presented only briefly in this book, another important aspect of household analysis is documenting the age and sex composition of the household. Using population census schedules for 1830 to 1850, Mason (1983) was able to observe changes through time in the age-sex structure of frontier and postfrontier households in the project area and to compare these with findings from other areas of the United States.

To complete the analysis of frontier settlement systems at the initial level we analyze the subsistence practices of rural households by focusing generally on the agricultural development of the region as the system moved from primarily providing day-to-day subsistence to producing a surplus, and specifically on agricultural holdings of families from one locality within the project area and on faunal remains that were recovered from archaeological excavation of several early residences. Based on information from a wide variety of historical sources, we propose that, though the basis of early frontier subsistence was agriculturally oriented, significant amounts of time and energy were expended on nonagricultural subsistence activities such as hunting and fishing. The by-products of consuming the results of these pursuits should be evident in the archaeological record.

The Farmstead

The second level of analysis encompasses the household and adds two further dimensions: the components of the rural *farmstead* and their spatial organization. Early farmsteads were for the most part self-contained units that functioned relative to various modes of production in practice at the time. As markets were established closer to colonial settlement and agriculturists became involved in commercial production, farmsteads reflected this development. Theoretically, we should be able to document a continuum in farmstead complexity through time as new elements were added and to relate these changes to increased wealth of landowners.

However, several factors have worked against our ability to completely carry out such detailed analysis. One factor is the time span covered by the research reported here—1818 to 1850. Many early farmsteads dating to this period either were demolished and replaced by later construction or were so modified by later additions that the original structural fabric is difficult, if not impossible, to define. Also, reservoir clearing razed a considerable number of structures before they were documented. Hence much of our effort is directed toward describing what little early rural architecture remains. Nevertheless, many useful data pertinent to the farmsteads of this era do exist and are presented in subsequent discussions.

The Community

At the third level of analysis, the community, we investigate several aspects of the formation and organization of early-nineteenth-century communities in the project area. One important aspect of our work involved delineating early communities and isolating spatial configurations of socially linked farmsteads. Early colonial communities are of particular interest because they represent the settlement of a relatively unknown area and can be examined in a "pristine state," excellent documentary information exists on their formation, and little is known of early-nineteenth-century Euro-American communities in the Midwest. Of particular interest are the roles both physical and cultural environmental factors play in determining the location of landholdings and farmsteads. The former include, among other things, timber density, proximity to water, and soil fertility; the latter include kin ties, commonality of place of emigration, and religious affiliation. These variables, acting alone or in concert, all acted to influence settlement decisions and to shape the formation and development of communities across the region.

The Settlement Pattern

The fourth level of analysis, regional patterns of settlement, involves investigation at the macrolevel, where we view the entire region as a whole and study broad trends in settlement. This analysis is intricately tied to that of individual communities, but it also involves another aspect of settlement: the use for which land was brought into production. It also is tied to events that were extraregional in scope, such as cyclical periods of easy credit, land speculation, and banking failures. These national trends were also distinct at the regional level, and some of them provided the impetus for emigration from Kentucky and Tennessee during the early nineteenth century and continued to affect development of the Salt River valley throughout its history.

For comparative purposes, and because they were linked directly to the colonization of the Salt River valley, two other regions are discussed in terms of environmental characteristics and settlement pattern: the Bluegrass region of central Kentucky in the late eighteenth and early nineteenth centuries, and the early-nineteenth-century Boonslick region of central Missouri. The Bluegrass region was of considerable importance to the social and political development of the central Salt River valley, for it sent tens of thousands of emigrants to Missouri before the Civil War. To understand the reasons for this prolific emigration, we develop an overview of the environment and the social development of the region before the emigration period. The Boonslick region, composed of rich alluvial bottomland and terraces along the Missouri River, was among the first locales to be settled by emigrant Kentuckians and Virginians who chose to bypass the urban center of St. Louis during the first and second decades of the nineteenth century. Various written accounts from this period note the similarity between this fertile area and portions of the Bluegrass region. It would be only a few years before many colonists of this area moved northward into the newly opened Salt River territory, being joined there by emigrants who bypassed central Missouri and headed directly to the Salt Valley. Thus, the settlement of this region is important for understanding early-nineteenth-century settlement decisions.

Summary

The approach we used to reconstruct the dynamic picture of frontier settlement in the central Salt River valley and to understand the mechanisms involved in the cultural development of the region is ecological and spatial and is derived in part from theory and method developed in the fields of historical analysis, geography, and anthropology. To clarify problems in terminology, we introduced the concept of settlement system to emphasize the systemic nature of settlement, in which certain elements operate in concert to effect change in the overall system. Such a concept emphasizes process and function as well as form and discourages the formation of settlement models that emphasize environmental and technological dimensions over social dimensions. In general, a settlement system can be thought of as containing three basic elements whose forms are mappable: the structure, the community, and the overall pattern of settlement across a region. Each element can also be examined as to the function it plays in the system, how it came into being, and how its role in the system changed through time as the system responded to physical and cultural stimuli.

To ground the study of settlement systems in the Salt River valley on a theoretical foundation, we present a formal model of settlement evolution and change in the following chapter. The model, adapted from ecological theory, contains a host of elements that have been postulated as being important in conditioning frontier settlement. Adopting theory from other fields should not be of great concern if one adheres to the principle that Hudson (1969) refers to as the discriminating use of ''morphological laws.'' In assessing the role played in anthropology by theory developed outside the discipline, Struever (1971:131) states that the introduction of ecological theory and systems theory has made the elucidation of culture process an operational problem, not simply a slogan. Despite the introduction of these theories into anthropology and the recent interest archaeologists have paid to processual studies of settlement systems, research strategies seldom are planned and carried out ''explicitly to maximize recovery of data pertinent to defining these systems'' (Struever 1971:136). We believe that the Cannon Project research strategies were planned and carried out to maximize data recovery, the analysis of which has added significantly to an understanding of frontier settlement systems. While we have not been able to investigate every aspect of the frontier and have tended to highlight some aspects over others, we hope to show that, despite the complexity of factors that shaped the frontier, it is possible to isolate, measure, and assess the significance of some of the factors and to understand something of the processes that contributed to its dynamic nature.

A Model of
Frontier Settlement

Robert E. Warren and
Michael J. O'Brien

In the preceding chapter we noted that the historical period research undertaken by the Cannon Project is oriented toward understanding frontier settlement pattern and process in the central Salt River valley. The objective of this chapter is to evaluate the significance of several factors that shaped the settlement of the region through time and to propose general expectations in terms appropriate to understanding human behavior in the region. To this end we construct a model of cultural development in the region and derive implications from the model that are testable using data drawn from documentary sources and archaeological excavation. The model presented here is abstracted from a variety of sources, including environmental studies of the Salt River valley, previous analyses of frontier development in other sections of the trans-Appalachian West, and our own perspectives on cultural adaptation and change. The model provides a series of hypothetical constructs that in later chapters are contrasted with findings in the project area to determine how well results conform to expectations derived from the model.

A model can be thought of as a simplified representation of reality (Harvey 1966:373) or as an attempt to "codify what has gone before" (Haggett 1965:23). In its simplest form, a model is a classification scheme that in itself asserts a set of "primitive" laws concerning the structure of reality (Braithwaite 1960:1). Importantly, the operating characteristics of a model may be derived either deductively, inductively from empirical observation, or by a combination. Developing a formal model and deriving testable implications from it are important steps toward understanding culture change and represent a significant advance over the normative pattern approach common in the geographical and archaeological literature. We agree with Harvey's (1966:374) appraisal that "ultimately we need models of evolution of spatial pattern rather than static equilibrium models."

The basic framework of the model presented here is adapted from a theory of rural settlement location developed by John C. Hudson (1969). Hudson's theory employs several important ecological concepts and focuses on changing locational behavior from the perspective of human geography. The theory, part of which Hudson tested using modern data from the heart of the Prairie Peninsula in eastern Iowa, recognizes three processes of rural settlement. The processes are sequential, have differential effects on locational patterning, and are presumed to represent the dynamics of colonizing behavior among a wide variety of plant and animal species.

Hudson's theory is particularly useful here in that it is predictive, is explanatory, and, in its synthesis of several geographical and ecological principles, incorporates both the form and the process of dynamic rural settlement. However, several aspects of the model require revision or expansion to fit the exigencies of *human behavior* in any *specific environment*. First, it is questionable whether Hudson's formulation can explain all configurations of rural settlement, since it does not seem to account for the complexities of human social and economic behavior. Central to Hudson's model is an ecological analogue based on observations of the dispersion, reproduction, and stabilization of noncultural plant and animal species in new territories or new environments. To the extent that human locational behavior in the Salt Valley does not conform to the behavior of noncultural organisms, we should anticipate patterns and processes of settlement that differ in form or cause from those outlined by Hudson. In an attempt to remedy these potential deficiencies, we discuss the effects of several anthropological factors on configurations of settlement, including kinship, commonality of origin, religious affiliation, transportation routes, and proximity to markets.

Second, Hudson (1969) provides a lucid account of the way environmental variables interact with populations to define the "place" of a population in its environmental context, but his model provides no clues as to which environmental variables will influence settlement in any given area. Since the Salt River valley was not environmentally homogeneous during the nineteenth century, there is little reason to expect that Hudson's theory can explain all the settlement variability we will observe in the project area. This is by no means an indictment of the location theory, which focuses on the form rather than the context of rural settlement. After all, theories predict and explain observations only under certain conditions. In Hudson's theory rural settlement patterns are predicted within those unknown parts of the environment exploited by Euro-American agriculturists. It is left to regional analysts to determine what those biophysical contexts were in different environmental provinces, and how and why they may have changed through time. This can be done inductively. However, previous attempts to determine the environmental contexts of rural settlement in the Prairie Peninsula help guide our investigations and allow us to address several alternative hypotheses (Warren, McDaniel, and O'Brien 1982).

In this chapter, then, we revise and expand Hudson's theory to incorporate the cultural and environmental dimensions of settlement. This provides a comprehensive model of locational behavior—one that deals with the form, process, and environmental context of rural settlement in the region. Our empirical research, presented later, will necessitate revisions of the model. Nonetheless, the result should foster a better understanding of the potentially universal processes of adaptation in social and biophysical environments on the frontier.

A Theory of Rural Settlement Location

Hudson's (1969) theory encompasses three processes of rural settlement, each of which has a distinct manifestation in space. In reality the three processes tend to overlap in time, but their modes of relative importance are generally sequential, and they can be thought of as phases or stages of frontier occupation.

The first process, *colonization,* involves the expansion of a population into a new area. The second process, *spread,* is a spatial correlate of population growth in the new area whereby spaces between early settlements are filled in as established colonial populations grow and the density of rural settlement increases. The final process, *competition,* appears because of limitations imposed by the environment. As competition increases over finite amounts of land and resources, weak competitors are forced out, population density decreases, and the settlement pattern stabilizes.

The actual number of stages in the settlement process can vary, depending upon how they are perceived. Hudson (1969:367) states that in practice there may be only two stages; colonization and spread can be considered aspects of the compound process of diffusion. However, separate analysis of the processes is simpler and more illuminating, since fewer parameters are needed in each case and the different spatial effects of the two processes can be examined in isolation.

As mentioned earlier, each stage of settlement should have a distinct, but not necessarily a discrete, expression in space. Two types of space are important to our discussion: *biotope space* and *niche space* (Hudson 1969:367). Biotope space, or physical space, is composed of a nearly limitless set of m environmental variables. It is a real-world phenomenon that can be mapped three dimensionally. Niche space, however, is a theoretical space viewed from the perspective of variables instead of land area. It is composed of a set of n analytical vectors, upon whch are aligned an equal number of linearly independent sets of interdependent environmental variables, reduced from the original set of m variables that constitute biotope space (thus, $n < m$). Niche space is conceptually similar to R-mode principal components space, in which a series of independent factors reduces variance among a larger array of *m* variables by aligning all interdependent variables on *n* dimensions (Warren, O'Brien, and Mason 1981).

Hardesty defines the multidimensional, or "Hutchinsonian," concept of ⌐ the ecological niche as "a [E]uclidian hyperspace whose *dimensions* are defined as environmental variables and whose *size* is a function of the number of values that the environmental variables may assume for which an organism has *positive fitness"* (Hardesty 1975:71, emphases in original; see also Hutchinson 1965). One problem with the concept of the Hutchinsonian niche is that it is difficult to apply to the real world (Hardesty 1975:72). For any organism the number of environmental variables affecting it is large, compounding the problem of measuring the size or width of the niche. For humans, adding cultural variables to the milieu multiplies these difficulties (Hardesty 1975:72). Nevertheless, the concept provides an indispensable heuristic framework for discussing behavioral trends in a theoretical sense.

There is an important distinction between types of niche: the *fundamental niche,* occupied by organisms under conditions of no competition or population stress, and the *realized niche,* occupied by organisms under varying degrees of competition and stress (Hutchinson 1965). A third type of niche, the "partial" niche, was proposed by Vandermeer (1972) to identify niche space that results from a particular competitor or population pressure.

Although the niche size of a population in a given biotope can be defined (at least theoretically) by the limits of environmental variables that condition the fitness of that population (i.e., the variables comprising the realized niche), the niche cannot necessarily be mapped in biotope space, since a complex function may be required to make the transformation (Hudson 1969). Nevertheless, the boundaries of a realized niche *can* be approximated in real space when one or a few factors explain a significant proportion of variability within the niche, and those factors tend to co-occur in space (Warren and O'Brien 1982:96).

Colonization

During the colonization phase of rural settlement, a population extends itself into new areas (Hudson 1969). The total size of the population remains constant in the source and target areas combined, but density decreases in the source area and increases in the target area owing to an outward shift of the population's magnitude function over space. The areas into which a population migrates may be new environments, unexploited parts of old environments, or new territories. Because midwestern environments have been relatively stable during late Holocene times, only the latter two possibilities apply here. It is important to distinguish between them, since each has different implications for both the scale and the evolutionary significance of different kinds of migration.

There are several possible outcomes of migration into unexploited parts of old environments. When viewed from the perspective of niche space these include: (*a*) the expansion of settlement along all preexisting vectors of the realized niche—such as into areas with less desirable soils, slope positions, and vegetation—that generally increases niche width; (*b*) the shift of settlement along one or a few preexisting niche vectors—such as toward sparser and drier upland forests—that quantitatively alters niche width along select dimensions of the environment; and (*c*) the shift of settlement along a new vector of the realized niche—such as into previously unoccupied prairies—that qualitatively alters the basic composition of the niche. In all three cases the scale of migration may be small, yet significant technological or behavioral adaptations may be necessary to exploit the environment efficiently.

Migration into a new territory is the most appropriate model for initial frontier settlement in the Midwest. However, the possible outcomes of large-scale movements are more varied and depend to a large extent on environmental differences between the old and new territories. When environmental characteristics of the source and target areas are essentially the same, any of the three outcomes just mentioned (*a–c,* above) could result. However, considering that survival in all these cases might require costly cultural innovations, it seems likely that settlers would follow a more conservative course of action. For instance, settlements in both the source and target areas could potentially cluster along identical ranges of the same niche dimensions and essentially duplicate in the new territory the realized niche of the old one. Settlers could thereby avoid readaptation to the physical environment of the target area. Beyond this, the net decline of settlement density in the source and target areas combined would allow settlers in the new territory to contract toward the centroid of all preexisting niche dimensions. This would decrease niche width to include an "optimum" spectrum of environmental conditions and maximize the chances of farmstead survival. On the other hand, when there are fundamental differences between the biotopes of source and target areas it is less likely that the realized niche could be duplicated. In this case settlers might be forced to effectively redefine both the vectors and the width of the realized niche and adjust their adaptations accordingly.

As Hudson (1969:368) noted, the concepts of niche and population magnitude provide a heuristic framework for determining both the density and the environmental context of colonial settlement. However, factors associated with neither of these concepts can by themselves determine all aspects of the spatial pattern of rural settlement during the colonization phase. Patterning on a regional scale is, of course, influenced in part by environmental heterogeneity and the tolerance limits of a population with respect to the environmental

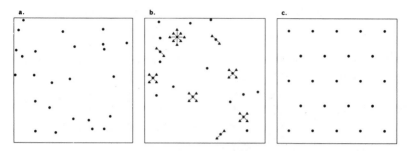

2.1. Farmstead distributions predicted by Hudson's (1969) ecological model for three phases of rural settlement: (*a*) random configuration during the colonization phase (twenty-five points); (*b*) compound random (denoted by ●) and clustered (denoted by ▲) configurations during the spread phase (fifty points); and (*c*) regular configuration during the competition phase (twenty-five points). Note that all three distributions assume a homogeneous environment or a realized niche that is wider than the areas shown.

variables that make up its realized niche (Greig-Smith 1979; Haggett, Cliff, and Frey 1977:104–5). Analysis of the biophysical niche of settlers is therefore important here. However, patterning may also be influenced by factors that are independent of variation in the biophysical environment. In this case patterning would occur *within* the mapping of the realized niche in biotope space, and the arrangement of farmsteads in this space would be unrelated to gradients of the biophysical environment.

There are three basic types of point patterns that farmsteads[1] can form during the colonization of homogeneous environments. On a scale of increasing aggregation these include regular, random, and clustered arrangements (see Pielou 1977). In a perfectly regular arrangement all points are uniformly spaced and maximally distant from their nearest neighbors (fig. 2.1*c*). Frequencies of points drawn from a regular grid are "underdispersed" in comparison with a Poisson distribution (Kershaw 1963), and the variance of point frequencies is less than the mean. In a random arrangement each point is located independently of all others (fig. 2.1*a*). Point frequencies are compatible with a Poisson distribution, and the variance of point frequencies equals the mean. Clustered or contagious arrangements occur when points are clumped into groups and nearest-neighbor distances are minimal (fig. 2.1*b*). Point frequencies are "overdispersed" with respect to a Poisson distribution, and the variance of point frequencies exceeds the mean.

To the extent that farmstead locations can be modeled as points, then, we

---

1. In this book we use the term farmstead to refer only to the primary residential locus of a farm. Euro-American farmsteads are normally the staging areas for farm operations and include areas and buildings for domestic activities, production, and storage.

would expect mutual avoidance among settlers to generate a regular arrangement of farmsteads, independence among the locational decisions of settlers to generate a random arrangement, and mutual attraction among settlers to generate a clustered arrangement. But which of these alternatives should we expect during the colonization phase of rural settlement? Hudson's theory does not deal directly with this issue. He suggests in his classic paper, however, that new colonial farmsteads should be "somewhat repelled" by older colonial farmsteads "under conditions of contiguous landholdings of approximately equal size typical of most homesteading in the United States" (Hudson 1969:370), and he concludes that this process should eventually result in a somewhat regular spacing of farmsteads. On the other hand, a recent summary of Hudson's original model by Hodder (1977) suggests instead that colonization-phase settlements in homogeneous environments should be arranged randomly, and a review by Haining (1982:212–13) suggests a clustered distribution. In fact, it is the random hypothesis that Hudson originally intended to impart as a general expectation for colonial settlement (J. C. Hudson, personal communication).[2]

There are several reasons we might expect a random arrangement of farmsteads during the colonization phase of rural settlement. First, randomness can be construed as the most parsimonious of the three alternative patterns. It requires no assumption of interdependence among the locational decisions of colonial settlers, and it is the only one of the three patterns that can be said to lack spatial trend. From a methodological perspective, then, randomness can be considered the "null hypothesis" of rural farmstead location. Second, random patterns are often regarded as the most appropriate ecological analogues for the initial colonizing behavior of relatively sedentary plants and animals. For instance, Kershaw (1963) reviews literature on vegetal colonization and postulates that plants generally undergo three phases of pattern development: early colonizers tend to assume random arrangements; clustered arrangements are later produced by the reproductive spread of offspring from colonizers via short-distance dispersal of seeds, stolons, or rhizomes; and greater regularity in the spacing of individuals is eventually caused by the expansion and stabilization of populations at or near carrying capacity.

Despite the potential merits of these arguments, it should be emphasized that both are somewhat problematic. The random null hypothesis, first of all, is actually little more than an arbitrary assumption. It is, somewhat to its credit, an assumption founded on a hypothesis of proximate causality. (As postulated earlier, independence among the locational decisions of colonists causes random patterning, whereas interdependence causes either clustered or

2. July 1982.

regular patterns depending on whether the interactive process among colonists is one of attraction or repulsion.) Nevertheless, selection of the null hypothesis as an empirical expectation is more of a methodological convenience than a choice grounded in knowledge of human behavior. This issue is an important one, and we shall return to it presently.

A problem with the second argument arises from the fact that the three-phase pattern sequence outlined by Kershaw (1963) may well be a general one but is by no means universal. As Barnes and Stanbury (1951) point out, random patterns should be expected only for colonizing species whose dispersal mechanisms favor independence among individuals during the process of translocating offspring from parent to substrate. This is often the case for plants dispersed by water or wind (Boughey 1973:23), but it is clearly not the case for plants dispersed as aggregates of seeds in fruits transported by animals. Interdependence among dispersing offspring generally produces clustered arrangements, and such clusters have been documented among the early colonizers of new environments (Barnes and Stanbury 1951). Moreover, regular patterns, which are admittedly rare among most plant and many animal species, have been demonstrated for the nest locations of some colonizing birds (Pielou 1977:160). Thus there are clear biological precedents for all three locational patterns in natural colonizing populations.

The importance of this point does not stem from its most immediate implication. To document regular, random, and clustered spatial patterns among nonhuman colonizers implies, at one level, only that a variety of arrangements are possible in frontier rural settlement. This we already know. Of greater interest is the less direct and less obvious implications that the three patterns, viewed as survival strategies, might differ in adaptive value for frontier immigrants. So far we have considered only functional explanations involving the *proximate* causes of the different processes of colonization—the differential effects on spatial pattern of independent and interdependent mechanisms of dispersal. Beyond these considerations is a more fundamental question of *ultimate* causality: Do any of the three dispersal mechanisms and their associated spatial patterns have a selective advantage over the others in colonial contexts, and, if so, would it be reasonable to assume that the most advantageous spatial pattern could actually appear given the means of obtaining land that were available to colonizers during the early nineteenth century?

The first part of this question forces us to refocus our attention downward to decision making at the level of the individual. Here the issue becomes one of interfarmstead distance: maximizing distance produces regular patterns, minimizing distance produces clustered patterns, and random patterns are produced when the distance to neighboring farmsteads is not a significant factor in locational decisions.

Upon reflection, there seem to be relatively few advantages to the strategy of maximizing distance (regular pattern) among market-oriented agriculturists in frontier contexts. Spatial regularity in nature usually indicates either relatively high population density and keen competition for resources (Pianka 1974:105) or highly territorial or allelopathic individuals (Pielou 1977:165). By definition, levels of density and competition are both relatively low during colonization, so we can discount the importance of these factors. Territoriality may be an appropriate model for frontier hunters and trappers with extractive economic orientation, but it seems nonetheless to be a poor model for midwestern colonial farmers who produced goods on much smaller, titled parcels of land. This leaves us with the factor of allelopathy, a rather curious characteristic of certain plant species that secrete toxic chemicals that inhibit the growth of nearby plants. Allelopathy hardly seems an appropriate analogue for frontier settlement, especially in light of the theory that most allelopathic substances evolved as defenses against animal predators or pathogens and that the inhibitory effect on other plants is incidental to the defensive function (Whittaker 1975:256). On the other hand, allelopathy does enable individuals to avoid contact and competition with other individuals, and this aspect of the process has parallels that might have been perceived as advantages by frontier farmers. For instance, isolation would enhance the likelihood that colonists with limited capital could eventually expand their landholdings contiguously (thereby maximizing the efficiency of future farm operations) by minimizing the risk that later immigrants would acquire the desired property before the original settler could do so. Isolation would also reduce the likelihood of interpersonal contact, and this could have been perceived as an advantage by the legendary asocial frontiersman. Nevertheless, it is doubtful that either of these strategies would have been sufficiently advantageous to have had a widespread impact on frontier settlement, and both pale in comparison with the potential advantages of distance minimization.

There are a variety of advantages to colonists who minimize interfarmstead distance (clustered pattern), and these seem to far outweigh the benefits of isolation. For instance, aggregation would enable farmers to minimize transportation costs to local markets and supply and service centers; maximize defense capabilities, an important consideration in many American frontiers; maximize the potential for large-scale public or private projects; facilitate the maintenance of social ties arising from common kinship, religious affiliation, or area of origin; and maximize the efficiency of communication networks. All these factors would be beneficial either economically or socially, and it is not difficult to imagine that midwestern colonists would have perceived them in that light.

In answering the first part of the question of ultimate causality, then, we are inclined to postulate that clustered patterns would indeed have a selective advantage over regular ones in colonial contexts. However, this is not to say that we expect exclusively clustered arrangements of farmsteads during the colonization phase of settlement in the Salt River valley. In fact, there are at least two good reasons to doubt this possibility. First, it seems unlikely that all immigrants were of one mind on the benefits of aggregation. Settlers migrating as independent nuclear families may well have considered only biophysical factors in making their land-purchase decisions. To the extent that distances to established farmsteads were ignored, of course, an important stochastic element would have been introduced into the regional land-selection sequence, resulting in a random arrangement of settlements within the realized niche.

Another reason to doubt exclusively clustered patterning revolves around the second part of the ultimate causality question: the available means of obtaining land during the early nineteenth century in the Midwest. Of interest here are several legal and geometric factors that could in themselves have had significant effects on farmstead arrangement.

The first factor arises from the fact that titles of exclusive ownership of nineteenth-century midwestern farms ordinarily did not allow land purchased from the federal government to be repurchased from the government once it had passed into private hands. When viewed from the perspective of sampling design, this means that farmsteads were purchased (sampled) without re-placement, so that the pool of available federal land shrank with every purchase. Only when samples are drawn *with* replacement can one guarantee a random distribution (Blalock 1972:143). What effect does sampling without replacement have on spatial pattern? To answer this question we simulated colonization in a gridded one hundred unit area that is comparable in structure to the township and range framework of land survey used historically in many parts of the Midwest (fig. 2.2). Units of constant size were sampled randomly, but without replacement, in three sequential series. Each series represents a sample of purchases made in a different time period so that we can observe the effect of increasing density on spatial pattern. At time I there are fifteen farmsteads, and 15% of the area is settled; at time II there are eighteen new farmsteads and fifteen old farmsteads, and 33% of the area is settled; and at time III there are forty-four new farmsteads and thirty-three old farmsteads, and 77% of the area is settled.

To measure degree of aggregation we used nested-block analysis of $\angle$ variance, a technique developed by Greig-Smith (1952, 1964) that accounts for potential change in degree of aggregation at different scales. The first step in the procedure is to determine the frequencies of farmsteads in each grid unit and in progressively larger sets of adjacent grid units (which in our case range in size from one to one hundred units) for each of the three time periods.

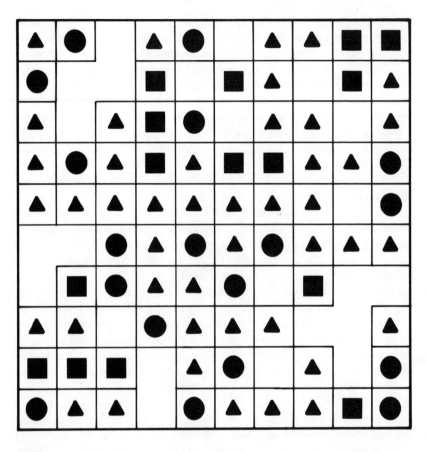

2.2. Simulated time-series distribution of randomly placed farmsteads in a 100-block area. At time I there are fifteen farmsteads (denoted by) and 15% of the area is settled; at time II there are eighteen new farmsteads (denoted by ●) and 33% of the area is settled; at time III there are forty-four new farmsteads (denoted by ▲) and 77% of the area is settled.

These grid units and sets of grid units, termed blocks, increase in size and decrease in number with increasing scale. For instance, at block size 1 there are one hundred square blocks, each block comprises one grid unit, and the number of farmsteads contained in each block can vary from zero to one; at block size 2 there are fifty rectangular blocks, each block comprises two adjacent grid units, and the number of farmsteads contained in each block can range from zero to two; at block size 4 there are twenty-five square blocks, each block comprises four adjacent grid units, and the number of farmsteads contained in each block can range from zero to four; and so on. The second step is to calculate, for each time period, the mean and variance of farmstead frequencies in progressively larger blocks. As we noted earlier, variance is respectively less than, equal to, and greater than the mean in regular, random, and clustered spatial patterns. It follows that the variance/mean ratio is a direct measure of degree of aggregation and can be used to compare the general characteristics of patterns at different scales and densities. The final step, then, is to calculate variance/mean ratios for each block size by time period.

The results of our simulation are shown in figure 2.3 as a graph of variance/mean ratio against block size. As the figure indicates, among the smaller block sizes (block size < 25 units) there is a progressive decrease in ratios through time. At time I (low density) the ratios range between 0.85 and 1.32 for the smaller block sizes; at time II (medium density) the range is 0.31 to 0.67; and at time III (high density) the range is 0.04 to 0.23. This suggests that spatial patterns become increasingly regular as density increases within a regular grid. This is confirmed, even for most of the larger block sizes, by the upper and lower 95% confidence limits of random distributions reported by Greig-Smith (1961). The low-density values are consistently random, the medium-density values tend to fluctuate around the lower limit of randomness, and the high-density values are consistently regular. The medium-density values are of particular interest in light of the fact that they border on regularity when only one-third of the sample area is in private hands. Results of the simulation indicate, then, that even if the locational decisions of settlers are independent of one another during colonization, a perfectly random distribution of farmsteads of constant size may be possible only during the initial stages of settlement.

A second factor that could have affected farmstead arrangement involves the geometric attributes of farms. It is obvious that farms are not composed simply of pointlike farmsteads; they also include relatively extensive tracts of land that can vary greatly in size and shape. Less obvious, perhaps, is the possibility that size or shape variation could influence farmstead location independently of other factors. This possibility is implied in an ecological study that models the spatial arrangement of plant populations as a function of the density and size variations of individuals (Pielou 1960). Pielou's study simulated the colonization of a homogeneous environment by randomly locating individual points, allowing preemptive circles drawn around the points to vary in size within limits that differed in each of three separate trials, and calculating variance/mean ratios of point frequencies at different densities. She found that degree of aggregation, as measured by variance/mean ratio, correlates directly with both the density and the size range of individuals. The positive density correlation is somewhat surprising, since it

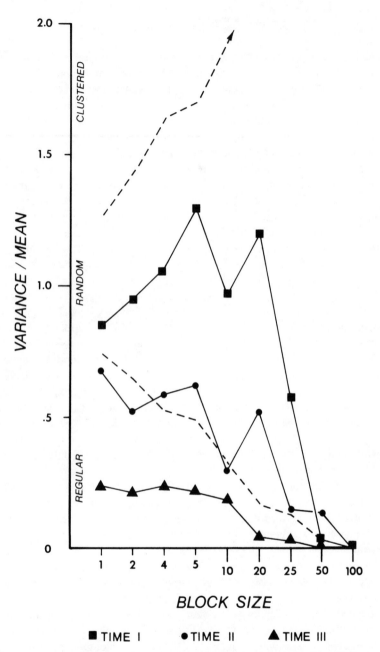

2.3. Graph of variance/mean ratio against block size of the time series of randomly placed farmsteads shown in figure 2.2. At time I (denoted by ■–■) there are fifteen farmsteads and 15% of the area is settled; at time II (denoted by ●–●) there are thirty-three farmsteads and 33% of the area is settled; at time III (denoted by ▲–▲) there are seventy-seven farmsteads and 77% of the area is settled. Dashed lines show upper and lower 95% confidence limits of random distributions.

seems to contradict our results (figs. 2.2 and 2.3). However, the discrepancy is explained by the fact that individuals in Pielou's simulation were made as large as possible within the prescribed size limits without overlapping previously drawn circles, whereas farmsteads in our simulation were of uniform size. Thus, Pielou's individuals generally shrank in size as density increased, and small individuals were able to establish themselves in dense clumps between the spaces occupied by the older, larger individuals. This process also helps explain the correlation between aggregation and size range: as individuals were allowed to range in size within broader and broader limits (the size ranges of large:small individuals were 12.25:1, 100:1, and 400:1 in Pielou's three trials), there was a greater potential for packing numerous small individuals among the relatively few large ones.

The relation that Pielou (1960) demonstrates between the size range of individuals and degree of aggregation forces us to question the assumption of uniform farm size in our first simulation. As one might suspect, colonial land purchases in the Midwest varied noticeably in area. In the project area, for instance, the first land entries of early settlers ranged from 40 to 640 acres (Mason, Warren, and O'Brien 1982), though most (86%) were 80 or 160 acre units. To test the effect of size variation on spatial pattern under more realistic conditions, we simulated colonial settlement a second time (fig. 2.4). In this case farms ranging in size from one- to four-unit areas were randomly plotted in an ordered sequence of three farm sizes (i.e., in three-farm cycles of small, then medium, then large, etc.), and farmsteads within the two- and four-unit farms were randomly plotted in one of the constituent units. Samples were drawn until the remaining space prohibited the completion of additional plot cycles. At time I there are fifteen farmsteads (five of each of the three sizes), and 35% of the area is settled, and at time II there are a total of thirty-three farmsteads (eleven of each of the three sizes) and 77% of the area is settled. Variance/mean ratios, calculated as before for the two time periods, are shown in figure 2.5. The results, somewhat surprisingly, are very similar to those for the first two time periods in the previous simulation (fig. 2.3). The low-density values are consistently random in both cases, and the higher-density values border on regularity. This seems to imply that the arrangements of randomly drawn, variably sized farmsteads become more regular as density increases, and this trend is essentially unaffected by farm-size variability. However, the proportion of a region occupied by settlers is probably a more appropriate measure of the extent of colonial settlement than farmstead density, and from the former perspective there is a clear difference between the two simulations. Time II in the first simulation (33% of area settled) actually corresponds to time I in the second (35% of area settled), while time III in the first simulation equals time II in the second (77% of area settled in both cases). Moving from the first to the second simulation, then, we see measurable increases in variance/mean ratios and a tendency toward greater aggregation. Since there is only one significant difference between the two simulations, we can conclude that farm-size variability correlates directly with degree of spatial aggregation and that this relation is powerful enough to counteract the trend toward greater spatial regularity that accompanies increases in density among farms of uniform size.

These results raise an additional question: At what point along the gradient

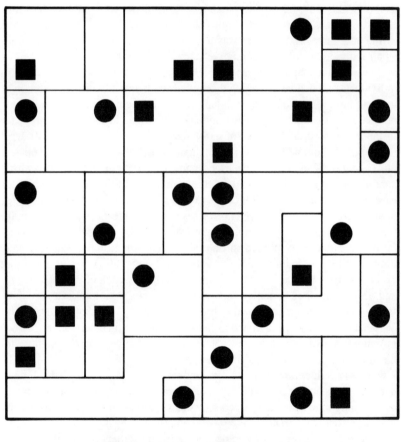

■ TIME I ● TIME II

2.4. Simulated distribution of randomly placed farmsteads, representing farms of different sizes, in a 100-block area. At time I there are fifteen farmsteads (denoted by ■) and 35% of the area is settled; at time II there are eighteen new farmsteads (denoted by ●) and 77% of the area is settled.

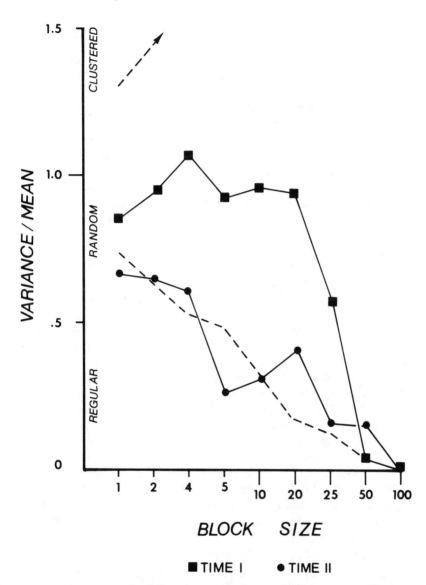

2.5. Graph of variance/mean ratio against block size for the time series of randomly placed farmsteads shown in figure 2.4. At time I (denoted by ■–■) there are fifteen farmsteads and 35% of the area is settled; at time II (denoted by ●–●) there are thirty-three farmsteads and 77% of the area is settled. Dashed lines show the upper and lower 95% confidence limits of random distributions.

of size-range variation will patterns become clustered owing to size variation alone? Experimental simulation is unnecessary here, since, in simple cases at least, maximum potential variance/mean ratios can be determined directly from the size relations and proportions of large to small farms. For instance, when there are two farm sizes (e.g., five-unit and one-unit farms) and their area relation is known (e.g., 5:1), population variance in a packed region always peaks when half the region is in large farms (e.g., one farmstead in a ten-unit region) and half is in small farms (e.g., five farmsteads in the same ten-unit region), regardless of the total number of farms. Means are also stable under these conditions, so it is a simple matter to calculate variance/ mean ratios for different size ranges of farms. A graph of variance/mean ratios against a series of area relations (1:1 through 10:1) indicates that there is a continuous and nearly linear increase in aggregation with increasing disparity between the sizes of large and small farms (fig. 2.6). Furthermore, in comparison with the 95% confidence limits for random distributions, the trend demonstrates a progression from regular through clustered patterns and indicates (with one important qualification) that large farms must be more than six times the area of small farms for size-range variation to effect clustered patterning. The qualification to be noted here is the rather unwieldy assumption that regions are evenly divided in area between large and small farms. This condition maximizes variance but does not ensure maximum variance/ mean ratios, since the latter vary asymmetrically in relation to the proportion of an area occupied by large farms. In fact, the points plotted in figure 2.6 underestimate to varying degrees the maximum possible ratios for each size relation. This is illustrated in graphs of variance/mean ratio against proportion of area in large farms for the 6:1 and 7:1 size ranges (fig. 2.7). The first graph (fig. 2.7*a*) demonstrates that clustered patterns *are* possible owing solely to size variation at the 6:1 area relation, but only when large farms occupy about 60–80% of a packed region. This range expands to about 40–90% for the 7:1 size relation (fig. 2.7*b*) and increases further for all higher size ranges. However, it must also be emphasized that these trends pertain only to regions that are completely settled and in which the arrangements and sizes of farms are perfectly suited for maximizing variance/ mean ratios. Neither of these conditions can be expected during the colonization phase of rural settlement. Moreover, the size range and proportion of most early land purchases in the project area (mentioned above) fail even to approach the minimum conditions effecting clustered settlement during colonization of the region.

[An idealized three-dimensional model summarizes the interrelations demonstrated here between the factors of farmstead density, farm-size variation, and degree of spatial aggregation (fig. 2.8). As we have seen, farmstead arrangements become more regular as density increases among farms of

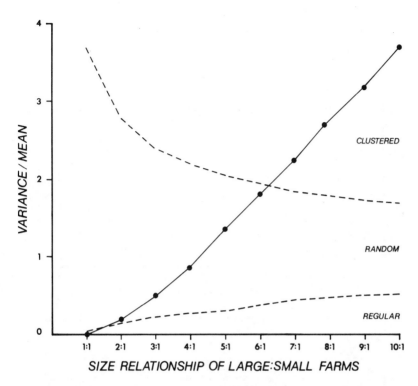

2.6. Graph of variance/mean ratio against size variability of large and small farms. Dashed lines show upper and lower 95% confidence limits of random distributions.

uniform size, and high-density arrangements become more clustered with increasing variation of farm size. These two relations imply that arrangements must also become more clustered as density increases among farms of diverse size. (It is worth noting that this particular association is supported by the locational simulations of Pielou 1960: table 1, rows 13-15.) Together these trends can be viewed as a fundamental predictive framework of rural settlement pattern.) As we noted earlier, nineteenth-century farms in the project area were fairly uniform in size. Thus the model predicts a random arrangement of farmsteads during the early phases of settlement and greater regularity thereafter. However, recall that cultural factors may impart signifi-cant selective advantages to settlers who locate near one another. To the extent that these advantages influenced the locational decisions of early settlers, we would expect clusters of colonial farmsteads in the region. Actually, there is little reason to doubt that the configuration of colonial settlement was dualistic, with both random and clustered arrangements of farmsteads

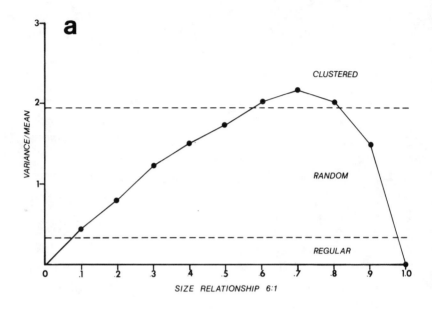

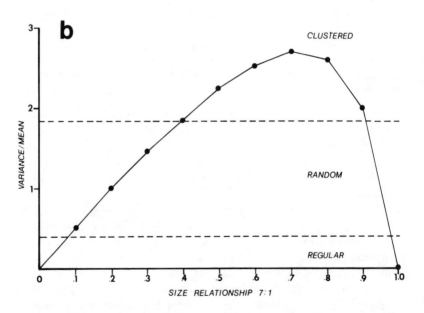

2.7. Graphs of variance/mean ratio against proportion of area in large farms for two size relations of large to small farms: (*a*) 6:1 size relation and (*b*) 7:1 size relation. Dashed lines show upper and lower 95% confidence limits of random distribution at the 0.5 proportion.

represented in the same region (cf. fig. 2.1*a*). This would have shifted upward the median degree of colonial farmstead aggregation, though subsequent increases in density would eventually have effected a more and more regular configuration of settlement.

Spread

During the spread phase, settlements increase in number, owing to population growth, and fill up the realized niche (Hudson 1969). If technological advances occur at the same time, the niche itself may expand and allow settlement of new parts of the environment. In either case the spread process ends when populations approach ʿcarrying capacityʾ and physical and ⁊ cultural pressures cause a leveling off or a reversal of growth.

There are two processes that account for increases in population density during the spread phase. It is important to distinguish them, since each has a distinct effect on settlement pattern. The first arises from reproduction. As the surplus offspring of colonists reach maturity, they ordinarily disperse from the

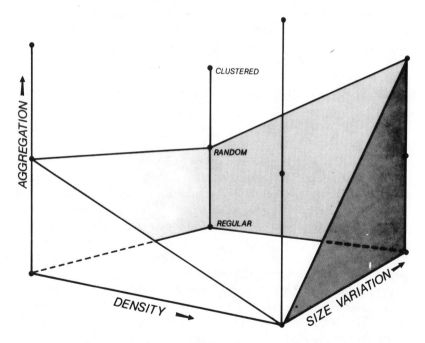

2.8. Trivariate model showing the effects of farmstead density and farm-size variation on degree of farmstead spatial aggregation. Based on simulations of randomly placed and ideally placed farmsteads (figs. 2.2–2.6).

parent household and establish new households elsewhere. Citing an extensive body of ecological and geographical research, Hudson postulates that in rural contexts this budding or diffusion of new farmsteads takes place over limited distances so that the probability of encountering a budded farmstead increases as one approaches a parent farmstead. This short-distance dispersal results in clustered arrangements of related farmsteads (fig. 2.1*b*), and it is worth emphasizing that the individuals occupying these farmsteads would benefit from many of the same social and economic advantages enjoyed by colonial immigrants who settled near one another.

The second process is a carryover from the colonization phase of rural settlement. Hudson (1969:370) states that "a principal determinant of increasing density in many frontier zones is not spread but continued migration to the frontier from outside the area." The spatial effects of continued immigration should to some extent mimic those predicted above for the colonization phase (i.e., overlapping random and clustered arrangements of farmsteads). However, the locational constraints imposed by increasing farmstead density must eventually outweigh the effects of independent and interdependent migration (fig. 2.8). As the realized niche becomes filled there is less opportunity for new settlers to exercise free choice in acquiring public lands. Interfarmstead distances must eventually become more uniform and settlement configurations more regular. This process would affect budding farmsteads in the same way and probably at the same rate. Thus the spread phase should be a dynamic interval in which both random arrangements and old and new clusters of farmsteads give way to more regular configurations.

Competition

The spread phase ends roughly when all agriculturally productive areas of the biotope have been acquired by individuals and the upper limits of rural population are approached. Density-dependent conditions that could affect this limit include both soil exhaustion and the lack of available public land. At this point a third process, competition, becomes a dominant force affecting population density and settlement pattern. Competition is a struggle among farmers to keep their landholdings intact and to increase their net productivity and economic return. One direct method of accomplishing this goal is to increase the size of one's holdings. When the realized niche is filled, however, farmers are forced to compete for one another's land. This favors the expansion of large farms at the expense of smaller ones. As Hudson (1969:371) notes, "there is a lower limit on the size of the farm that can be operated economically." Although an increase in the price of farm products may temporarily revitalize some smaller farms, the process inevitably is checked, and the long-term survival rate of small farms is relatively low.

Thus, as landholdings change hands during the competition phase, large farms ⌐ get larger, the total number of farms decreases, and rural population may decrease as well.

These trends have important spatial correlates that should reinforce changing rural settlement patterns. Although economic stability and the potential for competitive expansion may be greatest among settlers with relatively large landholdings and abundant assets, it is unlikely that expansionist farmers would fail to consider the effect of production costs on the potential gross revenues to be generated by additional land purchases. Since production costs increase at a higher rate than gross revenues as the distance between home and field increases (Found 1971:70-71), optimal purchase choices for most kinds of farming operations are those nearest the original farmstead and within the realized niche. In addition, production costs per unit of output are generally U-shaped across a scale of increasing farm size (owing to varying efficiencies of management, supply, equipment, communication, and transport), and the relative inefficiency of very small and very large operations favors farms of intermediate size, in which unit production costs are lowest (Barlowe 1978:149-51). Over time these two processes would select for farms of roughly equal size in which farmsteads are near the centers of landholdings. Thus, as Hudson (1969) argues, the ideal rural settlement pattern of the competition phase is a hexagonal lattice of landholdings with equidistant midpoints and a regular spacing of farmsteads (fig. 2.1c).

Sociocultural and Economic Factors

In our discussion of the colonization phase we mentioned several sociocultural and economic factors that could have had important effects on patterns of settlement in early frontier contexts. In most cases these factors favor minimizing interfarmstead distance and tend to effect clusters of interacting farmsteads. Since sociocultural and economic factors are not incorporated into Hudson's (1969) ecological model, and because their effects differ from those postulated by Hudson for initial phases of frontier settlement, they deserve special emphasis.

Of the many sociocultural and economic factors that could have acted ⌐ singly or in concert to condition frontier settlement, five are mentioned here—kinship, commonality of origin, religious affiliation, transportation routes, and proximity to market and service centers. The benefits accruing from settling near kin are numerous and include facilitating neighborly sharing of labor for intensive tasks and maintaining existing social ties between related nuclear families or between interdependent groups colonizing parts of a region contemporaneously. Also, fear of Indian reprisals may have persisted among some newcomers to northeast Missouri (though native groups had largely evacuated the area by 1820), and these fears could have favored some clustering of settlements for defensive purposes (Warren, O'Brien, and Mason 1981:22).

For the reasons presented above, persons from the same general area in the source region may also have settled near each other out of a feeling of "kinship," whether or not the social units were related by affinal or consanguineous linkages. The role of religion in conditioning settlement may have been similar to that of commonality of origin. If church ties in the source area were strong before emigration, members of the same church or denomination may have chosen to maintain those ties in the frontier region by settling near one another.

- Transportation routes, especially well-maintained roads, could have greatly affected the locations of rural farmsteads throughout the region. As we discuss in chapter 5, transportation networks developed rapidly in the project area after 1825, connecting the region with external markets to the south, east, and northeast. The advantages gained by locating one's farmstead along these routes should have been significant in reducing the time, effort, and risk of transporting goods. In similar fashion, there would have been several advantages to selecting land in proximity to market and service centers (cf. Hall 1966; Losch 1954), including minimizing field-to-market costs of transporting agricultural products, minimizing travel time to obtain goods and services, and maximizing information exchange with other area residents.

Together these factors seem to constitute a strong argument for clustered settlement, especially during the early years of colonization. Moreover, their economic and social advantages should have been evident to many migrating colonists both in and behind zones of frontier settlement. Thus we postulate that a process we call *interdependent immigration*—the migration of linked multifamily social units to a frontier context—could have had a strong impact on the proximal spacing of frontier farmsteads (Warren, O'Brien, and Mason 1981). An alternative process, termed *independent immigration,* would have effected less-aggregated patterns of settlement among colonists who considered only biophysical factors in making land-purchase decisions. In combination, the two processes are expected to generate a compound configuration of clustered and random colonial settlement.

Physical Dimensions of the Realized Niche

Hudson's model predicts changing configurations of settlement within an abstract realized niche. For obvious reasons, though, it does not attempt to isolate the *dimensions* of the realized niche in any specific environmental province. Nonetheless, biophysical factors can be assumed to influence the locational decisions of settlers in all but the most homogeneous environments, and it is imperative that our model of frontier settlement isolate the factors that may have been influential in the project area.

The biophysical dimensions considered here are biome (prairie versus ↙ forest), forest density, slope susceptibility to flooding, and soil quality. Based on the available literature, biome was a major determinant of frontier settlement. There is a widespread notion that early settlers avoided prairies, and we examine in detail several published analyses of early settlement to assess the validity of this proposition. While it is relatively easy to model settlement relative to individual dimensions such as biome, it is more difficult to model it against the sum of all dimensions. As will be seen, the complex interrelations among these dimensions preclude efforts to construct a simple predictive model for settlement. We can, however, posit certain general expectations regarding human settlement vis-à-vis these postulated physical dimensions of the realized niche.

The suitability of land for crop production undoubtedly was a central concern of pioneer agriculturists, regardless of the region being settled. Upon arriving in a frontier area, the colonist was faced with the decisions on how much land, and which tracts of land, to purchase. We speculate that the immediate concern of the frontier settler was to satisfy perceived needs with a minimal investment of time and energy. Ignoring for the moment the role of cultural factors in conditioning these decisions, we assume that a person would choose the best land available for his purposes. There are standard methods for determining the "best," or most productive, land, but modern measurements may not correspond to dimensions that were important to frontier agriculturists (Warren, McDaniel, and O'Brien 1982). Because of differences between the "ideal" as it exists in modern quantitative measurements and as it existed in potentially different frontier perceptions, our model attempts to balance both etic and emic perspectives. For this reason, our discussion occasionally turns to narrative accounts of historical settlement in other areas of the Midwest, especially studies that have investigated what might be termed the "preferred" environmental characteristics for settlement.

Prairie and Forest

Agricultural technology in the upper South was based on wood (McManis 1964). Farmers made their houses, barns, fences, implements, and wagons from wood, especially in frontier situations (Bidwell and Falconer 1925:162). In the early nineteenth century, cornfields were first plowed with a light moldboard plow with an iron tip, and often a wooden harrow was used to complete soil preparation (Bidwell and Falconer 1925:342). Brick or stone houses were rare in frontier areas of the upper South; a characteristic wooden house-construction style in both log and frame was developed instead. Given this wood-based orientation, one might argue that colonists would choose forested areas over prairie for settlement. In fact, Bidwell and Falconer (1925:158) recognized long ago that frontier settlements in the Prairie Peninsula were distributed nonrandomly with respect to features of the environment. They suggested that early frontier settlements were biased toward forest locations and proposed that agriculturists consciously avoided prairies owing to scarcity of timber needed for construction and fuel, lack of usable surface water, and dense prairie sod whose cultivation usually required a prohibitive investment of money and labor.

Based on information from historical accounts, there may be reason to suspect that in some areas of the trans-Appalachian West colonial settlement was directed primarily at wooded environments. For instance, Michaux (1904:220), while crossing the sparsely timbered Barrens of south-central Kentucky in 1802, encountered only eighteen houses in 60 miles of road. The Kentucky legislature, hoping to counter the forest bias, offered 400 acres free to every man who would settle in the Barrens (Flint 1828, 2:175). When taken at face value, however, historical accounts often are misleading. Sauer (1927:34–35), after studying the settlement pattern of the Pennyroyal section of the Barrens, concluded that the fringes of the Barrens were settled early, possibly before 1790, and that frontier settlers recognized the value of the prairie.

This brings our discussion to an important point—differing opinions on the relative merits of forest versus prairie settlement. Jordan (1964:205) states:

In an effort to emphasize the effects of the obvious contrast between forest and prairie, many scholars have created the erroneous impression that there were only two types of land—that covered with timber and that devoid of timber. In fact, however, there was a land between the forest and the prairie, a land which shared the attributes of both, where the settler could have timber as well as grass on his land.

Jordan also notes that the differences in types of prairie have long been recognized. For example, a guidebook to Illinois published in 1837 (cited in Jordan 1964:205) divided prairies into healthy or bushy, alluvial or wet, and undulating or dry prairies, in addition to oak openings. Other contemporary sources made similar classifications. For his analysis of settlement in sections of Kentucky and the Old Northwest. Jordan recognized the following vegetational zones: openings; fringes of small dry prairies; fringes of small wet prairies; fringes of large prairies; large dry prairies; large wet prairies; interfluvial forests; and fluvial forests. He reduced these zones to three major vegetational patterns—forest, open prairie, and prairie-forest mixture—a classification that more accurately represents the true nature of the Prairie Peninsula than does the simple dichotomy between timber and prairie (see chap. 4).

Since the publication of Bidwell and Falconer's (1925) so-called prairie-avoidance hypothesis, a number of geographers and historians have attempted to revise this idea. A leader in this attempt is Jordan (1964, 1975), who, along with others (e.g., Birch 1971, 1974, 1979; Hewes 1950; McManis 1964; Peters 1970, 1973), has proposed that, rather than avoiding prairies, frontier agriculturists sought access to prairie-timber borders or oak savannas where forest resources were accessible yet laborious clearing of timber was unnecessary and native pastures were available nearby for grazing. Jordan presents an interesting as well as plausible answer to the question why upper South frontier settlers attained the reputation of being prairie avoiders. Southerners approached the Old Northwest from the south (Kentucky), which according to Jordan (1964:211) was the forested portion of the territory. Indian claims there were extinguished years before those to the north, in the mixed vegetational areas. In addition, the Ohio River and its tributaries were widely used as a link in the migration system of the late eighteenth/early nineteenth centuries, "and these waterways guided [settlers] to the forested areas, allowing little contact with the grasslands. The interfluves were the last to be taken, whether they were the forested interfluves of southern Indiana and Illinois or the prairie interfluves of central Illinois" (Jordan 1964:211). Thus the location of the forests of southern Illinois and Indiana adjacent to Kentucky, and the "guiding function" of the river, may have led early Kentucky emigrants to settle in forested areas. Jordan speculates that southern emigrants, once they came into contact with the prairie-timber margins, quickly realized the value of the mixed areas.

Both Jordan (1964) and McManis (1964) believe that frontier agriculturists' major objection to prairies was a lack of timber rather than a belief in the infertility of prairie soils. Accounts of prairie land, such as that by Timothy Flint (1828, 2:68) on Missouri's prairies, support this notion: "But this state alone has lands already fit for plough. . . . Prairies of hundreds of thousands of acres . . . covered with grass, and perfectly free from shrubs and bushes, invite the plough."

Most accounts Jordan studied note that houses were built in wooded areas on the edges of prairie and that crops were grown in the prairie margin. McManis used land purchase records as well as narrative sources to study select settlement locations in Illinois, and he concluded that timbered land sold earlier than prairie and that land on the edge of prairies sold before land in prairie centers. By the 1830s, only timbered areas and prairie edges had been sold, the latter apparently serving as pasture as well as cropland (McManis 1964:92).

An earlier study of settlement location in southern Illinois supports the opinion of Jordan and McManis. Pooley (1908) demonstrated that large prairies were avoided by agriculturists from Kentucky and Tennessee, who favored the edges of prairies. They built cabins at the forest edge and fenced parts of the prairie for cultivation. Thus small prairies were brought into production, and "every man could, figuratively speaking, keep his back to the timber and his attention on the prairie" (Pooley 1908:324). A letter from the project area written in 1831 by a Greenup County, Kentucky, emigrant to his family in Kentucky gives us a rare opportunity to examine land purchase strategies in the Salt River valley. Richard D. Powers bought an 80 acre tract with improvements (18 acres already were cleared and fenced) for $300, purchased an additional 80 acres for $250, and entered another 160 acres for the minimum price of $200. Of the total, 60–80 acres were in prairie and the rest was in timber and brush. Powers considered the soil quality to be excellent—"very black," "loose," "of considerable depth."

Unfortunately, few attempts at revising the prairie-avoidance hypothesis are grounded in systematic regional methods of sampling or analysis (Warren, McDaniel, and O'Brien 1982), and it is difficult to evaluate either the relative importance of prairie and timber in settlement decisions or changes in settlement decisions through time. They do, however, present us with an opposing view of colonial land preference, whose implications can be tested using data from the project area. Based on these reviews of the prairie-avoidance hypothesis, we speculate that it was not the grassland biome that was avoided but rather the *center* of the open prairies, "for only there did the prairie problem really begin" (Jordan 1964:216). There are three environmental contexts of prairies in the project area (chap. 3): moderately sloping valley sides and gently rolling uplands; flat, seasonally ponded upland marshes, or "swamps"; and areas near the ecotone, which contained scattered hardwoods and often dense thickets of scrub oak and hazelnut. We suggest in chapter 4 that until the adoption of drainage tiles Euro-American agriculturists avoided "wet prairies," leaving the two other prairie types as possible locations for settlement. We suggest that, owing to its proximity to forest resources, ecotonal prairie would have been the preferred prairie type for early frontier agriculturists.

It should not be construed from these statements that ecotones are "microcosmic Edens" that exhibit extraordinarily high resource potential and thereby attract human settlement (Warren and O'Brien 1982:88). They merely are zones of transition between different ecosystems that usually support reduced densities of certain species present in the major biomes and perhaps a few of their own. Nevertheless, settlements along narrow transition zones can be expected in response to the diverse resource needs of diffuse or mixed economies. For example, prairie edges may have attracted frontier agriculturists because they provided access to construction material, pasture, fuel, game, and sparsely timbered soil that did not require much clearing. Thus, though ecotones are not necessarily productive or are productive only seasonally, they can serve as staging areas from which the critical resources of adjacent communities can be tapped efficiently (Warren, McDaniel, and O'Brien 1982:18).

Forest Density

Forest density may have conditioned responses in the same way that biomes did, since lightly timbered areas could have attracted settlement owing to the ease of clearing land for cultivation. We note in chapter 4 that timber density in general forms a unimodal, bell-shaped curve that peaks strongly on steep valley sides, decreases gradually into lower slopes, bottomland terraces, and upland rims, and drops off sharply into level upland forests and prairies. There also were patches of anomalous low-density forests in the region, perhaps caused by presettlement fires. Thus a wide variety of land types were available to frontier settlers, and settlement choices must have been conditioned by individual perception and need. It might be argued, however, that, given the relative ease with which lightly timbered areas could be cleared, these areas would have been selected before more densely timbered areas.

Slope

Slope classes in the project area range from flat uplands and valley bottoms to steep talus slopes. As noted in chapter 4, between these extremes are valley sides with more moderate slopes. Although each of these classes is found in all sections of the project area, relief in the northeastern part is relatively severe. Steep slopes, combined with shallow, rocky soils, limit the value of these areas for settlement. Agriculturists generally prefer farming level to moderately sloping land. Schroeder's (1968) analysis of settlement location in Howard County (chap. 3) demonstrates a high correlation between early (pre-1820) settlement and moderately to gently sloping terrain. Gently sloping uplands were relatively easy to farm and also contained perched water tables (because of clayey subsoil) that could be tapped for potable water (Schroeder 1968:7).

One major disadvantage to farming many flat landforms in the project area is seasonal or annual wetness. Although the soil productivity of many upland prairies is high (see below), without adequate drainage this portion of the biosphere was inaccessible to early agriculturists.

Flooding

Flooding by the Salt River and its tributaries, which is severe at times (chap. 4), can seriously affect agricultural yields and damage farmsteads. Owing to the soil composition of bottomlands, often containing large amounts of clay particles, fields can remain wet for several weeks and prevent cultivation. Sauer (1920:113–14) notes a number of historical references to the "malarial" nature of the Missouri River bottomlands (cf. Flint 1828, 2:79), and Lewis Beck, an early traveler in the Salt Valley, noted that "the banks of Salt River have always been considered unhealthy" (1823:315). Thus, colonists of the region may have avoided wet bottomlands for both economic and health reasons.

Soil Quality

Historical accounts that refer to soil quality and preferred soil characteristics often discuss accompanying vegetation—both its density and its composition. As noted in chapter 3, soil fertility of estates in the trans-Appalachian region of Kentucky and Tennessee was ranked by the presence of certain species of trees (Michaux 1904:229). In addition, these accounts often refer to topography, suggesting that frontier agriculturists were cognizant of the interrelations between various environmental dimensions and that their perceptions of soil quality were conditioned by a variety of indirect indicators.

Regarding the Powers letter from the project area mentioned earlier, Mason (1983) notes that, with the exception of oak and "sugar trees," all trees Powers listed as occurring on his land appear in Michaux's list of taxa denoting first-class land in Kentucky. In the same vein, Flint (1828, 2:65) described the Boonslick region in terms of "extensive tracts of that fine kind of timbered upland alluvion, which constitutes the finest central portions of Kentucky." Regarding upland areas, he noted that they "are timbered with the same trees, which the alluvions bear. Like those, they are surmounted with grape vines, and are free from underbush. The graceful pawpaw, the persimmon, and the wild cherry tree, all denoting rich soils, abound in these regions; and they are nearly as fertile as the bottoms of the Missouri, or the Mississippi" (Flint 1828, 2:65). Based on these and other historical accounts, we suggest that the distribution of various types of timber may have conditioned colonial settlement decisions by providing an indirect index of soil productivity.

Information Flow

Having discussed several potential physical dimensions of the realized niche, we now consider the processes by which environmental information was transmitted to frontier agriculturists. General Land Office plats, showing the locations of natural features such as rivers, swamps, and the prairie-timber boundary, were sent by surveyors to the federal land office in St. Louis (Schroeder 1981:22). Since the land surveys were checked against individual surveyors' field notes by clerks in the St. Louis office, it is conceivable that the notes also were available for public inspection. If so, settlers had access to valuable information in the soil-quality assessments of the surveyors and data on the locations of important species of plants (chap. 4), and locational decisions could have been based on this information. Once colonial settlements were established and colonists had the opportunity to observe the environment firsthand, this information could also have been transmitted to newcomers to help them make wise purchase decisions.

It is also possible that some colonists, instead of using land-office data, traveled to the Salt River region to personally evaluate the physical composition of the environment and choose tracts of land. These early entrants may not have had friends or kin in the region to assist them in their decisions, and it may have been difficult to locate individual tracts. Richard Powers, who in 1831 arrived in a section of the project area that had attracted considerable settlement over the previous twelve years, had difficulty finding specific areas: "before we got it [the tracts of land] we had to experience some of what is called ups and downs for the want of someone to show us land and give us the numbers. Myself and Thomas [a brother-in-law] rode at least one hundred miles before we got any satisfaction about it for want of some acquaintance who would show us" (Powers 1931).

Niche Size

While discussion thus far has centered on the potential environmental factors constituting the realized niche, it should be pointed out that the realized niche may change radically across time and space as a function of culture change. For instance, technological innovations may allow exploitation of new parts of the biosphere and can thereby cause expansion of the realized niche or a reordering of the economic importance of its vectors (Warren, O'Brien, and Mason 1981:21).

Important technological innovations were introduced into the project area several decades after initial settlement, and these probably expanded the realized niche of frontier agriculturists. For instance, drainage tiles allowed removal of standing water from wet upland prairies—areas that previously could not have been tilled or planted successfully. With steel plows settlers were able to efficiently break the tough prairie sod and thus cultivate its fertile soil. These and many other devices (see Bidwell and Falconer 1925) not only enabled farmers to do more work in less time but could have brought extensive components of the environment into full crop production for the first time.

As noted earlier, social linkages among immigrating households, such as preexisting affinal kinship ties or cooperative economic arrangements, should have selected for spatial clustering of frontier farmsteads. Thus socioeconomic factors may have been as important as physical environmental factors in defining the composition and size of the realized niche. These linkages, if expressed locally, would cause a varied configuration of contemporary settlement across a region.

A Synthetic Model

Having discussed Hudson's theory of frontier settlement, several economic and sociocultural factors that can affect settlement decisions, and possible physical dimensions and sizes of the realized niche, we now synthesize our findings and present a comprehensive model of historical settlement in the project area.

Stage I

The tendency of a population to expand throughout the space available to it, the necessity of adapting to variation within its habitat, and the competitiveness of the migration process are the prime characteristics of colonization (Casagrande, Thompson, and Young 1964:283). Human colonization often involves movement into areas that are already occupied, though often sparsely, by peoples having technologically less complex cultures. Thus the intrusive population generally is able to exploit the physical environment more intensively than are resident groups. Because agriculturists entering the central Salt River valley in 1818 were preceded by French salt producers and native hunter-gatherers (chap. 3), and because many environmental characteristics of the region differed from those of source areas, the region represented both an unexploited portion of an old environment and a new territory. Resources in the region were virtually untapped, and we assume that immigrants attempted to maximize their access to beneficial environmental characteristics when they settled. Locational decisions may have been conditioned to some degree by individual or group perceptions of economic potential formulated in areas well behind the frontier (chap. 3). We therefore propose that the realized niche of colonists in the Salt Valley was similar to those in regions from which they emigrated.

7   As discussed previously, Hudson (1969:370) suggests that the morphology of colonial settlement will be random in space. However, this assumes that frontier zones are environmentally homogeneous, which the project area was not. Given that environmental zonation in the project area is composed of bands that parallel major streams (chap. 4), and assuming that this gradient was important to immigrants, then the realized niche of colonists in the region should be expressed as linear bands. The geographic arrangement of settlements, which Hudson suggests is random, should therefore be expressed *within* these linear bands. In other words, settlement morphology should *not* be random across the region as a whole. Rather, settlements should associate with distinct subsets of the physical and cultural environment. Population

density should be low and landholdings small, and settlements should correlate with restricted niches in biotope space.

One problem with the random spacing of farmsteads proposed by Hudson is that it ignores the potential benefits of settling near other farmsteads, whether these units exist or are planned. Considering the benefits mentioned earlier (sharing labor, maintaining social ties, and defense), we suggest that early locational strategies took into account proximity to neighboring settlements and that colonial settlements were clustered in some areas owing to interdependent immigration and random in others owing to independent immigration (fig. 2.9).

Stage II

Hudson (1969:370) recognized two distinct processes that operate during the spread phase—reproduction and independent immigration. As in most frontier regions, immigration into the central Salt River valley continues for many years after the founding of colonial settlement units. Thus during stage II new immigrants were colonizing previously unsettled areas of the biotope and establishing farmsteads that in many instances were independent of those in existence. We also propose that some colonial family units were composed of nearly mature offspring who began buying land of their own soon after arriving in the Salt River valley. Influenced by the social advantages of settling near their kin, these offspring probably settled land near the farmsteads from which they had budded.

We therefore expect the continuation of two distinct but overlapping settlement patterns. Population growth attributable to reproduction should be reflected in small settlement clusters within the niche space, while continued independent immigration should be reflected in a random arrangement of farmsteads between the clusters (fig. 2.10).

We further suggest that during stage II there was continued interdependent immigration by families related to groups already residing in the frontier area. This should be reflected in larger clusters of settlement units within the realized niche (fig. 2.10).

Two additional settlement patterns also are possible. First, as regional service and trade centers are established, they function as magnets that attract settlement to their peripheries. In places where agricultural conditions are favorable, we expect dense settlement surrounding these centers (fig. 2.10). Second, we suggest that agriculturists took advantage of existing roads in selecting tracts for purchase and that linear arrangements of farmsteads might transect the realized niche (fig. 2.10).

Together, these five components of stage II of the model—continued independent immigration, continued interdependent immigration, budding, attraction of service and trade centers, and linear settlement along roads—

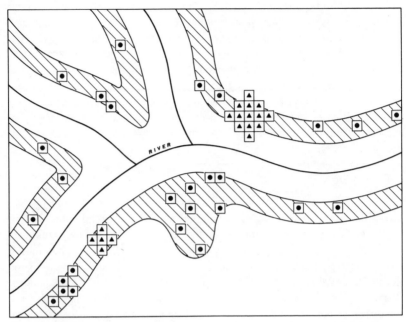

2.9. Model of farmstead distribution during the colonization phase (stage I) in the Cannon region showing the realized niche as a subset of biotope space (shaded) and compound random and clustered configurations of forty-five farmsteads. The locations include twenty-seven farmsteads situated at random within the niche owing to the process of independent immigration (denoted by ●) and eighteen farmsteads clustered owing to the process of interdependent immigration (denoted by ▲). Note that in most places the realized niche is narrow, parallels streams, and is defined by environmental characteristics that co-occur along the slope-position gradient. The exception, a protuberance near the center of the figure, represents a habitable area created by fire or some other localized disturbance of the ecosystem.

should be expressed in space as a fairly random distribution of settlement units interrupted in several places by small and large clusters as well as by linear arrangements of settlement units. However, our simulations indicate that this pattern must have changed through time as early clustered settlement units were hemmed in by new immigrants, creating a more regular spacing. Concurrently, the realized niche probably expanded as technological innovations (such as the steel plow and drainage tiles) allowed exploitation of new portions of the biotope. In summary, these conditions suggest that stage II was a dynamic phase during which population grew and dispersed along several trajectories. However, each trajectory had real limits imposed by constraints on the carrying capacity, and settlement trends shifted as stress increased (Warren and O'Brien 1982:98).

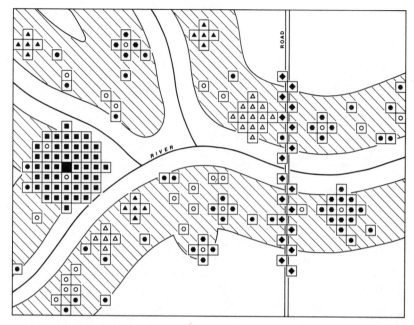

2.10. Model of farmstead distribution during the spread phase (stage II) in the Cannon region showing the realized niche (shaded) and compound random, clustered, and linear configurations of 178 farmsteads. The locations include: twenty-seven new farmsteads situated at random within the niche owing to continued independent immigration (denoted by ●); fifteen new farmsteads clustered owing to continued interdependent immigration (denoted by ▲); twenty-eight new farmsteads clustered owing to budding from established farmsteads (buds denoted by ◆); forty-five new farmsteads clustered for access to a new town (farmsteads denoted by small ■, town denoted by large ■); eighteen new farmsteads arranged linearly for access to a new road (farmsteads denoted by ◆); and forty-five old farmsteads established during the earlier colonization phase (denoted by ○ and △). Note that niche width has increased owing to technological change.

Stage III

During stage III, or Hudson's competition phase of the settlement process, the realized niche is occupied completely, there are no unexploited portions of the productive biotope, and agriculturists are forced to compete for each other's land. We suggest that the more agriculturally productive a portion of the biotope is, or the closer a tract of land is to a regional center, the more valuable that area or tract becomes. Hence, competition within select areas may begin earlier than in adjacent areas that are still in the process of spread.

Once certain technological advances such as the steel plow allowed exploitation of prairie soil—highly productive portions of the biotope—

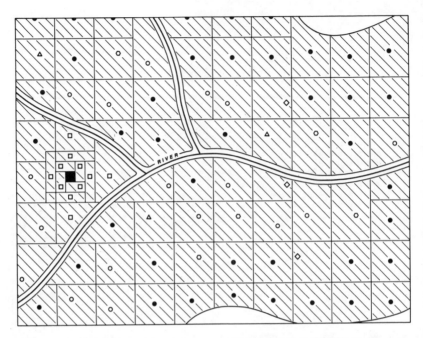

2.11. Model of farmstead distribution during the competition phase (stage III) in the Cannon region showing the realized niche (shaded) and compound regular and clustered configurations of seventy-seven farmsteads. The locations include thirty-eight new farmsteads (denoted by ●); thirty-one old farmsteads established during the colonization or spread phases (denoted by ○, △, ⬡, □, and ◇); and eight old farmsteads clustered for access to an old town (farmsteads denoted by small □, town denoted by large ⬛). The sixty-nine farmsteads in the first two groups are situated for efficiency near the centers of landholdings that have increased greatly in size, producing a regular distribution across much of the region. Note that although niche width has increased further owing to technological change, many old farmsteads have not survived competition, and there is a net decrease in farmstead population.

competition for these soils should have been keen. Because of the flat terrain, prairies were easier to farm than undulating, sloped land, a factor that should have been an added attraction to the prairie biome. The ease of cultivating flat prairies may have led agriculturists to sell tracts of land in other environmental zones and to concentrate their holdings on or along the prairie. In any event, competition must eventually have reinforced the trend toward settlement regularity that first became evident during stage II (fig. 2.11).

Summary

The model of Euro-American settlement presented here serves both as a guide to research and as a source of testable hypotheses. It employs several important ecological concepts and focuses on changing locational behavior based on the perspective of settlement geography. The model is adapted from Hudson's (1969) theory of rural settlement location, which is aimed at explaining changes in settlement configuration through time. Hudson's theory recognizes three stages, or processes, of rural settlement: colonization—the expansion of population into a new area; spread—the filling in of gaps between colonial settlement; and competition—the bidding for limited space and resources.

To Hudson's basic framework we added several economic and sociocultural dimensions that should also have been important determinants of settlement morphology, and also physical environmental dimensions of the central Salt River valley. In light of the potential importance of these two sets of dimensions, we revised Hudson's model to isolate those physical and cultural factors that may have been important dimensions of the realized niche in the project area. Associating these sets of variables with the theory of rural settlement serves to introduce the factors that we examine empirically later in this volume to determine the relative power of each in explaining observed patterns of settlement.

3

The Roots of
Frontier Expansion

Michael J. O'Brien

The history of westward expansion of the American frontier is by nature tied to the history of points east. Likewise, the forces that shaped the frontier and promoted the settlement and growth of frontier regions had their roots in the more established areas that produced the colonists of the frontier. So it is with the Salt River valley, viewed from the perspective of its being both a frontier zone and, later, a developed region. To understand the settlement of the central Salt River valley we must trace the history of developments that led to its colonization and then to its growth. This chapter deals directly with the first goal by presenting an overview of historical events and frontier settlement dynamics during the late eighteenth and early nineteenth centuries that relate directly to the eventual immigration of colonists to the Salt Valley. Emphasis is placed on describing events that helped shape colonists' decisions to emigrate from the East and on developing an understanding of the processes that effected the patterns of land purchase and community development seen in the project area. Thus this chapter sets the stage for the analysis of Salt Valley settlement in chapters 5 through 7 by tracing the advance of the frontier and its settlers through the Bluegrass region of Kentucky, across the Ohio River and into portions of the southern Prairie Peninsula, across the Mississippi River into central Missouri, and finally northward to the Salt River. An understanding of the trajectories along which colonists of the Bluegrass region—and later of central Missouri—aligned themselves, even in a preliminary sense, is important to the analysis of settlement along the Salt River because it allows us to preview various decisions the settlers made on settlement location. Hence these data contribute directly to the testing of the model of frontier settlement presented in chapter 2.

One point that is central to the discussion below is the significant advantage that the frontier always offered—inexpensive or free land. Almost without exception, when all the many possible variables that influenced decisions to immigrate are reduced to a single common denominator, that factor is land. Because of the importance of land in the settlement and development of the western frontier, much of the discussion in this chapter revolves around issues such as the availability of land, laws regulating the disposal of public lands, and, where such data exist, the types of land early frontier settlers selected within a given region. For ease of organization and presentation, these topics are dealt with during discussion of specific geographic areas, as we trace chronologically the westward movement of the frontier, beginning with the Bluegrass region of Kentucky.

The Bluegrass Region

River valleys in central and northeastern Missouri were part of what a number of authors (e.g., Jordan 1967; Kniffen 1965; Mitchell 1972, 1978; Voss 1969-70) have referred to as a pre-1860 ''upper South'' cultural and agricultural region, composed in large part of emigrants from Kentucky and Virginia (Mason, Warren, and O'Brien 1982). A study of original places of residence reported in patents and biographies of project area residents (National Historical Company 1884; Owen and Company 1895) showed that of the families for which a specific eastern county of origin is known, 63% were from a thirty-four-county area of Kentucky known as the Bluegrass region (as defined by Davis 1927). This region was one of two focal points for early settlement west of the Appalachians (the other being the Nashville Basin), receiving a few colonists from Virginia as early as the 1770s. Early access to the area was difficult, but the fertile soil of the Bluegrass led thousands to brave both the difficult passage over the highlands to the east and the constant danger of Indian attack to take advantage of the new opportunity to gain free or inexpensive land (Davis 1927:4–5). The preeminence of the region in the agricultural history and development of Kentucky has continued unabated for the past two hundred years. For comparison with the physiography of the Salt River area (chap. 4), the setting of the Bluegrass region is discussed briefly below.

The Physical Setting

Depending on how the region is defined,[1] the Bluegrass encompasses between 8,000 and 9,000 square miles of north-central Kentucky (fig. 3.1). The roughly circular outline of the region is a result of structural uplift and the work of weathering agents that have produced various soils and topographic conditions. The physiography of the region is conditioned by the positioning

1. Davis (1927) includes thirty counties in his list of those located in the Bluegrass region but actually shows thirty-four counties in his regional map.

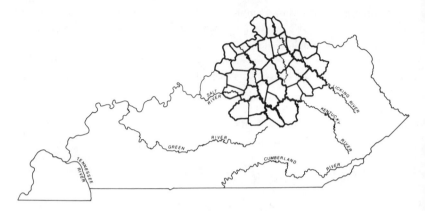

3.1. Location of the Bluegrass region of north-central Kentucky.

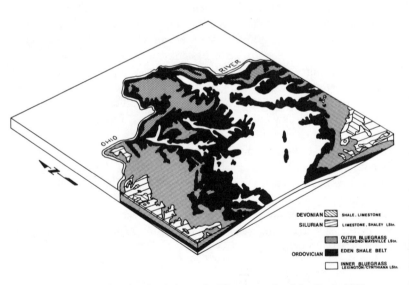

3.2. Position of the Cincinnati arch relative to the Bluegrass region (after Davis 1927).

of the Cincinnati arch, a low, broad anticline that trends northeast-southwest across the center of the state (fig. 3.2). Erosion has stripped younger strata from the central portion of the dome, exposing Ordovician limestone and shale beds that become increasingly more recent in age toward the margins of the Bluegrass. Because of the fairly concentric nature of erosion relative to the arch, Ordovician beds form belted arrangements of rock and overlying soils that surround the center of the arch. This central portion, or Inner Bluegrass (fig. 3.3), is underlain by highly phosphatic limestones that contribute directly to the excellent quality of the soil. Topography in this area is gently rolling except along the borders of the larger rivers (discussed below). The Eden Shale belt, which encircles the inner dome, is distinctly different from the Inner Bluegrass; owing to severe erosion of the less resistant shale beds, the area more closely resembles the mountainous regions to the east. Hills often terminate in sharp ridges, and valleys are narrow and V-shaped (Davis 1927:12). Surrounding this belt is the Outer Bluegrass, which is similar in nature to the Inner Bluegrass subregion. Erosion-resistant limestone beds contribute to the flat to gently sloping topography and support dense stands of grass and trees. The periphery of this subregion abuts a semicircular bank of hills capped by erosion-resistant Silurian limestone beds. This area, known as the Knobs, is in sharp contrast to the fairly level terrain of the Outer Bluegrass.

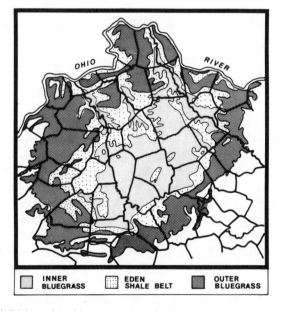

3.3. Major subdivisions of the Bluegrass region (after Davis 1927).

Maximum elevation in the Bluegrass region ranges from about 1,115 feet AMSL near Lexington to approximately 853 feet AMSL in Bath County (fig. 3.1). Drainage to a large extent is conditioned by the resistance of geologic beds and extensive faulting throughout the region (Miller 1919). Two river systems dominate the Bluegrass—the Kentucky in the west-central portion, and the Licking in the extreme northeast. Both are tributaries of the Ohio River and contain fairly large watersheds. Other drainages include the Dix River and several tributaries of the Salt River, in the western portion of the Bluegrass. Drainage in the Inner Bluegrass region is in large part underground, particularly around Lexington. Springs form along fault lines and in sinkholes and to some extent probably determined the location of many pioneer settlements (Davis 1927:12).

Two aspects of the physical environment are particularly important to our overview of settlement dynamics in the Bluegrass region—soils and vegetation. We expect that these two components of the biosphere, acting in concert with other aspects, to a large extent conditioned the location of frontier settlements in the Bluegrass region. Unfortunately, there are no data for this region comparable with those for the project area. Although modern soils data provide distributional information and a measure of relative productivity of different soil series, no systematic observations exist for the frontier period. No General Land Office (GLO) surveys were ever conducted in Kentucky; hence our knowledge of early vegetation is derived mainly from historical accounts and a few recent studies of specific areas within the Bluegrass. Despite these limitations, available data on soils and vegetation allow us to form a general picture of these aspects of the early frontier biosphere.

SOILS

Soil formation and fertility across the Bluegrass region are conditioned to some extent by the composition of the underlying bedrock. Since bedrock composition varies considerably from area to area, as does slope, the quality and the depth of soil vary accordingly. In general, soils in the Inner Bluegrass are superior to those elsewhere, followed by Outer Bluegrass soils and, at a distance, soils of the Eden Shale belt. Typical of soils in the Inner Bluegrass region is the Maury-McAfee association, composed of silt loams and silty clay loams. This association, which occupies approximately 55% of Fayette County, in the heart of the Inner Bluegrass, consists of undulating deep and moderately deep, well-drained soils that are high in phosphate (Sims et al. 1968:3). Under modern medium-level management, and on 0–12% slopes, soils in this association have modern average corn yields of between 50 and 90 bushels an acre (Sims et al. 1968:27). Soils of other associations in Fayette County yield similar quantities under similar conditions.

In contrast, Eden Shale belt soils, derived from siliceous, shaley parent rock, often are thin and of low fertility. Under cultivation the slopes erode quickly, leaving slabs of shale and limestone to litter cultivated hills (Davis 1927:25). Owing to the narrow (often less than a mile), irregular, ribbonlike configuration of the Eden Shale belt, it is difficult to map the distribution of soil associations across the region. However, one association that appears highly restricted to the shale belt is the Eden-Lowell, the soils of which formed mainly in material weathered from interbedded limestone, calcareous shale, and siltstone. In a few restricted areas at higher elevations they formed in material weathered from calcareous sandstone (Weisenberger, Blevins, and Hersh 1963:9–10). Most of the association currently is in pasture owing to the steepness of the slope. Where 6% to 12% slopes are cultivated, the modern average corn yield is roughly 50 bushels an acre. However, on the few level ridge tops, average corn yields can run as high as 100 bushels an acre (Weisenberger, Blevins, and Hersh 1963:65–66).

Outer Bluegrass soils generally are on a par with those of the Inner Bluegrass—they contain large amounts of phosphorous and often are quite deep. However, along the interface between the Outer Bluegrass and the Eden Shale belt—fairly rugged terrain—soils are thin and unproductive. In Bath County, modern corn yields for Outer Bluegrass soils average approximately 70 bushels an acre, with some soils averaging up to 110 bushels an acre (Weisenberger, Blevins, and Hersh 1963:65–66).

Thus, across the Bluegrass region soil formation is conditioned in part by parent material, with soils in the Inner and Outer Bluegrass containing high levels of phosphate owing to the limestone substrate. Eden Shale belt soils, conditioned by underlying shale beds, are high in siliceous material. Soil productivity across the Bluegrass also is conditioned in large part by slope, with Eden Shale belt soils being the most eroded and generally most unproductive in the three subregions.

VEGETATION

Most attempts at characterizing presettlement vegetation in the Bluegrass region are based on early historical accounts of travelers passing through the area. While these narratives provide glimpses of the physical environment of the time, they are biased by the predilections of the authors, are usually nonspatial in nature, and in some instances are contradictory. Hence they must be used with caution and should be evaluated against systematic analyses of presettlement cover. As mentioned previously, very few modern studies of presettlement cover have been undertaken, and the ones that do exist are not systematic. Therefore our assessment is little more than a distillation of narrative sources and a few modern observations.

According to many historical accounts, of which that by Flint (1828,

2:208) appears typical, early settlers arriving in central Kentucky found "a kind of open forest; in which the lawns were tangled with cane, and other luxuriant vegetation, and grass." Trees were "promiscuously arranged for the effect of a pleasure ground" (Flint 1828, 2:174). François Michaux, a French botanist who passed through the region in 1802, stated that there was little "herbage" between trees, which were spaced far enough apart that "a stag may be seen a hundred or a hundred and fifty fathoms off" (Michaux 1904:231).

The nature of this "herbage" has been debated for a number of years, especially with reference to the extent of canebrakes across the region. Based on a review of a considerable number of accounts and diaries from the late eighteenth century, Davidson (1950:14) concludes that portions of the region were covered with cane, "and cane only." Undoubtedly, extensive cane-brakes[2] did cover portions of the Bluegrass, and the locations of some often appear on early maps of Kentucky. For example, Filson, on his 1784 "Map of Kentucke" (McHargue 1941:5), indicates an extensive area between Cynthiana and Paris in Bourbon County as being "Fine Cane Land." James B. Finley, whose father settled in 1790 on "Cane Ridge" in Bourbon County, stated: "The land purchased by my father was a part of an unbroken cane-brake extending for twenty miles toward what was called the Little Mountain [now Mt. Sterling]. We had to cut out roads before we could haul the logs to build our cabins. The cane was so thick and tall, that it was almost impossible for a horse or cow to pass through it" (Finley 1853:39). Braun (1950:128) states that these canebrakes were not treeless and "must have contrasted strongly with true grasslands, which are distinguished on . . . [Filson's] . . . early map." In addition to canebrakes, early accounts often mention large areas of wild rye and clover: "Where no cane grows, there is abundance of wild rye, clover, and buffalo-grass, covering vast tracts of country" (Filson 1784:24).

Based on the number of historical accounts that mention "open forests" and the interspersion of grasses and flowers among forest trees, Davidson (1950) and Braun (1950) conclude that timber density across the Inner Bluegrass subregion probably was quite low. The Outer Bluegrass, in contrast, probably contained dense stands of timber (Braun 1950:128). Dense forests also may have existed over much of the Eden Shale belt, though no historical accounts specifically mention timber density for any recognizable areas of this subregion.

Presettlement forest composition of the subregions is impossible to assess quantitatively; hence we must rely primarily on observations made by mid-nineteenth-century geological survey teams. Based on data from these

---

2. Braun (1950:128) states that the cane referred to is *Arundinaria gigantea*.

surveys, approximately twenty-five species of trees were fairly prevalent over the Inner Bluegrass. Several species of ash (especially blue), bur oak, white oak, walnut, sugar maple, hickory, bristle-tip oak, wild cherry, black locust, and mulberry are mentioned frequently (Braun 1950:129). One community, composed of bur oak, blue ash, sugar maple, walnut, and a few additional species, appears to have occupied the "cane lands." The prevalence of bur oak indicates low tree density, since the species is shade intolerant. A study of fifteen remnant stands of "savanna-woodland" vegetation in various sections of the Inner Bluegrass (Bryant et al. 1980) revealed that bur oak and ash composed 70% of the remnant stands. Examples of five species were considered old enough to have predated human settlement: ash, elm, Shumar oak, chinquapin oak, and bur oak.

The Eden Shale belt today contrasts sharply with the Inner Bluegrass in terms of forest composition (Braun 1950:130). Based on a mid-nineteenth-century geological survey of Mercer County, which is bisected by the line dividing the two subregions, the dichotomy is at least a century old (Kentucky Geological Survey 1857, 3:81). There white oak, black oak, and hickory were present in much higher frequencies in the Eden Shale belt, while the Inner Bluegrass contained significantly higher frequencies of ash, black walnut, and white walnut. The contrast between the Bluegrass (either Inner or Outer) and the "oak land" (or Eden Shale belt) frequently is mentioned in the Kentucky Geological Surveys, the former referred to as being fit for crops and pasturage and the latter as suited for tobacco and hemp production.

Forest composition in the Outer Bluegrass is, and probably has been for at least the past few hundred years, similar to that in the Inner Bluegrass, as evidenced by Kentucky Geological Survey descriptions of vegetation in western Bath County: "locust, black walnut, black and blue ash, wild cherry, and some white oak" (1857, 3:133). Forests composed of beech, tulip tree, sugar maple, white oak, and red oak probably were prominent throughout the subregion, especially on rolling topography near the periphery (Braun 1950:130). Near the Ohio River, beech is today a locally dominant taxon (ibid.).

In summary, although data on early settlement vegetation are sketchy at best, it is evident that colonists of the Bluegrass region were faced with a complex mosaic of deciduous trees, understory, and grassland. To a large extent, the distribution of plant communities, and individual taxa within communities (such as bur oak, cf. Bryant et al. 1980), were conditioned by substrate—hence the general correlation of plant communities with the three subregions. At the time of settlement, the Inner Bluegrass could be character-ized as having been a savanna-woodland, with blue ash and bur oak as prominent taxa. Canebrakes were situated across the subregion, as were expanses of wild rye and clover. The Eden Shale belt contained stands of hickory and white and black oak, with beech and sugar maple on the lower slopes. The Outer Bluegrass, though somewhat similar in forest composition to the Inner Bluegrass, exhibited a higher tree density, especially along the reaches of the Licking and Kentucky rivers and their tributaries. Here, tree density may have approximated that found in certain densely forested locales in the Cannon project area.

Settlement and Population in the Bluegrass Region, 1772–1817

Before 1792, most of what is now Kentucky was part of Fincastle County, Virginia, created by the Virginia Assembly in 1772. Permanent colonization of central Fincastle County began in June 1774, when a group of adventurers led by James Harrod laid out the settlement of Harrodsburg near the headwaters of the Salt River (Hammon 1972). Although the settlement was soon destroyed by Indians, it was rebuilt the following year, coinciding with the founding of Boonesboro several miles to the east. These initial settlements were able to survive despite Indian attack and internal turmoil (Rohrbough 1978), and by the end of the decade new population nodes sprang up in several areas of the Bluegrass. By the summer of 1775, about 150 men were in Fincastle County (Greene and Harrington 1932:192), and approximately 200 acres had been planted in Indian corn (Rohrbough 1978:24). In the autumn of 1776 the Virginia legislature divided the trans-Appalachian region into three counties, with Fayette County encompassing the Bluegrass region.

The main attraction of the trans-Appalachian region to early immigrants was land. To be sure, the lure of adventure and the mystique of unconquered regions led a few persons across the mountains, but this attraction can most profitably be viewed as a minor factor in the true settlement of the area. On the eastern side of the Appalachians, years of poor farming practices had worn out many agricultural fields, and high prices of implements and land resulted in foreclosure for a considerable number of farmers (Rohrbough 1978:23). At the end of the immigrant road west, the pioneer settlers "began to discover the pleasing and rapturous appearances of the plains of Kentucky" (Walker 1854:152).

Although absolute population figures for the years before the first federal census of 1790 differ from source to source, the relative gains for Kentucky during the period 1775–90 are witness to the fantastic growth of the trans-Appalachian region during this fifteen-year period. Using a variety of federal and Commonwealth of Virginia sources, Greene and Harrington (1932:192) note a population growth for Kentucky from 150 men in 1775 to

73,677 persons in 1790. Of the 1790 total, 12,430 were slaves. Rohrbough (1978:25) attributes this rapid population increase in part to the richness of the soil but also to the fact that the lands were advertised widely in areas east of the Appalachians. Also, Virginia land warrants, issued between 1782 and 1792 for service in the French and Indian War and the Revolutionary War, were redeemable in Kentucky lands. The amount of land received via these warrants depended on the rank achieved in military service. A cursory examination of these grants shows that the minimum awarded was about 50 acres. The maximum amount ranged into the tens of thousands of acres, occasionally reaching 100,000 acres. These exceedingly high acreage figures may be the result of a person's having purchased the warrants of veterans who had no intention of claiming their settlements.

Land speculation was at fever pitch during this era, as was the need for large tracts of land for tobacco and hemp cultivation (discussed below). The attractive offer of land west of the Appalachians undoubtedly promoted development of the Bluegrass region. Before 1780 Kentucky land was offered for sale by the Commonwealth of Virginia for 40 pounds per 100 acres. Because of the resulting rush to buy land, in 1780 the price was increased to 160 pounds per 100 acres (Gray 1958:622).

By the late 1780s the population of Kentucky had reached the point that land in the Bluegrass region was becoming scarce and thus exceedingly expensive, and social and economic distinctions already were evident (Rohrbough 1978:32). Antagonism between owners of large tracts of land and pioneer settlers became increasingly pronounced, leading members of the latter group to petition the Virginia legislature, complaining that the rising class of large landholders were grabbing the more productive land, raising land prices, and trying to "shut out" the small farmers in the Bluegrass as they had in the Tidewater region (Byrd 1951:182). The need for a regional government to deal with such problems increased to the point that Kentuckians began petitioning for separate statehood. The distance between the western settlements and the central legislative offices of Virginia was great, and despite the representation of the western territory in the legislature, regional problems could not be handled adequately by that body. Thus in 1792 Kentucky was granted separate statehood. By that year nine Virginia counties had been formed within the boundaries of the new state (fig. 3.4), which contained approximately 100,000 persons including slaves (U.S. Bureau of the Census 1960:13).

One problem that had reached epidemic proportions by this time was the inaccuracy of land descriptions and locations, which resulted in multiple claims on the same piece of land. Unlike the regular grid system used after the Land Ordinance of 1785 to survey and map lands in the Northwest Territory

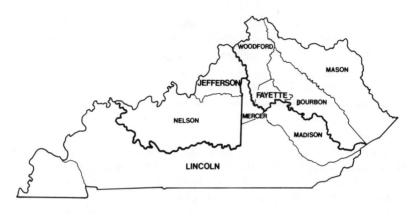

3.4. County subdivisions of Kentucky in 1792. Heavier lines delimit the original three counties (Fayette, Jefferson, and Lincoln) formed in 1776 out of Fincastle County, Virginia.

and regions west of the Mississippi River, landholdings were assigned and measured by the English metes-and-bounds system (Johnson 1976), with legal descriptions such as the following:

George Miller Enters 500 acres on part of a Tresury Warrant. . . . Beginning at a Beach [*sic*] Mark'd WI standing on the Bank near a large fork of said Southwardly running creek about ten Miles from the head of Creek thence from the above mentioned Marked Beech East to the Hills thence from the Beginning West to the Hills thence from each end of this line down the Creek on each side binding on the Hills and to Take all good Lands that Shall be deemed fit for Cultivation till the Qty. is Obtain'd. [Bourbon County, Kentucky, deed book, 29 August 1788]

The courts were constantly filled with petitions for titles and civil suits over rights of ownership (Flint 1828). Early surveyors of the trans-Appalachian region often were unskilled at their trade, adding to the confusion of locating claims in the largely unsettled wilderness (Clark 1979:45). The problem was by no means confined to the small, unknown pioneer settler. Daniel Boone, one of the preeminent men of his era, surveyed great expanses of Kentucky for the state of Virginia and claimed several large tracts for himself. He soon found out, however, that land "legally belonged to the man who could prove that he had been first to buy his warrants, make his surveys, file his claims, and get his certificates" (Bakeless 1939:341). Most land maps of those days are crisscrossed with "shingled" claims (fig. 3.5), so called because they overlap each other like shingles on a roof (Bakeless 1939). Undoubtedly, the trauma of losing land after they had cleared, cultivated, and defended it caused many settlers to abandon the region in search of new lands elsewhere.

The ties between the project area and the Bluegrass region can be traced

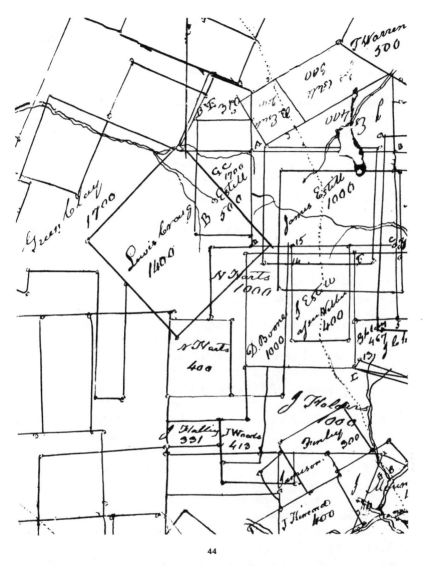

44

3.5. Typical late-eighteenth-century Kentucky plat showing shingled claims (note "D. Boone" in central portion of plat) (from Clark 1979).

through land patents and biographical data. Some of the most complete data we currently have are on persons originating in the counties of Bourbon and Bath (chap. 7), in the eastern portion of the Bluegrass region. Bourbon County was formed from Fayette County in 1786, and Bath from Montgomery (*ex* Clark, 1797; *ex* Bourbon-Fayette, 1793) in 1811. The development of towns and regional centers in the eastern Bluegrass area, like towns and centers elsewhere in the region, kept pace with county formation. Paris, the seat of Bourbon County, was founded in 1786, apparently in an area that would not compete with the use of the land for agriculture (Perrin 1882). By 1790 the town had a population of 358. Very little is recorded of the early history and development of Paris, though we speculate that it soon took on the necessary services (dry goods stores, mills, etc.) that previously had been available only at Lexington (one to two days' journey to the west) or Limestone (two or more days' journey to the north). Owingsville, the seat of Bath County, was founded in 1811; Sharpsburg, 12 miles northwest of the county seat, was laid out in 1814; and Bethel, in one of the richest livestock and agricultural sections of the county, was platted in 1817 (Richards 1961). One of the first industries to appear in Bath County was a carding factory at Owingsville, obviously constructed to process the considerable tonnage of hemp being produced in the area.

Cultural and Economic Development of the Bluegrass Region

The development of the Bluegrass region, in terms of its economy and cultural characteristics, can best be viewed as an amalgam of motivations of, and interactions between, two groups of agriculturists: "yeoman" farmers with small tracts of land and a class of "small planters" possessing from two to ten slaves (Mitchell 1978:83) and larger amounts of land. As the region became more densely populated, class distinctions and differences based on wealth and landholding became more and more apparent (Byrd 1951:184). By 1820 the constant interplay between the two groups had created a mature economic and cultural system that dominated the trans-Appalachian area for several decades. Germane to discussion here is the rapidity with which the system matured and the effect it had on the resident population.

The interplay between the two agricultural groups—the yeoman farmers and the small planter class—led to the development of what Mitchell (1972, 1978) and others have referred to as an "upper South" cultural and agricultural region. The fusion of elements from two "hearth" areas—southeastern Pennsylvania with its emphasis on corn, wheat, and livestock and the Chesapeake region with its tobacco, hemp, and slavery—occurred in western Virginia by 1750 and spread rapidly after 1780 into central Kentucky (Mitchell 1972:741, 1978;81). Concomitant with this spread there developed a class structure different from that seen in the North, owing to the presence of slavery (Mitchell 1978).

The extension of an upper South agrarian complex into the trans-

Appalachian region was virtually guaranteed by the immigration of settlers from western Virginia to the Bluegrass region. Slavery and its integration into the staple economy of the time created a desire in yeoman farmers who had been exposed to plantation slavery in Virginia to become members of the planter class, specializing first in hemp and then, in the 1790s, tobacco (Mitchell 1978:83). In 1972 at least 22.8% of Kentucky households (2,688 of 11,803) contained slaves, with an average slaveholding of about 4.3 (Coward 1979:37). Two counties in the heart of the Bluegrass (Woodford and Fayette) had slaveholding rates among households of 35.3% and 31.6%, respectively (ibid.). Because of the tax liability of slaveholding, these figures (derived from tax lists) probably underrepresent the true extent of slavery.

Mason (1983) states that slave ownership in the trans-Appalachian East probably was more important for its prestige value than for its economic contribution. This opinion follows that of Viles (1920) and Trexler (1914) on slavery in Missouri, but it may not have applied to early Kentucky. There slaves appear to have made a significant economic contribution to tobacco and hemp production. Tobacco necessitated year-round labor under close supervision, and hemp required heavy labor in breaking, drying, pressing, and baling (Gates 1960). Consequently, production of these commodities may have been restricted to persons owning more slaves than the usual few household servants.

In assessing the agricultural system of eighteenth-century Kentucky apart from tobacco and hemp, Mitchell (1978) characterizes it as having been broadly based and composed of corn, wheat, and rye cultivation. The evolution of the system can, in a simplified perspective, be seen as beginning in the 1770s with an emphasis on establishing crops that permitted self-sufficiency and that grew rapidly, producing a surplus for sale. Intricately tied to grain production was livestock specialization, especially in hogs and cattle. By 1790 the practice of fattening cattle on corn in open feedlots during the winter may have diffused from western Virginia to central Kentucky (Jones 1956), laying the foundations of midwestern Corn Belt farming during the nineteenth century.

Corn and pork could be produced by all farmers in the Bluegrass, whether or not they owned slaves, and any surplus could be shipped down the Ohio and Mississippi rivers to New Orleans, forming the basis of a market economy in Kentucky. By 1810 central Kentucky was participating in the triangular trade characteristic of the presteamboat era in the Midwest (Wade 1959). Agricultural products were shipped on flatboats to New Orleans, where the proceeds were used to buy cotton and sugar that were shipped by sea to New England markets. Sale of these commodities in northeastern cities allowed purchase of English-made goods that were transported by wagon to Pittsburgh. From there these goods, plus locally produced iron and glassware, were shipped down the Ohio River to Maysville (Limestone), Kentucky, then sent overland to Lexington (Mason 1983).

During the 1830s the Bluegrass region underwent a shift from commercial production of tobacco and hemp to livestock production (Gray 1958). One possible reason for this shift was depletion of soil by decades of overproduction with little or no effort at revitalization. Horses and mules were bred for sale, and cattle were fattened on cornstalks and bluegrass for eastern markets (Henlein 1959). The change to livestock production required larger farms, and during the 1830s stockmen purchased the lands of many hemp and tobacco producers (Gray 1958). By way of example, in 1835 Bourbon County produced 40,000 hogs, 10,000 head of cattle, 3,000 horses and mules, $50,000 worth of bacon and lard, and $70,000 worth of whiskey (Gray 1958:877). Despite this shift in agricultural emphasis among wealthy landowners —from tobacco and hemp to livestock—the majority of agriculturists, those without slaves, still supported themselves by raising corn, hogs, and a few cattle (Mason 1983). Corn was fed to livestock or distilled into whiskey because of the high transportation costs of grain (Bidwell and Falconer 1925:349).

In summary, many immigrants to central and northeastern Missouri possessed a relatively homogeneous cultural background formed in the Bluegrass region. Upper South culture, though based on corn and hog production, emphasized acquiring land and slaves as a means of increasing one's social status. From the discussion above we can speculate on possible reasons for emigration from the region. First was the rapid decrease in available land as people continued to pour across the Appalachians after the turn of the century. Landholdings of most settlers probably were small, and with the filling up of the region offspring would have had to move away from home, possibly onto poorer land, or subdivide the homestead. If the soil was being depleted by continuous cropping and poor management, the latter alternative would not have been promising. The problem may have been exacerbated by the spread of stock raising and tobacco/hemp production, both requiring large amounts of land. With the capital needed to purchase land concentrated in the hands of major producers, small farmers may have been forced to sell out. On the other hand, rising land values connected with the general economic expansion of the late 1820s and early 1830s may have made the sale of small farms economically attractive (Mason 1983).

Second, the uncertainty over land titles may have spurred movement west. With the faulty system of land survey and boundary descriptions in practice at the time, multiple claims on the same tract of land were the rule rather than the exception. As people lost their claims on land that they in good faith had improved and cultivated, they probably desired to vacate the region and move to an area that had been surveyed in a sensible manner.

Third, the opportunity to acquire large tracts of land in other, less crowded areas could have satisfied aspirations of becoming "landed gentry" (Mason 1983). Slaves could always be purchased for a reasonable price, but if one did not own enough land to work the slaves efficiently, there was little economic gain in owning them. The opening of public lands in the West presented at least a potential solution to the problem of how to move upward socially as well as economically.

The Movement West

Closely connected with the issue of land and the western movement of the frontier in the late eighteenth century was a new force that significantly influenced trans-Appalachian settlement: the authority of the federal government (Rohrbough 1978:90). This authority was first set forth in a series of ordinances (e.g., the Land Ordinance of 1785 and the Ordinance of 1787) that established a system of government's providing for the development of a territory into a state and was ratified by the adoption in 1789 of the Constitution, which provided for a strong central government. With a series of diplomatic and military triumphs during the decades before and after 1800, especially negotiation of the Louisiana Purchase in 1803, the new government gained respect and confidence (Rohrbough 1978:90).

With the establishment of formal territories north of the Ohio River (Northwest Territory [Ohio], 1787; Indiana Territory, 1800; Illinois Territory, 1809), waves of immigrants, many from Kentucky and Tennessee, began a steady assault on the newly opened lands. It is impossible to state with any degree of precision the numbers of immigrants that resided in these areas at any given time. Migration patterns constantly shifted as new lands were advertised and word from previous emigrants reached family and friends back home. By 1820 Ohio had a population of over 581,000 persons, or 17,000 more than Kentucky (U.S. Bureau of the Census 1960:13). This figure for Ohio represents an increase of more than 350,000 persons from that given in the 1810 federal census, and more than a tenfold increase from the 1800 census (ibid.).

The settlement of lands north of the Ohio River was made somewhat easier and safer by the retreat of Indian groups in the face of federal forces and organized territorial militia (Boggess 1908; Horsman 1970) and by the development of larger river boats and better road systems. Land in these northern territories varied in price from $2 an acre at the federal land office up to $50 an acre from individuals (Boggess 1908:105). To assist the colonization of lands north of the Ohio River, Congress in 1804 passed an act that reduced the minimum amount of land a person could buy from 640 to 160 acres. To assist the settler Congress also regularly passed relief acts to extend the time during which payment could be made (Carter 1936, 7:173–84). These relief measures would last until 1820, when the credit system was abolished (discussed later in this chapter).

The subsistence economy of the Northwest Territory was similar to that noted for Kentucky. Power (1953) describes immigrant Kentucky pioneers in Indiana in terms of characteristic corn and hog culture, with little interest in orchards or dairy products. One significant difference between lands north and south of the Ohio River was the virtual absence of slavery to the north (Horsman 1970:79; Mitchell 1978:83). This greatly affected the agricultural development of the Northwest Territory, so that by 1815 farming was still little more than a subsistence-level activity (Horsman 1970:149).

The purchase in 1803 of the vast expanse of land west of the Mississippi River ushered in a new era of western frontier settlement. The United States controlled not only the strategic west bank of the river and the soon-to-be important port of St. Louis, but the rich mineral resources as well. Immigration to this relatively unknown region proceeded at a fantastic rate, as documented below. Although settlement after 1803 occurred in several areas of what is now Missouri, such as along the Mississippi River south of St. Louis and in the rich bottomlands near the junction of the Missouri and Mississippi rivers, we focus on developments farther west, along the north bank of the Missouri River in what was known as the Boonslick region. Settlements here attracted thousands of settlers before 1820, many of whom used the region as a staging area for their move into the central Salt River valley.

Central Missouri and the Boonslick Region

The importance of the Boonslick[3] region in the growth and development of central Missouri is perhaps best summed up in the often-cited statement by Wetmore (1837:78): "The Booneslick country for many years, in the early settlement of Missouri, was the point of attraction for emigrants; and it was deemed headquarters, to which the traveller, with an indefinite idea of a new home, repaired. Here it was customary to halt, and look about for a location." The Boonslick area encompassed a large expanse of rich bottom-lands and alluvial terraces along the Missouri River (fig. 3.6) and was fairly accessible by both river and overland route. The geographical limits of the area were never specific, but varied from description to description. An early

---

3. The spelling of this region differs from author to author (e.g., Boone's Lick, Boon's Lick).

definition is given in the Franklin *Missouri Intelligencer* (27 August 1819) as both sides of the Missouri River from the mouth of the Osage River to the western Indian boundary (Schroeder 1968:2).

The Physical Environment

The Boonslick region is the first area of deep, loess-derived soil west of St. Charles, Missouri, and as such represented an ideal location for agriculturally related frontier settlement. Historical narratives of the period (e.g., Flint 1826, 1828; Wetmore 1837) attest to the region's attraction for frontier settlers. The Boonslick proper (situated entirely within the bounds of present-day Howard County) was just east of the extensive prairie that continued unabated across the central Great Plains. Moreover, it was situated in the farthest west extension along the Missouri River of the continuous forest environment that settlers had followed from the East (Schroeder 1968:2). The prairie represented a major visual environmental change for colonial settlers (Schroeder 1968:3) and an environment they may have been hesitant to enter: "Despite the excellent loess soils and gentle slopes which

3.6. Howard County and the Boonslick region of Missouri.

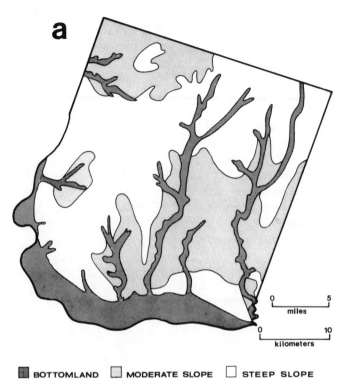

BOTTOMLAND   MODERATE SLOPE   STEEP SLOPE

3.7. Maps of Howard County, Missouri, showing (*a*) slope and (*b*) soils ratings (after Schroeder 1968).

continue upvalley on both sides of the Missouri River to Kansas City and beyond, it was only in the Boonslick where these deep and productive soils were extensively combined with the familiar forest environment'' (Schroeder 1968:3). Despite the eventual broad spread of settlement out from the Boonslick proper—first eastward, then southward across the Missouri River, then westward into the prairie—discussion here is limited to the physical environment of the region encompassed by the present-day boundary of Howard County. The county boundaries encompass the areas of initial settlement; in addition, the county has been studied intensively from the standpoint of relations between colonial settlement and physical environmental variables (Schroeder 1968).

Terrain across the county is hilly, except for the large expanses of bottomland (up to 4 miles wide) along the Missouri River. Slope angles vary considerably, depending on the degree of glaciation, erosion, and stream

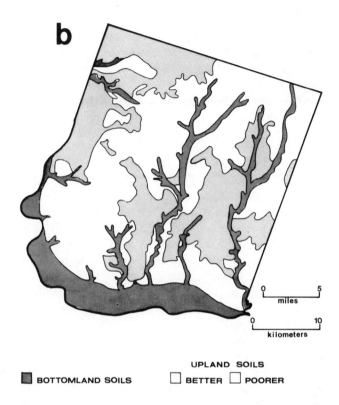

UPLAND SOILS

■ BOTTOMLAND SOILS   □ BETTER □ POORER

downcutting a particular area received. In simplified form slope percentage can be reduced to the three classes shown in figure 3.7*a*. Two distinct areas of moderate to gentle slopes are immediately obvious—one in the extreme northwest corner of the county and one in the east-central area. Both contain stream networks that through alluviation have produced small, flat flood-plains. Steeper slopes occur over the remainder of the county, becoming pronounced along the Missouri River bluffs and upper reaches of tributary streams.

During the early nineteenth century springs were fairly common across the region (Wetmore 1837:79). Dissection of the land by gullies and low-order streams resulted in the interception of the water tables so that on practically any quarter section of land water was obtainable at shallow depths (Schroeder 1968:7). Saline springs also occurred in the region and attracted salt producers during the first few years of the nineteenth century.

SOILS

Soils vary considerably across the county in texture, color, composition, and drainage. Based on modern productivity ratings (Scrivner 1961), soil associations can be subdivided into bottomland soils, better upland soils, and poorer upland soils (fig. 3.7*b*). Because of the effect of slope on soil productivity, the areas of better upland soils correspond closely to areas of predominately moderate to gentle slope in our simplified scheme (compare figs. 3.7*a* and *b*).

The alluvial soils of the extensive Missouri River bottomlands and the narrow bottoms of tributary streams, although easy to cultivate, pose certain problems to modern farming—problems that occasionally would have been severe for nineteenth-century agriculturists. Some bottomland soils are seasonally wet, with restricted subsoil aeration, and often must be totally avoided. In contrast, other more sandy soils drain too rapidly for agricultural use (Scrivner 1961:9). All bottomland soils are subject to seasonal innundation, which can last weeks at a time. Intense flooding can remove several feet of topsoil or deposit extensive blankets of coarse sediment across the bottomlands. Under management that does not provide for artificial drainage or soil conservation, average corn yields vary from 10 to 60 bushels an acre, depending on soil composition.

Poorer upland soils, formed under forest cover from loess and glacial till, are found along the Missouri River bluffs and adjacent uplands, usually in areas of fairly steep slopes. Soil fertility varies from extremely low to moderately high, with soils in the latter category being restricted primarily to high ridgetops and high stream terraces. The least productive soils are found in the northeast corner of the county and are fit only for pasturage or timber growth. Modern average corn yields for poorer soils range from 10 to 35 bushels an acre, with yields for soils in the northeast corner nearer the minimum figure (Scrivner 1961).

Better upland soils occur in the northwestern and east-central portions of the county, their position being determined in large part by depth of loess deposits from which they were derived (Scrivner 1961). Along the bluffs of the Missouri River in the northwestern corner of Howard County, and extending several miles to the east, loess deposits average 20 feet or more in depth. Soils in this area, especially those on ridgetops and upper slopes, are extremely fertile, and modern average corn yields range from 40 to 60 bushels an acre with no soil management. In the east-central portion of the county, more weathered loess deposits range up to 3 feet in depth. On moderate to gentle slopes soils produce average corn yields of 35 to 50 bushels an acre.

In summary, upland soil fertility in Howard County is conditioned in part by slope and, importantly, by the depth and amount of weathering of underlying loess deposits. Loess-derived soils are friable, thus facilitating drainage, and can be farmed on fairly steep slopes. Bottomland soils, derived from undifferentiated alluvial material deposited by the Missouri River and its tributaries, generally are fertile but often become waterlogged or, alternatively, do not retain moisture.

VEGETATION

Schroeder (1968:4) notes that at the time of settlement virtually all of Howard County was covered by timber. As described by Wetmore (1837:80), there were only two small patches of "wet prairie" in the Missouri River bottomland and two small pieces (actually a single patch; see Schroeder 1981:33) of upland prairie along the northern edge of the county. Schroeder's (1981) reconstruction of prairie boundaries from GLO survey records confirms these locations, but given that several soils in Howard County classified as "prairie soils" (Grogger and Landtiser 1978) were timbered at the time of the GLO surveys, we conclude that timber encroached onto these soils before Euro-American settlement, thus restricting the sizes of the upland prairies noted by both Wetmore and the GLO surveyors. In contrast to this forested environment, the region west of Howard County was predominantly prairie at the time of survey, as was the area several miles to the north (Schroeder 1981).

Data concerning forest composition and timber density at early settlement have not been generated from the GLO records for Howard County, but several general studies of Boone County (adjacent to the east) have been completed. Based on GLO survey data, Howell (1955) suggests that the most densely timbered sections of Boone County were in bottomlands and creek valleys and on lower slopes (see also Howell and Kucera 1956). The most important taxon represented there is white oak, followed by several species of hickory and other oaks and by sugar maple. Together, seven oak taxa composed slightly over 58% of the GLO witness tree composition of Boone County.

Based on a few historical narratives, rushes were abundant in Missouri River bottomlands. Bradbury (1904:42) specifically notes that early settlements along the river were placed to take advantage of these areas of rushes, probably to supply winter feed for livestock (Schroeder 1968:5).

Comparisons between the Boonslick and the Bluegrass are tentative at best, but we can suggest the following: First, there is no indication that forests in the Boonslick were of the "open" type that apparently covered most if not all of the Inner Bluegrass. Second, forest composition differed between regions, often significantly, depending upon the subregion of the Bluegrass. In the Inner Bluegrass, blue ash and bur oak were among the dominant taxa, followed by black walnut and hickory. In Boone County, ash species played decidedly less dominant roles in presettlement forest composition, while white oak, hickory, and sugar maple occurred with considerable frequency—

much as in the Outer Bluegrass. Third, though Boonslick bottomlands contained stands of rushes interspersed among bottomland tree taxa, there is no apparent correlation between these stands and the extensive canebrakes of central Kentucky.

Comparing the forest composition of Boone County with that of the Cannon project area, we note striking similarities. White oak constituted 39% of GLO sample trees in both areas, while other oak taxa constituted 19% and 30% of the sample for Boone County and the project area, respectively (chap. 4). Ash (all species) constituted 4% and 1.6%, elm 8% and 8%, and sugar maple 5% and 2%, respectively.

Early Settlement

Presettlement incursions into the Boonslick region by the Spanish and French are documented (National Historical Company 1883), but whether parties simply passed through the area or were attracted by saline springs is uncertain. By 1806 members of the Boone family were extracting salt from the springs bearing the family name. Permanent settlers arrived in 1808, but owing to Indian hostility throughout the region they retired downstream to a more defensible position. The first permanent settlement began in 1810 when a party headed by Colonel Benjamin Cooper settled along the Missouri River in an area that became known as Cooper's Bottom (ibid.). Problems with local Indian groups in 1812 forced the group, which had grown to about 500 persons, to construct a series of crude forts (Houck 1908, 3:137–38), which probably were nothing more than cabins grouped around fortified courtyards. Schroeder (1968:9) states that these five forts can be taken as the location of virtually all settlers in the immediate area at the time. He also notes that with the cessation of Indian troubles settlers began to disperse, and the forts gradually lost their central-place function and disappeared.

The population of the Boonslick reached upward of 1,000 persons by the end of the War of 1812 (Sauer 1920:110). Immigration to the area tapered off significantly during the period of hostilities, as it had across the entire territory (Anderson 1938:159–60), but by 1817 the adult male population was over 3,300 (*Missouri Gazette,* 10 April 1818) and the need for local administration was recognized. In 1816 the territorial government created Howard County, which encompassed all lands above the Osage River to a line parallel to, and just south of, the Des Moines River (fig. 3.6). Franklin, on the north bank of the Missouri River—central to the Boonslick settlements—became the county seat. By 1820 the population of Howard County was about 14,000 (based on federal census figures cited in Ronnebaum 1936:96) and that for Cooper County (subdivided from Howard County in 1818), across the Missouri River from Howard County, was about 7,000 (Ronnebaum 1936:96).

Schroeder (1968:2) attributes the attraction of early settlers to the Boonslick in part to the well-respected Boone family name and the presence of salt springs, but more importantly to the loess soils: "this fact may have been largely responsible for the settlement frontier jumping from St. Charles to the Boonslick with only isolated settlements in the intervening one hundred miles along the Missouri River." Even the most casual observer in St. Louis or St. Charles must have had the same thoughts as John Peck, an itinerant missionary to frontier Missouri, who witnessed the immigration up the Missouri River to the Boonslick: "It seemed as though Kentucky and Tennessee were breaking up and moving to the 'Far West.' Caravan after caravan passed over the prairies of Illinois, crossing the 'great river' at St. Louis, all bound to the Boone's Lick" (*Missouri Historical Society Bulletin* 1950:468). Voss (1969–70:68) views these settlers to Missouri as upper South immigrants (cf. Mitchell 1978), many of them former landowners who had left worn-out fields in search of rich soil. He notes that one attraction Missouri had for these immigrants over the Northwest Territory was that it did not prohibit slavery.

The increasing immigration of slaveholders to central Missouri was noted in several newspaper accounts such as the following:

Notwithstanding the great number of persons who are held in check by the agitation of the slave question in congress, the emigration to Missouri is astonishingly great. Probably from thirty to fifty wagons daily cross the Mississippi . . . an average of four to five hundred souls a day. The emigrants are principally from Kentucky, Tennessee, Virginia, and the states further south. They bring great numbers of slaves, knowing that congress has no power to impose the agitated restriction, and that the people of Missouri will never adopt it. [*St. Louis Enquirer,* 10 November 1819]

The persistence of slavery in the newly created territory was another link in the common southern heritage of immigrant settlers. Commenting on the influence of the upper South on Missouri, Voss (1969–70:68) notes the extraordinary similarity between the constitutions of Missouri and Kentucky, particularly in the articles granting the states the power over slavery.

LAND AND LAND-RELATED PROBLEMS

As the steady flow of immigrants continued to pour into the sparsely settled central Missouri region, Missourians happily reaped the benefits of an ever-expanding population. Land prices soared in some areas, and the local economy flourished (Foley 1967:173). With this increase in status, consideration for statehood could not be far behind.

However, this population increase caused severe land-related problems for a new system ill equipped to handle them. Although some of the problems the government faced in disposing of land in Howard County were particular to that area, an analysis of these problems is important because their solution affected the settlement system in central Missouri during the decade 1810–20, and because it probably laid the groundwork for the subsequent orderly disposal of lands in the Salt River valley.

One driving force behind the rapid settlement of central Missouri may have been the high prices for farm products seen at the end of the War of 1812, with the subsequent lifting of the trade embargo against England. If the estimates of numbers of immigrants passing through eastern Missouri on their way west are anywhere near correct, and available census figures indicate that the relative magnitudes are, then one can speculate that competition for land increased considerably by the end of the second decade of settlement. And, if Voss (1969–70:68) is correct in his statement that many of the immigrants were men of means who "expected to own a large amount of land, establish a plantation, and become the social, economic, and political leaders of the region," then competition for the choicest land must have been fierce at times.

Firing the matter further were the laws regarding land speculation. Under the contemporary system a person needed to pay on the day of sale only for the land survey, the application, and one-twentieth of the selling price—at that time $2 an acre. One-fifth of the sale price was due within forty days, but the next quarter was not due until two years from the date of sale (Treat 1910:102–4). Land speculation reached fever pitch throughout the territory, leading Flint (1826:198–99) to comment while a resident of St. Charles between 1816 and 1819:

During the first winter and all the second and third years of my residence here, the rage for speculating in their lands was at the highest. . . . I have often been at collections, where lands were at sale for taxes and by orders of court, and at other times, where there were voluntary sales at auction. The zeal to purchase amounted to a fever. . . . The surveyors of course were very important instruments in this business, and a great and fortunate land-speculator and land-holder was looked up to with as much veneration by the people, as any partner in the house of Hope in London, or Gray in America. . . . A very large tract of land was cried by the sheriff for sale, when I was present and the only limits and bounds given were that it was thirty miles north of St. Louis. A general laugh ran through the crowd assembled at the courthouse door. But a purchaser soon appeared . . . undoubtedly with a view to sell it to some more greedy speculator than himself. . . . There were people who offered immense tracts of land, the titles to which were contingent, and only in prospect. Often the same tract was offered for sale by two and even three claimants.

The writer of an editorial in the *St. Louis Enquirer* (22 December 1819) was outraged that the evils of land speculation had even reached the federal government:

I have lately seen a number of patents for military bounty lands, each one of which is accompanied with a printed advertisement couched in these terms, "A map of the bounty lands, and a description of this lot, its quality, situation and timber, may be had by sending one dollar to the general land office." This advertisement is attached to the parchment of the same great seal which alone gives authenticity to the patent, and consequently is put there by the officers of government.

The height of land speculation probably did not reach as far west as Howard County until just after the official opening of the Missouri Territory for sale in 1818. For several years Missourians had agitated for the disposal of public lands, and as the hunger for land pushed speculation in private holdings to new heights, the campaign to bring Missouri's public land into the market gained momentum (Foley 1967:185). The announcement of the opening of public land sales appeared in the 5 June 1818 edition of the *Missouri Gazette and Illinois Advertiser*. President James Monroe ordered the sales to begin in St. Louis on the first Monday in September of that year. Federal law fixed the minimum price at $2 an acre; land was to be sold to the highest bidder, with a minimum purchase of 160 acres.

Sales opened on schedule in St. Louis but were delayed several months in Howard County because of the late arrival of the registrar of land titles (Foley 1967:185). Local newspapers reported brisk bidding and high prices (*St. Louis Enquirer*, 31 March 1819; see Foley 1967:185 for additional references). Apparently land speculation was so widespread that President Monroe suggested that the minimum land price be raised to counteract the practice. Howard County residents strongly protested any such action (*Missouri Gazette and Public Advertiser*, 20 February 1820), however, and the proposal was dropped.

The problems involving speculation were only the last in a long series of land-related dilemmas in Howard County that faced both the federal and the territorial governments. Several problems stemmed directly from the fact that before the opening of public land sales in 1818, no clear titles to land existed. Many immigrants simply "squatted." Following the practice established during the early colonization of the trans-Appalachian East, settlers selected a tract of land, settled there, and hurriedly made a few improvements. It was widely recognized that as soon as a first crop was harvested the settler could lay claim to the land. Unfortunately the law often did not view the situation in similar manner, and to protect their landholdings claimants began filing for rights of preemption. A similar procedure was followed by people in Howard County who held Spanish grants to what often were huge tracts of land. Foley (1967:177) states: "The Spanish land-claimants criticized Congress for failing to go far enough [in recognizing the claims], while at the same time opponents of the Spanish claims in Missouri condemned the national legislature for recognizing what they termed worthless and fraudulent titles."

He also argues that these conflicting opinions merely reflected the struggle between two groups of competing speculators over Missouri's fertile land.

It had become common practice for the General Land Office to grant preemption rights to settlers residing on public lands before their sale, a practice confirmed by an act of Congress in 1814 for the Territory of Missouri (Carter 1951). However, as Schroeder (1968:10) notes, in 1818 Secretary of the Treasury William H. Crawford ruled that since Howard County was still Indian territory in 1814 when the act was passed, the act did not apply to that county and preemption rights therefore were void. In the face of utter outrage, Crawford reversed his ruling, and in March 1819 Congress passed an act confirming the applicability of the preemption act to settlers of Howard County who had been in residence on or before 12 April 1817. A full draft of this act appeared in the Franklin *Missouri Intelligencer* on 30 April 1819. The significant role of John Scott, territorial delegate to Congress, in securing passage of this act is documented in editorials and letters in the *St. Louis Enquirer* on 31 March 1819.

In addition to the problems of validating Spanish land claims and settling preemption rights in Howard County, the federal government also was faced with the problem of New Madrid claims. Areas in southeast Missouri had been devastated by a major earthquake in 1811 and its aftershocks in 1812. As a relief measure Congress in 1814–15 passed an act authorizing persons owning land in those areas to relocate on lands elsewhere, with an upper limit of 640 acres per claim. This led to speculators' buying land from unsuspecting New Madrid residents until a law was passed in 1820 prohibiting the transfer of claims. Before passage of this protective measure, the relief act, coupled with the earlier ruling against the right-of-preemption in Howard County, essentially opened all lands in central Missouri to claims by holders of New Madrid titles (Foley 1967:181). With the reversal of that ruling the problem of land titles was thrown into even greater chaos. The relief act of 1814–15 failed miserably in its attempt to aid New Madrid residents; out of 516 certificates issued, only 20 were used by original residents. Most (385) were held by speculators who resided in St. Louis, one of whom had 40, another 33, and a third 26 (Saalberg 1966; Schroeder 1968).

Saalberg (1967) points out that contemporary land values in the Boonslick region were greater than in any other part of the state, so it was natural that many certificates would be used there. Land was selling on the average for $4 an acre at the Franklin (Howard County) land office, while it averaged only $2.84 an acre at St. Louis (March 1967, 1:247). As a result, more than 66 square miles (42,360 acres) of New Madrid claims were made in Howard County, or nearly one-fourth (121) of the total claims (Schroeder 1968:12). As a final note on the problems involving New Madrid claims, it took six acts of Congress to settle claims that arose from the original act (Saalberg 1967:72).

Having presented an overview of various land-related problems in central Missouri during the period 1810–20, we turn our attention in the following sections to patterns of settlement in the Boonslick region between 1818 and 1829. During these years, there was a steady stream of emigrants from central Missouri to the Salt River valley, so that we need at least a preliminary understanding of the dynamics of settlement, the kind of land purchased (in terms of the environmental characteristics of parcels), and the rates of purchase. Although there has been no statistical analysis of land purchase in central Missouri relative to physical and cultural environmental dimensions such as that discussed later for the Salt Valley, Schroeder (1968) presents an excellent analysis of some physical and cultural factors that encouraged settlement in the Boonslick area. The following discussion is adapted from his work.

Patterns of Settlement, 1818–29

After the opening of the land office at Franklin in February 1819, the local agent began the long process of registering claims and parcels sold at auction that year. The distribution of land entered by the end of 1819 is shown in figure 3.8. The enormousness of the total amount entered by 30 September 1819 is evident in the figure Viles (1923) gives for the receipts taken in by the land office for that period—close to half a million dollars. These initial entries were in three general regions: (*a*) The entire Cooper's Bottom and parts of the adjacent uplands and major tributaries. These lands, representing the oldest continuously occupied areas of the county, were close to or adjoined the river link with larger population centers downstream and surrounded the newly established town of Franklin. (*b*) Along a wide band trending northwest–southeast and running through the central portion of the county. This band of settlement conformed closely to areas of fairly well-drained upland soils (fig. 3.7*b*. (*c*) The northwest corner of the county, where loess soils are exceptionally deep and fertile, though most slopes range from moderate to steep. Creek valleys in this area open up to the Missouri River along steep bluffs, and the deep water provides excellent landings.

These three general settlement locations exhibit a relatively high correlation with better soils, regardless of slope. Conspicuously absent from occupation are the western third of the county with its poor soils, steep slopes, and saline waters; the northeast corner of the county with its poor soils, steep slopes, and considerable distance from the Missouri River; and the rugged bluffs in the extreme southeastern corner of the county.

Although not mentioned by Schroeder in his correlation of land entries with environmental variables, the locations of numerous salt springs in the Boonslick region may have been important in land entry decisions. However,

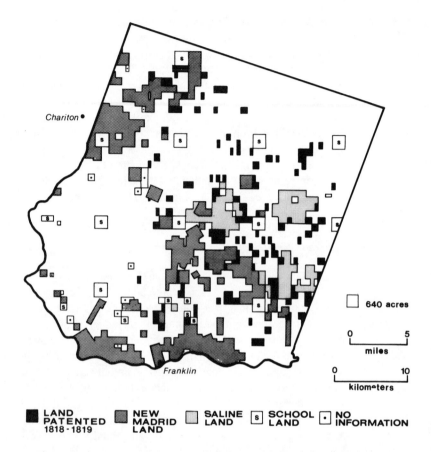

3.8. Land entered in Howard County, Missouri, by 1819 (after Schroeder 1968).

the magnitude of their importance is difficult to assess, since all but one major spring (Boon's Lick being the exception) were in areas Schroeder rates as having "better" soils. There appears to be a slight tendency for 1819 purchases to be adjacent to saline lands that in 1821 were withheld from sale and opened to the public for salt procurement. This tendency may be coincidental, however. As Schroeder (1968:17) notes, the saline land reserves largely were failures. Salt never became such a valuable commodity that the price it commanded overrode the expense entailed in extracting it on a small scale. Salt from as far away as western Virginia was inexpensive enough in the Missouri Territory that most salt springs in Howard County were seldom used, and then only by the local residents for private consumption (*Missouri*

Intelligencer, 9 July 1819). All reserved saline lands finally were put up for sale in 1831 (*Missouri Intelligencer,* 27 August 1831).

Economic Development and Patterns of Settlement, 1820–29

During the third decade of the nineteenth century the Boonslick region witnessed phenomenal growth. This growth spilled over into adjacent areas to the west, south, and east so that in 1820 the territorial legislature created additional counties, carving up portions of Howard County into Boone, Callaway, and Saline. It is evident from a cursory examination of dates of entries and sales of land made in the Boonslick area by later residents of the Salt River area that many entrants had little or no intention of remaining in central Missouri. Rather, they simply used the region as a staging area for later movement north or west. Franklin, and Howard County in general, benefited from being the northern terminus of the Santa Fe Trail, which opened in 1821–22 (Schroeder 1968; Voss 1969–70). From 1820 until its destruction by the Missouri River in 1826, Franklin was the center of transportation and trade in central Missouri. The determinants that caused its rise to prominence would be the stimuli for the growth of other towns in the region:

The role of being the main transportation terminus of the West, of being a market for goods to the South and Southwest, of dominating state politics . . . would prove important for the growth of other towns in Central Missouri. In the background was the heritage of the upper South. This tradition would play an important role in determining which political, social and economic choices the region and its towns would make in the future. [Voss 1969–70:80]

The development of Franklin as a commercial center and port assured agriculturists of a transportation point for their harvests of tobacco and hemp. Tobacco was well suited to the rich alluvial and loessial soils and soon became an important cash commodity. However, its cultivation apparently became so intense that some formerly fertile lands began to wear out and erode (Schroeder 1968:15–16). Hemp was widely used throughout the South for cotton baling, and steady shipments made their way down the Missouri and Mississippi rivers from the Boonslick region.

Intricately connected with both the stability of commodity prices and the influx of easterners to central Missouri in search of large tracts of land were social and economic developments in the East. Toward the end of the 1820s opponents of slavery were gaining momentum in eastern states—not because of any humanitarian feelings but because of economics. Years of poor agricultural practices had depleted the soil to the point that large tobacco producers were earning smaller and smaller profits, despite having the manpower (slaves) to produce greater amounts of tobacco. Meanwhile, western states and territories where slavery was accepted began to make considerable inroads into the tobacco market, finally to the point where eastern producers began to liquidate their holdings and move west with their large slaveholdings (Schroeder 1968; *St. Louis Globe-Democrat,* 2 July 1899). This westward emigration of tobacco producers, which reached its height during the late 1820s and early 1830s, effected new settlement patterns not only in central Missouri but in northeastern Missouri as well.

The settlement of Howard County during the 1820s also was influenced by economic cycles that affected not only central Missouri and the Appalachian states but the entire nation. A period of economic expansion followed the War of 1812, and the succeeding years witnessed a continual emigration west. This expansion was facilitated by easy credit terms offered by banks and by federal land policy. However, in 1818 the Second Bank of the United States curtailed credit, called in notes from state banks, and forced the state banks to resume payment in specie. This sudden policy change led to the Panic of 1819, whose effects did not reach Missouri until late in 1819. Much of Missouri's economy before this time was based on supplying new immigrants with goods until they became established (Dorsey 1935:79). As long as immigration continued, the Missouri economy remained relatively stable. The first evidence of trouble was the failure late in 1819 of the Bank of St. Louis (Cable 1923:56).

Failure of the banks meant that all currency previously issued was worthless. Without the means to buy land, the number of immigrants dwindled and the economic boom collapsed. Prices of commodities and land declined, and speculators who had purchased large tracts of land on credit had no one to sell it to and no way to make payments to the government (Dorsey 1935). By the end of 1820 the unpayable debt on public land sales was $23 million (Rohrbough 1968:138). On 24 April 1820 a law was passed (effective 1 July 1820) that replaced credit sales with a cash-only system (Peters 1845). Under this new law land was offered in 80-acre tracts for a minimum of $1.25 an acre. The change in policy did not seem to hurt land sales in Howard County, since more land was sold in the five years immediately following the change than at any other time (Schroeder 1968:16). It is unclear whether more established areas of Missouri exhibited similar growth.

Although he does not distinguish speculators from actual residents, Schroeder (1968:18) notes in general that the great increase of population in Howard County during the decade 1820–29 caused almost continuous settlement over the county (fig. 3.9). By fall 1823 the population center of the county had shifted northward, and Fayette became the new county seat. After the destruction of Franklin, its remaining functions were moved to Boonville, across the Missouri River in Cooper County, or to New Franklin, a town

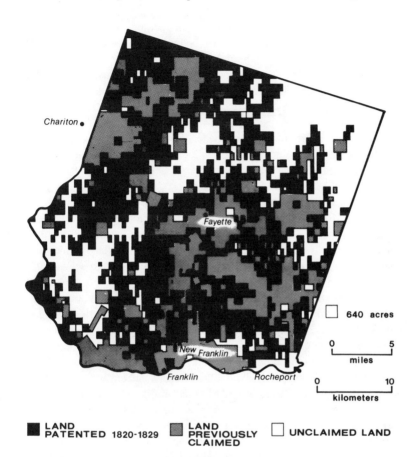

3.9. Land entered in Howard County, Missouri, during 1820–29 (after Schroeder 1968).

platted in 1828 on low bluffs to the north of the old site of Franklin (Schroeder 1968:19).

By the end of 1829, 70% of the public land in Howard County had been disposed of. Areas of the county still not settled included the poor-quality soils running northeast–southwest through the western half of the county, the steep slopes and poor soils in the northeast corner, and the steep bluffs in the southeast corner (fig. 3.9). In the following decade land sales slowed considerably as immigrants to Missouri turned increasingly to good soils in counties away from the Missouri River or upriver from the Boonslick (Schroeder 1968:19). Land entered after 1829 tended to be in areas of poor soils but adjacent to regions of better soils. Schroeder (1968:19) speculates that land patented after 1830 was entered by landowners who wanted to increase their holdings, offspring of original settlers who desired to remain close to home rather than to emigrate to better land elsewhere, and speculators who continued to operate in the most prosperous county in central Missouri. During this decade the average land parcel entered decreased from 120 acres in the early 1820s to 50–60 acres. This was due in part to a law enacted on 5 April 1832 that allowed entry of 40 acre parcels as opposed to an earlier minimum entry of 80 acres (Peters 1846:503). Thus an entrant could be more selective in his choice of land (Schroeder 1968:20). There was a stipulation in the 1832 act that required an entrant to sign an affidavit that the land entered was to be used solely for cultivation *by the purchaser.* This provision was repealed on 8 May 1846 (Minot 1854:9).

In summary, comparing Howard County land entry locations by period with physical environmental variables allows us to construct a preliminary model of settlement decisions for a frontier area. Although to date no multivariate analysis of land entry locations relative to environmental variables has been carried out for Howard County, and though social variables have not been treated in depth, Schroeder's (1968) work is important for illustrating trends in settlement configuration. These trends in turn can be used as a baseline from which to assess developments to the north, in the central Salt River valley. Pre-1812 settlement in the Boonslick region was confined almost exclusively to the present-day boundaries of Howard County. The major trajectory along which settlement occurred was defined by the agricultural potential of the rich alluvial bottomlands and terraces along the north bank of the Missouri River. By 1812, small fortified settlements had spread out across the alluvium. We can speculate that decisions on where to farm within this region were governed in large part by the distance from these fortified locations. As the population grew and Indian groups moved out of the region, consideration for safety probably decreased.

By the middecade mark much of the better agricultural land, especially previously unsettled areas along the Missouri River and in the productive loessial deposits in the northwestern part of the county, was owned by persons (mostly speculators) holding New Madrid claims. That they picked these prime areas indicates that speculators were actual residents of Howard County and thus had prior knowledge of the location of prime agricultural land; were nonresidents who, upon arriving in the region quickly assessed the situation; or were nonresidents who had agents in the region who gave them advice on which land to enter.

Land entry progressed throughout the remainder of the second and third decades, with suitability for agriculture being one strong determinant of land entry location. In light of one significant debate in settlement geography—the attractiveness of timber versus prairie for settlement—it would be interesting to have statistics on forest density in Howard County during the early settlement period, but at present these data unfortunately are not available. Based on Schroeder's (1981) map of prairie distributions in Missouri, derived from GLO field notes, there is a virtual absence of prairie within the county; hence settlement decisions may have been based partially on forest density, but certainly not on the presence of prairie-timber ecotone.

The role of the major producer (tobacco and hemp) in the development of central Missouri was discussed briefly; what are missing are data on the types of land producers purchased. Were the physical variables perceived as being desirable for tobacco and hemp production the same as those conducive to grain production? What was the minimum amount of land necessary for commodity production to return a profit? These data would significantly enhance the present picture of settlement dynamics in an important area of the Midwest.

Movement into the Salt River Valley

Diaries, narratives, and newspaper articles written during the second decade of the nineteenth century are testimony to the rising interest among frontier settlers in the Salt River valley:

After a while the Boon's Lick current began to dispart, and a branch of it to sweep off towards Salt River. In a little while Salt River, —a river of the Upper Mississippi, —became the pole-star of attraction. [Flint 1826:203]

An hundred persons have been numbered in a day passing through St. Charles, either to Boone's lick, or Salt river. [Flint 1828:110]

A number of rich farmers had sat down in the neighborhood of Salt River waiting for the opening of the Land offices. [*Missouri Gazette*, 11 January 1817]

The motion of the Tennessee and Kentucky caravans of movers, flowing through our town [St. Charles] with their men servants and maid servants, their flocks and their herds, remind the citizens of the patriarchal ages. As in the days of our father Abraham, some turn to the Boons Lick, some to the Salt river—lands of promise. [*Missouri Gazette and Public Advertiser*, 9 June 1819]

Settlers arriving in the Salt Valley in the few years before 1820 were not the first colonists of that relatively unknown region. Holcombe (1884:128) refers to an early fur trader named Maxent who explored the lower valley from the Mississippi River as far west as the junction of the main stem and North Fork of the Salt River. The first recorded settlement in the region was established in 1792 by Maturin Bouvet of St. Louis for salt production (Holcombe 1884:130–31). The small settlement, situated in the northeast corner of the project area about 1.5 miles from the Salt River, consisted of a salt furnace, warehouse, and residence. A band of Sac Indians destroyed the works in the winter of that year (during Bouvet's absence), and Bouvet made no further attempt to occupy the region until 1795. In that year he petitioned the Spanish governor at St. Louis for a grant of 20 arpens around the salt spring. This was granted, and he rebuilt his house and works. Because of the uncertainties of navigation on the Salt, he moved his warehouse to Bay de Charles, on the Mississippi, where he was granted 84 arpens. A settlement was established with up to 25 persons, several houses, fields, and gardens (Holcombe 1884:133–35). Salt was transported to St. Louis until 1800, when Bouvet was killed during an Indian raid.

At least three other attempts to produce salt along various reaches of the lower Salt River met with failure owing to Indian attacks (Holcombe 1884; Megown 1878). Apparently there were one or two agriculturists in the region at this time (Holcombe 1884) who also were driven out by Indians. The first permanent occupation appears to have been that of Giles Thompson, in an area north of the Salt River known as Freemore's (Fremon's) Lick (Holcombe 1884:143). He was visited in September 1817 by a party of five men from Bourbon County, Kentucky, who had traveled from the Boonslick region in search of a place to settle. They had found the Boonslick settlements "considerable crowded, and all of the desirable locations taken up" (Holcombe 1884:143). Some chose locations near the Salt River and then returned to Bourbon County—probably influencing many from that area to immigrate to the region (Mason 1983).

By 1818 population density along the lower Salt River had reached the point that Pike County was formed from St. Charles County. The area covered under this newly created county extended from the Mississippi River west to the Howard County line and northward from Lincoln and Montgomery counties into present-day Iowa. The town of Louisiana, just south of the mouth of the Salt River, was founded as the county seat. Farther north and inland from the Mississippi River, the town of New London was founded in 1819. It soon became the seat of Ralls County, which was formed in December 1820 from a portion of Pike County (fig. 3.10).

By the end of April 1818 almost all land in the project area had been divided into townships and ranges and subdivided into sections by GLO surveyors, and on 30 April 1818 the following presidential proclamation was issued:

Therefore, I James Monroe, President of the United States, do hereby declare and make known, that public sales for the disposal (agreably [sic] to law) of certain lands in the territory of Missouri, shall be held as follows, viz: At St. Louis, in the said territory, on the first Monday in August, October, December, February and April next, and three weeks after each of the said days, for the sale of lands in the land district of St. Louis. Thirty townships shall be offered at each sale, commencing with the most

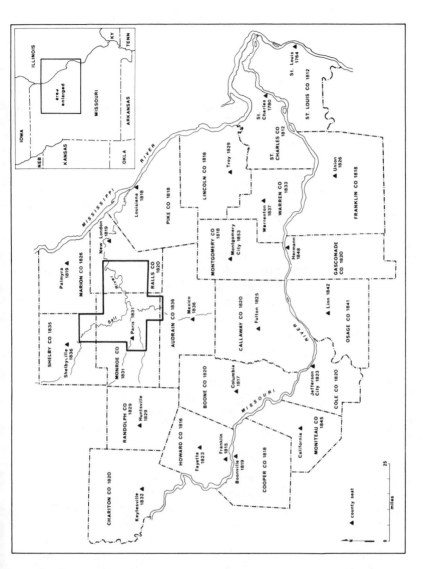

3.10. Map of northeast Missouri, showing locations of counties and county seats and dates of county formation (from Mason 1982).

eastern ranges west of the fifth principal meridian line, and proceeding westerly. [*Missouri Gazette and Public Advertiser,* 1 January 1819]

The project area fell within the land district of St. Louis, which included all lands north of T34N between the Mississippi River and the west line of R10W. Public land sales in the project area began 7 December 1818, when land in T54N, R6-8W was offered. Land in T54N, R9-10W was offered for sale on 1 February 1819, and land in T55-57N, R6-9W was first offered on 5 April 1819 (*Missouri Gazette and Public Advertiser,* 1 January 1819). At the February sales in St. Louis the average price of land was $2.52 an acre (Rohrbough 1968:134).

It is probable that most project area land sold in 1819 went to speculators who did not intend to settle it (Mason 1983). Based on our identification of residents, it is clear that many 1818–19 entrants did not become residents (chap. 5), but whether they actually were speculating in land is open to question. By the end of 1819 there were at least two clusters of settlement established by residents. The Ely settlement, founded by a small number of interrelated families from Bath County, Kentucky, was situated in T55N, R6W, south of the Salt River. The Smith settlement, also settled by emigrants from Bath County, was north of the Middle Fork in T54N, R9W. Both settlements are mentioned by name in 1823–24 Ralls County road records.

Thus by 1819 settlement in the central Salt River valley had begun in earnest. The Boonslick region continued to receive a substantial influx of immigrants from the East, but sharp competition developed between it and the newly settled area to the north. One striking aspect of the movement west of peoples from Kentucky and Tennessee, and the subsequent growth and development of portions of Missouri west of St. Louis, was the short time involved. The population of Kentucky in 1775 was approximately 150; in forty-five years the combined population of Tennessee and Kentucky had reached almost a million (U.S. Bureau of the Census 1960:13). During this short time span, the frontier had moved rapidly westward, leaving in its wake highly developed agricultural regions and commercial centers. By 1800 one leading edge of the frontier had pushed northward across the Ohio River into the vast expanse of grassland and forest now known as the Prairie Peninsula, while another turned west to timbered tracts along the Missouri River. By 1819 the latter edge had split and the frontier once again headed into the Prairie Peninsula. In the following chapter we examine in detail the physical context of the project area portion of the Prairie Peninsula, with particular emphasis on certain key elements of the environment as they existed on the eve of frontier settlement.

4

The Physical Environment:
A Context for
Frontier Settlement

Robert E. Warren

Euro-American immigrants to northeast Missouri entered a diverse and extensive environmental province similar to both the mesophytic forests of the eastern United States and the relatively dry grasslands of the Great Plains. This province, called the Prairie Peninsula, is a complex mosaic of two major biomes that protrudes eastward from the bluestem prairies of Nebraska to the beech-maple forests of northern Indiana (fig. 4.1). The Prairie Peninsula was formed about 10,000 years ago by a unique set of climatic conditions and is distinctive for its long history of ecological variability in space and time. This variability is of particular interest here, since it was an important aspect of the physical context of frontier settlement and undoubtedly had a significant effect on Euro-American cultural adaptations in the middle Salt River valley.

The project area lies on the southern margin of the Prairie Peninsula in an area composed of level upland prairies, timbered valley sides, and rich bottomland forests along meandering streams. In this chapter[1] we explore the inherent variability within and among these ecosystems, focusing on environmental variables that may have been important to the land-use practices of nineteenth-century settlers. Together these variables form the basic structural elements of a general model of the regional environment—a model that allows us in later chapters to examine the changing physical dimensions of the human niche during historic times.

Climate

Climates in the Prairie Peninsula are affected by four major streams of air (Borchert 1950; Bryson 1966): cold, dry Canadian air that forms mean frontal zones along the northern edge of the Prairie Peninsula during winter;

1. This chapter is substantially revised from Warren (1982).

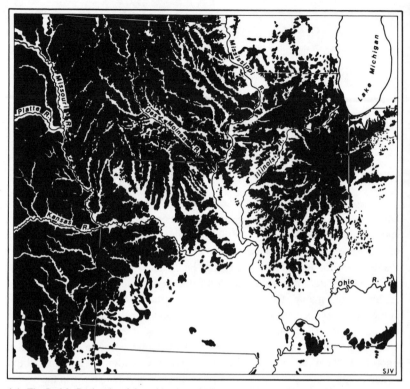

4.1. The Prairie Peninsula of the midwestern United States (from Warren 1982).

cool, dry Pacific westerlies from the northern Rocky Mountains that push across the Prairie Peninsula in winter but usually decrease in strength and abandon the Prairie Peninsula by midsummer; a warm, dry Pacific air mass, from the Great Basin and southern Rockies, that usually increases and decreases in strength with the cooler westerlies; and relatively hot, moist air from the Gulf of Mexico that moves across the southeastern United States throughout the year. The Gulf air mass is weakest in winter, when its leading edge meets the strong Pacific air masses along the southern margin of the Prairie Peninsula. But as the westerlies subside tropical air pushes farther west and north. By midsummer it flows over the eastern Plains and most of the eastern United States (including the Prairie Peninsula), meeting the Canadian air mass in a long frontal zone that stretches eastward from southern Manitoba to Newfoundland.

Borchert (1950) has shown how the varying seasonal effects of these airstreams give the Prairie Peninsula a distinctive climate. During winter, when strong westerlies drive a deep continental wedge between the Canadian and Gulf air masses, the Midwest is relatively dry. To the northeast is a steep gradient of increasing snowfall, and to the southeast is a steep gradient of increasing winter rainfall. During summer, when tropical air pushes northward, mean precipitation is more uniform across the east. The prairies are again distinctive, however, since rainfall is more variable than in areas to the north and south. In contrast to the Great Lakes region, showers tend to come in shorter bursts, and there are longer dry intervals between rains.

The prairies also are distinguished by relatively frequent and severe droughts. When winter westerlies fail to subside in summer, the dryness typical of winter persists in the Midwest and often reaches critical proportions during July and August. Temperatures increase as well, and hot, dry winds produce severe evaporative stress in a giant wedge coincident with the boundaries of the Prairie Peninsula.

Effects of these processes are reflected in weather records for northeast Missouri. The area has a humid continental climate with warm summers and moisture throughout the year, but there is a great deal of seasonal variability, and each season has a distinct array of climatic features (fig. 4.2). Winters are usually cold and dry, with moderately strong westerly winds. Spring is progressively warmer and wetter, and winds peak in strength as the expanding Gulf air mass pushes its interface with Pacific air across the region. Summers are normally hot, humid, and still. Mean rainfall peaks in May and June, before the temperature maximums for July and August, then drops off sharply before increasing again in September. This symmetric dip in late summer precipitation is common across the Prairie Peninsula, reflecting the frequency and timing of summer dry spells. Rainfall during most years actually peaks in July (Borchert 1950:14), but late summer droughts are severe enough and occur often enough to deflate these monthly means. Autumn months are progressively cooler and drier, and increasing wind speeds reflect the resumption of dominant westerlies.

Variation above and below these seasonal means is an important characteristic of Prairie Peninsula climate; in fact, few years can be expected to approximate normal trends. Major drought years occur, on average, every five years (Borchert 1950), and major drought periods (i.e., sets of three or more consecutive years of below-average precipitation) can be expected about every twenty years (Gribbin 1978). The effects of major droughts can be rapid and locally profound, influencing the cover, composition, and productivity of plants and the number and distribution of animals. By the end of the 1910–14 dry period, thousands of oaks had perished along prairie-forest borders in Illinois (Transeau 1935) and were replaced by prairie grasses. During the 1930s, short-grass associations displaced tall grasses in Iowa and other prairie

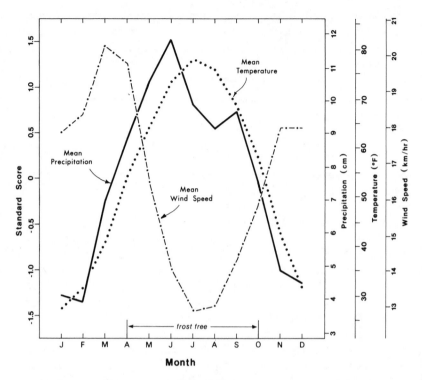

4.2. Seasonal variation of mean monthly temperature (....), precipitation (——), and wind speed (.._.) for northeast Missouri; based on means of records for Quincy, Illinois (1941–1970), Kirksville, Missouri (1937–66), and/or Columbia, Missouri (1931–60) (from Warren 1982).

states, migrating downslope in hilly areas (Tomanek and Hulett 1970) and eastward among upland interfluves in the heart of the Prairie Peninsula (Borchert 1950). These shifts, controlled by local moisture regimes, begin to reverse themselves with the return of summer rains. Ground cover can be reestablished quickly, but several decades of moisture may be necessary to restore some grasses to their predrought proportions, and succession toward the predrought compositions of plants can take much longer.

An important point emerges from these observations: year-to-year variability in weather patterns must be viewed as an integral component of the modern Prairie Peninsula climate. This variability has direct effects on local environments, usually keeping the interfaces between floral communities in a constant state of flux. Moreover, periodic droughts can be expected to reduce or eliminate crop yields in about one out of every five years—a rate of failure that could have been ruinous for specialized frontier agriculturists.

Water

Water resources vary in location and magnitude across northeast Missouri, reflecting local differences in geomorphic structure and fluctuations of climatic patterns through time. Several kinds of water sources are important in the project area: surface drainage systems, surface impoundments, and subsurface aquifers. Quantities of water in all these sources are controlled directly by rainfall and evapotranspiration rates within the Salt River basin. Because moisture patterns in the Prairie Peninsula vary greatly among seasons and from one year to the next, amounts of water in streams, lakes, and bedrock are also quite variable.

Surface drainages compose the most extensive network of potential water sources in northeast Missouri, and the Salt River has the largest catchment in the area. Streams form a dendritic pattern in the central and eastern parts of the basin; elsewhere they tend to flow north or south in trellislike patterns (fig. 4.3). Most of the Salt's major tributaries coalesce within the project area, and together they carry runoff from about 80% of the basin. Thus net stream discharge is relatively high within the project area, both compared with the remainder of the drainage basin and with respect to northeast Missouri as a whole.

Stream magnitudes also vary significantly within the project area, grading from small ephemeral tributaries in headwater ravines to perennial rivers associated with mature floodplains. Using the Strahler (1957) rank order technique to evaluate differences in stream magnitude, the Salt River mainstream, which originates at the confluence of Middle Fork and South Fork, is a seventh-order stream. Its five major tributaries (North Fork, Middle Fork, Elk Fork, Long Branch, and South Fork) are all rank orders 6 or 5. Progressively lower-order streams increase in abundance at a geometric rate, but they are also of lesser magnitude. All fourth-order ($n = 11$) or larger streams flow year round, as do most third-order streams (21/27), but very few second-order streams (13/127) and no first-order (0/651) streams are perennial. Nonetheless, there are only a few places in the study area where water is more than 1 or 2 miles away.

Stream-flow variability exerts a strong influence on local environments. High water can reshape land surfaces, destroy crops, and threaten man-made structures. Low water can cause stress among plants and animals dependent on streams for water or aquatic resources. As the climatic model presented earlier might lead us to expect, flow records for the Salt River show significant variability among seasons and from year to year. However, patterns of stream flow are not simple functions of rainfall or any other single climatic variable. Peak stream flow occurs during April, when the Salt is on average about 6 feet deeper than the annual mode. Rainfall is near the annual mean at this time, but rates of evaporation and transpiration are fairly low, ratios of runoff to infiltration are fairly high, and rates of ground water discharge are high owing to warming spring temperatures. Thereafter, flow drops off abruptly toward an August low point, when rates of evapotranspiration and infiltration are both relatively high and there is a dip in late summer precipitation. Discharge is fairly constant through autumn and midwinter but rises during early spring, somewhat in anticipation of spring showers, owing to snowmelt and surface thaw.

Times of abnormally high stream discharge generally parallel monthly means. Major floods (30,000 cubic feet per second or 23 feet above mean stream level) are most common during April, when they occur about once

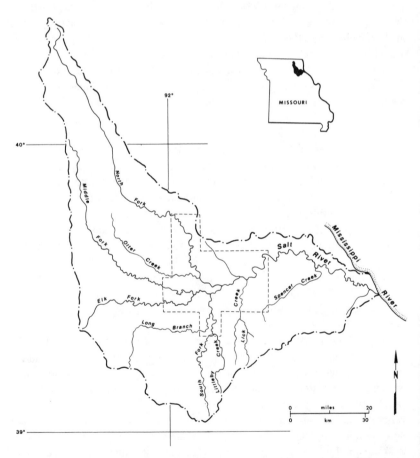

4.3. Major streams in the Salt River basin, showing the location of the project area (from Warren 1982).

every ten years, and are rare during January. The probability of a major flood during any given year is about 0.42, but the effects of most are quite localized, and even record floods normally return to bank level in a matter of days.

Abnormally low discharge is common during late summer and autumn. Although sporadic and infrequent flooding does occur during July, September, and October, stream flow more often is low during these months. Stream flow is also low during periods of drought. During the dry 1930s the Salt River itself reportedly degenerated into a series of small pools, most of which were, as a local resident states, "too shallow and hot to swim in."

Documented surface impoundments are uncommon in the project area. Several ponds were reported by early land surveyors, and a few oxbows persist today along the floodplains of major streams. Most are clustered in a few select localities, such as on wide bottomlands of the lower Salt and upper North Fork, and most are very small. Certainly none approaches the size of large backwater lakes observed along the Mississippi and Illinois rivers, and many probably shrank or dried up entirely during late summer dry spells or extended droughts.

Wetlands, which are documented in federal land survey and land sale records, occur in two distinct contexts: low-lying bottomlands subject to annual flooding and level upland flats with poor surface drainage. Most of the former are composed of small and widely scattered segments of active floodplains, but one fairly broad area of wetlands is evident in the northeast corner of the study area where the valley floor is notably wide and flat. Before construction of artificial drainage networks, wet uplands were widespread in the Prairie Peninsula on flat, glaciated interstream divides (Winsor 1975). Here the combination of level terrain, impermeable claypan soils, and sparse networks of small streams often prevented rapid drainage of spring and early summer rains. Extensive but shallow and impermanent "lakes" commonly appeared on the upland prairies, which made travel difficult, established breeding grounds for noxious insects, and discouraged cultivation (Klippel and Maddox 1977). Several upland "swamps" are known from the project area, including rather large parts of the broad, flat prairies east of North Fork and Lick Creek, and smaller portions of the rolling prairies east and west of South Fork.

Freshwater springs occur widely in the project area, but most perennial ones are concentrated in the northeastern part of the region along bluff bases on the Salt and its tributary streams. Here the terrain is relatively rough, and bedrock exposures below the water table are common. Spring discharge, ultimately regulated by rainfall patterns, normally fluctuates seasonally. Some springs flow more consistently than others, and a few reportedly were reliable and critically important water sources during the drought-stricken 1930s.

Saltwater springs are relatively rare in the study area proper, but they attracted eighteenth-century French entrepreneurs just a few miles downstream.

Landforms

The bedrock surface of northeast Missouri is composed of horizontally bedded limestones, sandstones, siltstones, and shales (Missouri Botanical Garden 1974). By late Tertiary times (about 1.8 million years ago) erosion had carved these deposits into a mature hilly landscape drained by several major east-flowing and south-flowing streams. But during the early Pleistocene the first of a series of glaciers moved across the area and sheared off prominent hilltops, filled valleys with debris, and mantled the new ground surface with a level layer of drift. During the million years since glaciers last covered the area, erosion has incised many new valleys into the glacial plain. Large amounts of glacial drift remain, however, and the overall landscape is immature. Broad upland flats are still a major feature of the area's physiography. Although most large streams follow meandering courses and are associated with well-developed terraces, bottomlands are generally flat or concave, and tributary valleys have youthful profiles with steep gradients. Signatures of Pleistocene glaciations are, then, quite evident on the modern landforms of northeast Missouri.

Landforms in the region reflect these general trends. Flat uplands, which dip slightly toward the east at a rate of about 1.5 feet per mile are preserved as level to gently sloping interstream divides (fig. 4.4). Valley bottoms, also with level to gently sloping surfaces, vary greatly in width and orientation depending on the resistance and erosional history of underlying deposits. Between these two extremes are valley sides with moderate (3-10%) to steep (10%) slopes. These slope classes are distributed widely across the project area; moderately sloping valley sides usually border upland flats, and steep valley sides often abut valley bottoms. However, steeper slopes are more common and more continuous in the northeast portion of the region, whereas gentler valley sides are more extensive to the west and south.

These topographic patterns occur because local relief increases significantly as one moves downstream. Extreme differences in local elevation range from 121 to 141 feet where each of the four major tributaries of the Salt River enter the project area from the north, west, and south, but relief is up to twice as great (240 feet) in the northeast corner of the region where the Salt makes its exit. Relatively steep valley sides not only occur more frequently along the lower Salt and its lateral tributaries, they are quantitatively steeper there as well.

Talus slopes greater than 45% are common, and vertical limestone cliffs often outcrop along the outer edges of modern stream meanders. These

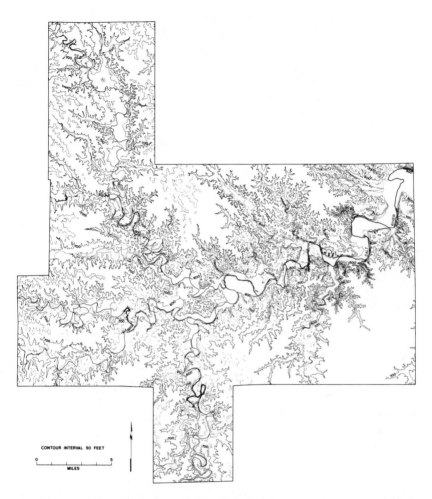

4.4. Topographic map of the project area (from Warren 1982).

differences in terrain correlate with other environmental variables and have important implications for human land use. Rugged landscapes, for example, tend to buffer the evaporative effects of dry summer winds, offer better protection from winter storms, and contain greater numbers of freshwater and saline springs. However, they also tend to associate with shallow, rocky soils and place greater constraints on transportation networks and on appropriate locations for residential or other types of settlements.

Bottomland terraces in the project area have a complex and poorly understood history. They probably were formed during the past million years or so, after meltwaters from the retreating Kansan ice sheets scoured at least parts of the valley to bedrock. After a rapid episode of alluvial deposition, it appears that there were several cycles of stream incision and partial refilling. An extensive program of geomorphological research, in which over two hundred terraces were mapped, trenched, and/or cored, has led to recognition of four major Pleistocene cycles (Huxol 1980). Each cycle is represented by the truncated remnant of a former floodplain. Together they are arranged steplike above modern streams. Attempts to date these terraces have not yet succeeded, but Huxol (1980) suggests that all terraces in the study area are middle to late Pleistocene in age. Other alluvial deposits, attributed by Huxol to the modern floodplain (i.e., periodically flooded surfaces less than 23–28 feet above modern streams, which compose about one-third the area of modern bottomlands), would date to the Twocreekan (12,800 to 11,500 B.P.) or Greatlakean (also termed Valderan, 11,500 to 10,000 B.P.) substages of the terminal Pleistocene, or to the more recent Holocene period.

Characteristic landform types in northeast Missouri tend to cluster along an upland-lowland gradient of slope position. In any given locality these features can be grouped within a mutually exclusive series of land areas precisely delimited by contour elevation boundaries. Further, by establishing controls for interlocal variation of relief, slope position categories can be expanded to a regional scale with a comparable degree of precision. Five slope position categories, termed *drainage classes,* have been defined for the region (Warren 1976, 1979). Each drainage class correlates with a discrete set of landform types and with a number of other important environmental variables as well (Warren and O'Brien 1981). Together they partition the project area into a series of five ribbonlike zones that roughly parallel the courses of major streams or cap upland interstream divides.

Boundaries between drainage classes are composed of elevation contours that are redefined, from place to place, to account for changing river elevations and variation of maximum local relief (fig. 4.5). Drainage class 5, which includes all lands less than 20 feet above the mean elevations of major streams, typically corresponds with flat to slightly sloping floodplains along major streams and lower tributaries. Its upper margin usually intersects the risers of high bottomland terraces. Drainage class 4 occupies all areas that are above class 5 and less than 60 feet above mean major stream level. It usually consists of level to moderately sloping bottomland terraces and sloping lower valley sides, rarely inundated.

Drainage classes 3 through 1 occupy areas successively greater in elevation than the upper limit of class 4, but they differ from classes 5 and 4 in that their vertical intervals vary directly with downstream increases in maximum local relief. The two boundaries that separate the three classes divide the vertical relief above class 4, and below the maximum upland elevation, into three

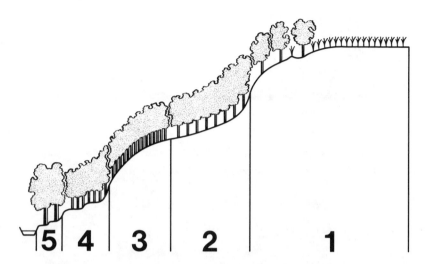

4.5. Idealized transverse section of the middle Salt River valley showing drainage classes and associated floral and topographic characteristics (from Warren and O'Brien 1981).

equal units. Thus drainage class 3, which occupies middle valley sides with moderate to steep slopes, covers all areas that are above class 4 and below contours that are one-third the vertical distance to the local maximum upland elevation. Class 2, which lies above class 3 and below contours that are two-thirds of the vertical distance to the local maximum elevation, is generally composed of moderately sloping land along the upper margins of valley sides. Drainage class 1 includes all areas above class 2 and typically occupies level to slightly sloping upland flats.

In summary, the drainage class technique subdivides valleys into a series of precisely defined slope position categories that form irregular linear bands running parallel to major streams (fig. 4.6). Classes generally contain distinct arrays of topographic features, and the technique is therefore a useful approach to landform classification in the project area. Further, tests have shown that drainage classes significantly reflect patterned variation of dominant biome distributions, forest species compositions, tree diversities and densities, soil characteristics, and prehistoric and historical period site locations (Warren and O'Brien 1981). Given this sensitivity to environmental and cultural variation, the technique has been used widely as a regional stratification device for a variety of studies in the project area.

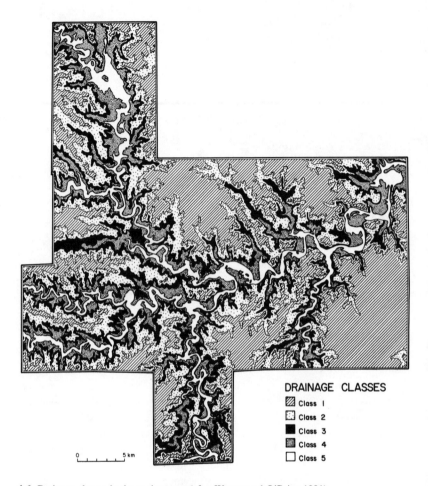

DRAINAGE CLASSES

▨ Class 1
⊡ Class 2
■ Class 3
▨ Class 4
☐ Class 5

0 ____ 5 km

4.6. Drainage classes in the project area (after Warren and O'Brien 1981).

Soils

Soils are formed, under the influence of topography, by long-term interactions of geological substrates with climates and plant and animal life. Soils are active components of functioning ecosystems that reflect the spatial variability of ecological processes and at the same time have varying degrees of suitability for different kinds of human behavior. Summarized in this section are soil characteristics that were important to historical use of the region. Also discussed are early historical period perceptions of soil quality, as a framework for interpreting the spatial patterning of frontier land purchases.

Five soil associations, defined as landscape units containing discrete sets of similar soil types, are recognized in the project area (Warren 1976; cf. Watson 1979). These units tend to conform spatially to topographic slope positions, running in bands parallel to streams or forming patches with recurrent landform characteristics (fig. 4.7). Similarities with distributions of drainage classes are as real as they are apparent (cf. fig. 4.6). Statistical tests show that soil associations covary significantly with drainage classes in Monroe and Shelby counties (Warren and O'Brien 1981), the only two counties for which modern soil surveys were completed by 1979.

Soil associations I–III occur on valley sides and interstream divides. The first, coincident with drainage class I, occupies extensive, level upland flats. Here soils are deep silt loams with mature profiles. Developed in loess under a

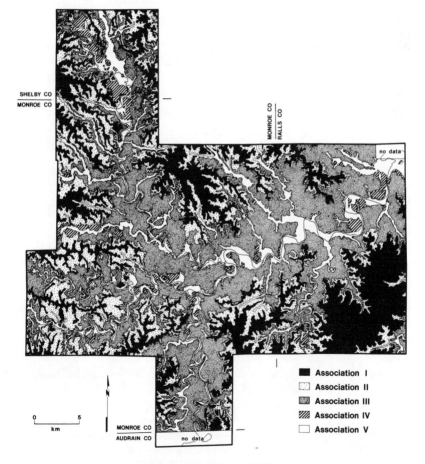

4.7. Soil associations in the project area (from Warren 1982).

flora of prairie grasses, they are naturally fertile and have moderately high productivity ratings for modern row crops (fig. 4.8). However, they also are poorly drained; those on the flattest landforms have dense claypan "B" horizons and are subject to seasonal ponding. Successful cultivation often required considerable investments of time, energy, and capital to establish systems of artificial drainage. Association II occurs downslope from I, usually along the gently sloping margins of upland flats. These are moderately well drained loams and silt loams derived from loess and glacial till. They were formed under prairie grasses or a transitional cover of mixed grasses and trees. They are slightly less productive than soils in association I, but standing water is not a serious problem. The third association occupies sloping valley sides. Soil textures here are quite variable, ranging from silty clay loams to cherty silt loams. Most developed under a forest cover in glacial till, and, though they are well drained, agricultural productivity generally is low.

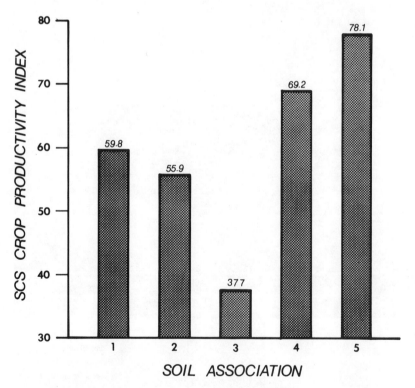

4.8. Variation of potential crop productivity among soil associations in the project area. The values are mean Soil Conservation Service productivity ratings of the soil series in each association weighted by the area proportion of each series within each soil association in the region.

Associations IV and V are formed from alluvial deposits in valley bottoms. Most soils in association IV are loams or silt loams occurring on high, level terraces once covered by forests or prairies. Some have surface drainage problems, but their productivity ratings are generally higher than soils in association I (fig. 4.8). Association V is composed of active floodplain soils subject to seasonal inundation. They follow the timbered courses of rivers and some intermittent creeks, and they range in texture from silty clays to fine sandy loams. Although they often are poorly drained, soils in association V generally have the highest agricultural productivities of any in the region.

During the early nineteenth century, General Land Office (GLO) surveyors laid out section corners and township and range lines across most of northeast Missouri. Following instructions by the surveyor general (see chap. 5), their field notes contain a rich variety of information, including explicit references to soil qualities observed along section boundaries. The project area was surveyed between 1816 and 1822 by ten survey teams, and soils were rated on all but a few section lines. Most references are brief general descriptions, and not all surveyors phrased their ratings in the same terms. All seem to have had one underlying variable in mind: the suitability of observed soils for frontier cultivation. Given this interpretation, all references can be classified within a three-level ordinal ranking: "rich" to "very rich," "excellent" or "first-rate" soils "fit for cultivation," "good" or "second-rate" soils "fit for cultivation," and "poor" to "very poor," "thin" or "broken and rocky" or "third-rate" soils "not fit for cultivation."

A map of these soils evaluations (fig. 4.9) shows a great deal of local continuity. Soils rated poor are most common in the central and eastern portions of the project area where the terrain is relatively rough. There are three general contexts for poor soils: sloping forested valley sides, poorly drained bottomlands, and level or wet upland prairies. Good and rich soils also occur in central and eastern areas, but only on high, well-drained bottomland terraces, level upland forests, or gently rolling uplands near the prairie-timber ecotone. To the west and north, where landscapes are much less rugged, high ratings are common in all but the steepest or wettest localities.

Vegetation

During the early nineteenth century, and throughout much of the Holocene, the Prairie Peninsula was composed of a mosaic of deciduous forest and grasslands. Both communities were made up of distinct arrays of plants and animals, and each offered a different set of resources to human residents in the area. Attempts to understand the properties of the two communities are therefore of great interest to our analysis.

Modern studies of Prairie Peninsula ecology face many difficulties. The

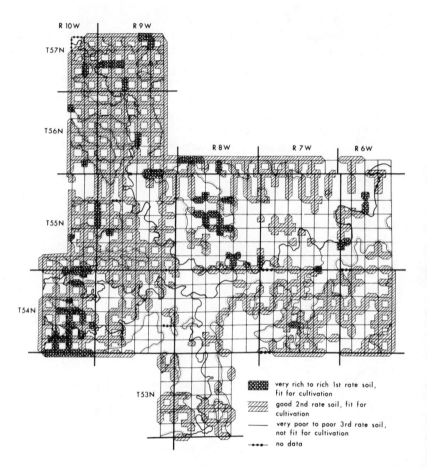

4.9. Soil-quality evaluations made by General Land Office surveyors along section lines in the project area (1816–22) (from Warren 1982).

area is today most often referred to as an agricultural region, the Corn Belt, rather than as a native floristic province. Consistent with this terminology, the original vegetation has been altered drastically by western economic pursuits. Most prairies have been replaced by extensive fields of corn, soybeans, and wheat. Many areas once forested also are now under cultivation, and most existing forests represent secondary regrowth on abandoned cropland or have been consistently logged, grazed, and protected from fires. Thus the modern ecology of the Prairie Peninsula is of an entirely new order, and attempts to reconstruct native communities based solely on contemporary observations are hazardous at best (Bourdo 1956).

Fortunately, a wealth of pertinent information is contained in the preserved field notes of early GLO surveyors. These surveys, designed to systematically establish permanent section corners and to document resources of interest to western development, were for the most part conducted in the project area several years before permanent Euro-American settlement (1816–22). Included in the records are detailed plat maps that depict prairie-forest boundaries and descriptions of the understory and overstory vegetation observed along section lines. The notes also provide valuable information on "bearing trees"—trees that were blazed to enable the relocation of section and quarter section corners—including their common names, diameters, and distances and directions from posts driven into the ground at each corner. These data enable the delimitation of prairie and forest communities and allow general studies of the composition, diversity, density, and resource potential of forests. Although biased in several ways (Warren 1976; Wood 1976), GLO records currently provide the best information available on presettlement vegetation patterns.

Prairie

Prairies originally covered about 30% of the project area (fig. 4.10). Most were restricted to upland contexts on broad, level interstream divides. A few occurred in bottomlands, most notably along the upper North Fork where upland ridges slope smoothly toward the valley floor, but bottomland prairies were nevertheless rare in comparison with larger river valleys elsewhere in the Prairie Peninsula (Zawacki and Hausfater 1969). Herbaceous species are not mentioned in GLO records, but prairies probably were dominated by bluestem and other perennial grasses and a variety of sedges, legumes, and composites.

Three types of prairie can be distinguished in the project area. The first includes flat, seasonally ponded upland marshes underlain by impermeable subsoils. These areas, referred to as "wet prairies" by GLO surveyors and as "swamps" by later settlers, were ill suited for agriculture before adoption of drainage tiles to facilitate runoff and were avoided by Euro-Americans well into the nineteenth century (Bremer 1975). The second and most extensive type of prairie, occurring on rolling uplands and moderately sloping valley sides, was stereotypic of well-drained midwestern grasslands. Here ponding was not a detriment to agriculture, but the dense root matrix of prairie sod discouraged extensive cultivation until the steel plow was invented and marketed in the Midwest.

A third type of prairie, common on narrow strips of grassland in the northwest part of the study area and near the prairie-forest ecotone elsewhere, contained a relatively diverse flora. Although dominated by herbaceous perennials, these areas also contained scattered trees and, in places, dense

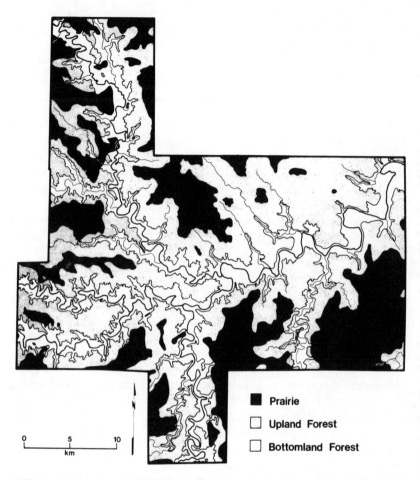

4.10. Nineteenth-century distributions of prairie and forest in the project area (from Warren 1979).

thickets of hazelnut, scrub oak, and grapevine. Most prairie trees were black oak (*Quercus velutina*), a species constituting about 72% of the bearing tree sample (a total of 130 trees). Also represented were a few pin oaks (*Q. palustris*), white oaks (*Q. alba*), elms (*Ulmus* sp.), hickories (*Carya* sp.), and blackjack oaks (*Q. marilandica*). In open areas oaks usually develop broad crowns and shade larger areas than their counterparts in forests. However, prairie trees were extremely sparse in the project area. Applying the "closest individual" method of Cottam and Curtis (1956) to post-to-tree distances we obtain a mean density of only 0.5 trees per acre. This is only about half the value ordinarily used to define the minimum density of open woodlands (Curtis 1959), suggesting that, although trees occurred in areas defined by GLO surveyors as prairie, the prairie trees were a minor component of the habitat.

Forest

Prairie Peninsula forests are normally limited to the bottomlands and dissected valley walls of perennial streams. During the early nineteenth century they covered about 70% of the region (fig. 4.10), dominating nearly all of the drainage classes 3 through 5, three-fourths of drainage class 2, and nearly one-third of class 1. They were most extensive in the northeastern portion of the project area, where relief is greatest, and they tended to become narrow upstream.

The sample of GLO bearing trees from forested parts of the region includes a total of 1,955 trees at 981 section and quarter section corners; an average of about two trees per corner. Also available is a sample of 73 streamside witness trees used by surveyors to map positions of the right and left banks of the Salt River along a 14 mile course in the northeastern part of the project area. Thirty distinct taxa are represented in the forest sample, including twenty-six distinguishable at the species level and four at the level of genus.

A variety of approaches has been used to analyze vegetation data derived from GLO records. One inherent problem with the records is that datum points are widely spaced at half-mile intervals along section lines, and it is not possible to generate conventional tables that describe homogeneous *and* contiguous stands of trees. Thus, samples must be stratified for comparative analysis.

Of primary concern here is the intraregional variability of forests as a framework for understanding local environmental differences within the project area. Using a variant of direct gradient analysis (see Whittaker 1967), the Missouri Botanical Garden (1974) has shown that modern remnant forests in the region are sensitive to topographic variation along an upland-bottomland gradient of slope position. Since drainage classes represent a formalized sequence of slope positions that correlates strongly with available soils and landform data (see above), drainage classes were used to subdivide the sample of forest bearing trees into five units. Two additional samples, prairie bearing trees and bearing trees reported from the banks of the lower Salt River, are appended to opposite ends of the continuum.

COMPOSITION

Presettlement forests in the project area were dominated by six major taxa: white oak, black oak, hickory, elm, pin oak, and sugar maple. Together,

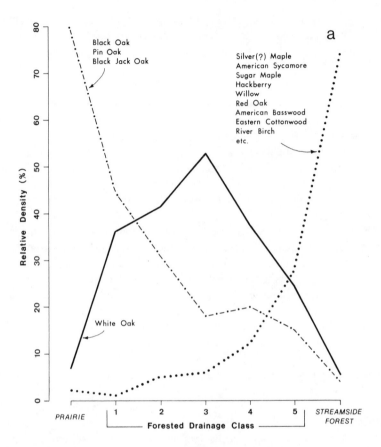

4.11. Compositional variation of early historical forests along a gradient of slope position. The data are relative densities of (*a*) three dominant and (*b*) three subdominant modal groups of important GLO bearing tree taxa (from Warren 1982).

they compose almost 90% of forest bearing trees. As shown in table 4.1, the relative frequencies of these and other taxa are quite variable along the drainage class gradient. A summary of these trends appears in figure 4.11, which plots the relative densities of abundant GLO taxa (i.e., taxa with relative densities greater than 1% in at least one stratum) after consolidation of the taxa into six major "ecological groups" defined on the basis of shared modes (Whittaker 1975:127).

Group 1 accounts for most prairie trees and also dominates level to gently sloping upland forests (fig. 4.11). Included here are black oak, an early successional species tolerant of dry soils, and lesser numbers of pin oak and blackjack oak. Hickory, the only taxon in group 2, is most abundant on the

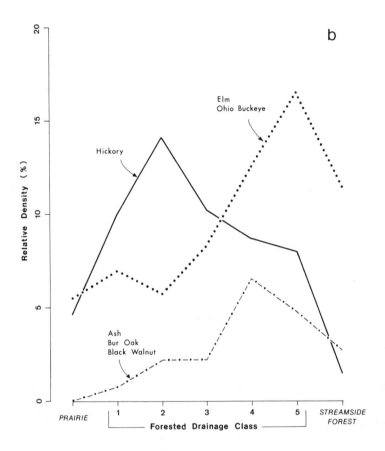

moderately sloping margins of upland flats. Modern vegetation studies show that shagbark hickory (*Carya ovata*) is by far the most common species of hickory in the project area today (Missouri Botanical Garden 1974). Moreover, it currently is most abundant in drainage class 2. The coincidence of slope position modes for *Carya* and *C. ovata* in presettlement and modern forests implies that shagbark hickory was an important element of early historical upland forests, and it may well have been the most common hickory species in the region as a whole.

White oak is the only species in group 3. It predominates in several drainage classes but apparently favors steeply sloping land on middle valley sides. Group 4 is a relatively minor unit, subdominant on high bottomland

Table 4.1. Relative Densities of GLO Bearing Trees in the Cannon Project Region

Taxon	Prairie sample: 130	Forested Drainage Class					Streamside Forest sample: 73
		1 sample: 287	2 sample: 638	3 sample: 488	4 sample: 329	5 sample: 213	
Willow	0.8	—	—	—	—	0.9	6.8
Eastern cottonwood	—	—	0.2	—	0.6	3.8	4.1
Black walnut	—	—	1.1	0.6	1.2	0.9	—
Butternut	—	—	—	0.4	—	0.9	—
Walnut	—	—	0.3	0.6	—	0.5	1.4
Black hickory	—	—	—	—	0.3	—	—
Hickory	4.6	10.1	14.1	10.3	8.8	8.0	1.4
Eastern hop hornbeam	—	—	—	0.2	—	—	—
River birch	—	—	0.6	0.4	0.9	1.4	2.7
White oak	6.9	36.2	41.7	53.1	38.6	24.4	5.5
Post oak	—	—	0.5	0.6	1.2	—	2.7
Bur oak	—	—	—	0.2	1.5	1.4	—
Blackjack oak	1.5	0.7	—	0.2	—	—	—
Black oak	71.5	40.4	27.3	16.6	18.8	13.1	4.1
Pin oak	6.9	3.5	3.8	1.2	1.5	1.9	—
Northern red oak	1.5	—	1.3	0.8	0.3	0.5	5.5
Oak	—	—	—	—	—	0.5	—
Elm	5.4	7.0	5.8	8.2	11.6	15.0	9.6
Hackberry	—	—	0.5	0.4	1.2	5.6	9.6
Red mulberry	—	—	0.3	0.8	0.3	0.5	1.4
American sycamore	—	—	—	0.2	0.9	2.8	12.3
Serviceberry	—	—	—	—	—	0.5	—
Black cherry	0.8	0.7	—	0.4	0.3	—	—
Kentucky coffee tree	—	—	—	—	—	0.5	—
Honey locust	—	—	0.2	0.4	0.3	—	—

Table 4.1. *continued.*

| | Prairie | Forested Drainage Class | | | | | Streamside Forest |
Taxon	*sample: 130*	*1* *sample: 287*	*2* *sample: 638*	*3* *sample: 488*	*4* *sample: 329*	*5* *sample: 213*	*sample: 73*
Locust	—	0.4	0.3	—	0.3	—	1.4
Sugar maple	—	0.4	0.6	1.6	3.7	6.1	9.6
Silver (?) maple	—	—	—	—	0.3	3.8	13.7
Ohio buckeye	—	—	—	—	0.9	1.4	1.4
American basswood	—	—	0.5	1.0	2.4	2.4	4.1
Black (?) gum	—	—	—	0.2	—	—	—
Blue ash	—	—	0.2	0.2	0.6	—	—
Hoop ash	—	—	—	0.4	0.6	0.5	—
Ash	—	0.7	0.9	0.8	2.7	1.9	2.7

Source: Data from Warren (1982).
Note: Figures represent percentage of stratum.

terraces, that includes ash (*Fraxinus* spp.), bur oak (*Q. macrocarpa*), and black walnut (*Juglans nigra*). Elm and Ohio buckeye (*Aesculus glabra*) peak on bottomland floodplains (group 5), while a great variety of taxa together dominate low, moist streamside forests (group 6).

The patterns formed by changing bearing tree percentages among slope positions strongly resemble the Gaussian or bell-shaped distributions that species tend to form when their abundances are measured along environmental gradients that are important determinants of reproductive success (Gauch 1982:96–102). In all cases there are persistent increases toward well-defined modes, and most intervals along the landscape gradient support the mode of a unique array of taxa. However, this does not mean that the modal groups comprise well-defined communities that intergrade either abruptly or continuously with adjoining communities. Plots of individual taxa show that each has a uniquely shaped curve along the gradient, and these patterns conform well to Gleason's (1926) individualistic hypothesis of species distribution.[2] Thus the patterns are not controlled by species adaptations to one another within integrated communities. Rather, they are functions of an important environmental gradient of some kind that varies from upland to lowland contexts.

There are two basic categories of gradients in midwestern forests: physical factors, composed of the many varying characteristics that distinguish one place from another in terms of the potential reproduction and growth of different species (e.g., microclimate, percentage slope, aspect, soil composition, moisture), and successional factors, composed of the varying biological responses of different species to different types of ecosystem disturbance (e.g., resistance to wind, fire, and disease, reproductive potential, shade tolerance, growth rate, longevity).

Although these two gradients are conceptually distinct, in practice they often are difficult to isolate. For example, in a classic analysis of variation among upland forests in the northern Prairie Peninsula, Curtis and McIntosh (1951) discovered that tree species vary individualistically in abundance when ordered along a one-dimensional gradient ranging from "pioneer" taxa (e.g., bur oak, black oak) in open-canopy forests with relatively sparse trees and saplings and abundant shrubs to "climax" taxa (e.g., eastern hophornbeam, sugar maple) in closed-canopy forests with denser trees and saplings and less abundant shrubs (Bond 1957). Subsequent research has shown that a wide variety of plants and animals vary in abundance along this same dimension (Bond 1957; Gilbert and Curtis 1953; Hale 1955; Loucks and Schnur 1976; Tresner, Backus, and Curtis 1954), and it is now widely regarded as a major

2. The sequence of important taxa in the region (from upland prairie to streamside forest contexts) is as follows: blackjack oak, black oak, pin oak, hickory, white oak, black walnut, ash, bur oak, elm, Ohio buckeye, eastern cottonwood, American basswood, sugar maple, river birch, hackberry, northern red oak, silver (?) maple, American sycamore, and willow.

successional gradient that measures the varying degrees of ecosystem recovery from fire and other agents of forest disturbance (Bray and Curtis 1957; Gauch 1982:121–34).

In light of these results it might be reasonable to propose that, because fire played a major role in determining the presettlement composition of southern Wisconsin forests, it was a predominant formation process throughout the Prairie Peninsula (cf. King 1978). This is a popular idea in many ecological and anthropological circles, and it might readily explain the variability of forest composition in the project area. However, in a multivariate reanalysis of the upland forests in southern Wisconsin, Peet and Loucks (1977) successfully isolated physical and successional gradients in factors that vary independently. In fact they discovered that the succession gradient actually explains less of the variation among their samples than does a moisture-nutrient gradient related to varying soil properties. Moreover, a comparison of species ranks ($n = 19$) on the two gradients indicates that the original climax adaptation sequence of Curtis and McIntosh (1951) correlates much more highly with the moisture-nutrient gradient ($r = .927$) than with the succession gradient ($r_s = .688$).[3]

Three important aspects of the study by Peet and Loucks (1977) deserve emphasis here. First, the successional sequences of species in the Prairie Peninsula can be expected to vary significantly in different physical contexts. On relatively moist sites there should be a natural progression among mesic species from shade-intolerant to shade-tolerant forms (e.g., red oak to sugar maple), whereas on drier sites the progression is from intolerant to tolerant xeric species (e.g., black oak to shagbark hickory). This indicates that both pioneer and climax GLO taxa will differ substantially along the project area slope position gradient, and most of the dry upland forests in which hickories were relatively abundant (i.e., drainage class 2) may have been in equilibrium at the time of Euro-American settlement.

Second, the "depth" (or species diversity) of successional sequences, as measured by the number of species involved in the development of a climax forest, increases markedly from xeric to mesic sites. Thus, in relatively moist contexts one would expect to see fluctuations in the abundance of a great variety of species through time, whereas in progressively drier contexts there will be fewer species involved. In fact, Peet and Loucks (1977) note that black

3. It is noteworthy that both correlations are significant at the $p < .01$ level $r_s = .549$), as is the correlation between species ranks on the moisture and succession gradients ($r_s = .621$). This indicates that, although the moisture and succession gradients are independent, the behavior of species on the two gradients is nonrandom. Early successional species tend to be abundant in dry and sterile contexts, whereas late successionals are relatively abundant where conditions are more mesic and fertile. This is especially true for species on either end of the two gradients, and these tendencies help explain the undue emphasis on the succession factor in one-dimensional ordinations of southern Wisconsin forests.

oak is both a pioneer and a climax dominant in the driest physical contexts examined in southern Wisconsin. Conditions there are too severe for other tree species to survive, and the open canopy required for the regeneration of black oak is maintained in climax stands. These findings indicate that the relative predominance of black oak in the Salt Valley prairies and xeric forests (i.e., drainage class 1) is as easily explained by moisture limitations as by forest disturbance.

Third, the two-dimensional representation of forest composition in southern Wisconsin is both classificatory and diagnostic (Peet and Loucks 1977:494). Although its denotative capabilities undoubtedly are greatest in the northern Prairie Peninsula, it can be used in similar ecosystems to evaluate the relative impacts of differing physical environments and disturbance histories on forest composition. Thus, if fire was a major determinant of the compositional variation within project area forests, there should be a significant relation between the sequence of GLO taxa on the project area slope position gradient and the scores of conspecifics on the succession gradient from southern Wisconsin. However, the rank orders of seven taxa, all of which are common in both regions, clearly indicate that this is not the case (table 4.2).[4] There is a weak correlation between the two sequences (r_s = .393) that is insignificant at the 5% level of probability. On the other hand, there is a strong and highly significant correlation between species ranks on the slope position and moisture-nutrient gradients (r_s = .893; p < .01). Together these relations indicate that physical context variables were much more influential than disturbance factors in determining the composition of presettlement forests in the project area. More specifically, the downslope increase in the availability of soil moisture (in the form of decreasing depth to the water table and decreasing distance to perennial streams) probably is the most important environmental characteristic of the slope position gradient. Assuming that fires had disturbed the early historical vegetation encountered by Euro-American settlers, it appears that their effects were either limited to open prairies or were local, rather than regional, in extent.

The strong patterning of bearing tree taxa indicates clearly that floral resources were not distributed evenly along the slope position gradient. However, we have little reason to assume that floral composition was constant

4. The seven taxa selected for comparison include all but one of the GLO taxa that constitute 1% or more of the forest bearing trees in the project area as a whole. The exception is ash (*Fraxinus* spp.), a genus that was rarely observed in the stands reported by Peet and Loucks (1977:487) and is represented by at least three species of unknown proportion in the project area (Steyermark 1963). The scores of shagbark hickory and American elm were selected to represent the hickory and elm genera in table 4.2, since modern vegetation studies indicate they are by far the most abundant representative species in the region today (Missouri Botanical Garden 1974:105, 142–52).

Table 4.2. Spearman Rank-Order Correlations between the Slope Position Modes of Seven Common Bearing Tree Taxa in the Cannon Region (Ranked Upland to Lowland) and Scores of the Same Taxa on Gradients of Moisture-Nutrients (Ranked Xeric-Sterile to Mesic-Fertile) and Succession (Ranked Early to Late) in Modern Upland Forests in Southern Wisconsin

Taxon	Cannon Slope Position Gradient	Wisconsin Moisture-Nutrient Gradient[a]	Wisconsin Succession Gradient[a]
Black oak	1	1	1
Hickory	2	2[b]	6[b]
White oak	3	3	2
Elm	4	4[c]	4[c]
American basswood	5	6	5
Sugar maple	6	7	7
Hackberry	7	5	3
r_s		.893[d]	.393[d]
p		$<.01$	$<.05$

[a]Data rescaled from Peet and Loucks (1977:492).
[b]Ranks of shagbark hickory *(Carya ovata)*.
[c]Ranks of American elm *(Ulmus americana)*.
[d]The Spearman correlation between the Wisconsin moisture and succession gradients equals .607 ($p<.05$) for these taxa.

within drainage classes across the entire region. As noted earlier, topographic relief and levels of effective moisture generally increase in the region from west to east. Since many taxa are sensitive to moisture variation, we might expect significant compositional variation along an upstream-downstream moisture gradient that parallels the patterns expressed among slope positions.

Maps of GLO bearing tree locations support this proposition (fig. 4.12). White oak, a mesic-xeric species tolerant of steep slopes in the project area (Warren 1976), appears to be disproportionately abundant in the north-central portion of the region and relatively sparse toward the west and north. Black oak, a xeric species less tolerant of steep slopes, apparently increases in abundance from southeast to northwest. The hickory complex is dominated in the project area by species with intermediate moisture requirements and preferences for moderate slopes. It is distributed widely but seems to be most common in the south-central part of the area and least common toward the northeast. Walnut and sugar maple, both relatively mesic forms, apparently decrease in abundance toward the west and north. Statistical analysis of frequency variation among sets of contiguous townships confirms these trends. There is a strong downstream progression of modes from black oak to hickory to white oak ($\chi^2 = 78.08$; df $= 20$; $p < .001$), and both walnut ($\chi^2 = 4.67$; df $= 1$; $p < .05$) and sugar maple ($\chi^2 = 6.67$; df $= 1$; $p < .01$) are, in comparison with aggregated frequencies for the white oak–

hickory–black oak group, proportionately more abundant in the eastern half of the region (ranges 6–8) than they are in the west (ranges 9–10). The reader will note that this progression of modes corresponds directly to the sequence of taxa observed along the slope position gradient. This confirms our hypothesis and indicates that there were in fact *two* significant moisture gradients in the region— upslope and upstream. The upstream decrease in effective moisture probably accounts, at least in part, for the relatively narrow gallery forests toward the west, and it may also indicate that locations upstream were somewhat less suitable for crop production than those downstream.

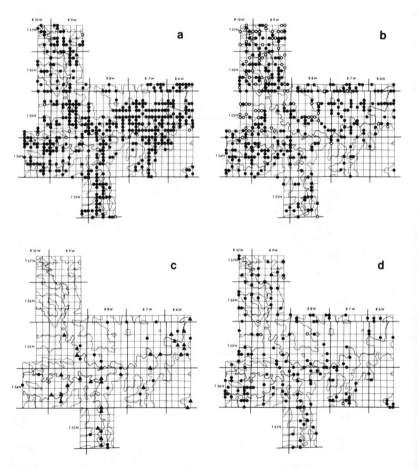

4.12. Geographic distributions of (*a*) white oak (*Quercus alba*), (*b*) black oak (*Q. velutina*), (*c*) sugar maple (*Acer saccharum*) (denoted by ▲) and walnut (*Juglans* sp.) (denoted by ●), and (*d*) hickory (*Carya* sp.). In (*a*), (*b*), and (*d*), ● indicates forest bearing trees and ○ signifies prairie bearing trees (from Warren 1982).

DIVERSITY

The relative densities shown in figure 4.11 imply that the taxonomic richness of presettlement forests increased downslope along the drainage class gradient. To test this proposition, we applied several measures of species diversity to GLO taxa. The results indicate clearly that trees were progressively more diverse downslope from prairies and upland forests to timbered floodplains (Warren 1982).

The downslope increase in forest diversity may simply reflect the fact that relatively few tree species in the midwestern United States are adapted to xeric habitats (Peet and Loucks 1977). It also is questionable whether tree diversity could have had an important influence on the settlement decisions or economic behavior of frontier immigrants. However, recent ecological theory—albeit controversial—indicates that a variety of pertinent factors commonly are functions of the diversity of primary producers. For instance, it has been proposed that floral diversity increases directly with degree of species dispersion (Margalef 1968), with the diversity of animal taxa (Whittaker 1972), with succession (Whittaker 1965), with community stability (Connell and Orias 1964; MacArthur 1955), with primary productivity (Brown 1981; MacArthur 1972), and so on (see Pianka 1978:286–300). Assuming these relations are valid, we may propose that terrestrial biota in the Cannon region ranged from aggregated and homogeneous forms in upland prairies to relatively dispersed and varied forms in floodplain forests, and that bottomlands were relatively stable and highly productive of energy and biomass. Although most of these relations probably hold in the Salt Valley, recent research has demonstrated that diversity and productivity are not always directly correlated (Whittaker 1975). In homogeneous ecosystems diversity may cycle out of phase with productivity (Sprugel and Bormann 1981), while in temperate deciduous forests the two variables may peak together—but at intermediate points along gradients of environment and forest succession (Loucks 1970). Moreover, humans are selective consumers of energy, nutrients, and technological resources, and it would be unwise to assume that the spatial distributions of all possible resources, biotic or otherwise, were of equal importance to human adaptations. It is for these reasons that we now turn to the absolute densities of forest taxa and attempt to translate those values into units of measurement that theoretically were important to historical settlers in the Cannon region.

DENSITY

Tree densities can be calculated from GLO records as an inverse function of distances between corner posts and bearing trees. Using the "closest individual" technique of Cottam and Curtis (1956), 1,016 distances to trees nearest posts were added to the radius of each nearest bearing tree, stratified by biome and drainage class; averaged; and transformed into mean densities per stratum (see Warren 1976). Along the slope position gradient these values form a unimodal bell-shaped curve peaking strongly on the steep valley sides of drainage class 3 (30 stems per acre). Densities decrease gradually into bottomland classes 4 and 5 (81% and 64% of maximum) and upland class 2 (71% of maximum) but drop off sharply into level upland forests and prairies (34% and 2% of maximum, respectively). Although resulting density estimates are probably only small fractions of actual values owing to the bias of the GLO surveyors against small trees (Bourdo 1956), results show clearly that forest densities varied a great deal in the project area and that this variability was partially a function of landscape position and steepness of slope.

When considered in geographic terms, the apparent correlation between forest density and ruggedness of terrain implies that forests were densest in the northeastern portion of the project area and on sloping valley sides near major streams, but that they were relatively sparse on dry upland interfluves and along the upper courses of small streams. Tests of these propositions should be illuminating, since spatial variation of forest density has several interesting implications. First, because density is correlated inversely with openness of the forest canopy and penetration of sunlight onto the forest floor, density variation across space should associate with distributions of understory flora adapted to varying degrees of shade tolerance (Whittaker 1975). Open woodlands generally contain proportionately greater amounts of biomass in the form of understory shrubs and herbs than do dense forests, thereby attracting important browsers such as white-tailed deer and many other terrestrial or ground-nesting vertebrates seeking concealment in dense brush (King and Graham 1981). Second, historical narratives indicate that sparsely timbered forests could be cleared and cultivated more easily, in less time, and at lower cost than either dense forests or open prairies (Bidwell and Falconer 1925:158–59, 267–71). They may therefore have attracted early frontier settlers who required direct access to lumber and, at the same time, fields that could be rapidly prepared for planting (Warren, O'Brien, and Mason 1981). Third, high-density forests are relatively mesic and insensitive to minor climatic change (Asch, Ford, and Asch 1972). Thus, patches of sparse forest that conform to dry physiographic contexts may reflect areas sensitive to climate-induced fluctuations of the prairie-forest ecotone. On the other hand, anomalous patches of sparsely timbered forests (i.e., patches that transgress distinct zones of humidity) may signify local disturbance caused by some catastrophic event such as fire.

To test the geographic implications of variation in forest density and evaluate any patterns that might occur in the region, a tree density map was generated from GLO records using transformed distances between corner posts and trees nearest posts. One problem with this approach is that GLO records constitute an open lattice of datum points. Values for center points of sections ($n = 296$), a class of information not documented by GLO surveyors, therefore were interpolated using means of all available post-to-tree distances occurring along the four surrounding section lines. A second problem, less common in GLO records, is missing data. Missing values ($n = 12$) were estimated using means of all available "nearest distances" from the surrounding square-mile area. The resulting matrix, comprising 1,147 distances, was then plotted and locally smoothed by substituting for each value the mean of its nine or fewer nearest neighbors in the surrounding one square mile block. Smoothed distances were then transformed into densities ("closest individual" technique of Cottam and Curtis 1956), assigned Cartesian coordinates, and stored on computer tape. Finally, prairie-forest boundaries and courses of major streams were digitized, and a spatial interpolation routine was used to project densities into between-point contexts.

The statistical distribution of results is fairly smooth and ranges from 1 to 211 stems per acre, signifying continuous variation from very sparse to very dense forests. The project area mean of 20.5 stems per acre, projected from a mean post-to-tree distance of 23.03 feet, cannot be compared with results of most modern studies because of GLO surveyor bias toward large-stemmed bearing trees. However, estimates from other GLO samples indicate that the Cannon region as a whole was of moderately low density. Early historical forest in the Black Belt region of western Alabama averaged 83 stems per acre (Jones and Patton 1966). Mean densities ranged from 37 to 71 stems per acre in a five-county area of mesic white oak forests along the Missouri River in eastern Missouri and averaged 53 stems per acre for the River Hills region as a whole (Wuenscher and Valiunas 1967). Closer to the project area mean are estimates of 26 stems per acre for oak-hickory openings on dry alkaline soils in Alabama's Black Belt (Jones and Patton 1966), 24 stems per acre for upland white oak forests along a tributary of the Missouri River in central Missouri (Reeder, Voigt, and O'Brien 1983), 20 stems per acre for upland post oak forests in southwestern Missouri (King 1978), and 14 stems per acre for disturbed bur oak woodlands in the prairie-forest border region of southwestern Wisconsin (Cottam 1949).

Although forests in the project area as a whole were of moderate density, the statistical distribution of locally smoothed values implies that up to 40% of project area forests were as dense as many heavily timbered regions in the central and southeastern United States. This proposal is strongly supported by the project area forest-density map (fig. 4.13), which shows a remarkably well defined concentration of high-density datum points. Consistent with our expectations, the most extensive area of dense forest associates with heavily dissected terrain in the central and eastern sections of the region. Here density levels 4 and 5 form a nearly uninterrupted patch of dense timber that spans the bottoms and steep valley sides of the Salt River and penetrates the lower reaches of its lateral tributaries. Upstream are smaller pockets of dense forest. Most of these also occur in dissected contexts, and they often are linked by strips of medium-density forest (level 3) that tend to parallel the courses of major streams.

In contrast, low-density forests (density levels 1 and 2) occur consistently on gently sloping upland divides, often in association with small patches of upland prairie. They also are common along the upper reaches of tributary streams and near the prairie-forest border, where the line descriptions of GLO surveyors often note areas of "thick bush" or "thin timber." In many of these areas the line descriptions also mention hazelnut in the forest understory. This is important because hazelnut is a shade-intolerant shrub that normally is found along the prairie-forest ecotone or in early successional phases of disturbed forests (Jones 1963; Loucks and Schnur 1976; Mohlenbrock 1975). Since it also grows well in a variety of moisture regimes and in both upland and lowland contexts (Steyermark 1963), hazelnut is a good indicator of open-canopy or low-height woodlands. The distribution of hazelnut across the project area correlates well with inferred locations of low-density forests. To the east, where trees were densest, it was common only along the ecotone and in patches of sparse forest, whereas it was widespread in forest and ecotone habitats toward the west (Warren 1982). Oak understory, which in youth is relatively tolerant of shade (Fowells 1965:635), shows a complementary distribution. It was most common in the central and eastern parts of the region and was relatively rare toward the west and north. In general, then, the indicated locations of high- and low-density forests are quite consistent with physiographic variation and understory distributions in the project area, and it is probably safe to conclude that major trends in nineteenth-century tree density variation are accurately portrayed in the forest-density map.

Given this conclusion, attention should be focused on two rather anomalous patches of low-density (level 1) forest that transect distinct zones of moisture and slope position. The first is a large ovoid area (3.7 miles north–south by 3.1 miles east–west) near the southwestern corner of the study area. It projects northward from an upland prairie, crosses the lower Elk Fork, and terminates along north-facing slopes of the lower Middle Fork valley. The second is a wedge-shaped area along the lower South Fork (3.1 miles north–south by 3.7 miles east–west) that extends eastward from a peninsula of upland prairie, crosses the South Fork, and intersects upland prairie on the east side of that river. Both areas are unique in that their datum points signify extensive level 1 forests, yet they cut across level uplands and steep valley sides in the same fashion. By contrast, valleys of the lower Middle Fork and Elk Fork are virtual mirror images of one another in terms of stream

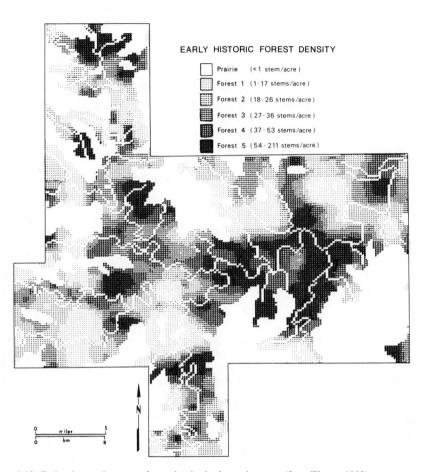

EARLY HISTORIC FOREST DENSITY

	Prairie	(< 1 stem/acre)
	Forest 1	(1 - 17 stems/acre)
	Forest 2	(18 - 26 stems/acre)
	Forest 3	(27 - 36 stems/acre)
	Forest 4	(37 - 53 stems/acre)
	Forest 5	(54 - 211 stems/acre)

4.13. Early-nineteenth-century forest density in the project area (from Warren 1982).

magnitude, topography, and soils, yet the bank of medium- to high-density forest that runs along the former is not reflected along the Elk Fork.

It is possible that these so-called anomalies are nothing more than random spatial aggregates of large post-to-tree distances. The two patches of sparse forest are defined by only thirty-eight datum points, and it is reasonable to suppose that they cluster in space merely by chance. However, several independent lines of evidence are consistent with the low-density forest proposition. First, hazelnut, an indicator of open-canopy forests, is mentioned in nearly two-thirds of the line descriptions in these areas (61.5% of thirty-nine line descriptions), whereas it occurs in fewer than half of the forest line descriptions in the remainder of the region (45.6% of five hundred descriptions). A univariate chi-square test indicates the statistical probability is less than 5% that this difference is due to chance alone ($\chi^2 = 3.99$; df $= 1$; $p < .05$). Second, there are several other line descriptions of the western patch that refer to oak "bushes" and "thickets" of oak and hickory "brush," and a number of section lines in the eastern patch are described as "B. jack roughs" composed of blackjack oaks (*Quercus marilandica*), hazelnut shrubs, and briers. Both sets of line descriptions imply that mature trees were relatively sparse, since aggregates of brushy or shrubby forms of overstory taxa are often indicative of disturbed, open-canopy forests (Braun 1950:117, 343; Cottam 1949:271–72)[5] and since blackjack oak is a small, shade-intolerant tree that typically occurs in open and relatively dry communities (Harlow and Harrar 1969:329; King 1978:46). Third, the species composition of GLO bearing trees in the two localities is significantly different from that in other forests in the region (table 4.3). Hickory, pin oak, and six other taxa are at least twice as abundant as in the remainder of the region, whereas white oak and several others occur at reduced rates. Of interest here is that six of the eight overrepresented taxa are shade-intolerant genera or species that are adapted to habitats with widely spaced trees and abundant penetration of sunlight below the forest canopy.[6] Moreover, ordering taxa by shade tolerance

5. Although we postulate here that the oak and hickory "bushes" noted by GLO surveyors were stump or root sprouts sent up by downed or injured trees, many of them may instead have been mature individuals of shrubby taxa. Dwarf chestnut oak (*Quercus prinoides*) is a small, shrubby plant that is widespread and fairly common in dry, open forests of Kansas and western Missouri (Stephens 1969; Steyermark 1963), and it occurs in similar contexts eastward to the Atlantic coast. In the Pine Barrens of New Jersey it is a dominant species in the dry, low-canopy pine-shrub oak transition community (Whittaker 1979), and it readily invades taller and more mesic communities disturbed by fire (Little 1979; Olsson 1979). Thus, even if the oak "bushes" in the Cannon forests were *Q. prinoides,* the environmental indication provided by this species' habitat is essentially the same as that implied by the sprout hypothesis (i.e., sparsely timbered, open-canopy or low-height woodlands), and the conclusion remains the same.

6. Despite decades of research on the process of ecological succession, a strong unifying synthesis has not yet appeared, and the interrelations among successional variables are often poorly understood (Golley 1977). One such variable is the shade tolerance of forest trees. Foresters have used field observations to order species on ordinal gradients of tolerance. These have been revised from time to time with additional observations, but experimental research that might lead to a less subjective and more quantitative framework was proved difficult. As a result, there occasionally is a lack of congruence among the evaluations of different observers. The primary source used here for taxonomic ordering is the tolerance table of Baker (1949). Fowells (1965) and Harlow and Harrar (1969) were consulted for taxa not discussed by Baker. The major discrepancy between these sources is the scaling of hickory (*Carya* sp.). Baker characterizes the genus as intolerant of shade. Although Fowells (1965:113) repeats Baker's generic characterization, he notes the ability of two species to reach climax status and states that shellbark hickory (*C. laciniosa*) and shagbark hickory (*C. ovata*) are very tolerant and moderately tolerant of shade, respectively (pp. 130, 134). This is an important issue here, since shagbark hickory probably was a major upland species in the project area during the early historical period and, by implication,

shows that 36.2% of the eighty bearing trees in sparse forests are intolerant of shade, whereas only 16.6% of 1,875 forest bearing trees elsewhere in the region are shade-intolerant. A bivariate chi-square test indicates that this difference can be expected owing to chance fewer than once in 1,000 times ($\chi^2 = 20.49$; df $= 1$; $p < .001$). Together these data offer firm support for the proposition that forests in both the lower Elk Fork and lower South Fork localities had anomalously low tree densities and were, indeed, open-canopy woodlands at the time of Euro-American settlement.[7]

ECOTONE

Zones of transition between prairie and forest often were relatively narrow (1-3 feet) in the central and southern Prairie Peninsula and were composed of slender, contiguous bands of small trees (e.g., plum and hawthorn), shrubs (e.g., dogwood, hazelnut, and grape), and tall herbs (e.g., sunflower and goldenrod) (Shelford 1963). Plat maps compiled by GLO surveyors imply that transitions in the project area also were abrupt (fig. 4.14). This may well have been true in many localities, particularly where sharp topographic breaks occur along the margins of level uplands. However,

---

was relatively abundant in the sparse Elk Fork and South Fork forests. Consistent with Baker's conclusion is a multivariate character analysis of seventy-five species of eastern broadleaf trees that gives *C. ovata* a relatively low score on a complex factor of light absorption (Wells 1976). Additionally, Peet and Loucks (1977) have argued that although *C. ovata* may become a climax dominant in midwestern forests, it can be expected to do so only in relatively dry contexts where very tolerant species with high moisture and nutrient requirements are unlikely competitors. It is for these reasons that Baker's (1949) original evaluation is followed here.

Taxa ranked intolerant or very intolerant in the project area include hickory, post oak, blackjack oak, pin oak, American sycamore, honey locust, willow, eastern cottonwood, black walnut, butternut, walnut, black hickory, black cherry, Kentucky coffee tree, and locust. The first six of these occur in the sparse forests along the lower Elk and South forks.

7. Granting that this conclusion is valid, the question of cause naturally arises. Since the low-density patches of forest crosscut different landforms and moisture regimes, are very localized, and tend to be bordered by steep gradients of tree density, it seems reasonable to assume that the agent involved was catastrophic and had a circumscribed impact in time and space. A variety of processes can disturb forest ecosystems, including such abiotic factors as wind, drought, ice, and fire and such biotic factors as senescence, insects, and disease (White 1979). Few of these alternatives can be tested rigorously with available data, but several lines of evidence suggest that fire was the most likely cause. For instance, trees in the sparse forests have a curiously bimodal size distribution (scaled in 4 inch interval diameter classes) with strong peaks at 11 and 19 inches, whereas tree diameters in the remainder of the region are more normally distributed with a single mode in the 11 inch class. It is provocative that fire-sensitive taxa (including hickory, elm, honey locust, and sugar maple: Fowells 1965; Starker 1934) are relatively small and compose most of the 11 inch mode, while relatively fire-resistant taxa (including white oak, black oak, pin oak, and red oak) are larger and make up most of the 19 inch mode. Chi-square tests of stem diameter versus fire-resistance show that sensitive taxa are

several lines of evidence indicate that transitions in many other places were more gradual, perhaps reflecting forest invasion of prairie owing to Neo-Boreal climatic changes (Warren, McDaniel, and O'Brien 1982). First, trees in forested level uplands were less than half as dense as forest in general, and many upland forests enclosed isolated patches of prairie (fig. 4.10). Second, surveyor line descriptions indicate that transitions themselves were sometimes diffuse and uncharacteristic of either prairie or timber. Several of these refer to intervening brushy zones dominated by hazelnut, plum (*Prunus* sp.), and blackjack oak. Others note areas of mixed prairie and forest. Third, a number of gaps occur in mapped GLO prairie-timber boundaries (fig. 4.14). Although these gaps could merely represent incomplete portrayals of the ecotone, a striking number of them occur in localities containing soil series that are transitional between soils developed under prairie and under forest. Thus it seems likely that many gaps signify areas in which zones of prairie-timber contact were fuzzy and difficult to map. Finally, as noted earlier, prairie trees were sufficiently common near forests that surveyors used them to mark section and quarter section corners at nearly one-fifth of all prairie corners. In sum, these data suggest that characteristics of the prairie-timber ecotone were highly variable in the region. Transitions apparently were gradual in some areas, were composed of dense brush in others, and may have been relatively abrupt in the remainder.

Fauna

Faunal resources were vital to prehistoric hunter-gatherers in the Salt Valley (Bozell and Warren 1982) and probably were of considerable importance to early Euro-American settlers as well. Evaluation of the diversity, abundance, distribution, and seasonal availability of these resources is therefore an important step in delineating the historical setting of the region.

---

significantly smaller than resistant taxa in the sparse forests (χ^2 = 22.61; df = 2; $p < .001$) and are also somewhat smaller than fire-sensitive taxa in the remainder of the region (χ^2 = 5.08; df = 2; $p < .10$), whereas resistant taxa are significantly larger than sensitive taxa in the sparse forests (see above) and are also significantly larger than fire-resistant taxa in the remainder of the region (χ^2 = 8.24; df = 2; $p < .025$). Moreover, the fire-sensitive taxa also have a secondary mode in the 19 inch diameter class—in addition to the much stronger 11 inch mode. These data are entirely consistent with the fire hypothesis, and, given this conclusion, the most likely scenario is a runaway prairie fire of medium intensity that entered the forest and killed most young trees, some fire-resistant trees, and all but the largest fire-sensitive trees about sixty to ninety years before settlement. The 11 inch trees reported in 1816 would represent maturing secondary regrowth (primarily hickory and other "gap-phase" taxa: see Bray and Curtis 1957:344; Peet and Loucks 1977:497), while the larger trees were individuals that survived the fire either because of their age or because of their species' natural resistance to fire (see Brown and Davis 1973:49, 51).

Table 4.3. Compositional Differences between Sparse Level 1 Forests along the Lower Elk and South Forks and Other Forests in the Cannon Region

Taxon	Sparse Forest Frequency	Percentage	Other Forest Frequency	Percentage
Hickory	17	21.2	198	10.6
White oak	24	30.0	786	41.9
Black oak	15	18.7	446	23.8
Pin oak	7	8.7	42	2.2
Elm	7	8.7	160	8.5
Others[a]	10	12.5	243	13.0
Total	80	99.8	1875	100.0

Source: The data are 1955 GLO bearing trees at forested section and quarter section corners.
Note: $\chi^2 = 24.39$; df = 5; $p < .001$.
[a]Post oak, blackjack oak, northern red oak, American sycamore, honey locust, sugar maple, Ohio buckeye, and blue ash.

However, animals are less tractable than plants, and there is no detailed nineteenth-century sample of faunal observations comparable with the information contained in GLO records. Further, the habitats of many species have been altered or eliminated by western development, and results of modern studies are at best hazardous guides to the past. Thus discussion of faunal resources is far less comprehensive than the topic deserves, and we must supplement data from the project area with information from other sources.

Inventories of modern taxa, including one short-term study in the project area and many others in the greater Midwest, indicate that a variety of native forms still occur in the region. These include about 30 species of freshwater mussels, 57 of fish, 15 of amphibians, 40 of reptiles, 170 of birds, and 47 of mammals (Missouri Botanical Garden 1974; R. D. Oesch, personal communication). Of this total, only about one-third are common or abundant in the region today. Many others, including a variety of secondary and tertiary producers that now are extirpated from the region or occur in limited numbers, formerly were more abundant and played important roles in the local ecosystem. In contrast, habitats of prairie/forest edge species, such as cottontail rabbit and white-tailed deer, have expanded owing to land clearing and the reduction of natural predators so that modern populations are potentially larger than those of early historical times. Thus modern census data are skewed strongly by modern environmental contexts, and estimates of primeval faunal composition and abundance must be either forgone or tempered with healthy margins of error.

Faced with these same problems in a study of the lower Illinois River valley, Styles (1981) used criteria developed by Jochim (1976) and others to

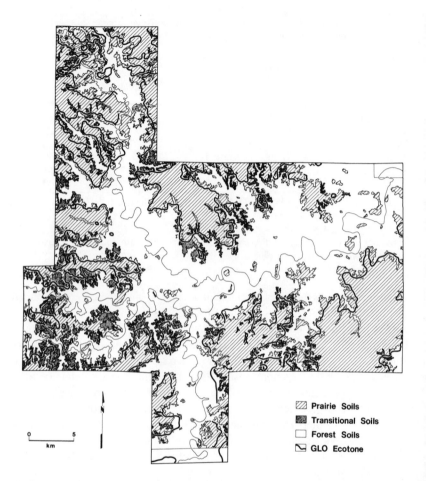

4.14. Distributions of early-nineteenth-century prairie-forest ecotone and soils developed under prairie, forest, and transitional floras (after Warren, O'Brien, and Mason 1981).

estimate which species or sets of species would have been more or less useful and accessible to local prehistoric hunter-gatherers. By synthesizing results of floral reconstructions with studies of the niches, behavioral characteristics, and potential utilities of faunal resources, Styles ranked taxa along a scale of predicted economic value. Given the proximity of the Illinois River valley to the project region (ca. 60 miles) and strong environmental parallels between the two areas, Styles's rankings are of great interest here.

Five highly productive taxa well suited for human exploitation emerge as "first line" resources in Styles's (1981) analysis. The first of these is white-tailed deer (*Odocoileus virginiana*), a large browser with high individual meat yields. Early accounts indicate that deer were generally abundant in midwestern forests (Shelford 1963). Modern research suggests that groups were relatively large in comparison with other megafauna but had small home ranges and fairly low mobility (Schwartz and Schwartz 1981). Thus, deer constituted an attractive resource that was fairly predictable and available all year long. Accessibility probably was enhanced during autumn when herds aggregated to feed on upland acorn mast, and also during winter when they often yarded during storms (Smith 1975). Wild turkeys (*Meleagris gallopavo*), characterized by fairly large body sizes and clutch sizes, also were common in the Midwest (Shelford 1963). Groups tend to aggregate in upland forests to feed on autumn mast and are readily exploitable during winter flock formation. A third important species, raccoon (*Procyon lotor*), is relatively dense in bottomland forests. Meat yields and pelt values are both high, groups have relatively small home ranges, and the species is active and available all year (Schwartz and Schwartz 1981).

The two remaining "first line" resources are composed of multispecies taxonomic groups—fish and migratory waterfowl (Styles 1981). Both were abundant in and along the Mississippi and Illinois rivers, but because of significant environmental differences between these areas and the Salt River valley they probably could not have functioned as "first line" foods in the project area (Warren 1982). White-tailed deer, turkey, and raccoon, on the other hand, are much more likely to have provided yields comparable with unit areas of larger valleys. All are abundant today in the project area, and ample browse produced in relatively sparse nineteenth-century forests should have sustained fairly dense populations in the past. Nevertheless, absolute abundances of these and other forest-dwelling taxa, when measured as numbers of animals per unit length of river valley, probably were relatively low. The far greater breadths and diversities of habitats along major rivers undoubtedly could have supported larger and more closely packed populations of animals than could have been sustained along smaller, narrower tributary valleys such as the Salt.

Conclusions

Information discussed in this chapter indicates clearly that the historical setting of the central Salt River valley was environmentally varied, both in time and from place to place. Four points deserve emphasis. First, climatic configurations in the southern Prairie Peninsula are susceptible to rapid and recurrent change, often causing short-term droughts that tend to check forest expansion and ensure the persistence of prairies. Second, the primary dimension of ecological variability within the region apparently is expressed along an upland-lowland gradient of slope position. This model is strongly supported by distributions of landform types and major soil associations, by early historical and modern plant compositions, and by modern faunal distributions, hydrographic data, and outcrops of geologic formations. Thus project area microenvironments are best viewed as a series of narrow parallel, contiguous bands that form concentric zones surrounding major streams and reflect increasing biotic diversity downslope. Third, variability also is expressed along an upstream gradient of decreasing topographic relief, increasing moisture stress, and decreasing proportions of mesophytic species. This trend probably is a general one that extends from the mouth of the Salt River to its headwaters, and it highlights the rather profound differences in resource abundance and diversity that distinguish the region from the larger river valleys to the east. Finally, one important variable—tree density—shows an element of randomness in its distribution. Presettlement forest tended to be densest in midslope and downstream contexts where relief and isolation were greatest, but several anomalous low-density patches of forest have been identified in certain localities. These localities appear to have been disturbed during the eighteenth century by fire or some other catastrophic and highly localized event, and dense, steady-state forests had not yet reappeared by the time Euro-Americans entered the region. Since low-density forests probably were highly valued by many frontier agriculturists, these areas may have attracted settlers to places that would be difficult to predict knowing characteristics of the upslope and upstream gradients alone.

In summary, the physical setting of the region represented a diverse and challenging context for historical settlement. Many aspects of this diversity were patterned in space and time and can be summarized by a few major environmental dimensions. However, other important characteristics of the environment were more random in distribution, compounding the problem of explaining frontier human behavior in the southern Prairie Peninsula.

5

General Patterns of Settlement and Growth in the Central Salt River Valley

Jacqueline A. Ferguson and
Michael J. O'Brien

As we noted in chapter 3, by 1819 the central Salt River valley had become a major focal point of settlers migrating westward. This new frontier, while in some respects quite different from the physical environments of the source areas in the East, must have at first glance reminded the immigrants of the fairly rugged, timbered terrain they had recently left. Their perceptions of the environment, in conjunction with their cultural background, conditioned to a large extent where they settled within the frontier zone. The complex mosaic of grassland and deciduous forest found in this portion of the southern Prairie Peninsula provided for almost limitless combinations of resource zones for settlement. The analysis of these land-selection decisions through time forms the basis of this chapter. We discuss land purchase and preferred environmental characteristics for six time periods, beginning with initial settlement in 1818 and ending with the sale of the last tract of public land in 1858.

Additionally, entrants are divided into three groups—residents, nonresidents, and speculators—to determine if the patterns of land entry for each group are distinct. The general overview presented here sets the stage for a more detailed, multivariate approach to settlement analysis presented in chapter 6 and an in-depth analysis of social dimensions and settlement presented in chapter 7. Taken together, these three chapters offer a test of the implications of the settlement model in chapter 2.

Also included in this chapter is a discussion of the growth and development of the region, both politically and economically. As we discuss settlement under each time period, we attempt to relate settlement both to trends in the national economy and to the development of the regional structure—township formation, founding of regional centers, growth of industry, and the like.

Finally, we examine several early (pre-1830) settlement clusters that are readily identifiable from inspection of land purchase maps (presented below). Many of these clusters were the nuclei both for later expansion by offspring

Patterns of Settlement and Growth

5.1. A congressional township and its subdivisions, as laid out by General Land Office surveyors.

and for interdependent immigration (chap. 2), and will be analyzed in more detail in chapter 7.

Background Data

The sources used to compile settlement data for the project area are varied and range from documents found in county courthouses to records stored in state and federal archives. These sources are discussed below in terms of their content, how they were integrated into the analysis, and potential biases in the sources.

Land Entry Data

The rectangular grid system upon which federal lands were surveyed subdivided the midwestern United States into a series of congressional townships, each ideally containing 36 square miles. Each township then was further subdivided into thirty-six sections, and each section was given a set number designation depending on its position within the township (fig.5.1). Sections were subdivided into quarter sections, each ideally containing 160 acres. This was the minimum amount of land sold before 1 July 1820. After that date, for twelve years, two quarter quarter sections, roughly 80 acres, was the minimum amount sold.

Land in the project area was sold by the federal government beginning in 1818, with the exception of all sections 16 (reserved for school revenue) and tracts designated by General Land Office (GLO) surveyors as swampland. These reserved tracts were ceded to the territory (later state) of Missouri. Sales continued until the last tract of federal public land was sold in 1858. Land entries (tracts purchased from the federal government) were mapped by the land office on plat books, which were eventually transferred to the office of the recorder of deeds in each county courthouse. Pages in the plat books show entry location, the name of the entrant, and the entry date for each purchase within a given congressional township. For our analysis, it then became a matter of simply transferring the legal descriptions of purchases, names of entrants, and dates of purchase into a master file for the project area. There are, however, a number of problems in using the data, as discussed below.

In analyzing land entry data for a larger region of the central Salt River valley than is included in the project area, Mason (1983) used purchases of individual entrants as basic analytical units and focused his analysis on the amount of acreage purchased through time. While methodologically acceptable, his approach assumes that the purchase units (quarter quarter sections, or sixteenth sections) each contained 40 acres or multiples thereof. The plat maps clearly indicate that this is an erroneous assumption. Especially in the most northern row of sections in T55N, R6-10W, where numerous adjustments were made to compensate for oversized sections, the amount of acreage biases any analysis in a manner that at present is of unknown magnitude and that may significantly skew the results.[1]

To avoid confusion in the present analysis a *land unit* is defined as the smallest piece of land that legally could ever be sold by the federal government. In most cases land units equal quarter quarter sections (roughly 40 acres), but in a number they do not. In contrast, a *purchase unit* refers to contiguous land units purchased by an entrant on a single day regardless of the number of land units included. If noncontiguous units were purchased on the same day, these are referred to as separate purchase units. A *settlement unit* refers to the first tract of land purchased by a person identified as an actual resident of the project area. The rationale behind this decision is that a person resided on the initial tract of land purchased.[2]

There are 6,631 land units identified in the project area. This figure does not include sections 16 (school land) or swampland, but does include 72 units ceded to the Hannibal and St. Joseph Railroad (discussed later). We decided to include railroad land because it was available for entry by other purchasers until 1852, when a large amount of land was granted to the railroad to help finance its construction. Neither school land nor swampland was included because units in these areas were not available for entry during all time periods.

PATENTS

Patents are deeds issued by the federal government for public land entries. Copies of some patents can be found interspersed through deed books in the county recorder's office. At least one patent was found for approximately two-thirds of the original entrants in the project area. Patents verify that the entrant became the actual owner of the land and list the entrant's county of

1. The region used in Mason's (1983) analysis includes approximately 10% more land than the project area. Although we do not use the acreage figures he presents for amount of land sold per year because of the larger area used in his analysis and the inaccuracy of assuming 40 acres per land unit, his results are of interest here. During his analysis he computed the number of individual entrants—residents, nonresidents, and eastern speculators—per year as well as the number of entrants per year who made first purchases. Instead of recalculating the population for only the project area and computing land-entrant frequencies, we use figures from Mason's analysis to illustrate general trends in number of entrants. Examining sample years using both populations has shown that neither the direction nor the magnitude of the trends is skewed by this approach.

2. Support for this assumption comes from the fact that of thirty house locations known to date to the pre-1830 period of settlement, twenty-seven are on first purchases (in a few cases a first purchase was from another individual rather than from the federal government: Mason, Warren, and O'Brien 1982:373).

residence at the time of entry. In most cases the county of residence listed was one of three local counties: Ralls, Monroe, or Shelby. This suggests that the entrant either was a resident of the area or intended to become one. Nonlocal counties, both within and outside Missouri, are listed for a number of entrants for whom at least one patent is available. These nonlocal patent residences allow identification of points of origin of immigrants to the area (if it can be demonstrated that they became residents of the project area), and land speculators from eastern states.

Census Schedules

Manuscript schedules of the federal census for the years 1830, 1840, and 1850 (the schedule for 1820 apparently was lost by the federal government), at the State Historical Society of Missouri in Columbia, were consulted for information on household composition. The 1830 census lists the name of the head of household and number of household members by sex and age groups, as well as slaves by sex and age groups. The 1840 census lists similar data plus the number of persons engaged in agriculture, commerce, or manufacturing. "Learned persons" in each household also are identified. The 1850 census lists the name, exact age, and state of birth of each household member, plus occupations of these members, if any, and the value of real estate owned. For 1850 there also exist separate schedules for slaves, products of agriculture, and products of industry. The agricultural schedule lists the value of a farm, number of improved and unimproved acres, amount of livestock owned, and crop yields for each farm that produced over $100 worth of commodities (Wright and Hunt 1900:235) during the previous year (1849–50). While the population schedule lists the value of land owned by an individual, the agricultural schedule lists the value of the land actually put into production.

Since the boundaries of the project area do not correspond to local political boundaries (counties or political townships), it is difficult to use census data to determine the population of the project area. The 1830 and 1840 censuses were taken by township and the 1850 census was taken by county. Since certain townships fall almost completely within the project area, and since most residents also were original entrants during the first years of settlement, the problem is not as great for 1830 and 1840 as it is for 1850. In his analysis of the regional population structure, Mason (1983) made several decisions to lessen this problem. For 1830 and 1840, lists were compiled of all persons in townships falling within, or mostly within, the project area whether or not they were original entrants. For 1850 it was assumed that the order of appearance in the census schedule represents the route of the census enumerator and that people listed close together in the census schedule lived near each other (this was tested for known locations of some original entrants and appears to be a valid assumption; cf. Conzen 1971). The presence in the census schedule of original entrants was used as an indication that people appearing near them in the schedule also lived in the project area. Although it perhaps biased the list of project area residents, Mason followed the rule that if more than four consecutive names were not original entrants, it was assumed that they lived outside the project area.

Other Data

Other sources of data include poll books, probate records, county road records, county marriage records, writs of *ad quod damnum*, tombstone inscriptions, family genealogies, oral interviews, and letters and business documents in the Western Historical Manuscript Collection of the State Historical Society of Missouri, Columbia. Similar sources in the Kentucky state archives and the Kentucky Historical Society were consulted to obtain background data on immigrants to the project area.

Poll books were used to determine how soon before a census was taken some original entrants became residents and to identify residents who did not remain until the 1830 census was taken. Probate records were used to determine dates of death of known residents and to identify as residents those persons who arrived between censuses and died before the next census was taken. Road records, besides allowing tentative reconstruction of early county road systems, also mention early communities, local landmarks, and house locations. County marriage records were used to establish interfamily ties and, in instances where the marriage ceremony was performed by a minister, the religious affiliation of families.

Writs of *ad quod damnum* were petitioned for by persons desiring to build dams on state rivers and streams, usually in conjunction with planned construction of water-powered sawmills and gristmills. The law requiring this procedure was passed by the state of Missouri General Assembly on 3 December 1822. Under the law, a petition was filed with the circuit court, which then appointed a jury of twelve men to visit the site of the proposed dam to determine the extent of any possible damage that construction posed to structures or agricultural fields. If the jury report was favorable, a writ was issued. Mason (1983) notes that these early "environmental impact state-ments" allow determination of locations of proposed mills, but other records must be checked to verify that the mills actually were built.

General Land Office Survey Data

One important source of data concerning the presettlement physical environment of the project area is the GLO survey of the region conducted between 1816 and 1822. Survey records have been used primarily to reconstruct native vegetation patterns (chap. 4), though the data are applicable to other research problems. The advantage of these records is that surveys were conducted before extensive western settlement and were completed according to specified procedures that permit qualitative as well as quantitative analysis (Warren 1976).

Instructions issued in 1815 by the surveyor general for lands in the Northwest Territory (land north of the Ohio River) read, in part, as follows:

You will be careful to note in your field book all the courses and distances you shall have run, the names and estimated diameters of all corner or bearing trees, and those trees which fall in your line called station or line trees, notched as aforesaid, together with the courses and distances of the bearing trees from their respective corners, with the letters and numbers marked on them as aforesaid; also all rivers, creeks, springs, and smaller streams of water, with their width, and the course they run in crossing the lines of survey, and whether navigable, rapid or mountainous; the kinds of timber and undergrowth with which the land may be covered, all swamps, ponds, stone quarries, coal beds, peat or turf grounds, uncommon natural or artificial productions, such as mounds, precipices, caves, etc., all rapids, cascades or falls of water; mineral, ores, fossils, etc.; the quality of the soil and the true situation of all mines, salt licks, salt springs, and mill seats, which may come to your knowledge are particularly to be regarded and noticed in your note books. [Tiffin 1815; quoted in Dodds et al. 1943:24]

In addition, points along section lines at which major changes occurred, such as prairie-timber boundaries, were to be reported and measured from section corners (Bourdo 1956). However, instructions given to GLO surveyors varied through time, and modern applications of survey data must be made in accordance with techniques used in the specific area of interest (ibid.).

Survey procedures followed in the Midwest resulted in the gathering of two types of data that have important implications for our analysis of historical settlement: soils-related information and data on floral composition. There are four basic kinds of floral data: the common names of two or more trees used to mark each section and quarter section corner; descriptions of overstory and understory vegetation observed while traversing section lines; records of the nature and location of resources encountered, such as watercourses and geologic and topographic features; and township plat maps illustrating legal boundaries and major shifts in vegetation cover (fig. 5.2).

A rich variety of soils-related data also are contained in GLO surveyor field notes, including explicit references to soil qualities observed along section lines. Most references are brief, general descriptions, and not all surveyors used the same terms to rate soils. All seemed to have one principal variable in mind, however: suitability for cultivation. Given this interpretation, references can be classified within a three-level ordinal ranking: "rich" to "very rich," "excellent" or "first-rate" soils "fit for cultivation," "good" or

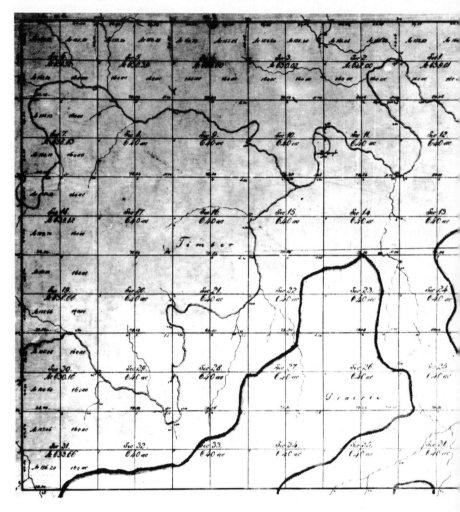

5.2. General land office plat map of T54N, R9W.

"second-rate" soils "fit for cultivation," and "poor" to "very poor," "thin" or "broken and rocky" or "third-rate" soils "not fit for cultivation" (chap. 4).

Patterns of Land Entry and Regional Growth

Land in the project area was available for purchase directly from the federal government from 1818, when the land was first opened to the public, until 1858, when the last piece was entered. For analysis, this forty-one year span has been subdivided into six periods: 1818–20, 1821–25, 1826–29, 1830–34, 1835–36, and 1837–58. Percentages of land units purchased during the six periods—classified by biome[3]—are shown in figure 5.3 and table 5.1. We note that national economic cycles had considerable effect on when land was entered. The first entries were made under the credit policy during the speculative period before the Panic of 1819. Between 1818 and 1820, 3.2% of available units in the project area were purchased. This period was followed by a five-year decline in land sales when the nation plunged into a severe depression. This economic downturn, coupled with a cash-only land policy, limited the percentage of land units purchased between 1821 and 1825 to 0.8%. When the national economy began to expand in the mid-to-late 1820s, land sales increased dramatically, culminating in the boom in land speculation during 1835–36.

A progression from the entry of 7.0% of the project area in 1826–29 to 29.7% for 1830–34, and finally to 47.6% for 1835–36, yielded a total of 84.3% of the project area that was entered during that eleven-year period (1826–36). By the end of 1836, 88.3% of all federal land had passed into private ownership. Swampland, school land (sections 16), and the remaining 11.7% of the land units were sold throughout the next twenty-two years. With these general trends in mind, we now turn our attention to the analysis of settlement dynamics during each of the six periods.

Initial Colonization: 1818–20

Before the 7 December 1818 opening date for the sale of land in the project area, there were few persons actually residing in the region. In contrast to the furor in the Boonslick over preemption rights (chap. 3), only one person (Jesse Burbridge) in the project area filed for preemption. Burbridge entered the northeast quarter of section 29 in T54N, R7W on 26 November 1818.

With the formation of Pike County in 1818, the entire middle and lower

---

3. A land unit was determined to be in prairie or timber if it was completely encompassed by one or the other of these two biomes as shown on GLO plat maps of the project area. An ecotonal status was assigned if both prairie and timber occurred within the same unit.

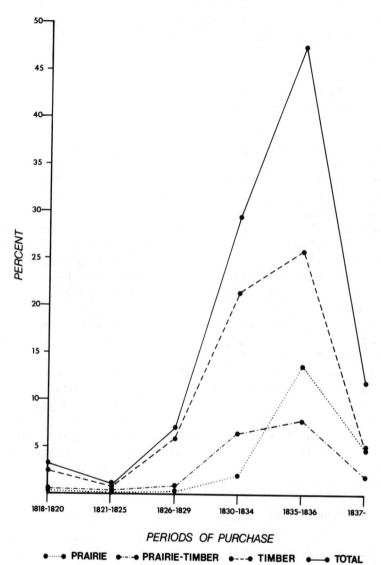

PERIODS OF PURCHASE

●·····● PRAIRIE   ●---● PRAIRIE-TIMBER   ●---● TIMBER   ●——● TOTAL

5.3. Percentage of land entered in the project area by biome, during six periods.

Salt River valley came under the jurisdiction of a local goverment, but this does not appear to have had an immediate effect upon settlement in the project area. Early land sales were made at the St. Louis land office, which was a considerable distance away, and though land along the central Salt River was advertised—both in newspapers and by word of mouth (chap. 3)—sales to persons who actually resided on the land were slow. Of the 210 land units entered during this period (3.2% of the units available), residents entered 98 units (46.7%) and nonresidents enterd 112 (53.3%) (table 5.1).[4] The percentage of land units entered by residents for this period is inflated owing to the entrance of a large amount of land in T54N, R7–8W by Andrew Rogers, who purchased 17.1% of all land entered during the period. If his purchases are excluded from consideration, the percentage for residents drops from 46.7% to 35.6% and the percentage for nonresidents rises from 53.3% to 64.4% (table 5.1). Several nonresidents listed St. Louis on their patent registrations as their place of residence. In view of the fact that nationally this was a period of speculation aided by a policy of credit, we assume that a number of these entries were made for speculative purposes.

REGIONAL GROWTH AND DEVELOPMENT

By 1820 settlement was spread widely but sparsely across the region (fig. 5.4). As discussed later in this chapter and in chapter 7, initial settlement was by several independent as well as several interdependent family units. Of the seven settlement clusters to be discussed in a subsequent section, four (Mt. Prairie, Lick Creek, Smith, and Ely) were founded by 1820.

Apparently the population to the east of the project area—and its economic requirements—had grown sufficiently that the need for a regional commercial center was realized in the platting of the town of New London in 1819 (fig. 5.5). Later it became the county seat when Ralls County was formed on 16 November 1820 (chap. 3). The new county was created from a portion of Pike County and originally extended north to the Iowa border and west to the

4. Residents are defined as persons who were listed in any population census, had a local county (Ralls, Monroe, or Shelby) listed as place of residence on a patent, appeared in any Ralls County poll book for the 1820s, or were listed in county probate records. Speculators are identified as persons not already defined as residents and who listed Pennsylvania, New York, New Jersey, or Connecticut as places of residence on their patents. Since nearly all entries made by persons in this group occurred on eight days during 1835–36, those persons for whom no patent was found but who made large purchases on those days and were not identified already as residents also were classified as eastern speculators. Nonresidents include all persons not identified as residents or speculators. For the larger region Mason (1982) identified 1,164 residents, 110 eastern speculators, and 280 nonresidents. It should be noted that many persons in the latter category could have been Missouri-based speculators.

Table 5.1. Frequencies and Percentage of Land Units Entered in the Project Area by Entrant Class, Period of Entry, and Biome

Date, Entrant Class, and Biome	Percentage of Entries by Biome	Percentage of Entries by Entrant Class and Biome	Percentage of Project Area Entered
1818–20			
Residents (100)[a]			
Prairie (6)	6.00	2.83	0.09
Timber (70)	70.00	33.02	1.06
Ecotone (24)	24.00	11.32	0.36
Nonresidents (112)			
Prairie (0)	0.00	0.00	0.00
Timber (99)	88.39	46.70	1.49
Ecotone (13)	11.61	6.13	0.20
1821–25			
Residents (53)			
Prairie (1)	1.89	1.89	0.02
Timber (49)	92.45	92.45	0.74
Ecotone (3)	5.66	5.66	0.05
1826–29			
Residents (436)			
Prairie (7)	1.61	1.51	0.11
Timber (387)	88.76	83.41	5.84
Ecotone (42)	9.63	9.05	0.63
Nonresidents (28)			
Prairie (0)	0.00	0.00	0.00
Timber (23)	82.14	4.96	0.35
Ecotone (5)	17.86	1.08	0.08
1830–34			
Residents (1,723)			
Prairie (101)	5.86	5.13	1.52
Timber (1,252)	72.66	63.55	18.88
Ecotone (370)	21.47	18.78	5.58
Nonresidents (244)			
Prairie (30)	12.30	1.52	0.45
Timber (164)	67.21	8.32	2.47
Ecotone (50)	20.49	2.54	0.75
Eastern speculators (3)			
Prairie (0)	0.00	0.00	0.00
Timber (1)	33.33	0.05	0.02
Ecotone (2)	66.67	0.10	0.03
1835–36			
Residents (1,736)			
Prairie (358)	20.62	11.33	5.40
Timber (1,059)	61.00	33.52	15.97
Ecotone (319)	18.38	10.10	4.81

Table 5.1. *Continued.*

Date, Entrant Class, and Biome	Percentage of Entries by Biome	Percentage of Entries by Entrant Class and Biome	Percentage of Project Area Entered
1835–36			
Nonresidents (266)			
Prairie (63)	23.68	1.99	0.95
Timber (156)	58.65	4.94	2.35
Ecotone (47)	17.65	1.49	0.71
Eastern speculators (1,157)			
Prairie (494)	42.70	15.64	7.45
Timber (507)	43.82	16.05	7.65
Ecotone (156)	13.48	4.94	2.35
1837–58			
Residents (565)			
Prairie (230)	40.71	29.75	3.47
Timber (241)	42.65	31.18	3.63
Ecotone (94)	16.64	12.16	1.42
Nonresidents (132)			
Prairie (74)	56.06	9.57	1.12
Timber (37)	28.03	4.79	0.56
Ecotone (21)	15.91	2.72	0.32
Eastern speculators (4)			
Prairie (0)	0.00	0.00	0.00
Timber (4)	100.00	0.52	0.06
Ecotone (0)	0.00	0.00	0.00
Railroad (72)			
Prairie (10)	13.89	1.29	0.15
Timber (55)	76.39	7.12	0.83
Ecotone (7)	9.72	0.91	0.11
Total 6,631			100.03

*a*Number of units entered.

border of Chariton County, which at that time was the line between R9 and 10W (Megown 1878:9).

Integral to the functioning of any political unit are its transportation networks. During most of this period there were few roads. The one road (probably no more than a rough trail) known to be in existence led from Franklin, in the Boonslick area of Howard County, to New London, passing through Middle Grove, a settlement established in 1820 in T53N, R12W by Ezra Fox and others from Fayette County, Kentucky. The road passed within a few miles of two other settlement clusters before reaching New London (Mason 1982).

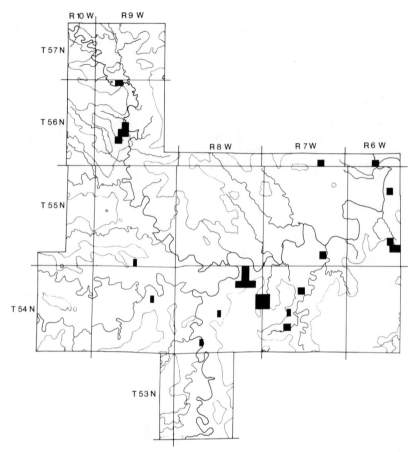

5.4. Resident land entries in the project area made during 1818–20.

LAND ENTRY

In the course of time, many new entrants were able to base their entry decisions on more than the information given in the land office, owing to communication with those already living in or near the project area or with persons who had visited it. Friends or relatives could inform potential entrants of the local environmental, political, economic, and social conditions. However, during the earliest period there were no established settlements or ties that outsiders could depend upon for information. Therefore entrants chose land based on their perceptions of the importance of various physical environmental dimensions, such as proximity to streams, prairie, timber, or the prairie-timber ecotone, land slope, and soil fertility. Information regarding many of these dimensions was included on the plat maps available in the land office. We now discuss the strategies residents and nonresidents used in entering their land units during the initial colonization period. At this general level of analysis we are concerned primarily with two dimensions of the physical environment—biome and forest density. Although we introduce other dimensions, analysis of their full impact on locational decisions is reserved for chapter 6.

At the outset of the sale of land in the project area in 1818, there were 1,374 land units in prairie (20.7% of the total), 4,104 in timber (61.9%), and 1,153 on the ecotone (17.4%). If purchases were made randomly, we should find that units were being entered in roughly these percentages during each of

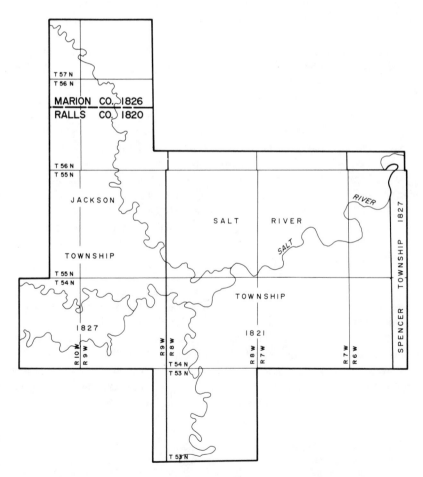

5.5. Local political boundaries before 1831, with dates of formation (after Mason 1983).

the six periods. However, figure 5.4 and table 5.1 show that during the early periods there was a decided preference for timbered tracts and an avoidance of prairie tracts. During the first four periods, land on the ecotone sold at a rate at least three times that of prairie land.

Examination of purchases during 1818–20 (table 5.1) shows that residents entered 98 land units, of which 68 were timber-only tracts, 6 were in prairie, and 24 were on the ecotone. The 6 prairie units, however, were all part of larger purchase units situated on the ecotone. Nonresidents entered 112 units, of which 99 were in timber, none were in prairie, and 13 were on the ecotone. Although these figures indicate a decided bias against prairie on the part of early colonists, they alone do not yield much insight into what they perceived as desirable environmental dimensions. To add another dimension to the analysis, we now examine land purchases relative to forest density, as shown in figure 4.14.

The largest contiguous blocks of settlement for this period are along, and just west of, the headwaters of Pigeon Roost Creek, in T54N, R7–8W (fig. 5.4). These tracts, totaling 1,440 acres, were entered in 1819 by Andrew Rogers. For the most part Rogers's land lay along the ecotone, bordering a large expanse of prairie that projected into the project area from the south. However, a sizable portion of the northern block extended almost to the Salt River and included some of the densest timber in the region.

To the east, in T55N, R6W, early entries were made by a group of related persons from Bath County, Kentucky (discussed later). Their purchases began in 1819 when one member entered a 160 acre tract in T54, R7W, in a heavily timbered area (53–211 stems per acre) near the ecotone. Possibly because of difficulties in clearing the timber, the group made additional entries the next year along the ecotone in T55N, R6W. Timber density on these tracts was light, ranging from 1 to 26 stems per acre.

In addition to the 1819 purchase mentioned above, two other tracts were purchased along Lick Creek (along with Burbridge's preemption). One was in the highest density-level forest, and one was on the ecotone. Burbridge's claim contained areas with both low and high timber density.

In 1819 two tracts of land of approximately 80 acres each were entered in the western third of the project area—one in T54N, R9W and one in T55N, R9W.[5] The tracts were purchased by members of a Bath County family that figures prominently in our analysis of both the social dimensions of settlement and the organization of frontier households. One unit abutted a large finger of

---

5. It is unclear why less than quarter section tracts were being sold when the minimum allowed for sale by federal law was a quarter section. Our conclusion is that the land agent at the St. Louis land office allowed the purchase of two noncontiguous half quarter sections rather than one contiguous quarter section, and the entry of the split purchase by two related persons.

prairie that entered the project area from the west and extended into dense timber; the other was several miles to the south and east, in a lightly timbered area (see fig. 4.13). Although not shown in figure 5.4, a third 80 acre tract—purchased by the family in 1819 from a nonresident—was situated just east of the more northern tract, also in heavy timber but adjacent to the ecotone. Thus, within a single family we note two different land purchase strategies, with two members opting for heavy timber but proximity to the ecotone and one choosing lightly timbered land.

Two separate purchases were made in T56N, R9W—one of 14 land units and one of 4 units—on or proximal to the ecotone (fig. 5.4). The larger purchase contained a considerable amount of prairie and lightly to moderately timbered (< 36 stems per acre) land (fig. 4.13). The smaller purchase was in a moderately timbered area adjacent to the ecotone.

Four purchase units entered between 1818 and 1820 were bisected by either the main stem of the Salt River or one of its major tributaries. Another purchase unit was bisected by a permanently flowing stream, and seven were within half a mile of a permanent water source. The three remaining purchase units were more than a mile from permanent water sources.

In summary, land purchase strategies by residents during the earliest phase of colonization were mixed, though there was a strong tendency to locate either along the ecotone or in areas of light timber density. Proximity to permanent water sources was also an important settlement consideration.

This pattern is mirrored by nonresident purchases (fig. 5.6). Most purchase units entered by this class were either in low-density timber or along the ecotone. We conclude that, though these entrants did not become project area residents, their considerations of desirable environmental dimensions indicate that many of them originally intended to become residents or to resell their land to residents.

Gradual Expansion: 1821–25

While the previous period was characterized locally and nationally by economic expansion spurred by easy credit, the period 1821–25 was one of economic depression. A cash-only policy made it difficult for people to purchase land and left many speculators owing money for land they could not resell. Although the population level in the central Salt River valley was low, the region was involved significantly enough in national economics that it was profoundly affected by the economic depression. Although the regional land office was moved to Palmyra in 1824, only two land units were sold during that entire year. We conclude that economic conditions were at an all-time low, and that these conditions affected land sales more than did the distance between the region and the land office.

During the five-year period, residents entered 53 land units, or 0.81% of

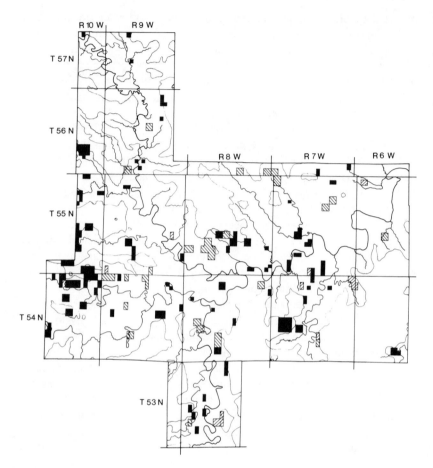

5.6. Nonresident land entries in the project area made during 1818–20 (▨), 1826–29 (▩), and 1830–34 (■).

the total number of units in the project area (table 5.1; fig. 5.7). There were no entries by nonresidents or speculators. The low percentage of entries is a considerable decrease over the 3.2% entered by all purchasers during the previous three-year period. Additionally, all land entries during the period 1821–25 were made by first-time entrants. During this five-year span, 17 residents entered approximately 2,200 acres, but no existing farmsteads were enlarged. We speculate that the depressed economy and the lack of well-established transportation routes (discussed below) contributed to this conservative attitude.

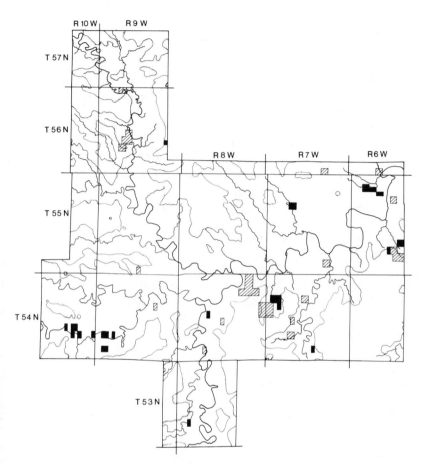

5.7. Resident land entries in the project area made during 1821–25 (hatched areas indicate prior entries).

REGIONAL GROWTH AND DEVELOPMENT

Despite the effects of the depressed economy during the early 1820s, some very important political developments influenced events in the project area. The most significant of these occurred in 1821 with the entrance of Missouri into statehood. On the local level the Ralls County court in 1821 divided the county into four political townships: Spencer, Salt River, Mason, and Liberty (fig. 5.5). In 1822 Union Township was formed. These developments indicate the changing needs of a frontier society as population grew and residents desired more localized government.

Strong county government with political townships as internal subdivisions was characteristic of political organization in the South and upper South, where leadership was provided by a wealthy elite or planter class. In early Missouri, county political power was concentrated in the county court, composed of three or more county judges. County judges were appointed by the governor before 1824 and between 1828 and 1831. From 1824 to 1828 county judges were elected by, and chosen from among, the justices of the peace in the county. After 1831 county judges were elected by eligible voters in the county (Megown 1878:10). County judges established roads, set taxes, appropriated funds, organized political townships, set polling places, issued business licenses, and acted as a probate court. Other county officials included the county clerk, treasurer, collector, assessor, and sheriff. Each county also had a circuit clerk, who was the local representative of a circuit court that served several counties.

Each political township within a county had several justices of the peace, a constable, and a polling place. At first justices of the peace were recommended by the county court for appointment by the governor, but in later years thay were elected by residents of the township. Justices decided simple legal cases, performed marriages, and acted as notaries public. One of their number was appointed each year by the county court to divide roads in their township into districts and to assign people to maintain them.

Roads played a significant role both in the settlement of the project area and in its development by permitting contact with extraregional commercial centers. The rapidity with which various rural areas were connected to newly formed towns and these towns to external markets indicates the degree to which access to markets was sought from the very beginning of settlement (Mason 1982).

Competition was keen over the location of new roads through recently settled portions of the region. Individuals and groups could petition the county court to locate branch routes through or near their purchases, and inspection of county road records indicates these petitions were numerous. It is obvious from following the descriptions of early roads that the routes frequently were directed past the farmsteads of wealthy landowners. In ranking the wealth of successful road petitioners on a scale of 1 (richest) to 10, Mason (1983) noted an average rank of 2.7.[6]

Another factor in the approval and routing of roads appears to have been social position and wealth of the county road commissioners. The mean wealth rank of commissioners examined by Mason (1983) was 3.2. The more affluent members of the county, who controlled county government, appointed

6. Wealth was based on property listed in the 1850 agricultural census; only persons appearing in that census who were listed in the 1830 population census were used (Mason 1983).

road commissioners of similar status and wealth, thus assuring themselves access to roads leading to external markets.

As mentioned previously, the earliest overland route through the area was a long-distance road from Franklin and Fayette in Howard County to New London. By the mid-1820s, a road was constructed from Columbia in Boone County to a point just west of New London, where it joined the Franklin/Fayette–New London road. The Fayette–New London road was formally cleared and slightly rerouted in 1825 by order of the Ralls County court.

Roads connecting the Fayette–New London road with two emerging settlement clusters—the Smith settlement in T54N, R9–10W and the Ely settlement in T55N, R6W (both discussed below)—were established in 1824 and 1825, respectively. The road through the Ely settlement led to Bouvet's Lick in the northeast corner of the project area, where it joined roads to Hannibal and New London. The road through the Smith settlement led northeast to Palmyra. All three towns were founded in 1819 and later became major regional centers.

LAND ENTRY

The severe economic depression of the 1820s resulted in the purchase of only 55 land units in the project area between 1821 and 1825. All purchases were made by residents (table 5.1). With respect to purchases by biome, 51 units were in timber, 1 was on the prairie, and 3 were on the ecotone (fig. 5.7). Because of the small number of land units purchased, we can easily examine the distribution of entire purchase units to determine the possible bias of looking only at land unit and biome. For example, figure 5.7 shows that the single prairie unit (in T55N, R6W) actually was part of an ecotonal purchase.

Comparing figure 5.7 with figure 4.13 shows that most entries were in areas of light to medium timber density ($<$ 36 stems per acre). Exceptions to this trend were two large blocks of land—one in T54N, R7W and one in T55N, R6W—situated in dense timber. The former was adjacent to a large tract purchased earlier by Andrew Rogers; possibly the purchaser—Stephen Scobee—was a relative. The latter tract was a subsequent purchase by Isaac Ely, who with two brothers and a brother-in-law had earlier settled along the eastern border of the project area. The distribution of land entered by the Ely group provides an excellent case study of early land purchase decisions in the region.

The Ely settlement, mentioned by name in the Ralls County road records as early as 1823, was begun by three brothers—Joshua, Thomas, and Isaac Ely—and their brother-in-law, Conrad See, all from Bath County, Kentucky (Owen and Company 1895). Joshua Ely first entered land in 1818, in section 9, T54N, R7W. The quarter section was in a heavily timbered area (53–211 stems per acre) but adjacent to the ecotone (fig. 5.7). A year later he entered approximately 240 acres 7 miles to the northeast, along the eastern boundary of the project area, adjacent to land entered that year by his brother Thomas. A few years later they were joined by their other brother and their brother-in-law. By 1823 the group had entered approximately 720 acres (and more to the east) in T55N, R6W, all of which either bordered prairie or actually lay on the ecotone (fig. 5.7). Timber density in the immediate vicinity of these entries was light, ranging from 1 to 26 stems per acre. Surprisingly, further entries made by Isaac Ely in 1823 and by Benjamin Ely, Jr. (probably a nephew), in 1825 were 3 to 4 miles north of the original settlement locus, in an area of moderate to heavy timber density several miles from the ecotone. Similarly, Benjamin Ely, Sr., entered land 7 miles west of the original settlement, in an area of moderately dense forest. Thus we see on the part of the Elys a shift in focus away from heavily forested locations (Joshua Ely, 1818) to ecotonal-prairie/lightly timbered locations (the settlement cluster) and, at least for some of the family, a shift back to moderately to heavily forested environments.

Another settlement cluster that appears in figure 5.7 was situated along Elk Fork, in T54N, R9–10W. This cluster was composed in part of colonists from Bath and Mercer counties in Kentucky, who arrived after 1820. The earliest resident entrant was Mary Smith Johnson, the daughter of Joseph H. Smith, Sr.; in 1819 Smith had been assigned land along the southern margin of T55N, R9W. She was joined in 1824 by her sister-in-law and the latter's husband, James Mappin, who entered a timbered tract a quarter mile east of her entry. To the south of Mary Johnson's tract, John McGee of Mercer County, Kentucky, entered a quarter section in 1823. His was the first of many entries made by a large group of interrelated families from Mercer County (chap. 7). To the west, in T54N, R10W, five separate purchases were made during this period. Although data concerning possible relationships among these individual family units are lacking, the proximity of the entries suggests some established relation.

Land entry along Elk Fork appears to have followed two patterns— proximity to permanent water and location in sparse timber. Six of eight purchase units touched or crossed Elk Fork, and all were in stands of timber with fewer than 36 stems per acre; four purchases were in areas of 1–17 stems per acre. As mentioned in chapter 4, the central portion of the Elk Fork drainage exhibits anomalously low timber density relative to most portions of the project area. One plausible explanation for this anomaly is presettlement fire (see chap. 4, note 7). Whatever the reason, the anomaly crosscuts all physiographic features in the area so that bottomlands as well as interstream divides contain low timber density. Thus, from the standpoint of ease of clearing, the central Elk Fork locale could have been viewed as advantageous for immediate cultivation.

Economic Recovery and Continued Immigration: 1826–29

During 1826–29 the central Salt Valley, as well as the rest of the nation, began to recover from the effects of the economic depression that had slowed growth and development over the previous five years. Recovery was slow, as evidenced by the fact that only 7.01% of the project area (464 units) was purchased during the four-year period. Of the 464 units sold, 436 were purchased by residents and 28 by nonresidents.

REGIONAL GROWTH AND DEVELOPMENT

Despite the slow recovery, several changes within the structure of Ralls County served to shape the region's development. During 1818–25 the regional population increased to the point that in 1826 Marion County was formed from a portion of Ralls County (fig. 5.5). The latter county was again subdivided in 1827, when Jackson Township was inserted between Salt River and Union townships.

Road construction figured prominently in the more settled eastern portion of the area. In 1828 and 1829 two roads connecting the Ely settlement with the Fayette-New London road were built, linking this growing area with the major east-west transportation route through the region. Smaller roads undoubtedly were constructed in other parts of the project area. One reason for the increased need for good roads was the sudden rise of the milling industry, which began within the project area boundaries around 1827 with the construction of a water-powered mill on Lick Creek, near the Fayette-New London road.

Evans (1974) suggests that mills served as transitional links between subsistence and market economies; a miller served as grain buyer, middle-man, and merchant. The appearance of mills signaled the beginning of rural residents' participation in a market economy, or at least the potential for their participation (Mason 1983). For many the mill served only to process grain into meal or flour for home consumption, but for surplus producers it provided a local outlet for bulk grain that was too expensive to transport any distance. As will be seen subsequently, by 1840 mills were ubiquitous in the project area. The importance of milling may be appreciated, in part, by realizing that the rationale behind the eventual location of Florida—one of two large pre-1840 trade centers in the project area—can be traced to Peter Stice's construction in 1829 of a mill on the South Fork (Gregory 1965).

LAND ENTRY

By 1826 approximately 96% of the project area was still available for purchase. Between 1826 and 1829 residents entered 436 land units; 387 were in timber, 7 were on the prairie, and 42 were on the ecotone (table 5.1). Nonresidents entered 23 timbered units, 5 ecotonal units, and no prairie units. These frequencies compare favorably with those of earlier periods. For the three periods discussed so far, the percentage of timbered units ranges from 70% to 89% of the total units purchased during each period, regardless of the class of entrant (resident versus nonresident). The percentage of ecotonal purchases ranges from 6% to 24%. By the end of the third period 15.3% of timbered units had been purchased, compared with 7.5% of ecotonal units and only 1% of prairie units (table 5.1). In all cases, regardless of entrant class, prairie units entered through 1829 were part of ecotonal purchases. Similarly, many timbered units also were part of larger purchase units situated on the ecotone.

During 1826–29 a significant percentage of purchase units entered by residents were along the ecotone (fig. 5.8), especially in T55N, R6–8W and T54N, R7W. There also was scattered settlement in fairly heavily timbered areas, especially in the Ely settlement, in T55N, R6W, and along the South Fork, in T53N, R8W. In these timbered areas it appears that agriculturists were taking advantage of small but fertile river bottoms, whose soils were rated good to excellent by GLO surveyors (fig. 4.9).

Several spatial trends are evident in the pattern of land entries made by residents between 1826 and 1829 (fig. 5.8). One significant trend is that many purchases tend to cluster around previous entries—in some instances owing to previously established relationships between entrants. Several of these settlement clusters are discussed below.

One area that received a considerable influx of settlers during this period was the east half of T54N, R10W and the northwest half of T54N, R9W. Early settlement began along the Elk Fork in 1819 and continued sporadically throughout the next six years. By 1829 these early entries were connected by a continuous spread of settlement from below the Elk Fork almost to the North Fork. The heart of the settlement expanse was the low-density timber zone that crosscut both the Middle and Elk forks of the Salt River. Although by 1830 the settlement cluster appears as a single expanse, examining entry dates for individual purchases demonstrates that there actually were two nuclei from which settlement radiated outward. Because of the excellent information we have concerning kinship and intermarriage among members within each settlement cluster, we postpone discussing in detail the dynamics of settlement in this section of the project area until chapter 7. It is sufficient here to point out that much of the clustering evident is due to two processes discussed in chapter 2: proximal budding and interdependent immigration.

Another settlement cluster for which we have some data other than entry dates is situated along the middle and upper reaches of Pigeon Roost Creek. What we have termed the Mt. Prairie settlement began in 1819 when Andrew

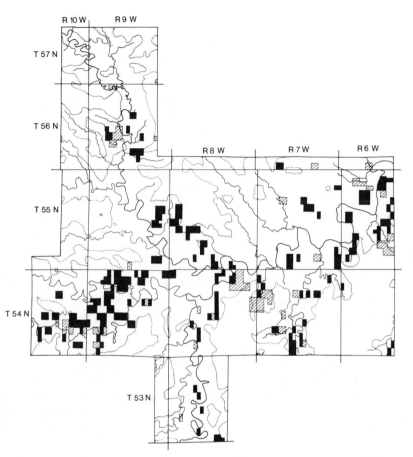

5.8. Resident land entries in the project area made during 1826–29 (hatched areas indicate prior entries).

Rogers entered two large blocks of land totaling approximately 1,440 acres in T54N, R7–8W (fig. 5.4). As discussed previously, Rogers's land abutted the ecotone, with one large projection extending into dense timber.

Rogers was joined in 1825 by Stephen Scobee, Sr., who entered a half section to the north and west of Rogers's southern block. Rogers expanded his holdings in 1827, adding two more units to the southern block, along the ecotone. In 1828 Rogers's brother Ariel purchased a quarter section along the ecotone, approximately a mile south of Rogers's southern block. In 1830 Aleri Rogers, possibly a third brother or a son, entered approximately 80 acres, also along the ecotone and abutting the southern block. Several other pre-1830 entries were made along the ecotone, including that of Stephen Scobee, Jr., who in 1829 entered approximately 80 acres to the northwest of his father's holdings.

Field survey of the Mt. Prairie settlement successfully located the sites of seven original farmsteads, all represented by standing structures or identifiable foundations. Six of the seven can be tied to individuals appearing in the 1830 census;[7] the seventh—that of Joseph White—was constructed about 1832. The distribution of farmsteads is remarkably consistent; all occur on upland margins overlooking Pigeon Roost Creek or a neighboring stream, and most are in forest but are also near the ecotone (fig. 5.9). Together the sites tend to form a U-shaped configuration that surrounds the upper reaches of Pigeon Roost Creek and generally parallels the ecotone. We do not have detailed data concerning social and kin relations of members of the settlement beyond that for the Stephen Scobees and Andrew and Aleri Rogers, but the coincidence of several other surnames of early residents (e.g., Hanna), and also time of settlement implies that social interactions were common before settlement. Further, we know the settlement maintained a post office until at least 1831 that served colonists in distant areas (Powers 1931). We therefore suggest that the Mt. Prairie settlement functioned as a distinct socially interdependent community composed of economically independent individuals.

Although never mentioned formally in county records, there was an early cluster of settlement along the middle reaches of Lick Creek, extending westward along the northern bank of Burbridge Creek (fig. 5.8). Three settlers entered land in 1819, all choosing locations on or adjacent to the ecotone. By 1829, ten other settlers had moved into the area, seven choosing ecotonal land. Importantly, none of the entries made by that date were more than a quarter mile from either creek. Owing to the proximity of the ecotone to the creeks (fig. 5.8) and to the general low density of forest (fig. 4.13), this portion of the project area was ideally suited for early settlement. Historical data on early colonists living in the settlement cluster are scant, but several entrants were found in the 1810 federal census for Kentucky, several of which were from the Bourbon-Montgomery counties area of the Bluegrass region.

Another early settlement cluster never formally mentioned in county records was west of Shell Branch, between the North Fork of the Salt River and the ecotone (fig. 5.8). A small tributary of the North Fork—Buck Branch—separated the settlement cluster into two groups of entries. In 1819 several nonresidents entered nearly contiguous blocks of land that lay either along the ecotone or along a small strip of isolated prairie between the upland

---

7. Andrew Rogers apparently was living with his brother Aleri.

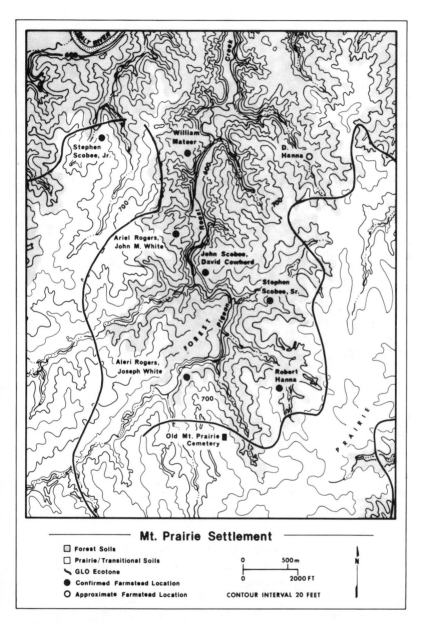

5.9. Map of Mt. Prairie community showing known and probable locations of early-nineteenth-century farmsteads (from Warren, O'Brien, and Mason 1981).

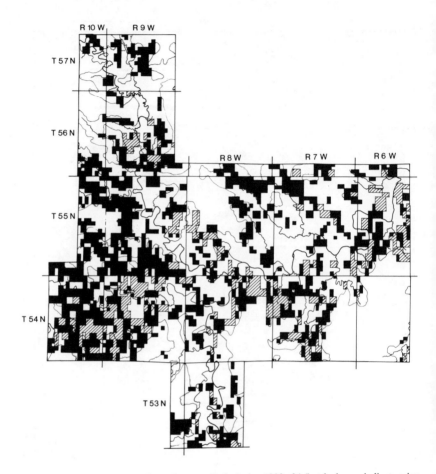

5.10. Resident land entries in the project area made during 1830–34 (hatched areas indicate prior entries).

prairie and the North Fork (fig. 5.6). This land changed hands during the 1820s, but it was not until the end of the decade that further entries were made. Settlement to the east of Bucks Branch centered on the edge of the upland prairie and the eastern edge of the isolated prairie strip. Entry locations were coincident with two rather large spurs of transitional soils that projected south from the upland prairie (fig. 4.14). To the west of the creek, three entrants purchased large contiguous tracts of land that extended from a half mile south of the upland prairie to the mouth of Buck Branch (fig. 5.8). Kin and social relationships among settlers in this area are not well known. We do note, however, that by 1834 William Wilkerson's five sons, who had emigrated with their father from Clark County, Kentucky, had entered land in the vicinity. They possibly were related to established residents who had come from the same area.

Economic Prosperity: 1830–34

Between 1830 and 1834 several events occurred that left a permanent mark on the region. It was during these years that the early frontier society began to stabilize as a visible extension of the upper South. This nascent society benefited from continuing improvement in the national economy that had begun within the previous five years. Increased economic activity led to the purchase of almost three times as much land during the period as had been bought during the previous twelve years. A little under 30% of land in the project area was purchased between 1830 and 1834, including, for the first time, entries by eastern speculators. Land sales increased dramatically for two years before declining in 1832, and the influx of new residents resulted in the formation of a new county and several regional centers.

The new growth was not uniform across the project area. Several portions grew rapidly during the period, but none as greatly as the western third of the region (figs. 5.6 and 5.10). Because of the founding of Paris in 1831 as the county seat of newly created Monroe County, a considerable amount of available land surrounding the site (situated in section 11, T54N, R10W) was bought between 1830 and 1832. The net effect of this rapid purchase was that by 1834 little land remained unsold within a 4 mile radius of Paris. Other settlement clusters also expanded, so that by the end of the period an almost unbroken string of settlement connected the eastern and western edges of the project area (fig. 5.10).

One factor responsible at least in part for the upward surge in land entry was another change in land-sale policy. On 1 May 1832 the land sales act was amended to further reduce the minimum entry to 40 acres if the purchaser filed an affidavit swearing that he would cultivate the land (Peters 1846:503). This amendment made it possible for new, less wealthy immigrants to purchase land and allowed established residents to increase their holdings for a minimum investment of $50 ($1.25 an acre). The effect of the amendment on average entry size was dramatic. Between 1 July 1830 and 30 April 1832, approximately 50% of resident entries were for two quarter quarter sections (approximately 80 acres); between 1 May 1832 and 30 July 1835, approximately 30% were for two quarter quarter sections and 41% were for single quarter quarter sections. The average size of all first entries decreased from about 120 acres in 1831 to 100 acres in 1832 and to approximately 88 acres in 1833 (Mason 1983).

REGIONAL GROWTH AND DEVELOPMENT

As a response to continued population increase in the central Salt River valley, the state General Assembly created Monroe County on 6 January 1831. It included all of Ralls County west of a line that ran north and south one mile west of the R6–7W line (fig. 5.11). The northern boundary was the Marion County line, which ran between T56 and 57N; the western boundary was the Randolph County line, which ran between R12 and 13W; and the southern boundary was the line between T52 and 53N (fig. 5.11). The area south of this line (which later became Audrain County) was attached administratively to Monroe and Callaway counties.

The first county court met on 16 February 1831 in the home of Green V. Caldwell, on the Fayette–New London road in section 24, T54N, R10W. Caldwell came from New London, Missouri, and had opened a store in his house, probably hoping it would become the site of the Monroe County seat (National Historical Company 1884:132–33). As Mason (1983) notes, Caldwell's location was a logical choice for the county seat, since it was one mile west of the intersection of the Palmyra and Fayette–New London roads. The original and new (1829) routes of the Fayette-New London road diverged at his house.

The county court met at Caldwell's home on at least five occasions. At the first meeting (16 February 1831) several wealthy residents of the county presented commissions from the governor to serve as county judges, including John Curry of the Elk Fork settlement and Andrew Rogers of the Mt. Prairie settlement. The latter had entered large tracts of land in 1819, along the middle and upper reaches of Pigeon Roost Creek (see previous discussion), and had served as county judge of Ralls County (Megown 1878:10).

By the time of the next meeting (1 May 1831) Caldwell had died, and the commissioners appointed to choose a site for the county seat did not select the area surrounding his house and store but instead chose a site 2.5 miles to the northwest, on the south bank of the Middle Fork. The land selected (the west half of the northwest quarter of section 11, T54N, R10W) had been entered on 3 January 1831 by James C. Fox, a son of Ezra Fox, an early resident of the county. Fox donated 45 acres of his two quarter quarter sections to the commissioners on 3 June 1831, and James R. Abernathy sold 9 acres of an adjacent two quarter quarter sections to the same body for $25. An additional 25 acres was sold by Hightower T. Hackney for $100. Fox's wife, Ann Smith Fox, was "permitted the honor of naming the new town, which she called Paris, after Paris, Kentucky, her old home" (National Historical Company 1884:133). Apparently there was some dissension among the county judges regarding the location of the county seat, as evidenced by the removal of two of them before the 1 May meeting. We speculate that upon the death of Caldwell Fox immediately seized the opportunity both to influence the commission to locate the county seat on his land and to have dissenting county judges removed from office. These judges normally served four-year terms, but two of them (William P. Stephenson and John Curry) served less than three months. Stephenson apparently was from the Middle Grove community and possibly wanted the seat located in that area. Andrew Rogers, who escaped replacement, lived along Pigeon Roost Creek and may have had no real preference about the location (see Mason 1983).

At the 1 May 1831 meeting of the court, the county was divided into three townships, each approximately 10 miles wide: Jefferson to the east, Jackson in the center, and Union to the west (fig. 5.11). At the 4 June session Fox was appointed commissioner for the sale of lots in Paris, and Abernathy was

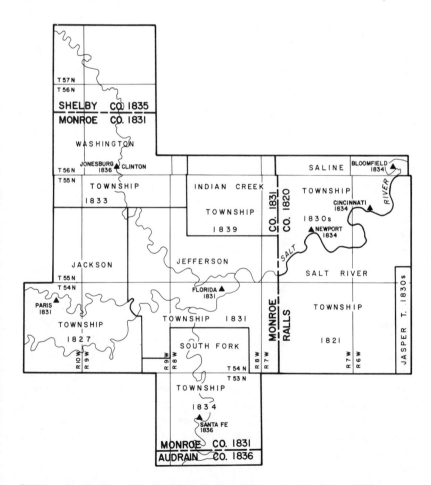

5.11. Local political boundaries in 1840, with dates of formation (after Mason 1983).

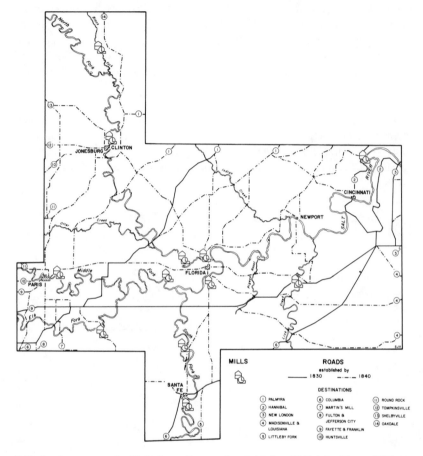

5.12. Roads, towns, and mills in the project area founded before 1841 (after Mason 1983).

appointed commissioner of school lands. This position involved selling section 16 land in each congressional township and collecting the proceeds to support a school system. John S. McGee (chap. 7) was appointed county surveyor (he already had been appointed assessor) and ordered to survey the town of Paris. Monroe County court records indicate that lots in Paris were sold at auction on 12 September 1831, on credit, with payments due six, twelve, and eighteen months after the date of sale. The sale was very successful, with 127 residential lots selling for $20 to $30 and lots along Main Street and around the town square selling for $50 to $150 each. More lots were platted and offered for sale in September 1835.

At the 1 August meeting of the county court, Fox presented the town plat of Paris to the court. Other business conducted at the meeting included establishing road districts for existing roads and studying petitions for new road locations to link Paris with existing roads.

In 1832, a year after the founding of the county, the Monroe County court established seven roads with a total length of 44 miles; a year later it established six more roads having a combined length of 43 miles (Mason 1983). These roads connected Paris with the Fayette road, with Florida and Hannibal to the east, with Columbia to the south, and with various points north and west (fig. 5.12). Roads also were established linking Florida with the Fayette road, with the Palmyra road, with Hannibal, and with points northwest.

Apparently the earliest industries associated with the newly formed town were water-powered gristmills on the Middle Fork (fig. 5.12). On 25 June 1831 John Saling, a previous partner in a mill just south of Florida (discussed below), petitioned the court for permission to build a mill and dam about 2 miles west of Paris. The mill was in operation in 1833, when the county court approved a road connecting it to Paris. The second mill was built early in 1832, a mile east of Paris on the Paris-Florida road.

The town of Florida, situated at the confluence of the North and South forks of the Salt River in eastern Monroe County (fig. 5.12), actually was the first town platted in the county, predating Paris by several months. The town site, the plat for which was recorded on 24 May 1831, contained 94 lots in 15 blocks. It was in the south half of the northwest quarter of section 3, T54N, R8W and was purchased at the Palmyra land office on 10 February 1831 by six residents of the project area: Hugh A. Hickman, John T. Grigsby, William Keenan, William W. Penn, John Witt, and Richard Cave.

Peter Stice's mill on the South Fork was sold in 1830 to Hugh A. Hickman and John Saling for $1,000. They rented a portion of it to William Penn, who operated a store there for several years (National Historical Company 1884:92). Hickman bought out Saling's interest in 1835 and soon after began to ship flour to the port of Louisiana on the Mississippi River and to transport commodities such as sugar and coffee back to Florida (Wetmore 1837). In 1830 Richard Cave constructed a mill on the North Fork of the Salt River, just north of the future site of Florida (fig. 5.12), and in 1833 Benjamin Bradley built a third mill about a mile upstream of Florida.

The desire both for reliable transportation networks and for increased commercialism in the Florida vicinity led to several schemes to make the Salt River navigable from the Mississippi River to Florida. In 1831 entrepreneurs in Florida successfully petitioned the General Assembly to enact legislation prohibiting the damming of the Salt River below the town. In 1834 the Monroe County court appropriated $500 to clear the river between Florida and the county line. The dream of making the river navigable reached its height in

1837, when the General Assembly chartered the Salt River Navigation Company to dredge the river and construct locks and dams along its reaches. Although the venture failed for lack of capital, it illustrates the lengths to which residents were willing to go to secure links with external markets (Mason 1983).

Although roads were vital links in the regional economy, it was the two nodal points in the network—the towns of Paris and Florida—and their services that determined the success of the economic system. These centers were the interface between an economy based on rural manufacturing and agriculture and one more national in scope. A brief comparison of the rise and early development of the two centers is of interest, if for no other reason than to highlight the diverse reasons behind their founding.

The location of Florida was determined by its proximity to both the North Fork and the main stem of the Salt River. As mentioned above, several mills had been constructed in the area before the actual date of platting, making it a logical choice for a commercial center. Paris, on the other hand, appears to have been located for political reasons. Although several mills were planned in the vicinity of its ultimate location, these probably were the result of prior knowledge of where the eventual town site would be. Given the density of settlement in T54N, R9W (the Elk Fork and Smith settlements) and the presence of a store and blacksmith shop, that area would have been the natural choice for the site of the county seat.

Court records for the few years following 1831 indicate that numerous commercial licenses were issued in Monroe County, but without a more detailed study it is impossible to tell whether these licenses were for establishments in Paris or Florida. Several liquor licenses were issued during 1831 for the private sale of spirits. The first tavern license for Paris was issued in 1832 and the first for Florida in 1833. During the first six months after county formation, four merchant's licenses were issued. It was not until 1833, however, two years after the founding of Paris and Florida, that the first grocery was licensed. Mason (1983) speculates that there may have been less demand initially for food, which could be grown locally, than there was for imported manufactured goods and commodities such as sugar and coffee. After 1833, however, there was considerable competition and turnover among grocers in Paris and Florida, as evidenced by the issuing of twenty-two licenses between 1833 and 1840.

PATTERNS OF LAND ENTRY

Comparing land entries made by residents between 1830 and 1834 with entries made during the previous twelve years (fig. 5.10) reveals that new settlement tended to abut older purchases in the easternmost four townships;

the southwest corner of T55N, R8W; T56N, R9W; the southern half of T53N, R8W; and most of T54N, R9–10W. In contrast, land entries also were made in portions of the project area not previously settled, including the northeast half of T55N, R8W; T57N, R9–10W; the west half of T55N, R9W; and T55–56N, R10W. As we mentioned earlier, the portion of the region that received the greatest influx of settlement was west of the R8–9W line, primarily owing to the founding of Paris as the seat of newly created Monroe County.

Based on the assumption that the founding of Paris as the seat of Monroe County affected patterns of land entry in the immediate vicinity, this locale is examined in some detail. Figure 5.13 illustrates the pattern created by entries made during each of the years 1829 through 1833. Paris was selected as county seat on 1 May 1831. The land for the town was donated by James C. Fox, who had purchased it on 3 January 1831—three days before the creation of Monroe County. Fox's role in influencing land purchase in the vicinity of the future commercial center should not be underestimated. We already have discussed his manipulation of the county court to secure the location of the county seat on his land. In addition, in 1833 he helped a Columbia, Missouri, merchant foreclose on a tract of more than 80 acres that abutted the southern edge of Paris. This obviously was one of the choicest tracts in the county, and its subdivision into lots allowed the town to expand to the south.

Figure 5.13 shows that a considerable amount of land was purchased in what became the vicinity of Paris during 1829 and 1830. A significant percentage of these entries were made by nonresidents. The clustered nature of the resident and nonresident entries suggests that there may have been an early expectation that Monroe County would be formed and that the county seat would be located in that area.

Included in figure 5.13 is the distribution of entries made around Paris for three periods during 1831: January through July, August, and September through December. During the first period most land was entered south of the Middle Fork. Paris was on this side of the river, and it was logical, given the difficulty of constructing bridges and keeping fords passable, that entrants would prefer to reside on the town side. These entries, together with those made during earlier years, filled up most of the area south of the river. Thus entries made after July 1831 were concentrated on the north side.

The frequency of land entry within a 4 mile radius of Paris was considerably higher during August 1831 than during any other month. The explanation for this is that Paris was platted during that month. The formal platting of the town and subsequent sale of lots made that locale and its surrounding land much more attractive to entrants who previously may not have been convinced that entry near an unplatted county seat was worth the economic risk—especially if the land was less desirable for agriculture than land available elsewhere.

In contrast to the clustered settlement evident around Paris, the area around Florida—which was platted three months before Paris—does not exhibit a similar pattern. It is logical to assume that if settlement clustering is a normal consequence of a town's being platted, it should have occurred first around Florida, then around Paris. To the contrary, clustering began before the platting of Paris and never occurred around Florida, except as a natural consequence of land entry over time. This suggests that the administrative and governmental functions that belonged to Paris as the county seat were strong settlement attractions.

Viewing resident land entries across the region relative to environmental dimensions, we note several significant patterns. First, there was still an avoidance of the prairie. Of the 1,723 land units entered between 1830 and 1834, 1,252 (72.6%) were timber-only tracts, 370 (21.5%) were on the ecotone, and only 101 (5.9%) were on the prairie. Inspection of a large sample of the prairie tracts documented the fact that a vast majority of these tracts were part of ecotonal purchases. The area that contained most purchase units was contained roughly within a 4 mile radius around Paris (fig. 5.10). A desire for proximity to the regional center apparently offset any perceived or real difficulties in bringing prairie land into agricultural production.

Nonresident entries accounted for 12.4% of the land purchases between 1830 and 1834. The land entry pattern of this class of entrants was quite similar to that of residents. Of the 244 units entered, 164 (67.2%) were in timber, 50 (20.5%) were on the ecotone, and 30 (12.3%) were on the prairie (table 5.1). The percentage of prairie units was considerably higher than percentages seen previously for nonresident entries in that biome. Large purchase units containing prairie were entered around Paris—possibly for speculative purposes—as well as in T54N, R7W and T56N, R9–10W (fig. 5.6).

For the first time since the central Salt River valley was opened for sale, entrants who definitely can be tied to eastern states began purchasing land. The number of units entered, however, was small (three units, composing 0.04% of the project area). The low frequency of eastern speculator entries for this period is in sharp contrast to what would follow during the next two years.

The Speculative Period: 1835–36

The years 1835 and 1836 were the culmination of a ten-year period of economic upturn—a period characterized nationally by considerable westward expansion and locally by a tremendous population increase and the development of small but rapidly growing regional centers. The height to which the speculative fever rose during the mid-1830s is reflected in the amount of land entered between 1835 and 1836. During the ten-year period

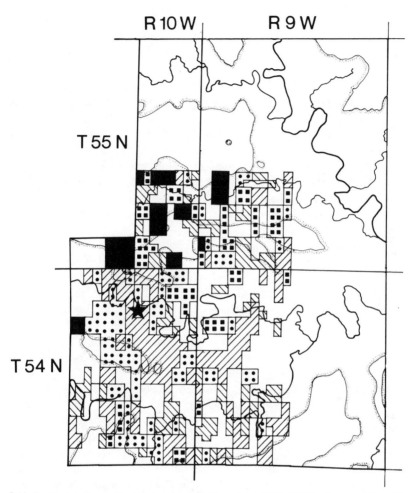

5.13. Resident and nonresident land entry around Paris during 1829–30 (▨), January–July, 1831 (⬚), August, 1831 (■), September–December, 1831 (⬚), and 1832–33 (◩).

1827–36, approximately 84% of the project area land was sold, with the years 1835–36 accounting for about 50%.

Resident purchases accounted for 1,736 (55%) of the 3,159 units entered. However, based on figures provided by Mason (1983) for the larger region, much of the land entered by residents consisted of secondary purchases. In 1835 the percentage of first land units entered (i.e., residents making their first entries) dropped below 50% for the first time, indicating that more than 50% of the units were subsequent purchases. Nonresidents entered 266 units

(8.4% of the total for 1835–36), and eastern speculators entered 1,157 units (36.6%). The number of entries by eastern-based speculators made during this period was unequaled during any other period.

REGIONAL GROWTH AND DEVELOPMENT

The rapid settlement of the region led to the founding of numerous small towns that the founders hoped would draw commerce and industry, thereby competing with Paris and Florida as trade centers. Three towns were platted in the eastern part of the project area late in 1834, though lots were not sold until 1835. All were located on the Salt River (fig. 5.12), but only one, Cincinnati, became a successful town. Newport, between Florida and Cincinnati, and Bloomfield, between New London and Cincinnati (fig. 5.12), may have been too close to established towns to compete as regional commercial centers (Mason 1982:137).

In 1836 towns also were platted in the newly created Washington and South Fork townships in Monroe County (fig. 5.12). Two towns in Washington township, Clinton and Jonesburg, were platted adjacent to each other. These two towns were on the North Fork, with only an alley separating them. Clinton was platted by two merchants and an operator of a sawmill/gristmill and ferry. Jonesburg was directly south of Clinton and was founded by a merchant who apparently had an ongoing enterprise before the town was founded. Competition between the two towns was reflected in conflicts over proposed routes of county roads (Mason 1982:139). Santa Fe was on the South Fork (fig. 5.12) and was platted in October 1836 by a local farmer-doctor. It remains today as a community.

By 1836 there was fairly regular spacing (about 12 miles) between most towns and villages. One exception to this spacing was Newport, located 6–9 miles from Florida and Cincinnati. Newport failed as a commercial center, which is not surprising since it was competing with its larger neighbors. Also, the lack of milling facilities created by the ban on damming the river below the forks at Florida hindered Newport's development and kept Cincinnati relatively small (Mason 1982:139).

LAND ENTRY

Resident land entry during 1835–36 occurred in all townships in the project area (fig. 5.14). However, because of the intense crowding around Paris owing to previous resident and nonresident entries, the large expanse of prairie (still largely avoided) in the southeast corner of the project area, and the variably timbered but dissected terrain (agriculturally poor) in portions of T55–56N, R6–7W, most entries were in a wide band of lightly to moderately timbered land running from T57N, R10W to T53N, R8W (fig. 5.14).

Owing to the high frequency of land entries made during this period, it is difficult to isolate environmental dimensions that influenced settlement. We note, however, that for the first time land units on the prairie were entered more often than ecotonal units. Of the 1,736 land units entered by residents, 1,059 (61%) were in timber, 358 (20.6%) were on the prairie, and 319 (18.4%) were on the ecotone (table 5.1). This increase in prairie purchases was due to the nonavailability of land perceived as better quality than prairie; the expansion of previous purchase units on the ecotone; and possibly a change in perceptions of the agricultural utility of the prairie.

The sale of prairie units also increased among nonresidents (table 5.1). Of the 266 land units entered, 156 (58.6%) were timbered, 63 (23.7%) were on

5.14. Resident land entries in the project area made during 1835–36 (hatched areas indicate prior entries).

the prairie, and 47 (17.7%) were on the ecotone. The distribution of nonresident entries is shown in figure 5.15.

Mason (1983) identified 107 eastern speculators, who purchased 1,524 land units (roughly 60,960 acres) during 1835–36. Speculators from New York, Pennsylvania, New Jersey, and Connecticut were identified from patent information. Most of the entries were made on eight days between 31 August 1835 and 31 August 1836—possibly because speculators used the same land agents in Palmyra (the location of the land office), who entered land for all clients on the same days (Mason 1983).

Speculator land was entered primarily in the eastern third of the project area (fig. 5.16), though there were clusters of entries in the eastern third of

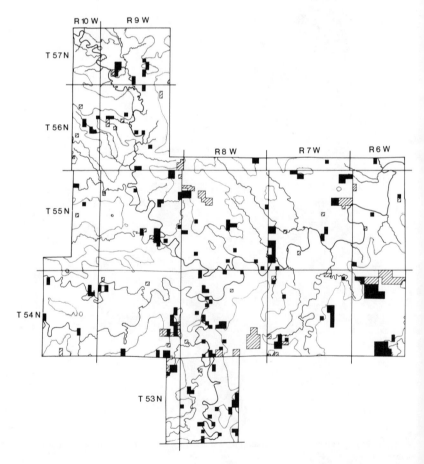

5.15. Nonresident land entries in the project area made during 1835–36 (■) and 1837–58 (▨).

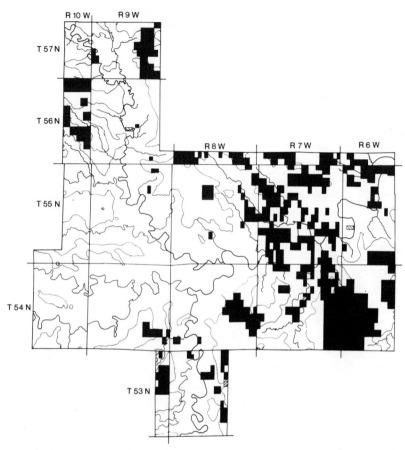

5.16. Eastern speculator land entries in the project area made during 1830–34 (▨), 1835–36 (■), and 1837–58 (▧).

T57N, R9W, in T56N, R10W, in T56N, R8–10W, and along the South Fork. Of the 1,157 units entered by speculators, 507 (43.8%) were in timber, 494 (42.7%) were on the prairie, and 156 (13.5%) were on the ecotone. It is evident from figure 5.16 that speculators preferred large, contiguous blocks of land units, and by 1835 most of the few locations left for large-block purchases were on the prairie. Another area in which large entries were made was the densely timbered, dissected land in the southwest half of T55N, R7W.

By the end of 1836, slightly over 88% of available land in the project area had passed into private ownership. With deteriorating economic conditions and the lack of availability of large tracts, land speculation essentially ceased at the close of the sale on 31 August 1836. Although there was still federal land for entry, it took another twenty-three years before the last units were sold. Thus in some respects the year 1836 signaled the end of the frontier period and the beginning of a period of internal adjustment. The scope of this adjustment is discussed below.

The Closing of the Frontier: 1837–58

The economic expansion that characterized 1826–36 triggered a national cycle of inflation and easy credit that resulted in a severe downturn beginning in 1837. Uncontrolled inflation began in 1834, coupled with an increase in both federal land speculation and the number of banks that issued unredeemable currency (Cable 1923:169). The situation was compounded by President Andrew Jackson's specie circular of 1836, which decreed that only gold and silver would be accepted as payment at federal land offices (ibid.). The effects of the specie circular were less severe in Missouri than in neighboring areas, apparently owing to a local belief in using "hard money" for business transactions (Mason 1983).

The Bank of the State of Missouri, chartered by the General Assembly, opened on 10 May 1837. Capital included state bonds and private notes, but loans were repayable only in specie. The bank took few risks and did little to expand specie circulation (Mason 1983). As a result, notes of other state banks circulated widely in Missouri even though they had been suspended. In November 1839 the Missouri bank declared that it no longer would accept notes not backed by specie. Missouri merchants holding unbacked notes retaliated by withdrawing deposits and withholding payments on loans from the Missouri bank (Cable 1923:179). The ban on acceptance of unbacked state bank notes was lifted in March 1841, and in 1843 the Bank of the State of Missouri filed suit against the Illinois state bank to recover the debt caused by acceptance of Illinois notes (Cable 1923:184). As Mason (1983) points out, this period of economic depression and attendant conservative banking practices inhibited regional development and commercial expansion, leaving merchants and other entrepreneurs to rely on unredeemable out-of-state bank notes.

REGIONAL GROWTH AND DEVELOPMENT

Although the growth and development of the central Salt region slowed considerably by the end of 1836, it did not halt. Continued immigration and in situ population growth increased the population density from about two persons per square mile in 1830 to eleven persons per square mile in 1840 (Mason 1983). Population levels along the southern margin of the project area and the region to the south had reached the point that on 17 December 1836

Audrain County was formed from territory that had been attached administratively to Monroe and Callaway counties (National Historical Company 1884:41).

Some settlers arriving in the region during the latter half of the 1830s probably were attracted by earlier road and town construction, so that economic development and local improvements were related to increased population in a positive feedback cycle (Mason 1983). Despite a general economic slowdown, by 1840 the length of improved roads per square mile in the project area was 0.75 miles, compared with the modern average of 1.4 miles. Taken another way, the 1840 figure indicates that the average maximum distance of any point from an improved road was about 1.3 miles. The highest density of roads in 1840 was south of Paris, in T54N, R10W (fig. 5.12), where the beginning of the ubiquitous Midwest grid system of roads is apparent (Mason 1982).

The economic downturn during the latter half of the 1830s may have been part of the reason many small towns failed to develop into regional centers. The head start that Paris and Florida had made it difficult for these newer towns to attract both providers and consumers of goods and services; economic depression made it difficult for people to purchase town lots and for potential craftsmen and merchants to gain the capital necessary to establish their businesses. Mason (1983) discusses the rapid decline of these centers, noting that few were able to compete even for lower-order business (e.g., groceries, dry goods). Although a few towns such as Newport (Joanna), Santa Fe, Clinton-Jonesburg, and Cincinnati were able to attract a few settlers and a small amount of business, they were totally eclipsed by the two larger centers. What goods and services were available in most towns were limited, necessitating a trip to Paris, Florida, Hannibal, New London, or Palmyra for anything but the most basic needs.

Perhaps the fact that most small towns did not attract industrial concerns explains the proliferation of rural manufacturing evident in the 1840 and 1850 population censuses. Conversely, the rise of rural industry may have prevented the growth of town-based industry. In either case, the 1840 census lists 13.4% of rural residents in the region as being engaged in at least part-time nonagricultural activities (Mason 1983). The percentage for 1850 was 12.8%. The distribution of rural, nonagricultural activities for 1840 (Mason 1982:fig. 8.4) is fairly random, though locations are near roads. The distribution of rural manufacturing for 1850 is similar to the pattern for 1840 except for a few clusters near the future communities of Indian Creek (platted in 1852) and Perry (platted in 1866).

Mason (1983) suggests that the phenomenon of rural manufacturing, especially by those engaged in it only part time, indicates that the rural location may have been determined by social relationships rather than by economic forces. The security of living with or near relatives may have outweighed the advantages of a central location. Alternatively, craftsmen not related to the household in which they were living may have participated in a patron-client relationship and may have contributed part of their time to agriculture. Poor transportation also may have promoted a rural dispersed distribution of some services, as with blacksmiths who worked on agricultural implements.

Mills operating in the region by 1840 were spaced 6–10 miles apart (fig. 5.12), so that most residents were within 3–5 miles of a mill. An exception to this was the north-central part of the project area, where some residents were up to 10 miles from a facility. All mills ground corn for local consumption, but apparently only Hickman's mill at Florida could grind wheat into flour (National Historical Company 1884:660). In 1837 at least two mills in Florida were employed in "merchant work" (Wetmore 1837:120). These apparently were the only mills capable of producing flour for export. The presence of so many mills near Florida suggests the beginning of a central place, with milling as a significant specialization. This probably was related to the expectation of steamboat transportation to the Mississippi River (Mason 1983).

By 1850 the fate of other small towns in the region finally caught up with Florida. In 1840 Paris and Florida contained almost equal populations (table 5.2), but soon after this date Paris began to expand at the expense of Florida, so that by 1850 the population of the former almost doubled that of the latter. By 1860, well after the period of interest here, Florida had almost disappeared while Paris had nearly doubled its 1850 population. By 1850 Paris had taken on service functions that began to distinguish it from lower-order places. With the exception of tailor shops, stage and freight depots, and a cigar maker in Florida, all activities located only in towns were found only in Paris (table 5.3). Specialized services there included a drugstore, a hatter, a brick mason, a silversmith, and a tinner. Paris also was the only town with a hotel and a newspaper. Its position as an administrative center also drew those engaged in

Table 5.2. Population of Missouri Towns at Various Dates

Town	1840[a]	1850[a]	1860[b]	1876[c]
Paris	289	572	1,000	1,400
Florida	281	316	160	100
Clinton-Jonesburg	88	99	—	—
Santa Fe	27	74	120	110
Cincinnati	60	50	?	?

Source: Data from Mason (1983).
[a]From manuscript census schedules.
[b]From Sutherland and McEvoy (1860).
[c]From Polk and Company (1876).

Table 5.3. Distribution of Types of Shops among Towns and Rural Areas in 1850

Shop Type	Rural	Town
Merchant	5	19
Druggist	0	1[a]
Peddler	1	0
Mill	10	4
Blacksmith	12	10
Carpenter	18	10
Cabinetmaker	2	7
Wagon maker	4	9
Cooper	7	4
Saddler	1	8
Shoemaker	3	3
Plasterer	2	2
Stone mason	2	1
Mechanic	1	1
Wheelwright	2	0
Gunsmith	1	0
Potter	1	0
Wool carder	1	0
Tobacco curer	1	0
Artist	1	0
Tailor	0	7
Transport	0	3
Brick mason	0	1[a]
Hatter	0	1[a]
Silversmith	0	1[a]
Tinner	0	1[a]
Printer	0	2[a]
Cigar maker	0	1
Hotel	0	1[a]
Doctor	10	12
Lawyer	3	7[a]
Teacher	15	5
Minister	9	3
Engineer	1	1
County official	0	1[a]

Source: Mason (1983).
[a]In Paris only.

the legal profession; all lawyers listed in the 1850 Monroe County census resided in or near Paris.

LAND ENTRY

By 1837 only 11.7% of the available federal land in the project area remained unentered (table 5.1), of which 5.1% was timbered, 4.7% was on the prairie, and 1.9% was on the ecotone. Of the 773 land units sold during the period 1837–58, residents entered 565 units, nonresidents 132, and eastern speculators 4, and 72 units were deeded by the government to the Hannibal and St. Joseph Railroad to finance construction of track.

To attract purchasers, on 11 February 1847 Congress passed the first military bounty act, which provided a warrant for 160 acres redeemable at any land office to noncommissioned soldiers who had served twelve months or more in the war with Mexico (those serving less than twelve months received 40 acres) (Minot 1854:123–26). On 28 September 1850 the right to bounty land was extended to officers who had served in the Mexican War and to all military personnel who had served in the War of 1812 or in any Indian war (Minot 1854:520–21). Most recipients of military warrants sold them to speculators, who resold them to settlers on credit with high interest rates (Gates 1942:325).

As further attraction, on 4 August 1854 Congress passed the Graduation Act, which reduced the price of land that had remained unsold for ten years or more (Minot 1866:574). If a unit of land met this criterion, it was to be sold for $1 an acre, and the price was to be reduced 25¢ every five years thereafter until it reached 25¢ an acre, after which no further reductions were made. To qualify for graduated land, entrants had to sign an affidavit affirming that the land was for their own use for settlement or cultivation and that they had not already entered more than 320 acres of graduated land.

The effects of the military bounty acts and the Graduation Act on the sale of public land in the project area were significant. Using Mason's (1983) figures for the region as a gauge, we note that between 1838 and 1847 the greatest number of land units entered during a single year was 60, in 1839. Except for the year 1841, when 33 units were entered, the next largest number entered was 22 (in 1847). However, for the five years following passage of the first bounty act (during which time the second act was passed), the number of units entered rose to 485. Sales during these five years, then, accounted for approximately 47% of all land remaining unsold after 1837. Sales in 1855—the year following the passage of the Graduation Act—more than quadrupled those in the previous year.

The percentages of timbered versus prairie units entered by residents after 1836 were almost equal (42.7% and 40.7%, respectively), while the percentage of units entered on the ecotone was low (16.6%). As indicated in figure 5.17, resident land entries were not clustered; owing to the intense infilling that had occurred before 1836, entries were scattered throughout the region. Two environmental zones that allowed for expansion of existing purchase units were the high bottomland terraces and slopes along the upper and middle reaches of the North Fork (fig. 5.17). Because of the difficulty of clearing timber (which was very dense in some areas) from the slopes, units in these locales may have been passed over previously.

The percentages of biome entered by nonresidents differ considerably from those entered by residents (table 5.1). Although the percentages of ecotonal units purchased by the two groups are almost identical, nonresidents purchased exactly twice as many prairie units as timbered units—a pattern not exhibited by resident entrants. Within the group of nonresident entries, the difference in frequency of prairie units entered over units entered in the other two biomes is significant ($\chi^2 = 33.58$; df $= 2$; $p < .001$). Additionally, the differences in frequencies of prairie and timbered units entered by residents as opposed to prairie and timbered units entered by nonresidents are also significant ($\chi^2 = 11.42$; df $= 1$; $p < .001$). The best explanation for these two patterns appears to be a desire on the part of nonresidents to purchase large blocks of land regardless of the location (fig. 5.15). Since fairly large chunks

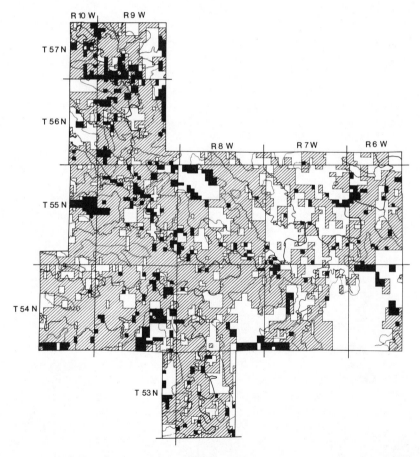

5.17. Resident land entries made in the project area during 1837–58 (hatched areas indicate prior entries).

of the prairie were still available, this was the logical biome in which to enter land. Conversely, residents—whether new entrants or previous entrants who were expanding their holdings—were not too particular about biome.

Eastern speculators entered only four units (all in timber) after 1837 (fig. 5.16), possibly having lost interest in the region owing to the economic depression of the late 1830s and 1840s and the lack of large, contiguous blocks of land for entry.

Summary and Conclusions

In this chapter we have presented a broad overview of settlement within an area of the central Salt River valley and have discussed the economic growth and development of the region between 1818 and 1850. Within this period the region underwent a rapid rise in population because of continued immigration from the trans-Appalachian areas of Kentucky, Virginia, and neighboring states. The influx of settlers gave rise to a number of political reorganizations that acted to draw more immigrants to the region. Influenced by national cycles, the region passed through a series of periods of economic growth and prosperity followed by times of stagnation. Towns were formed with the hope of their becoming flourishing communities—magnets that would attract population as well as commerce and industry. By 1840—a date that at this point in our discussion is somewhat arbitrary—it appears that the project area had passed through the frontier period and was well on its way to becoming an established upper South region.

In this section we summarize the discussion of settlement patterning and economic growth within the project area and draw tentative conclusions from the data presented thus far. The most important consideration here is the degree of correlation between the data and the implications of the model. While not all portions of the model can be tested at this point, these preliminary results highlight several areas of interest that we examine further in chapters 6 and 7.

Regional Growth and Development

As we have mentioned several times previously, changes in the character of the project area from the perspectives of economic development and population growth are intricately tied to cycles in the national economy and to local politics. At the political level, Missouri's change in status from territory to state and the subdivision of western Ralls County into political townships—both of which occurred in 1821—presented the populace with the opportunity for government at the local level. While normally such an event might bring about a dramatic increase in immigration, such was not the case in the central Salt Valley. A downturn in the national economy at the end of the second decade was so severe that few immigrants arrived in the region.

If one can believe the accounts of intense crowding and lack of available, affordable land in the trans-Appalachian region and, closer to home, the Boonslick area—and the evidence supports the accounts—then it would be reasonable to assume that as soon as the land surveys were finished immigrants would have flooded the Salt Valley. However, the poor shape of the economy, coupled with the virtual absence of any support structure (roads, towns, etc.) kept immigration slow during the first seven years.

By 1826 the feedback between population growth (although the growth rate was low) and a recovering economy led to further changes in the regional picture. Immigration increased considerably between 1826 and 1829, the road system throughout western Ralls County was greatly improved, and political boundaries were redrawn to compensate for shifts in population density.

By 1830 the region had grown enough that the impetus was there for a series of changes that would further fuel the feedback between economic development and continued population growth. Population levels, especially in the western half of the project area, had reached the point where it became economically feasible to establish towns from which to distribute goods and services. In turn, the founders hoped these centers would further attract commerce, industry, and immigrants.

First in a series of changes was the reorganization in 1831 of the boundaries of Ralls County and the subsequent formation of Monroe County. Population in western Ralls County had reached the level that the populace deserved a stronger voice in shaping the future of the region. The second event that significantly altered the region was the founding of Paris, also in 1831, as the seat of Monroe County. The town was located within a dense settlement cluster that began forming by early 1830. After the founding, the purchase of settlement units around Paris increased until by 1834 little land remained available within a 4–5 mile radius of the town.

In that same year, the town of Florida was founded near the junction of the North Fork and main stem of the Salt River. In contrast to Paris, its location was not politically motivated but was a function of the prior location of mills in the vicinity. Also in contrast to Paris, Florida did not attract dense settlement around it, nor did it attract the kinds of commerce and industry that the administrative center drew.

If we were to use a single word to characterize the region between 1831 and 1836, it probably should be *prosperity*. By 1835 land speculators from the East were entering large tracts of land in the project area, probably for quick resale to new immigrants and established residents desiring to expand their holdings. The resident population growth curve turned upward at a rate not seen previously[8] as continued immigration added more people to the pool produced naturally through childbirth.

This period of prosperity also produced a number of small towns to compete for trade with Paris and Florida. Within a few years, however, most of these planned communities were nothing but dreams in the minds of their founders. Given the established nature of the two larger centers in Monroe County and the proximity of eastern and northern residents to New London, Palmyra, and Hannibal—where goods were in better supply and probably cheaper—it is not surprising that small towns were not able to compete.

Throughout the boom years of the 1830s there was a concerted drive toward better transportation routes and links with external markets. While early settlement and milling sites often were proximal to the few roads through the southern and eastern portions of the project area, the location of later settlement determined where new routes were placed. By 1840 all but the most northern section of the project area was crisscrossed by an integrated road network.

The desire for improved transportation routes linking the region with external markets was not limited to roads, as witnessed by the ill-fated Salt River Navigation Company and the Florida and Paris Rail Road Company. The latter was incorporated in 1837 to join the two commercial centers— perhaps as a way to bolster Florida's ebbing economy—but, like its sister navigation company, it was caught in the recession of the late 1830s. Doubtless other transportation schemes met a similar fate.

The recession of the late 1830s/early 1840s, while slowing land sales in the region and contributing to the demise of smaller towns, possibly had less of an effect on the Salt Valley than on more established regions in other parts of the United States. During this period the population of both Paris and Florida increased significantly, as did the number of services offered by the two centers.

By 1840 settlement was virtually complete. Patterns of rural settlement and town location already were well established. As Mason (1982:139) points out, changes after that time were due largely to moderate increases in population density and competition among rural residents for land and among commercial centers for primary service functions. By 1850 Paris had won the battle for primacy.

Land Entry and Environmental Dimensions

By plotting land entries against biome for each of the six periods we determined that there was an early avoidance of the prairie proper that lasted until the speculative period of 1835–36. The one exception to this rule was the

8. See Mason (1983) for regional population figures for 1830, 1840, and 1850.

area within a 4 mile radius around Paris. There the desirability of proximity to the town apparently overrode concerns about farming the open prairie.

The earliest land entries—by residents as well as nonresidents—were along the ecotone or in timber. Unexpectedly, some of the entries were in heavily timbered areas as opposed to areas that could be cleared more easily. Between 1821 and 1825, however, little ecotonal land was purchased. Most entries made during that period were in lightly to moderately timbered zones. In the case of two resident entrants who entered land adjacent to that of a relation, the entries were on the ecotone. One settlement cluster that took advantage of low-density timber was situated along both sides of the Elk Fork, in T54N, R9–10W.

Throughout the remainder of the 1820s entrants continued to take advantage of the ecotone, entering sizable purchase units in timber but with access to the prairie. Enough land was still available that resident as well as nonresident entrants could be highly selective in their choice of location. It appears that timber density was not a prime determinant, since many low-density areas were skipped over. At least in T54N, R9–10W, highly productive soils as rated by GLO surveyors appear to have been more significant determinants.

During the first half of the 1830s the sale of timbered land continued to outdistance that of land in the other two biomes, though the percentage of timbered land decreased steadily. For the first time, prairie units constituted more than 10% of the total units entered by a single class of entrants during one period (12.3%, nonresidents). Additionally, the percentage of ecotonal land entered rose above 20% for the first time since 1820. Also for the first time, we note the presence of a few isolated land units situated entirely on the prairie, with no access to the ecotone. Their presence may signal the beginning of a cautious reappraisal of the grassland environment by resident entrants.

By the end of August 1835 the sale of public land in the project area was at an all-time high, with residents and eastern speculators entering sizable tracts of land in all three biomes. Residents preferred timbered land units—by about a 3:1 ratio—though there clearly was an increase in the number of isolated prairie units entered. Because eastern speculators wanted large, contiguous blocks of land, prairie was significantly overrepresented (42.7%) in their entries. Other large tracts of speculator land were entered in marginally productive (and hence previously unsold) areas in the northern and eastern extremes of the region.

Between 1837 and 1850 most of the remaining land was sold, though the last remaining unit was not entered until 1858. The number of prairie units and timbered units entered by residents was almost equal, but, significantly, nonresidents entered exactly twice as many prairie units as timbered units.

Table 5.4. Attributes of Environmental Dimensions Used in the Multiple Regression Analysis

Dimension	Attributes
Slope	1 0–5% (level or gentle slope)
	2 5–14% (moderate slope)
	3 14–30% (steep slope)
Vegetation	1 Timber-prairie
	2 Timber
	3 Prairie
	4 None (rocky)
Topography	1 Bottoms
	2 Low terraces
	3 High terraces
	4 Slopes and ridgetops
	5 Level uplands
Drainage	1 Moderately well drained; moderately well to well drained
	2 Somewhat poorly to moderately well drained; well drained
	3 Very well drained; somewhat poorly drained
	4 Poorly drained
	5 Very poorly drained

Source: Mason (1983).

While analysis and discussion thus far have centered on land entry in relation to biome, we recognize that other environmental dimensions surely were significant in deciding where to choose one's landholdings. For the early period of colonization we discussed the location of entries relative to timber density, and in some instances we included other dimensions such as soil fertility and proximity to permanent water sources. For the later periods, because of the large number of entries and the complex relation between entries and environmental dimensions, our discussion is inadequate for anything more than a preliminary assessment of preferred characteristics of biotope space. In the following chapter we focus our analysis on one area of the region—taking into account the location of entries relative to a number of dimensions—to obtain a clearer understanding of the nature of settlement decisions and how they changed through time.

As a preliminary step, we turn here to a multiple regression analysis Mason (1983) carried out to obtain a general overview of the relation between land entry and various environmental variables. The number of days a land unit remained unsold was the dependent variable, and four environmental dimensions were used as independent variables (see also Mason, Warren, and O'Brien 1982). These four dimensions—slope, vegetation type, landform, and soil drainage—vary with modern soil series and may have figured prominently in land-quality perceptions by early-nineteenth-century agriculturists. The attributes of the four environmental dimensions used in the analysis are listed in table 5.4; the twenty-six combinations of attributes (that form classes) actually occurring in the project area (i.e., that define actual soil series) are shown in table 5.5.

We must note, however, that the data used in this analysis were taken from modern Soil Conservation Service (SCS) surveys and as such are soil-based variables. For example, the Putnam series is described by the SCS (Watson 1979) as "deep, poorly drained, nearly level soils on uplands. These soils formed in silty and clayey material. The native vegetation was mixed prairie grasses." Despite its being a "prairie soil," we know that the Putnam series did support timber in some locales during the early nineteenth century. Timber encroachment onto prairie soils is not rare in the project area (fig. 4.14), as we determined from GLO survey records (chap. 4). Thus using modern SCS data can lead to erroneous conclusions, a fact that must be taken into account in

Table 5.5. Environmental Classes Used in the Multiple Regression Analysis and Percentage of Project Area They Occupy

Environmental	S	V	T	D	Soil Series	Percentage
1	1	1	1	2	Cedargap	0.1
2	1	2	1	1	Fatima, Kickapoo	2.7
3	1	2	1	3	Belknap	0.3
4	1	2	2	4	Moniteau	0.5
5	1	2	3	4	Auxvasse, Marion	1.8
6	1	2	4	3	Calwoods	1.9
7	1	2	2	5	Piopolis	6.4
8	1	3	1	4	Blackoar, Chequest	0.7
9	1	3	1	5	Wabash	0.1
10	1	3	2	3	Arbela	0.5
11	1	3	3	1	Vigar	0.1
12	1	3	3	3	Gifford	1.2
13	1	3	3	4	Chariton	0.4
14	1	3	5	3	Mexico, Kilwinning	16.3
15	1	3	5	4	Putnam	12.2
16	2	1	4	1	Gara	0.1
17	2	1	4	2	Armstrong	10.2
18	2	2	4	1	Keswick, Gosport, Weller, Winfield	15.1
19	2	2	4	2	Menfro	0.1
20	2	2	4	3	Gorin	4.3
21	2	3	4	3	Leonard, Sampsel	10.8
22	3	2	4	2	Goss, Lindley	13.1
23	3	4	4	3	Rockland	0.7
24					River, lake	0.1
25					Mine or quarry	0.1
26					No data	0.2

Source: Mason (1983).
Note: See table 5.4 for definition of attributes.

evaluating the settlement trends. Nonetheless, the approach does generate a preliminary assessment of settlement in relation to certain physical environmental dimensions—an assessment whose implications we examine in considerable detail in chapter 6 using more direct measures of the environment. Only the results of analyzing resident first entries are discussed here; results for the other entrant classes are discussed in Mason (1983).

Soil series that correlate most highly with pre-1830 resident first entries are Cedargap (level, timbered or prairie, moderately well drained bottomlands); Auxvasse-Marion (level, timbered, poorly drained high terraces); Armstrong (moderately sloped, timbered or prairie, differentially drained slopes and ridgetops); and Keswick-Gosport-Weller-Winfield (moderately sloped, timbered, moderately well drained slopes and ridgetops). Although significant, Cedargap soils are barely represented in the project area (table 5.5). Of more interest are the other three series that occur on timbered high terraces, moderate slopes with transitional vegetation, and timbered ridgetops and moderate slopes. Soil series that correlate with post-1830 first entries are Mexico-Kilwinning (level, prairie, variably drained uplands); Putnam (level, prairie, poorly drained uplands); and Goss-Lindley (steeply sloped, timbered, variably drained low terraces). Two other series—Belknap (moderately well drained, timbered bottomlands) and Chariton (level prairie and variably drained high terraces)—while displaying significant correlation, constitute only 0.3% and 0.4% of the project area, respectively (table 5.5).

Based on this preliminary analysis we conclude that timbered moderate slopes and ridgetops, timbered high terraces, and moderate slopes in mixed timber and prairie were preferred settlement locations (Mason 1983; Mason, Warren, and O'Brien 1982). Level, upland prairie and steep, timbered slopes were avoided until after the preferred locations were filled. Although the results of the analysis indicate preferred settlement locations, it is important to point out that the percentage of variance explained by the multiple regression is extremely low ($R^2 = .14$), meaning that variables not included in the analysis probably are affecting observed patterns. Included among possible variables are distance to roads and towns, proximity to kin, distance to permanent water sources, and so forth. These are discussed in more detail in chapters 6 and 7.

We also point out that using the amount of time a tract remained unsold as the dependent variable rests on the assumption that land with preferred characteristics was entered earlier than land with nonpreferred characteristics (Mason, Warren, and O'Brien 1982). In turn, this assumes that entrants knew the characteristics of the tract before they purchased it. As we pointed out previously, many entrants, through correspondence with family or friends residing in the area, may have gained some knowledge of these characteristics. On the other hand, a significant number of entrants may have

Table 5.6. Minimum Production Amounts Necessary to Be Considered a Market Commodity Producer for Various Commodities

Commodity	Unit	Minimum
Mules and asses		5
Swine		53
Cattle		33
Sheep		44
Milk cows		8
Corn	Bushels	1,441
Wheat	Bushels	168
Orchard products	Dollars	54
Tobacco	Pounds	1
Hemp	Tons	1
Flax	Pounds	169
Flaxseed	Bushels	7

Source: Data from Mason (1983).

had no more information than the locations of streams and prairie-timber boundaries, which were available on plat maps at the land office. Thus, after deciding to enter a timbered tract, for example, an entrant's further decision as to *which* tract to purchase may have approached randomness (with regard to physical environmental variables). Therefore we suggest that one reason for the low R^2 value is the unknown number of choices that were made without regard to specific environmental characteristics (Mason, Warren, and O'Brien 1982:378).

One explanation for early settlers' preference for the three environmental zones mentioned above might rest with the kind of agriculture a settler intended to practice. In chapter 3 we discussed the upper South agricultural complex, which was characterized by mixed farming with a balanced system of livestock and crops that emphasized corn, swine, and cattle (Mitchell 1972, 1978). In addition, there were major producers of commodities such as tobacco, hemp, and flax, as well as livestock producers who also grew large quantities of grain for feed. If this upper South complex were transplanted in the Salt River valley, then there might be a correlation between certain kinds of production and the type of land where a product is raised.

Unfortunately, the earliest quantifiable data that exist regarding agricultural production are in the agricultural census of 1850. In examining the census, Mason (1983) compiled data on the amounts of various kinds of livestock and produce grown in the region and identified major producers of certain items. He defined major producers as persons who produced a commodity in quantities beyond the mean amount of all producers plus one standard deviation (table 5.6), with the exception of tobacco and hemp. All producers of these two commodities were included, since the entire crop probably was produced for market (Mason, Warren, and O'Brien 1982:381). Using data on selected products from the agricultural census, we can examine the relation between the three environmental zones that correlated with early settlement and agricultural production.

Because of its high representation in the region (19.5% of the project area), the zone containing timbered moderate slopes and ridgetops correlates significantly with the locations of purchase units belonging to producers of several agricultural products, including hogs and corn. However, given that 99.9% of all households in the census were raising corn and 98.4% were raising swine, this correlation is spurious. The strategy followed by agriculturists in this zone probably consisted of clearing enough land for an initial crop, then clearing the remainder of the timber at leisure. A side benefit of having timbered land was that hogs could be turned out to forage on mast and then harvested as needed (chap. 9).

A high correlation exists between livestock production and moderate slopes in the prairie-timber zone. Using Mason's (1983) figures, 89.6% (78 of 87) of those producing grazing livestock (cattle, sheep, and milk cows) in 1850 for whom land entry locations could be determined owned purchase units on soils indicative of the prairie-timber transition zone. Of the 29 major grazing livestock producers listed in table 5.6, 28 had purchase units in this zone. Their strategy probably was to cultivate the lightly timbered areas and pasture their livestock on the prairie. Until general acceptance of the steel plow in the 1850s (Bidwell and Falconer 1925:285) facilitated prairie cultivation, pasturing livestock probably was the most efficient use of the prairie biome.

There is significant correlation between tobacco production and timbered high terraces along the North Fork and its tributaries—especially Crooked Creek—and along the main stem of the Salt River east of the confluence of the North and South forks. Both areas contain relatively large, high terraces that drain moderately well and are not subject to seasonal inundation (fig. 4.4).

Based on these casual observations, it appears that the most significant correlations between kinds of production and environmental zones are limited to purchases of major producers. Although more rigorous examination of the data is needed, we suggest that upper South agriculturists who planned to become major producers of livestock, grain commodities, tobacco, or hemp carefully considered their selection of land (discussed further in chap. 9). Because of the large amount of land needed for major production and the significant risk involved, major producers may have had different perceptions of optimal land than did most smaller operators.

CONCLUSIONS

Several conclusions can be drawn from our analysis of settlement dynamics and the spatial patterns they effected. First, environmental factors such as timber density and biome distribution strongly affected early settlement across the region. Throughout the pre-1835 period there was an avoidance of open prairie and a decided preference for ecotonal or timbered land. Early land entry decisions during this period were decidedly in favor of lightly timbered tracts or tracts on the prairie-timber boundary. As tracts with these preferred traits were removed from the public domain, and possibly as attitudes against moderately timbered land changed, the entry of tracts in heavier timber became commonplace. In some localities soil fertility appears to have become a significant consideration. There also appears to be major agricultural production, including the growing of hemp and tobacco and the raising of grazing livestock.

Second, a multitude of cultural factors likewise affected regional settlement. From the earliest stage of colonization, kinship and marriage bonds formed in various source areas contributed to the formation of settlement clusters in the frontier zone. One important process appears to have been interdependent immigration, whereby established social units moved westward simultaneously or at closely spaced intervals. Other cultural factors that influenced settlement include road development and town formation. The location of early settlement clusters was determined in part by the route of the single long-distance road through the region. As the region developed and population growth increased, the location of new roads became dependent in part upon the location of population aggregates. Conversely, these new routes became focal points of further settlement. The wealth of landowners also appears to have been a prime factor in road location. The magnetlike attraction of planned administrative/commercial centers to settlement is illustrated by the rapid entry of land around Paris before its founding. A similar pattern is not evident relative to other towns in the area, so we tentatively conclude that the addition of administrative functions to commercial functions was the key to settlement attraction.

Third, the economic forces that affected older, more established areas of the United States also affected frontier zones, though perhaps to a lesser degree. The history of land sales in the project area and the pattern of general regional growth accurately reflect national economic cycles.

In the following two chapters we analyze in considerable detail the various physical and cultural environmental dimensions examined here, relative to the settlement of a 56 square mile locality in the southwest portion of the project area. The results of these analyses provide a test of the conclusions reached thus far and will substantially refine our understanding of the processes behind the settlement of the central Salt River valley.

Environmental Dimensions of Settlement

Robert E. Warren,
Michael J. O'Brien,
and Chad K. McDaniel

Bidwell and Falconer (1925) recognized more than fifty years ago that frontier settlement of the Prairie Peninsula was not uniform with respect to physical environmental dimensions (chap. 2). They observed that early settlement was biased toward forested areas and that, for a variety of reasons, the open prairies were avoided. Since that time Jordan (1964) and others have attempted to revise the prairie avoidance hypothesis using personal accounts and other sources of historical data. We propose that, rather than simply avoiding prairies, frontier agriculturists were seeking access to timber-prairie borders or oak savannas where forest resources were accessible yet laborious clearing of timber was unnecessary and native pastures were available nearby for grazing (Hewes 1950; McManis 1964; Peters 1970). Unfortunately, few of these studies are grounded in systematic regional methods of sampling or analysis, and it is difficult to evaluate either the relative importance of different variables in settlement decisions or changes in settlement decisions through time (Horsman 1978). In addition, few attempt to deal with social or economic variables, though the potential significance of these factors is well known among cultural geographers (Swierenga 1973).

Previous studies of historical settlement in the central Salt River valley (Mason, Warren, and O'Brien 1982; Warren, O'Brien, and Mason 1981; Warren, McDaniel, and O'Brien 1982) have identified several important patterns. As illustrated in chapter 5, consistent with both the prairie avoidance and ecotone attraction hypotheses, grasslands were not settled extensively until after 1835 (some eighteen years after initial land purchases were made in 1818), and a majority of early purchases appear to have been in forests near the prairie-timber ecotone (Mason, Warren, and O'Brien 1982; Warren, O'Brien, and Mason 1981). However, there also were two clusters of early settlement in an anomalous context. These clusters, referred to together as the Smith settlement, were situated deep within forests along lower reaches of the neighboring Elk and Middle forks of the Salt River (O'Brien, Mason, and

Saunders 1982). In chapter 5 we hypothesized that sparsely timbered and readily clearable Neo-Boreal forests, which overlay productive grassland soils, attracted early settlement to the Smith locality. We also proposed that interdependent immigration of linked multifamily social units was responsible for settlement clustering.

In this chapter[1] we systematically examine changing distribution of early historical settlement in the anomalous Smith locality. In particular we examine the times at which lands in the area were purchased from the General Land Office (GLO). These sales represent the first transfers of land into private hands, and thus we are examining the order in which purchasers acquired these lands from the GLO. Other sales and land transfers between private landholders occurred during the period we consider, but in this instance we are looking only at the pattern of first entry onto any particular parcel. To test the settlement context hypothesis, we use soil productivity, forest density, and a variety of other physical and cultural variables to define contextual factors capable of discriminating between land purchases made during successive periods of the early nineteenth century. One cultural variable not used in this analysis is kinship, which is introduced in the following chapter.

The Data Base

The Smith locality is a 7 by 8 mile area in the southwest corner of the project area (fig. 6.1). It is drained by two perennial tributary streams—the Middle Fork and the Elk Fork—that join before entering the main stem of the Salt River several miles to the east. Presettlement vegetation was predominantly forest (fig. 4.14), but two broad fingers of prairie capped level interstream divides to the north and south (fig. 6.1). Landforms grade from upland flats to sloping valley sides to level bottomland terraces.

Independent (or discriminating) variables used in this analysis include nine measures of the physical environment and two of the social environment. The former are treated as static entities, while the cultural variables are dynamic measures whose scales are adjusted in time to account for constantly changing cultural contexts.

Static physical variables include: (1) Drainage class (DRANCLAS 1–5; fig. 6.2*a*), a topographic slope position and moisture gradient that ranges sequentially from dry level uplands in class 1 to moist bottomland floodplains in class 5 (chap. 4). Although this is an ordinal scale variable, drainage classes were coded as five presence/absence dummy variables. (2) Percentage slope (SLOPEDIP 1–3; fig. 6.2*b*), a gradient of slope steepness ranging from

---

1. Portions of this chapter are adapted from Warren, McDaniel, and O'Brien 1982.

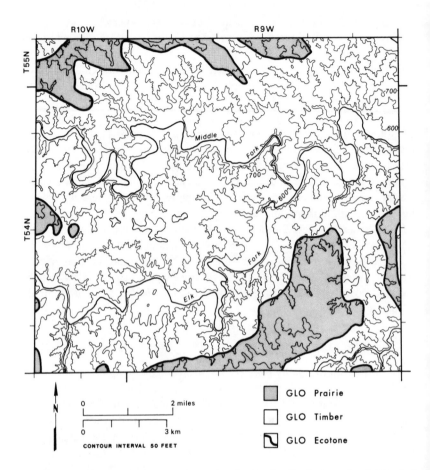

6.1. Topographic map of the Smith settlement locality showing distributions of early historical floral communities (from Warren, McDaniel, and O'Brien 1982).

gentle (less than 3%) to steep (greater than 10%) slopes. SLOPEDIP was coded as three dummy variables. (3) Distance to nearest perennial stream (PERENDIS 1–5; fig. 6.2c), an ordinal scale variable in which four of the five distance levels represent 0.5 mile intervals. It was coded as five dummy variables. (4) Distance to nearest border of prairie (PRAIRDIS 1–6; fig. 6.2d), an interval scale variable of 0.5 mile intervals coded as six dummy variables. (5) Tree density (TREEDENS 1–5; fig. 6.2e), an ordinal ranking of quintiles of tree density (stems per acre) calculated as a function of post-to-tree distances in GLO records (Warren 1982). TREEDENS was also coded as five dummy variables. (6) Presettlement biome (GLOBIOME; fig. 6.2*e*), a nominal variable from GLO plat maps denoting the (i) absence or (ii) presence of timber. (7) Soil Conservation Service (SCS) soil productivity (SOILPROD; fig. 6.2*f*), an ordinal scale measure of normal crop production of soils under modern soil management (O'Brien, Mason, and Saunders 1982). (8) Soil evaluations reported in line descriptions of GLO surveyors (GLOSOILS; fig. 6.3*a*). This is a three-level ordinal scale of surveyors' perceptions of soil quality or cultivation fitness that ranges from (i) very poor to poor third-rate soil, not fit for cultivation, to (iii) good or second-rate soil, fit for cultivation, to (v) rich to very rich first-rate soil, fit for cultivation (chap. 4). Section corners were assigned median values (ii or iv) if the two lines they contacted were rated differently. Since GLO records document observations only along section lines, locations (i.e., sixteenth section quadrats) were coded only if they contacted a section boundary. (9) Hazelnut in understory line descriptions of GLO surveyors (GLOHAZEL; fig. 6.3*b*). This is a nominal variable documenting (i) absence or (iii) presence of hazelnut (*Corylus americana*) in understory, a possible indicator of the relative openness of forest canopy. Section corners were assigned median values (ii) whenever adjacent lines were rated differently.

Dynamic cultural variables include distance to nearest contemporary road (ROADDIST) and distance to nearest previously purchased land unit (NEIGHBOR). Neither variable is simple to measure, since networks of roads and configurations of land purchases changed greatly during the course of settlement. Roads were constructed over a fourteen-year period (fig. 6.4), and first land entries were purchased more or less continuously between 1819 and 1855. True distances to nearest roads or neighbors from any particular place in the Smith locality would necessarily have changed through time. To control for these dynamic processes, all distance measures were transformed by scaling them against distributions of distances between all unpurchased quadrats and their nearest roads or neighbors as these existed when the given parcel was bought.

The dependent variables to be discriminated are groups of land units (sixteenth sections) ordered in time by dates of first land entry. Four periods of land purchase are recognized (fig. 6.5). The FIRST period (1819–25)[2] represents the earliest appearance of Euro-American agriculturists in the

2. It should be noted that the periods of land entry used in this analysis differs slightly from those used in chapter 5. We decided to reduce the number of periods from six to four to increase the number of land units in each period. Figure 6.6 shows that the general trends for the sale of land in the Smith locale are similar to those for the sale of land in the project area (including the Smith locale) and that the pattern is not significantly distorted by combining 1818–20 with 1821–25 and 1835–36 with 1837–59 and including 1834 with the latter aggregate period.

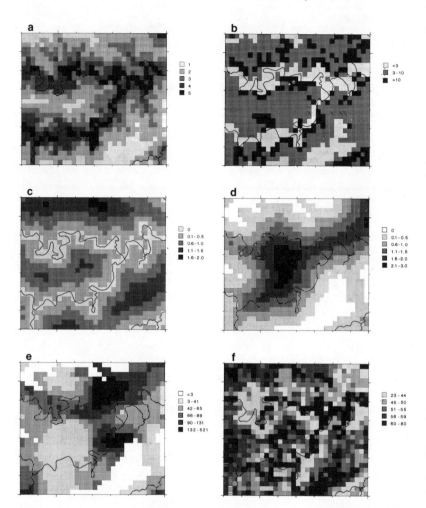

6.2. Maps of the Smith settlement locality showing coded distributions of: (*a*) drainage classes (DRANCLAS 1–5), (*b*) percentage slope classes (SLOPEDIP 1–3), (*c*) ranked distances in miles to nearest perennial stream (PERENDIS 1–5), (*d*) ranked distances in miles to nearest patch of early historical prairie (PRAIRDIS 1–5), (*e*) ranked early historical tree densities (stems per acre; TREEDENS 1–5) and presence of early historical timber (GLOBIOME), and (*f*) ranked scores on an SCS index of modern soil productivity (SOILPROD) (from Warren, McDaniel, and O'Brien 1982).

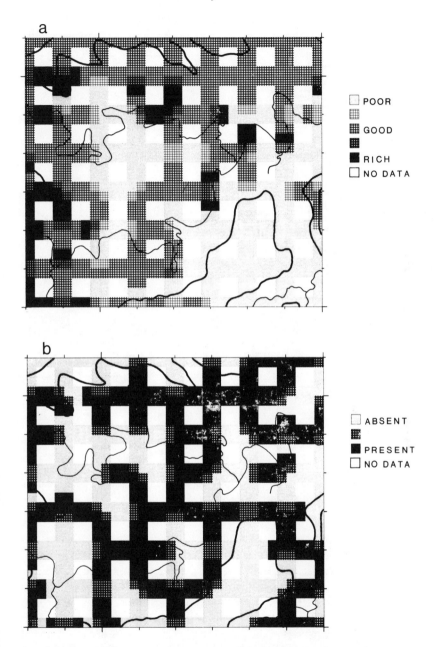

6.3. Maps of the Smith settlement locality showing coded distributions of: (*a*) early historical soils evaluations made by GLO surveyors (GLOSOILS) and (*b*) presence of hazelnut (*Corylus americana*) in early historical forest understory or brushy prairie (GLOHAZEL) (from Warren, McDaniel, and O'Brien 1982).

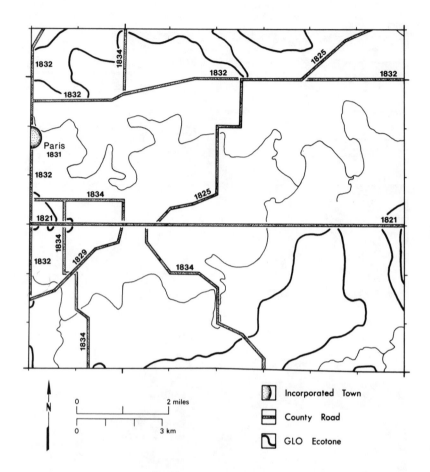

6.4. Early towns and roads in the Smith settlement locality, with dates of incorporation or construction (from Warren, McDaniel, and O'Brien 1982).

Smith locality, and contexts of land purchase may reflect the factors that attracted initial settlement. During the SECOND period (1826–29) rates of land purchase increased markedly (fig. 6.6), and a nearly contiguous chain of settlement was formed that ran diagonally across the locality from northeast to southwest. The THIRD period (1830–33) brackets the peak period of land purchase in the locality, when 44% of available land was entered in only four years (fig. 6.6). Purchases of the THIRD period appear to be dispersed around those made during the SECOND period, and there is a distinct node of dense settlement surrounding Paris, the newly formed seat of Monroe County (fig.

6.4). Purchase rates were generally lower during the FOURTH period (1834–55), but a secondary mode appeared in 1835–36 owing in part to purchases made by nonresident land speculators living in the eastern United States (Mason 1982). Many purchases made during this final period are concentrated in the southeastern portion of the locality on or near upland prairies.

Basic units of analysis are sixteenth section (roughly 40 acre) quadrats. In an attempt to control for the biasing effects of unequal availability (e.g., school land, railroad land, etc.) and the potentially randomizing effects of purchases made by nonresidents during the FIRST period, 57 of the 896 quadrats were excluded from consideration. Purchases made by other nonresidents and by eastern speculators in 1835–36 remain in the sample.[3] To avoid

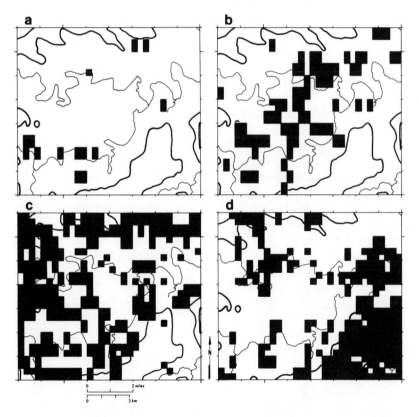

6.5. Distributions of first land entries in the Smith settlement locality by period: (*a*) FIRST, 1819–25 entries; (*b*) SECOND, 1826–29 entries; (*c*) THIRD, 1830–33 entries; (*d*) FOURTH, 1834–55 entries (from Warren, McDaniel, and O'Brien 1982).

problems of missing data for the GLOSOILS and GLOHAZEL variables (fig. 6.3), 224 quadrats positioned on section interiors also were eliminated. The resulting sample of 633 quadrats includes 19, 106, 275, and 233 units from the FIRST–FOURTH periods, respectively.

There are three basic questions we hope to answer with this analysis. First, are there significant differences among the characteristics of the quadrats being entered in each period? Second, which variables are most important for defining these differences, and how accurately can they predict purchase period groupings? Finally, what are the features of a model that accounts for observed trends, and how do these interpretations compare with results presented earlier? We use $n \times 4$ contingency tables and stepwise discriminant function analysis (with weighted prior probabilities and jackknife classification procedures; Jennrich and Sampson 1977) to answer the first two questions, and we use results of both procedures to deal with the third.

Results

As shown in table 6.1, thirty-two of the thirty-six variables used in the discriminant analysis are distinguished by deviant cells in eleven $n \times 4$ contingency tables of context variable by purchase period. Chi-square analyses indicate that all eleven context variables associate significantly with purchase periods at alpha $= .01$. Results of discriminant function analysis are consistent with these findings. Three canonical variables (CNV 1–3) were created from combinations of thirteen discriminating variables that entered the function, and the overall discriminating power of the canonical variables (as measured by an F-statistic of 14.65) is significant at a probability of less than .01 (table 6.2). Moreover, a matrix of F-statistics comparing pairs of purchase-period groups (not presented here) indicates that all groups are significantly differentiated from one another at probabilities of less than .01. Thus we can conclude that there are significant contextual differences among quadrats grouped by purchase period.

F-to-enter scores of discriminating variables denote the relative power of each for discriminating among purchase periods. These scores, used to order variables listed in table 6.1, indicate that soils evaluations made by GLO surveyors (GLOSOILS) are most powerful. Standard scores of purchase period means (also presented in table 6.1) suggest that purchasers during both

---

3. Because of the low frequencies of units entered in the Smith locality by nonresidents and speculators (chap. 5), land units purchased by these two groups of entrants were not excluded. However, a good case can perhaps be made for eliminating these quadrats as well, and we plan to do so in future analysis.

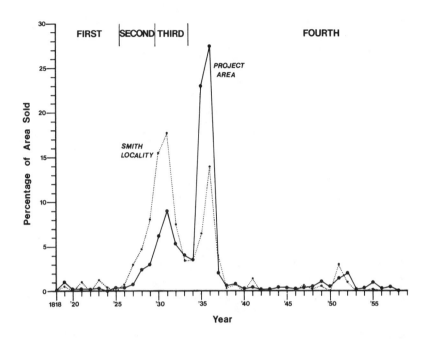

6.6. Percentage of federal land in the project area and in the Smith settlement locality entered during four periods.

the FIRST and SECOND periods selected for soils perceived as being of high quality, while those of the THIRD and FOURTH periods bought land progressively lower in perceived quality. What this appears to represent, however, is not a shift in the criteria by which buyers evaluated the land they purchased. Rather, shifts were due to changes in the pool of lands available for first purchase, since lands generally perceived as better were taken during the earlier periods.

It is notable that modern SCS evaluations of soil productivity (SOILPROD; rank 29) have considerably less discriminant power than do the nineteenth-century GLO soil evaluations, suggesting that perceptions of soil quality may have changed significantly since early historical times. Table 6.3 confirms this impression. It shows that while modern SCS soil evaluations are not randomly related with GLO soil productivity evaluations, the correlation between the two is very low (Spearman rank-order correlation = 0.158).

A strong selection for forested land among early purchasers is indicated by the second most powerful variable, GLOBIOME, which shows a monotonic decline in purchase period means from the FIRST to FOURTH periods. All

Table 6.1. Variable Patterning among Purchase Periods (Standard Scores), Relative Power of Variables for Discriminating Quadrats by Purchase Period (F-Statistic), and Order of Entry of Variables into Stepwise Discriminant Function Analysis

Discriminating Variables	Standard Scores of Purchase Period Means[a]				Discriminant Variable Entry		
	FIRST	SECOND	THIRD	FOURTH	F to Enter (step zero)	Entry Step	F to Enter (at entry step)
1. GLOSOILS	0.78[b]	0.86	0.66	-1.23	35.7	1	35.7
2. GLOBIOME	1.16	1.02	0.40	-1.03	23.3	2	21.5
3. NEIGHBOR 2	-0.86	0.92	0.59	-1.05	18.8	6	15.6
4. ROADDIST 5	1.83	-0.41	0.07	-0.05	14.7	5	17.1
5. SLOPEDIP 1	1.04	-0.95	-0.48	0.92	14.3	—[c]	—
6. SLOPEDIP 2	-0.57	1.18	0.46	-1.03	13.6	8	7.6
7. DRANCLAS 1	-1.25	-1.06	-0.31	0.96	12.7	—	—
8. ROADDIST 3	-0.65	-0.98	-0.61	1.22	11.7	—	—
9. PRAIRDIS 5	-0.70	1.46	0.02	-0.63	10.4	—	—
10. TREEDENS 5	-0.14	1.64	-0.05	-0.67	10.3	7	7.7
11. PERENDIS 3	-1.17	1.03	0.31	-0.74	8.5	—	—
12. PERENDIS 1	0.73	-1.33	-0.22	0.81	8.1	3	19.8
13. PRAIRDIS 1	-0.34	-1.58	0.86	-0.27	7.8	4	20.1
14. ROADDIST 1	-1.71	0.62	0.10	-0.26	6.9	—	—
15. GLOHAZEL	0.21	1.33	0.40	-1.10	6.8	—	—
16. NEIGHBOR 1	-1.67	-0.51	-0.35	0.78	6.7	—	—
17. DRANCLAS 3	0.24	1.69	-0.14	-0.63	6.2	—	—
18. NEIGHBOR 3	1.88	-0.27	-0.15	0.15	5.6	12	5.8
19. DRANCLAS 5	0.92	-1.13	-0.37	0.87	5.5	—	—
20. TREEDENS 3	-1.78	-0.69	0.63	-0.29	5.2	—	—
21. DRANCLAS 2	-1.81	0.06	0.50	-0.47	5.0	—	—
22. TREEDENS 4	-0.04	1.69	-0.16	-0.58	4.8	—	—
23. ROADDIST 2	0.52	1.54	0.11	-0.88	4.8	9	7.1
24. PRAIRDIS 2	1.72	0.68	0.19	-0.67	4.7	—	—
25. PERENDIS 4	-0.14	-1.63	-0.00	0.76	4.7	—	—

Table 6.1. *Continued.*

Discriminating Variables	Standard Scores of Purchase Period Means[a]				Discriminant Variable Entry		
	FIRST	SECOND	THIRD	FOURTH	F to Enter (step zero)	Entry Step	F to Enter (at entry step)
26. PRAIRDIS 3	-0.28	1.68	-0.45	-0.21	4.6	—	—
27. TREEDENS 1	1.86	0.79	-0.25	-0.22	4.6	—	—
28. DRANCLAS 4	1.95	0.11	0.00	-0.21	4.3	13	4.2
29. SOILPROD	1.84	-0.33	-0.20	0.24	4.2	11	6.1
30. PERENDIS 2	1.26	1.43	-0.17	-0.55	3.1	10	7.2
31. TREEDENS 2	1.30	-1.07	0.46	-0.16	3.0	—	—
32. PERENDIS 5	-0.74	-0.74	-0.74	1.26	2.3	—	—
33. PRAIRDIS 6	-0.34	1.66	-0.34	-0.34	1.7	—	—
34. ROADDIST 4	-1.70	-1.04	0.20	0.38	1.5	—	—
35. PRAIRDIS 4	1.96	0.29	-0.28	0.04	0.7	—	—
36. SLOPEDIP 3	-1.80	-0.85	0.12	0.40	0.6	—	—

[a]Scores were calculated using the grand mean of all cases on each variable, instead of the mean of purchase period means. Thus, sums of row scores may not equal zero.

[b]Italics denote deviant cells in n x 4 contingency tables (not presented here) in which cell chi-squares exceed minimum mean cell values of distributions that are significant at alpha = .01, and expected cell frequencies exceed 5.0.

[c]Variable failed to enter function owing to low discriminant power or preemption by a more powerful variable (or set of variables) with similar discriminating effects.

Table 6.2. Associated Eigenvalues, Percentages of Total Dispersion, Canonical Correlations between Discriminating Variables Entered and Dummy Variables Representing Purchase Period Groups, and Mean Purchase Period Coordinates of Each Discriminant Function

Canonical Variable	Eigenvalue	Percentage of Total Dispersion	Canonical Correlation	Mean Group Coordinates[a] FIRST	SECOND	THIRD	FOURTH
1	0.803	77.8	0.667	0.73	1.30	0.37	−1.09
2	0.141	13.7	0.352	2.07	−0.26	−0.02	−0.03
3	0.087	8.5	0.284	0.30	0.45	−0.31	0.14

[a]Approximate F-statistic $= 14.65$; df $= 39.0, 1,827.8$; $p < .01$.

variables except GLOHAZEL and SOILPROD are represented in the subsequent ten rankings, suggesting that a wide variety of both cultural and physical criteria were used in making land purchase decisions.

As implied by major discrepancies between the sequence of variables entered into the function and rankings of the potential discriminant power of discriminating variables, the list of variables entered is not a good indicator of variable importance. Stepwise discriminant analysis is an iterative procedure that selects variables capable of distinguishing between groups (purchase periods in our case) in light of the effects of variables already entered into the function. Variables failing to enter may have had low discriminant power to begin with (e.g., SLOPEDIP 1). Thus, thirteen variables are capable of distinguishing between purchase periods, but many more are needed to define all the significant patterning.

We also should emphasize that variables with good discriminant potential were not necessarily important considerations in land purchase decisions. Some may be accidental effects of others, and patterns among groups and variables must be examined to determine which are the variables of real significance. As indicated below, for example, TREEDENS 5 probably is a coincidental function of ROADDIST 1 and ROADDIST 2, since only the latter variables have consistent intergroup and intragroup patterns.

An important measure of the success of a discriminant analysis is the proportion of cases correctly classified by posterior classification procedures. After selecting discriminating variables and creating from them a new set of canonical variables, the program we used (BMDP7M) scores all cases on each canonical axis, calculates probabilities of group membership using data for all cases except the one being classified (jackknife procedure), and classifies each case into the most probable group. Our results, summarized in table 6.4, represent fairly good accuracy. Nearly two-thirds of all cases are correctly classified, and group proportions range from 42% to 72% correct. Nonetheless, we believe accuracy can be improved by adding new variables (e.g., proximity to towns; cf. figs. 6.4 and 6.5c), by refining certain context measurements, and perhaps by controlling the order of variable selection and entry.

Discussion

Distributions of mean group coordinates on canonical variables reflect important aspects of intergroup relations. If all group means fall on the grand centroid (i.e., coordinates 0,0,0), there probably are no significant differences among groups on the variables entered. If each group scores high on a unique canonical variable and lies on the centroids of most or all others (e.g., 3,0,0; 0,3,0; 0,0,3; 0,0,0), there are significant differences among groups, but there may be no intergroup relations that can be defined by linear combinations of one or more variables. However, if all groups grade from high positive to high negative scores on CNV 1 and have low scores on all others (e.g., 3,0,0; 1,0,0; −1,0,0; −3,0,0), there probably is a single linear combination of variables upon which groups are differentiated.

Mean coordinates of purchase period groups are plotted on canonical variables 1–3 in figure 6.7. Given the significant differences among groups documented earlier, it is no surprise that most groups are distant from the grand centroid. Of interest are the implications of intergroup relations. The FIRST period scores high on CNV 2 but is progressively nearer the centroids of CNV 1 and CNV 3, suggesting that initial purchases in the Smith locality differ from those of later purchases in some unique ways. Three entered

Table 6.3. Cross-Tabulation of a Soil Conservation Service Index of Soil Productivity (SOILPROD) on Early Historical Evaluations of Soil Quality by General Land Office Surveyors (GLOSOILS)

GLO Soil Evaluations	SCS Soil Productivity Index					Total
	23–44	45–50	51–55	56–59	60–80	
Poor	56^a	47	37	40^b	50	230
Poor/Good	6	12^a	7	11	8	44
Good	50	56	60	75	55	296
Good/rich	1^b	3^b	14^a	8	8	34
Rich	3^b	11	6^b	24^a	24^a	68
Total	116	129	124	158	145	672

Note: Data are 672 cross-classified quadrats in the Smith locality; $\chi^2 = 51.4$; df $= 16$; $p < .01$; $r_s = .158$.

[a]Cell overrepresented.
[b]Cell underrepresented.

variables correlate highly with CNV 2 (ROADDIST 5, SOILPROD, NEIGH-BOR 3), and two others correlate with both CNV 2 and CNV 1 (GLOBIOME, DRANCLAS 4).

In contrast, means of the SECOND, THIRD, and FOURTH periods are ordered monotonically from high positive to high negative scores on CNV 1 and show minimal associations with CNV 2 and CNV 3. This indicates that an important combination of associated discriminating variables is operating in the SECOND–FOURTH periods. Moreover, these variables may represent the adoption of a new conceptual model of desirable land distinct from that operating in the FIRST period. Variables correlating highly with CNV 1 include GLOSOILS, ROADDIST 2, and PERENDIS 2. Three others correlate positively with CNV 1 and negatively with CNV 2 (NEIGHBOR 2, TREEDENS 5, SLOPEDIP 2), one correlates negatively with CNV 1 and positively with CNV 2 (PERENDIS 1), and GLOBIOME and DRANCLAS 4 correlate positively with both CNV 1 and CNV 2. The only remaining entered variable, PRAIRDIS 1, correlates negatively with CNV 3 and depresses the THIRD period mean on that axis.

The results of discriminant function and chi-square analyses allow us to evaluate relations among groups and variables and to construct models of changing purchase period contexts. Quadrats purchased during the FIRST period were relatively distant from neighbors and roads, though both measures suffer somewhat from artificially high values of early purchases. After 1821 most purchases were near roads and neighbors, and the settlers' consideration of these factors appear to make a major contribution to the spatial clustering of settlements evident in figure 6.5*a*. Vegetation, soil, and landform variables have more consistent patterns. All FIRST period quadrats are in sparsely timbered or ecotonal forests (TREEDENS 1–2, PRAIRDIS 1), and this particular association is statistically significant at an alpha of .01 ($\chi^2 = 10.74$; df $= 1$). Most also have good ratings for GLO soils and high SCS

Table 6.4. Jackknifed Classification Matrix of Cases, in Which Classification Functions for Each Case Were Calculated Using Data for All Cases Except the One Being Classified

Group	Percentage Correct	Cases Classified by Group				Total
		FIRST	SECOND	THIRD	FOURTH	
FIRST	42.1	8	1	9	1	19
SECOND	45.3	0	48	51	7	106
THIRD	69.8	6	20	192	57	275
FOURTH	72.1	1	2	62	168	233
Total	65.7	15	71	314	233	633

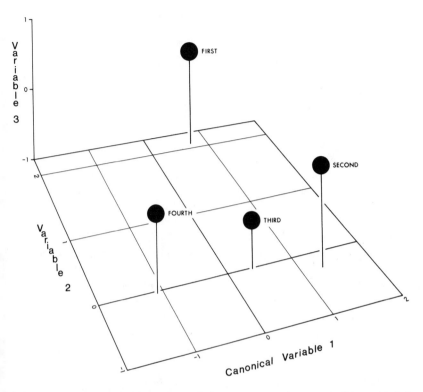

6.7. Three-dimensional plot of canonical variables evaluated at purchase period means (shaded circles), illustrating a linear configuration of the SECOND–FOURTH period means on variable 1 and an orthogonal relation to the others of the FIRST period mean on variable 2 (from Warren, McDaniel, and O'Brien 1982).

soil productivities, and a majority are in bottomland contexts near perennial streams. However, there were other places unsettled in the Smith locality that fit the latter criteria, suggesting that the forest variables were most critical.

Because the contexts of SECOND–FOURTH period quadrats are ordered along a single gradient, it can be argued that a common set of criteria influenced purchase decisions after 1825. Most SECOND period quadrats are in forests near roads and neighboring purchase units. The majority associate with good GLO soils on gently sloping valley sides, although these locations tend to have low SCS soil productivities. There also are statistically significant associations with certain TREEDENS and PRAIRDIS variables, but intra-group patterns are inconsistent. Both are incidental spatial correlates with ROADDIST 1 and 2, variables that characterize 80% of SECOND period quadrats and explain well the diagonal configuration of settlement shown in figure 6.5*b* (cf. fig. 6.4).

Quadrats of the THIRD period, positioned between those of the SECOND and FOURTH periods on CNV 1, tend to have intermediate scores on variables that distinguish earlier from later purchases. Cases in timber with good GLO soils and moderate slopes are still overrepresented. Quadrats tend to be near neighboring purchases (but not significantly nearer than cases in other groups), and significant numbers are on upland flats near prairie-timber borders. Also favored are locations within 2 miles of an incorporated town, though the relative strength of this variable has not been determined.

FOURTH period quadrats occur very near neighboring purchases in two distinct physical contexts: level upland prairies distant from streams and level floodplain forests near perennial streams. Both contexts have poor GLO soils evaluations but high SCS measures of soil productivity.

Patterns among purchase period contexts suggest that two distinguishable models of land value were used to make land purchase decisions in the Smith locality. Purchases by early frontier immigrants during the FIRST period focused on sparsely timbered or ecotonal forest with soils that contemporary observers judged to be of good quality. In comparison, later purchasers of the SECOND–FOURTH periods focused on locations near existing roads, towns, and previous purchases, ordinarily in forested contexts with perceived good soils. As purchase choices decreased through time owing to removal of desirable parcels from the pool of available federal land, there was a consistent progression away from optimum locations.

Conclusions

The question may be raised concerning how representative the Smith locality is of the central Salt Valley. As we discussed, from the aspect of forest density the area represents an anomaly when compared with the region as a whole. One reason for selecting the locality for intensive analysis was the low-density forest present over much of the 8 by 7 mile area. While other portions of the project area contain zones of similar low density, they are neither as large nor as continuous as in the Smith locality. Additionally, while the average density of timber across the 56 square mile area is indeed low relative to other areas of comparable size, there are pockets of timber along both the Elk and Middle forks with densities as high as any in the region. Several large areas with densities of 36 or more stems per acre occur on low bottomland terraces of the Middle Fork, and two areas (one approximately 1 square mile in size and the other approximately 3 square miles) of 53 or more stems per acre crosscut the drainages and extend up to the prairie edge. Thus, there is considerable variation in timber density—along with sizable pieces of prairie—within the locality.

Other reasons for selecting the area included the presence of settlement from 1818 on and the existence of considerable data concerning social relations. Given the time allotted for analysis, it would have been difficult to find another locality that was better suited to our immediate needs. For further analysis, we plan to expand the field of analysis eastward to include the early settlement around Pigeon Roost Creek—the Mt. Prairie settlement—to determine if our results from the Smith locality are substantially modified. As discussed in chapter 5, early farmstead locations in the Mt. Prairie settlement appear to be restricted to upland margins overlooking Pigeon Roost Creek (a perennial stream) or a tributary stream, and most are in forest but also near the ecotone. Hence our model undoubtedly will undergo future adjustments to account for the variability in settlement decisions as these variations are uncovered.

Irrespective of undiscovered trajectories of settlement, we can draw several important conclusions from this analysis. First, our results are consistent with an earlier hypothesis (Warren, O'Brien, and Mason 1981) that frontier settlement in the Smith locality was attracted by good soils that were sparsely timbered and could rapidly be cleared for cultivation. However, this combination of variables was important only during the initial phase of settlement and does not explain dense clusters of settlement during later periods. Second, recognition of two settlement decision models suggests that processes of early historical settlement in the Midwest are more complex than is often assumed. Initial settlers acquired timbered land of good quality that could be put into production rapidly and easily (often regardless of proximity to prairie-timber borders), while later settlers focused on good timbered land near routes of transportation, centers of commerce and service, and established land-holdings. Third, the importance of cultural distance variables to early land purchase decisions in the Smith locality affirms the significant effects of social and economic factors on patterns of settlement in midwestern frontiers (Bohland 1972; Mitchell 1977; cf. Hudson 1969). The importance of social factors is examined in the following chapter. Finally, discrepancies between the soil quality evaluations of GLO surveyors and modern SCS experiments indicate that perceptions of soil quality have changed during historical time and that modern soil survey data can be poor predictors of frontier settlement locations.

7

Social Dimensions
of Settlement

Michael J. O'Brien

In the two previous chapters our discussion centered on relations between frontier settlement and physical environmental dimensions. Although only brief mention was made in those chapters of the conditioning effects of various kinds of social relationships, our model of frontier settlement (chap. 2) predicts that kinship and other social relationships exerted considerable influence on settlement decisions. In chapter 5 we identified a number of early (pre-1830) settlement clusters across the lower half of the project area and discussed a few of the many known social relationships within certain clusters. In this chapter we examine two pre-1830 clusters in detail, along with one that developed in the early 1830s, in order to demonstrate that two distinct processes—budding and interdependent immigration—operated throughout the colonization phase, the latter lasting well into the spread phase. We also examine the processes that contributed to community growth, wherein settlement units expanded into adjacent areas and often were joined via intermarriage. Thus two distinct sets of kin-based social relationships are dealt with—those formed in the source areas and brought to the frontier, and those formed in the frontier by previously unrelated persons.

In addition to kinship, two other social dimensions have been predicted as having influenced settlement decisions in the Salt River valley—commonality of county of origin and religious affiliation (Mason, Warren, and O'Brien 1982; Warren, McDaniel, and O'Brien 1982)—but these predictions have never been adequately tested. Specifically, we predict that some settlement unit clusters were formed by unrelated families that shared a religious affiliation or were from the same county in Kentucky. If such patterning is found it remains to be determined whether the persons represented are tied by kinship bonds.

Kinship and Interfamily Relationships

During stage I, or the colonization phase of settlement, there are three spatial patterns that the distribution of farmsteads can take: random, clustered, or regular (chap. 2). Based on environmental considerations only, the model predicts an early tendency toward randomness, with a later tendency toward regularity. However, at this point the model ignores cultural factors that may impart significant selective advantages to settlers who locate near one another. It was predicted that some settlers—especially those immigrating in groups—took advantage of proximal settlement while others did not. Reasons for proximal settlement included cooperative labor, maintenance of existing social ties, exchange of food in times of stress, and defense. Therefore we expect to see a dualistic configuration, with both random and clustered farmstead arrangements in the same region. As shown in chapters 5 and 6, this indeed is the pattern noted.

During stage II, or the spread phase, we predicted that two phenomena—proximal budding and interdependent immigration—contribute to the growth of established farmstead clusters or the formation of new clusters. Also during this phase, as a result of continued immigration by families related to persons already established in the settlement and by unrelated families seeking an established settlement near which to settle, and because of the spread of settlement units through the purchase of additional land, the available niche space begins to fill up and settlement clusters begin to lose their spatial identity. Given the myriad social relationships that by that point have been formed and propagated, the settlement takes on the characteristics of an established community.

The settlement clusters examined in this section are the Smith settlement, which developed through interdependent immigration and intermarriage; the McGee settlement, composed of numerous interrelated families from Kentucky; and the Poage settlement, also composed of interrelated families from Kentucky. The three clusters are within or proximal to the 7 by 8 mile area used as a data base in chapter 6. Although our knowledge of intrafamily and interfamily relationships within these clusters is incomplete, we have a much better understanding of kinship ties within these groups than we do for other settlement clusters. As discussed in chapter 1, our decisions on which farmsteads to investigate archaeologically were based in large part on the amount of reliable information we had in 1977–78 concerning the interrelation of founding members of the Smith settlement (Henning, n.d.). Data relative to these relationships were checked thoroughly against records in Bourbon and Bath counties, Kentucky, and local Missouri counties and corrected where necessary. Information on residents of the McGee and Poage settlements was gathered from published and unpublished genealogies as well as from census records.

Additional research on these families undoubtedly would add substantially to our knowledge of interfamily relationships, but it also would be extremely time-consuming and expensive. In sorting out the individuals involved and their relationship to each other we have taken a conservative approach; for the most part we discuss only those persons whose identities we could establish with a high degree of confidence. Such an approach forces us to delete many entrants who, because of common surnames, probably were related to identifiable persons. Regardless, the data used are both reliable and strong enough to illustrate some of the social processes that conditioned settlement.

The Smith Settlement

The Smith settlement, situated in the northern half of T54N, R9W and along the southern border of T55N, R9W, was formed in 1819 by members of the Joseph H. Smith, Sr., family from eastern Bath County, Kentucky. Based on several lines of evidence, the Smith family was fairly prosperous. One bit of evidence is a Bath County court record that details a transferral of land from Joseph Smith to two purchasers sometime between 1815 and 1818.[1] During that period, Smith sold 208 acres bordering Slate Creek—a tributary of the Licking River—for $4,000. The Slate Creek area, in extreme eastern Bath County, is not by current standards a highly productive agricultural region. Steep slopes border a fairly narrow stream valley, and soil erosion is moderate to heavy. Based on the high sale price, we conclude either that there were substantial improvements to the property (farm buildings, fences, etc.) or that land prices in eastern Kentucky had reached outrageous levels by the second decade of the nineteenth century. A second indication of Smith's wealth is contained in his will (probated in Bath County in 1824), in which he bequeathed over $1,000 to his children.

Smith had four sons and three daughters, all except one of whom appear to have immigrated to the project area simultaneously. Two daughters were married before their arrival—Mary to John Johnson (Bath County, 1819) and Elizabeth to James Adams (date and place unknown). Except for Joseph H. Smith, Jr., who in 1824 married Jane Sidener in Bourbon County, Kentucky, the remaining children married after they arrived in the project area. The family made three purchases in 1819, each of roughly 80 acres: land entered in 1818 by Randolph Biggs (a nonresident) and later assigned[2] to Joseph Smith; an entry by Alexander Smith; and an entry by James Adams. Joseph

1. Suit for payment was brought against the purchasers by the Smith heirs in 1829, but the settlement papers (Bath County Court records, 17 July 1829) do not indicate the original purchase date.

2. An assignment was the transfer of the patent application from the original entrant (in this case Biggs) to the person who purchased the land from the entrant. It often took up to two years

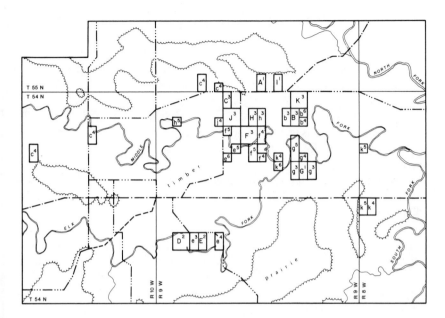

7.1. Locations of purchase units entered by members of the Smith, Mappin, and related families. Letters refer to individual entrants—capital letters denote first entries, and lower case letters denote subsequent entries (A, James Adams; B, Otho Adams; C, James C. Fox; D, Mary Johnson; E, James Mappin; F, Matthew Mappin; G, Alexander W. Smith; H, John B. Smith; I, Joseph H. Smith, Sr.; J, Joseph H. Smith, Jr.; and K, Samuel H. Smith). Numbers refer to period of purchase (1, 1818–20; 2, 1821–25; 3, 1826–29; 4, 1830–34; 5, 1835–36; and 6, 1837–59).

Smith's assignment and Adams's entry were a quarter mile apart, along the southern border of T54N, R9W (fig. 7.1). Alexander Smith's entry was several miles to the south, across the Middle Fork.

It is not entirely clear whether Joseph Smith, Sr., was ever an actual resident. Evidence against his residency includes the facts that early Ralls County tax records state that Alexander Smith paid the taxes on the property purchased in his father's name and that his will was filed and probated in Bath County, where he died. However, the way his will is worded leads us to conclude that he was a resident of Missouri but returned to Kentucky to file his will and live out his few remaining years. In his will he bequeathed ''unto my Daughter Mary Johnson the sume of Two hundred Dollars which I have already paid for the Quarter Section of land which She is living on''

---

from the date of entry to the issuance of a patent. During this interval, if an entrant resold the land, the patent office was notified so that an official assignment could be made. This bound the assignee to pay off the note if the land had been sold on credit.

(discussed below) and to "my son Samuel H. Smith & my son John B. Smith the Quarter Section of land which I have been living on and Two hundred & forty dollars out of my real & personal Estate to clear said quarter out of the land office." Thus he states that *he* had purchased his daughter's land at the St. Louis land office and that he resided on a quarter section of land. The latter point is an important one, because land in Kentucky was never surveyed on the rectangular grid system and is never referred to in land records in terms of sections. Both bequests therefore imply that he immigrated to the project area. Documentation of this is important to discussion of the budding process below.

There is a minor discrepancy between our records of land purchase—derived from plat maps and deed records—and Smith's will regarding the size of his landholdings. The records show that he owned only two quarter quarter sections (assigned from Biggs), but in his will he stated that he was living on a quarter section (160 acres). We have no answer for this discrepancy except to suggest that instead of buying two quarter quarter sections from Randolph Biggs in 1819 he actually purchased an entire quarter section. This would have joined his landholdings to those of his son-in-law, James Adams, instead of leaving a strip between the two.

The process of budding, whereby new settlement units split off from established ones, is illustrated by Mary Johnson's entry of a quarter section on Elk Fork in May 1821 (fig. 7.1). We assume that Mary and John Johnson resided with her family for the two years before her entry (paid for by her father) and then moved to the distant farm. This locale became a focus of interdependent immigration in 1824 when James and Aliazannah Johnson Mappin (John Johnson's sister) arrived from Bath County, Kentucky, and entered land to the east of the Johnsons' (fig. 7.1).

Beginning in 1827 the younger Smith sons began entering land: Joseph H. Smith (Jr.) entered a quarter section a mile southwest of James Adams's two land units; John B. Smith entered roughly 80 acres a quarter mile to the east of Joseph's holdings; and Samuel H. Smith entered a quarter section a quarter mile southeast of the family home (fig. 7.1). These entries, together with those of James Adams and Joseph Smith, Sr., formed a tight cluster of settlement along the north bank of the Middle Fork and on both sides of the road that had been built through the settlement in 1825. By this time several intermarriages had taken place, which led to changes in the settlement pattern. Two marriages involved the Smiths and members of a prominent family from the Middle Grove community a dozen miles to the southwest. In 1822 Ann Smith married James C. Fox, the son of Ezra Fox, who before 1820 had emigrated with his family from Fayette County, Kentucky, and founded the community at Middle Grove. In 1824 Alexander Smith married James Fox's sister Susannah. It was not until 1829, however, that James Fox entered land in the project area, finally purchasing a site that abutted the northern border of land entered by Joseph H. Smith, Jr. (fig. 7.1).

After John Johnson's death about 1826, his widow, Mary Smith Johnson, married Otho Adams (perhaps James Adams's brother), who in 1826 had entered land a half mile south of Joseph Smith, Sr.'s, assignment (fig. 7.1). In 1828 John Yates (place of origin unknown) purchased the Joseph Smith, Sr., assignment, and in that year his daughter Martha married Samuel H. Smith. In 1829 another Yates daughter, Sally, married John B. Smith, and in 1835 a third daughter, Nancy, married Ovid Adams, possibly a brother of Otho Adams or a son of James and Elizabeth Adams. Also during the 1820s, another resident of Bath County, Kentucky, Matthew Mappin, the brother of James Mappin, entered a quarter section bordering the Middle Fork. In 1826 Matthew Mappin married Eliza McGee, whose family settled along the Elk Fork (discussed in the following section).

The patterns followed by the Smiths, Mappins, and related families in making subsequent entries and purchases give some clues as to their desire to maintain the sense of community developed during the mid-to-late 1820s and their perception of the advantages of consolidating their landholdings for logistical reasons. For simplicity, we identify two basic patterns of land entry by an individual: *consolidated* (nucleated) and *dispersed.* If a person entered land more than a mile from his residence (defined as being situated on the initial entry) and there were no contiguous boundaries between the two parcels, we designate that pattern dispersed (O'Brien, Mason, and Saunders 1982:310). Conversely, if parcels are within a mile of each other, we designate the pattern consolidated.

One excellent example of consolidated landholdings is illustrated by the distribution of land entered by Alexander Smith (fig. 7.1). All entries were joined by common borders, creating a compact holding. Smith made additions to his initial 1819 entry in 1829 (160 acres), 1832 (40 acres), and 1835 (120 acres). The land, which lay south of the Middle Fork, was sparsely timbered, with soils rated by GLO surveyors as being of poor quality (fig. 4.9). Thus Smith's decision to consolidate his holdings was made at the expense of purchasing land with higher-quality soil, but the advantages obtained by entering interconnected land, which in his case was lightly timbered and easy to clear, clearly offset the disadvantages.

Another example of consolidated holdings is the distribution of land entered in sections 9 and 10 of T54N, R9W by Matthew Mappin (fig. 7.1). Between 1832 and 1836 Mappin entered land adjacent to, or within a quarter mile of, his original 160 acre entry. Mappin clearly was selective in his choice of land: in 1833 he passed up land adjacent to the 1828 entry in favor of another tract. It was not until 1836 that he purchased the 80 acres passed over previously. Matthew Mappin's 1833 entry appears to have been the result of a decision to enter land adjoining that of his brother James, who in 1832 sold his Elk Fork holdings, purchased the entire northern half of section 16 (school land), and relocated his farmstead there. Later entries by James Mappin were adjacent to the half section block and further solidified his holdings with those of his brother.

Most subsequent entries by other Smith sons and sons-in-law followed this consolidated pattern, though there were significant exceptions. For example, all of Samuel Smith's subsequent entries were several miles from his farmstead (fig. 7.1) and may have been speculative purchases. Speculation appears to have been the reason for James C. Fox's entries in T54N, R10W, one of which became the site of Paris in 1831 (chap. 5). If we exclude these probable speculative entries, the pattern of growth exhibited by the Smith settlement was one of consolidating holdings and filling in spaces between farmsteads. This presumably was the result of deliberate planning on the part of the interrelated families to maintain their social ties and take advantage of cooperative labor.

The McGee Settlement

Concomitant with the growth and development of the Smith settlement to the north was a growing array of settlements along the Elk Fork, whose origins provide important insights into the degree to which social relations conditioned the location of settlement units. Whereas the Smith settlement was formed only partially as a result of source-area marriages and subsequent interdependent immigration of family units, the McGee settlement developed from the immigration of several related family units, connected through many generations of intermarriage. It should be noted that this greatly compounded the problem of unraveling various relationships of community members, as did the number of identical first names and surnames listed in the archival material.

The first resident land entrant along that portion of the Elk Fork that fell within the heart of the McGee settlement—excluding Mary Johnson—was John McGee, who in 1823 entered a quarter section south of the river in section 31 of T54N, R9W (fig. 7.2). McGee was a member of a prosperous lineage that traced its roots in Kentucky back to the initial settlement of the state. His father, John McGee, Sr., came to Kentucky with James, Robert, and George McAfee, who in 1773 explored the central portion of Kentucky along the Kentucky River a year before James Harrod's heralded expedition. In 1775 McGee claimed 500 acres along the Salt River, in what was to become Mercer County, and constructed a cabin (McGee 1940). However, Indian raids soon forced the McGee-McAfee party to retreat to Virginia. In 1780, after the region had been made somewhat safer from Indian attack, the

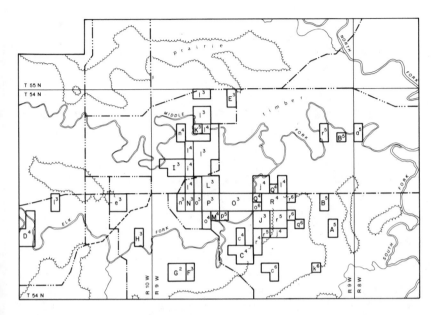

7.2. Locations of purchase units entered by members of the McGee, McKamey, Simpson, and related families. Letters refer to individual entrants—capital letters denote first entries, and lower case letters denote subsequent entries (A, George W. Cardwell; B, Wyatt Cardwell; C, John Forsyth(e); D, William H. McAfee; E, James J. McGee; F, Jane McGee; G, John McGee; H, John A. McGee; I, John S. McGee; J, Robert McGee; K, David A. McKamey; L, John McKamey; M, James B. Simpson; N, John M. Simpson; O, Robert Simpson; P, Walker D. Simpson; Q, Robert Smithey; R, William Smithey). Numbers refer to period of purchase (1, 1818–20; 2, 1821–25; 3, 1826–39; 4, 1830–34; 5, 1835–36; and 6, 1837–59).

McAfees and McGees settled the area permanently. John McGee, Sr., married Mary McCoun sometime before 1768, and Robert McAfee married her sister Anne about the same time. Thus was forged a bond among the three families that would continue across many decades and several frontier areas.

McGee received additional acreage from the Virginia Assembly, which gave him access to both sides of the Salt River in Kentucky. His land was bounded by that of George McAfee and James McAfee[3]—about 5 or 6 miles north of Harrodsburg (Mercer County). Within ten years McGee was able to replace his modest cabin with a stone house and to expand his landholdings (McGee 1940:315). Overlapping boundary lines, or shingled claims, which were prevalent in Kentucky at the time (chap. 3), ensnarled McGee, as they

3. McGee is listed in *The Certificate Book of the Virginia Land Commission 1778 & 9* as owning 1,400 acres (see the *Register of the Kentucky Historical Society,* vol. 21, 1923).

had other Kentuckians (ibid.; no mention is made of the disposition of the case). McGee died in 1810, leaving his wife and ten children. His widow and four of the children soon emigrated to Howard County, Missouri, and then to the central Salt River valley.

As had happened to countless immigrant families, tragedy struck the McGees soon after they arrived in Ralls County. In 1824, barely a year after he entered land south of the Elk Fork, John McGee, Jr., and his eldest daughter Mary were killed in a prairie fire while driving hogs overland from their previous home in Howard County. Undaunted, Jane McGee and her children and stepchildren[4] apparently continued to farm the quarter quarter section tract, and in 1826 she entered an adjacent two quarter quarter sections to the east (fig. 7.2). She soon was joined by her in-laws and their families: Robert and Peggy (McGee) Simpson in 1827, Jane (McGee) McGee and her husband Robert McGee (apart from being husband and wife, they also were first cousins) in 1828, and James and Polly (Wilson) McGee in 1828 (fig. 7.3). Along with Robert Simpson came his father and mother, John M. and Sarah Simpson, in 1827 and a brother, Walker D. Simpson, in 1828. A third brother, James Simpson, arrived in 1834. The Simpsons had lived on the Rolling Fork of the Salt River, in Mercer County, Kentucky. While the first entries of the McGees and Simpsons were not as clustered as those of the Smiths, all but one were south of the Middle Fork, in areas of low-density forest (fig. 7.2). The most clustered holdings were those of the Simpsons, whose first entries totaled approximately 560 acres, most of which lay along the northern bank of the Elk Fork.

Several other Mercer County families related by marriage to the McGees arrived in the project area in the late 1820s and early 1830s, including those of John McKamey and of his sister Margaret and her husband, John Curry[5] (possibly an older brother of Jane Curry McGee). The McKamey and McAfee families were united by several Mercer County marriages (fig. 7.4), including that of John McKamey and his first wife Margaret McAfee, the daughter of George McAfee. Immigrants related to the McAfees included Wyatt and George Cardwell (cousins) (fig. 7.5); Robert and William Smithey (brothers), who were married to Nancy and Martha Cardwell, respectively (Nancy was George Cardwell's sister and Martha was a cousin of Wyatt, George, and

4. John McGee, Jr., had been married twice, first to Mary Bingham (Mercer County, 1798), second to Jane Curry (Mercer County, 1816).

5. There are several Currys listed in *The Certificate Book* (see note 3) as owning land in what we can identify as Mercer County. James Curry owned land on the Salt River, adjacent to the holdings of Robert McAfee and William McAfee, and John Curry owned land on both sides of the Salt, adjoining land owned by Samuel Adams and William McAfee.

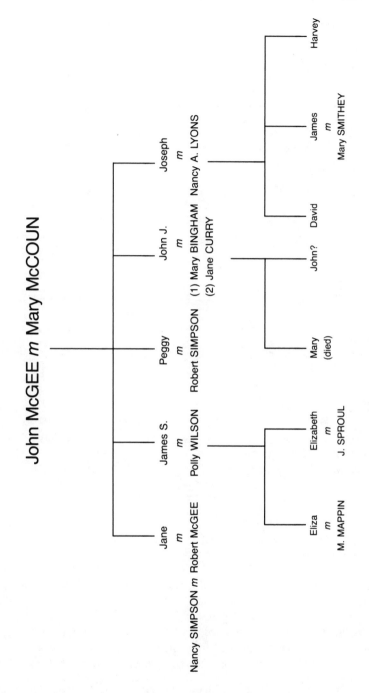

7.3. Diagram showing descendants of John McGee and Mary McCoun (McGee) and their marriages.

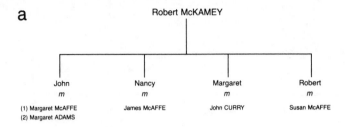

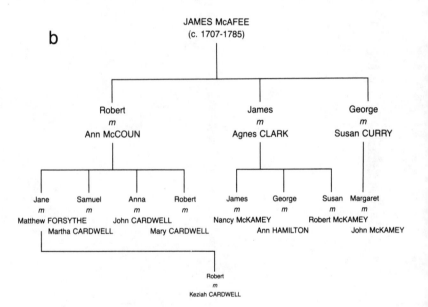

7.4. Diagrams showing intermarriage among McKameys, McAfees, and related families: (*a*) descendants of Robert McKamey and (*b*) descendants of James McAfee.

Nancy Cardwell) (figs. 7.4 and 7.5); and John Forsythe,[6] whose brother married a sister of George and Nancy Cardwell. Also during this period a number of other McGee families settled in and around the area. To simplify the myriad relationships discussed above, fig. 7.6*a* illustrates marriages between families that immigrated from Mercer County to the project area. Included are known marriages between persons who became residents of the

6. John Forsythe's father, Matthew Forsythe, settled near the McAfees in Mercer County and married Jane McAfee (daughter of Robert McAfee) in 1791 (Henning, n.d.). He also witnessed the will of John McGee, Sr., in 1808.

project area (solid lines) as well as those between family members who did not immigrate (dashed lines). The latter are included to demonstrate the degree to which certain families had intermarried in Kentucky.

Subsequent entries made by residents of the McGee settlement followed the trend noted for the Smith settlement, that is, a strong tendency for new entries or purchases to be adjacent, or in proximity, to initial entries. The pattern of land entry by John McKamey, the largest landholder in the settlement, documents some of the strategies a wealthy frontier agriculturist used in selecting land. In the five years before his death in 1833, McKamey

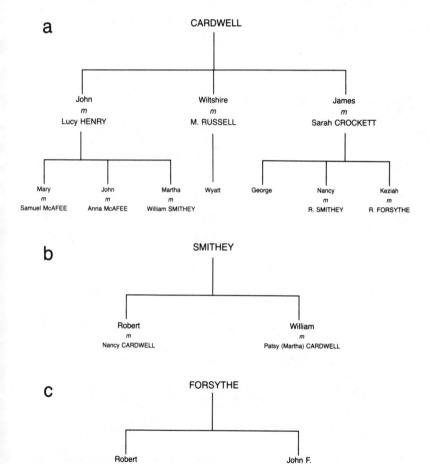

7.5. Diagrams showing intermarriage among (*a*) Cardwell, (*b*) Smithey, and (*c*) Forsyth(e) families.

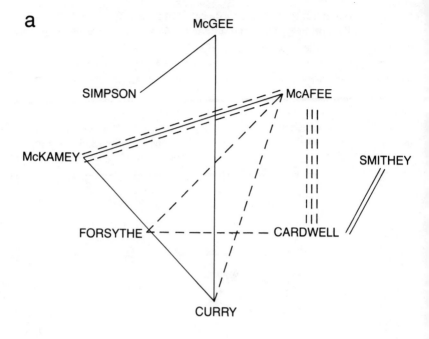

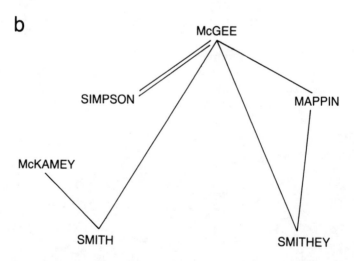

7.6. Diagram showing known marriages between families present in the McGee settlement: (*a*) marriages that predated immigration and (*b*) marriages that postdated immigration. In (*a*), solid lines represent a marriage of persons that afterward immigrated to the project area; dashed lines represent marriages of persons that did not immigrate.

entered more land (39 units, or roughly 1,560 acres) than any other five entrants in the Smith/McGee settlements combined. Except for a half section entered in T55N, R8W, his landholdings were consolidated and extended from the T54–55N line almost to the Elk Fork (fig. 7.2). McKamey's land was bounded by the three roads that were in existence by 1832, an advantage not claimed by any other area resident. As discussed elsewhere (O'Brien, Mason, and Saunders 1982:310), it appears that McKamey's goal was to consolidate his landholdings at the expense of entering land with more productive soil (based on GLO surveyor ratings) elsewhere in the general area. This strategy also was followed by the Simpsons and by John Forsythe.

Once the McGee settlement was established as a result of interdependent immigration, marriages between families continued (fig. 7.6b). For example, after the death of his wife Jane, Robert McGee married Nancy Simpson. There also were marriages between members of the Smith and McGee settlements, which by 1830 had begun to lose their spatial integrity as they spread toward one another. For example, in 1826 Matthew Mappin married Eliza McGee, the daughter of James S. McGee. By 1834 the number of Ralls County and Monroe County marriages among families discussed in this section was large (fig. 7.6b), and the interrelations were extremely complex. Interdependent immigration had effected a fairly tight spatial clustering of settlement units during the colonization phase—a clustering that continued through the spread phase as most entrants chose land near their initial entries.

The Poage Settlement

Beginning in 1830 a new cluster of settlement units formed just north of the Smith settlement, extending northward to Otter Creek (fig. 7.7). What is here termed the Poage settlement was composed of immigrants from Greenup County, Kentucky: six families consisting of sons and daughters of Colonel Robert Poage and his wife, Mary Hopkins Poage, and a related family, all of whom entered land along a narrow expanse of prairie that entered the project area from the west (fig. 7.7). Three families arrived in 1830: Thomas and Mary Ann (Powers) Poage, Richard D. and Harriett (Poage) Powers, and John and Ann (Poage) Stewart (fig. 7.8). All three families entered land that same year in addition to purchasing land with existing farmsteads and improvements. Powers's letter of 1831 to his parents in Kentucky (see chap. 5) states that for $300 he purchased 160 acres with a good cabin, loom house, stable, good cribs, and about 18 acres of cleared, fenced land. This is a significant statement, since the man from whom Powers purchased the land—Paul Herryford—had entered it only a year before.

Powers states that his brother-in-law, Thomas Poage, lived about a mile and a half from him; deed transactions indicate that he purchased the original Joseph H. Smith, Sr., homestead from John Yates, who had purchased it from

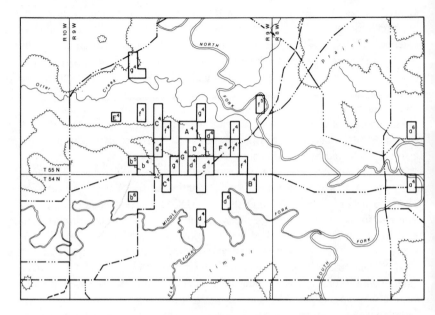

7.7. Locations of purchase units entered by members of the Poage family and related families. Letters refer to individual entrants—capital letters denote first entries, and lower case letters denote subsequent entries (A, Edmund Damrell; B, James H. Poage; C, Robert Poage; D, Thomas Poage; E, William Poage; F, Richard D. Powers; G, John Stewart). Numbers refer to period of purchase (1, 1818–20; 2, 1821–25; 3, 1826–29; 4, 1830–34; 5, 1835–36; 6, 1837–59).

the Smith heirs in 1828. He also states that Thomas "has as much land as I have." However, based on our data, Thomas actually had a bit more land. Powers also mentions his brother-in-law John Stewart as living about 2 miles away and owning 240 acres. This includes the 80 acre improved tract he purchased from James Adams.

Besides presenting us with information concerning the formation of the Poage settlement (and the environmental information cited previously), the Powers letter lends significant insight into various strategies of buying and selling land. He states that:

Each farm is partly prairie and all excellent land, though before we got it we had to experience some of what is called ups and downs for the want of someone to show us land and give us the numbers. Myself and Thomas rode at least one hundred miles before we got any satisfaction about it for want of some acquaintance who would show us.

We take this to mean that, coming into the frontier with no friends or acquaintances living there, they had no one to confer with on the availability

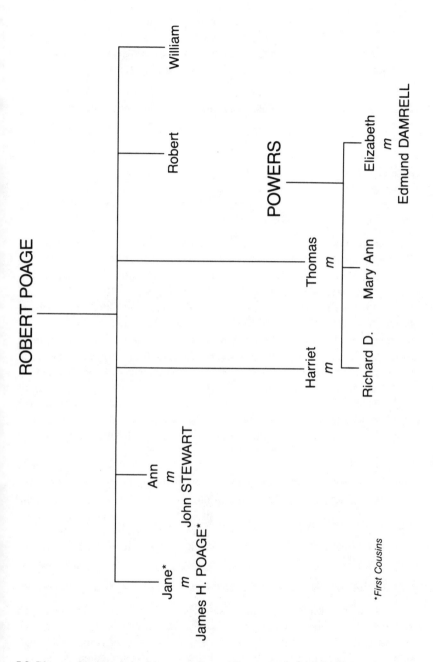

7.8. Diagram showing relationships among Poages, Powers, and related families.

or the price of land. Or his reference to "the numbers" might mean the rectangular grid demarcations. In any event, the deed records show that the three families bought the improved land before entering adjacent land.

Powers also gives us a clue as to the "selling mood" of established residents:

There is yet large portions of land of this description here yet to enter besides many places offered for sale second-handed at about the same rate that I purchased for. I would particularly speak of one piece of one hundred and sixty acres belonging to a Mr. Smith of this neighborhood, which he offers for four hundred dollars, which in point of soil nothing can exceed. The reason why so many are willing to sell is, that they may get money enough to enter two or three times as much as they sell. They frequently have other land in view of the neighborhood, and as soon as they pocket the money they are off to Palmyra to the land office.

We assume that the "Mr. Smith" he refers to is either Samuel, John, or Joseph Smith, Jr.

Shortly after their arrival, Poage, Powers, and Stewart were joined by four other related families: Robert and Ann Johnston Poage in 1831, Edmund and Elizabeth Powers Damrell (sister of Richard Powers and Mary Ann [Powers] Poage) in 1831, James H. and Jane Poage (she also being his first cousin and the daughter of Robert Poage) in 1832, and William and Ann McCormick Poage in 1833. Initial entries by these four families (there also may have been purchases of improved land) flanked those of the three earlier families and lay within 1.5 miles of them (fig. 7.7). Subsequent entries were made by six of the seven families, and except for later prairie entries by John Stewart and James H. Poage and an entry near the confluence of the North Fork and main stem of the Salt River by Edmund Damrell, the selected tracts lay in close proximity to the original settlement cluster.

In summary, the Poage settlement was similar to the Smith settlement in that the interdependent immigration of related families effected a strong clustering of settlement units in the frontier area. Unlike the situation in the Smith settlement, where marriage and proximal budding occurred during the latter half of the 1820s, Poage settlement members had married in Kentucky and brought developed family units with them to the frontier.

Commonality of Origin

In an effort to determine whether persons from the same counties in Kentucky or Virginia tended to locate near one another in the frontier, we plotted first entries of individuals with known counties of origin. Although only a small percentage of entrants listed non-Missouri counties as their residence on their patent applications, the number of entrants probably is sufficient to produce a significant pattern. As expected from previous discussion of interfamily relationships, there is a strong clustering, but one that is almost exclusively kin based. When settlement clusters that were the result of kinship and other family ties were removed from the plot, there was no clustering by county of origin. This significant lack of clustering might be the result of an inadequate sample, but a more plausible explanation is that the role of interdependent immigration, in which interrelated family units moved in a single group or in multiple groups, was so strong that it offset any need to find and locate near other residents from one's home county.

Religious Affiliation

The third social dimension considered here is religious affiliation, the implication being that persons of the same denomination tended to settle in clusters. Data concerning religious affiliation are rare, and our sample of residents of known denomination is small. However, a few church records are extant and have allowed us to form some preliminary conclusions. We preface the following discussion by noting that, while there are spatial clusters of individuals with like affiliation, the common denominator in most cases is interfamily ties. The exception may have been Catholics, who because of a general disdain of them, may have settled near one another.

An early Catholic settlement composed of interrelated families from Scott County, Kentucky, was situated along the prairie-timber boundary in the eastern portion of the project area. The settlement, which began in 1828, consisted of James Elliot and his sons (John and Matthew), Bernard Lynch, James and Raphael Leake (brothers), and Casper Hardy and his sons (George and Joseph). They were soon joined by several other families who located south of the earlier entrants. The Catholic community was served intermittently for many years by missionary priests from the St. Louis diocese, who offered mass in the homes of various residents. About 1840 a permanent church—St. Paul's—was erected in section 31 of T55N, R6W.

Another Catholic settlement was situated in T56N, R6–7W, only the southern border of which falls within the project area. Several entrants in this settlement were from Scott County, Kentucky, but because of the extent of the pre-1835 settlement and the fact that most of it lay outside the project area, our data on this imporant cluster are very incomplete. Mason (1982) notes that this Catholic settlement was not as compact as the one around St. Paul's, and that settlers of other denominations were interspersed among the Catholics. In 1845 the Catholic residents organized a parish and built St. Peter's Church; before this they probably attended the Catholic chapel in Cincinnati mentioned by Wetmore (1837:155).

A third Catholic settlement was situated along Indian Creek, in the northern half of T55N, R8W and the southern half of T56N, R8W. It began in 1830 with the arrival of nine families (three sets of two brothers [Green, Wimsett, and Miles] and one set of three brothers [Yates]). They were joined in 1835 by additional extended families (Pierceall, Carrico, and Hardesty). At least two families (Yates and Carrico) were from Washington County, Kentucky. The focus of this settlement was St. Stephen's Catholic Church, organized in 1833. The village of Elizabethtown (now Indian Creek) was platted in 1852 with the church at its center.

Several Presbyterian churches were founded in the region, the two most important to our discussion having been formed in the Smith/McGee settlement and in the Mt. Prairie settlement. The oldest church community in the project area was centered on the Pleasant Hill Presbyterian Church, just north of the Fayette–New London road in section 16, T54N, R9W. It was organized in 1828 by members of the McGee settlement; founding members were James McGee, Mary Ann McGee, John, Margaret, Elizabeth, Mary, and Rosannah McKamey, and Marietta, a "colored woman." Within two years the Powers and Poages had joined the congregation. Richard Powers mentions the church and its congregation in his letter:

As for society, we cannot complain; and there is Methodists, Presbyterians and Baptists, a few of each, but of the latter I believe the greatest number. There is a Presbyterian church constituted, I am told within a few miles of us [Pleasant Hill], consisting of eight or ten members. Indeed most of the people here seem to be sober, moral and orderly. We are all pleased with them.

The names of founding members of the Pleasant Hill Church, along with other residents of the McGee settlement, can be found in records of the New Providence Presbyterian Church in Mercer County, Kentucky. From the minutes of meetings held in 1821–22 (McAfee 1931), we were able to identify William and Thomas Smithey, John McKamey, and several families such as the Cardwells, McAfees, and Currys. The bond among members of the New Providence Church apparently was strong enough to induce the interrelated families to transplant their sense of religious community in the frontier area.

In 1831 a second Presbyterian church was established several miles to the east, in the Mt. Prairie community. Founding families included the Salings, Stuarts, Hickmans, Hannahs, and Meteers, some of whom lived several miles from the church site. By 1835, members of the Hannah families predominated in the rolls[7] of the church. In 1842 a third Presbyterian church was formed, at Paris, with most of the members coming from the Pleasant Hill congregation.

---

7. The Mt. Prairie Presbyterian Church record book is in the Western Manuscript Collection, State Historical Society of Missouri, Columbia.

Summary and Conclusions

We have proposed that three social processes—kinship, commonality of origin, and religious affiliation—contributed to the frontier settlement pattern observed in the project area. Of these, kin-based relationships were decidedly the strongest conditioning factors and, based on present evidence, subsumed the other two social dimensions. In summary, we note the occurrence of three processes in the formation of an early community: the interdependent immigration of families previously linked by source-area intermarriages; the budding off of family units and their settlement of proximal areas; and the intermarriage on the frontier of previously unrelated persons. Importantly, we note that the immigration of interrelated families was not necessarily accomplished in a single wave but continued well after initial colonization.

These findings generally support the predictions derived from the model of frontier settlement, but they also allow us to refine the model. One significant result came from analysis of the Poage settlement, where immigrants arriving in 1830 were able to purchase developed farmsteads for as little as half again as much as they paid for undeveloped land. Based on Powers's assessment of the mood of frontier colonists regarding resale of improved land, we conclude that while there was a spirit of community on the part of individual settlement members (in this case members of the Smith settlement) that kept landhold-ings in close proximity to one another during the early years of colonization, this feeling was easily replaced by a profit motive. In other words, once a community had developed past the formative stage and new relationships among its members were cemented, the advantages of settling near, or remaining near, kin may have decreased. In the case of the "intrusion" of the Poage-Powers-Stewart families into the Smith settlement, we speculate that after eleven years of living in proximity, its members had reaped the benefits of cooperative life and could afford to sell their improved land and move elsewhere.

Although such a lure existed and was seized upon by some members of the community, the fact remains that of the the original members of the Smith settlement only James Adams is known to have moved away from his initial residence, and, according to the scant data available, he left the region entirely. Census data and probate records indicate that most remaining members maintained their original farmsteads until death. The two excep-tions—Mary Johnson and James Mappin—both made moves that placed them closer to their kin and consolidated the sense of community in the Smith settlement.

Despite the fact that the three settlements discussed in this chapter formed at different times over an eleven-year period, they were remarkably similar in that they all consisted of related family units that immigrated within a few years of each other. However, we cannot assume that this phenomenon existed over the entire project area throughout all time periods. Although there is preliminary evidence that interdependent immigration was widespread throughout the colonization phase (keeping in mind that some areas of the region were colonized late)—for example, in the Ely and Leake settlement clusters in the eastern portion of the project area and in the Indian Creek settlement (chap. 5)—more detailed research is needed to evaluate such evidence.

Once settlement clusters were formed they grew rapidly through the budding off of individuals from the family unit, continued immigration, and the purchase of additional land by residents. Intermarriages between related and nonrelated members strengthened ties within the community, adding to or in some cases replacing existing social relationships. Ties among families of like religious affiliation probably developed similarly and would have led to cooperative arrangements and intermarriages, as evidenced by Monroe County marriages between members of the Poage and Mt. Prairie communities during the 1840s. Once these social dynamics were in force, individual settlement clusters across the region began to lose their spatial integrity, signifying the end of the colonization phase of settlement. The spread phase, which began in some areas much earlier than in others, then began in earnest, taking the settlement of the region out of the frontier period.

8

The Built Environment

*Michael J. O'Brien and
Dennis E. Lewarch*

The frontier farmstead, which included a house and usually residence service structures, fences, and various outbuildings such as barns and sheds, was the focal point of what we termed in previous chapters the basic settlement unit. As discussed in chapter 1, the description and analysis of this "built environment," that is, "the distribution of buildings by which people attach themselves to the ground" (Stone 1965:347), is one important aspect of settlement geography. But, given our interest in the function of settlement components, a mere description of the distributions of structural types falls short of our objective.

Our analysis of the built environment is conducted at several levels, beginning with the spatial arrangement of farmstead components and then narrowing to a discussion of dependency structures. Extant farmsteads in the project area dating to the pre-1850 era are rare, which hinders analysis of their components. Within the impact area of the Cannon Reservoir, several early farmsteads were maintained until the early 1970s, when they were purchased by the Corps of Engineers. When the land on which they were situated was sold, many farm structures were destroyed through vandalism and salvage operations. By the time site survey was carried out late in 1977, few outbuildings were standing. The few that did remain consisted mainly of heavy-timber barns that could not easily be dismantled or buildings that were in such poor condition that reusable materials could not be salvaged (O'Brien, Mason, and Saunders 1982). Many early farmsteads also have been modified by later construction and remodeling to the point that the original architectural form cannot be discerned. Although several structures remained long enough for us to study them in detail, our sample of farmstead components is woefully small. Thus we treat the structures as a sample of the architecture of the region, not as a complete inventory.

Spatial Arrangement of Farmsteads

The typical pre-1850 farmstead in the region consisted of a residence, house service structures, and farm dependency structures. The location of the residence and related structures usually was determined by topography, vegetation, or aesthetics (O'Brien, Mason, and Saunders 1982:312). The residence often was placed with the long axis (facade) parallel to the main access through the property, whether this was a public road or a private lane. The house usually was sited to take advantage of natural drainage, with service and dependency structures downslope from it. In a few instances the barn and barnyard were placed in front of the house because the terrain sloped to the rear.

Change in the economic status of a person or family often led to changes in farmstead composition and configuration, including replacing the house with a more elaborate one and upgrading other buildings. Although our data are not rigorous enough to adequately test the proposition, it is probable that the differences between farmsteads belonging to a subsistence farmer and to a farmer producing for a market economy were dramatic, the former consisting of a barn and a shed or two, and the latter including a variety of specialized structures (O'Brien, Mason, and Saunders 1982:312).

One well-documented example of modification in farmstead layout through time is the Samuel H. Smith farmstead, situated in the Smith settlement (fig. 8.1). The farm, which operated for over 140 years, exhibits a life history that is common in rural areas: the number of structures grows until a peak is reached, declines as modern farming practices replace older ones and electricity obviates the need for springhouses, icehouses, and smokehouses. The farmstead began about 1830 when Smith erected a single-pen log house on a quarter section he had entered in 1828. Within a few years he constructed a double-pen log house that abutted the original cabin (discussed later in this chapter). We presume the original barn sat on or near the site of a later transverse-crib barn. Over the years Smith (and eventually his son-in-law) added structures for hogs, sheep, and chickens, corncribs, a milkhouse, an icehouse, a smokehouse, and a root cellar.

Smith's ability to expand his farmstead was made possible by his acquired wealth, which may have been greater than that of his neighbors. This wealth was symbolized by the construction about 1850 of a large timber addition to his already massive log home (discussed later in this chapter). This created what must have been one of the most impressive pre-Civil War residences in the area, adding to Smith's prominence in the community.

Another farmstead over which we have fairly precise temporal control is that constructed about 1840 by Robert Eakin, a then-recent immigrant from Kentucky. The farmstead was situated along the upper edge of a steeply

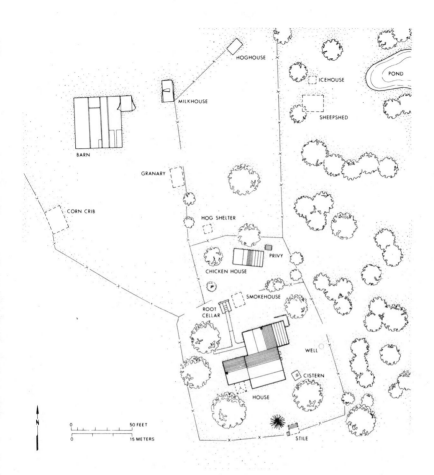

8.1. Spatial configuration of the Samuel H. Smith farmstead.

dropping terrace, overlooking the broad Middle Fork floodplain. The crop fields were to the south, in the bottomland; a small garden and orchard were to the west. As with the Smith farmstead, the house sat in a small yard enclosed by a wire fence, with the house service structures—a cellar, a smokehouse, and two sheds—close by (fig. 8.2). Farm-related structures were situated outside the enclosure in two clusters, out of the line of sight from the house: a transverse-crib barn to the east, and a hoghouse and a henhouse to the west.

A third intact early farmstead is that of Daniel Johnson, the son of John and Mary Smith Johnson (chap. 7), early settlers who entered land along the Elk Fork in 1821. The house and dependency structures (fig. 8.2) were construct-

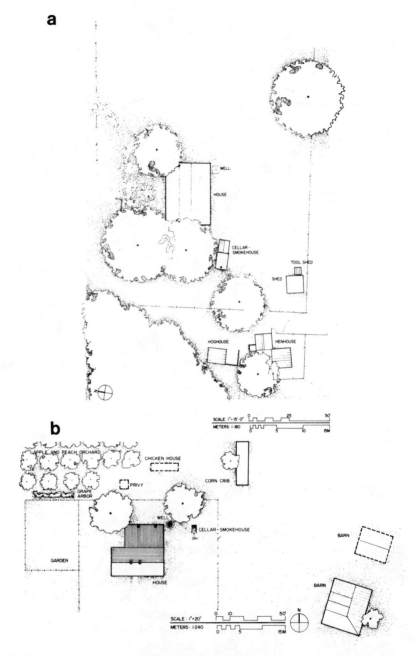

8.2. Spatial configurations of (*a*) the Robert Eakin farmstead and (*b*) the Daniel Johnson farmstead.

ed about 1840, in a large bottom south of the Elk Fork. The story-and-a-half log house was sited to face a steep hill and small tributary stream to the south; a well and cellar-smokehouse were placed to the east of the house. The yard surrounding the residence was fenced, and outside the yard to the north were a privy, a chicken house, and a log corncrib. To the east of the house was a large timber barn.

Farmstead Components

The remainder of this chapter examines the two major components of the farmstead—the barn and the residence. Since our sample of barns is extremely small, we make no effort to establish a formal classification of them but rather refer to established types. Three types of pre-1850 barns were noted in the project area: the transverse-crib barn, which predominates; the single-crib log barn, of which only one example is known from the area; and the bank barn, represented by a single structure. However, we can conclude from the deteriorated condition of most early farmsteads, many of which were abandoned in the early twentieth century, that the barns that exist today represent only a small sample of the original number of structures. Hence, vestiges of the truly early barns, which probably were little more than single-pen log structures, are gone forever. Thus our sample is skewed in favor of the more massive, well-constructed examples that do not represent the wide range of variation that existed during the early years of settlement.

On the other hand, our sample of residential structures is a more reliable indicator of variability. Because they represented a considerable investment of time and labor, cabins and houses were cared for and repaired when necessary. Often, original structures were incorporated into later renovation plans, so that the original structural fabric was preserved. For example, the original log house constructed about 1828 by Matthew Mappin was used as a summer kitchen after 1840, when a large, half-timber structure was erected abutting it. The log house was reroofed and the exterior covered with clapboards. Although the log house was demolished in 1893 to be replaced with a Victorian-style addition, a photograph taken shortly before demolition shows the log house and its detail, facilitating our interpretation of the site.

As we discussed above with regard to barns, our sample of early houses obviously includes only those that have withstood time and weather. Completely missing from the sample are the initial temporary structures that probably were quickly erected when a family moved into the region. A number of folk sources indicate that these could be built in a few days, with the construction of a more substantial residence delayed until more time could be dedicated to the project. In any event, the sample includes a wide range of

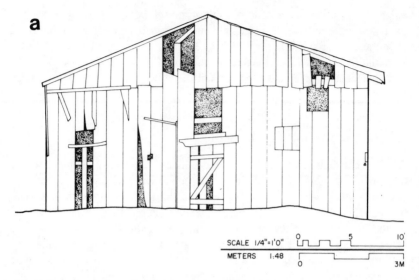

SCALE 1/4"=1'0"

METERS   1:48

8.3. (*a*) East elevation and (*b*) floor plan of the Mitchell Meteer barn.

single- and double-pen log houses, as well as half-timber structures, and is large enough that a formal classification is used to order the sample.

Barns

Marshall (1981:72) states in his excellent survey of folk architecture in Little Dixie[1] that, although no new house or barn types were developed in the region, one particular type of barn, known as the transverse-crib, is widespread across the area. Transverse-crib barns began in the East in the early nineteenth century, and the form was carried westward by emigrants (Kniffen 1965). Once established in areas such as northeast Missouri, it gradually replaced other early types such as the English and double-crib types (Marshall 1981). In form, the transverse-crib barn contains a long central passageway parallel to the gable that is flanked on both sides by stalls and grain storage bins. Montell and Morse (1976:70) note that most early transverse-crib barns in eastern Kentucky, whether constructed of logs, framing, or a combination of the two, are usually 20 to 50 feet long, with the flanking stabling areas usually divided at 8 to 10 foot intervals to produce individual stalls.

1. Little Dixie is a folk term for the region in north-central Missouri comprising Monroe, Ralls, Pike, Boone, Howard, Randolph, Audrain, and Callaway counties. It is based on shared cultural components of the upper South tradition.

b

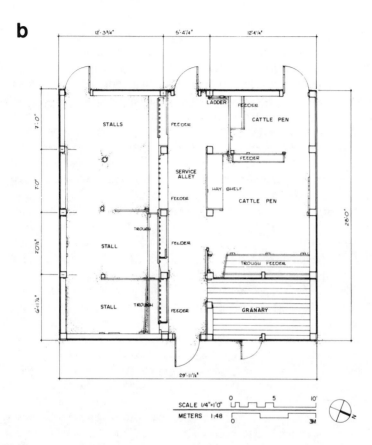

SCALE 1/4"=1'0"
METERS 1:48

The best-preserved transverse-crib barn that we can accurately date to the pre-1850 era is that built about 1847 by Mitchell Meteer. In 1978 the barn was one of only two remaining structures from the extensive farmstead Meteer constructed near the South Fork of the Salt River. The floor plan consists of a central service alley 4.5 feet wide and 28 feet long with a door at each end that runs the length of the structure; livestock stalls and a small granary flank the service alley (fig. 8.3).[2] Along one wall of the alley are feeders that allow feed to be passed through to troughs on the other side. Haylofts were created by laying boards across the joists above the stalls, with openings so hay could be dropped into the service area below. The only wooden flooring is in the granary; the rest of the barn has an earthen floor.

The structural system is an architectural masterpiece (fig. 8.4). Structural

2. The drawings and description of the Meteer barn are adopted from the Historic American Buildings Survey report.

members are circular-sawn white oak timbers that were joined using a combination of butted-and-nailed and pegged mortise-and-tenon construction. Twenty 8 inch square posts constitute the major support for the structure and define the spatial organization within, three bays by four bays (fig. 8.3). The barn is composed of five braced-and-framed transverse sections (bents) raised into place and tied by structural members running longitudinally (parallel to the gable). Columns on the longitudinal exterior walls are topped by 5 inch by 8 inch rafter plates, and the two rows of interior columns are topped by 5 inch by 8 inch rafter plates that receive the short secondary rafters. Four levels of 3 inch by 8 inch girts along the exterior walls provide blocking between the columns and carry the vertical plank sheathing. Each column is diagonally braced in at least one direction. Rafters (2 inches by 5 inches), spaced 24 inches apart on center, are notched at the plates and rest on shorter but more steeply pitched secondary rafters at the ridge. The rafters are joined at the ridge without the use of a ridge board. Flat-laid floor joists (3 inches by 5 inches, 16 inches on center) in the granary are notched at the ends and rest on notched sills. The major 3 inch by 7 inch joists for the hayloft are pegged into the columns, while the minor 2 inch by 6 inch joists that alternate with these (42 inches on center) rest on tapered horizontal strips nailed to the intermediate beams.

Like many transverse-crib barns in the region, the Meteer barn underwent several alterations of the original form described above, such as the addition of shed wings that have long since disappeared. Unlike many examples, this particular barn did not have interior doors that opened into individual stalls. Curiously, one entire bank of stalls could be entered only through a single outside door. Except for this peculiarity, the barn is quite similar to several structures illustrated by Marshall (1981) for the Little Dixie region, especially one in Randolph County that dates about 1850.

Kniffen (1965), in his often-cited article "Folk Housing: Key to Diffusion," states, "It was an easy transition from the four-crib barn to what is called here the transverse-crib barn, simply by adding cribs to occupy the side openings, leaving a long, gable-opening structure with passage through the center, stables and storage provided by the cribs on either side" (p.564). While no double- or four-crib barns were found in the project area, there is one recorded example of a single-crib log structure that subsequently was incorporated into an enlarged barn. The crib was part of a farmstead constructed about 1830 by Stephen Scobee, Sr., on the east bank of Pigeon Roost Creek, in the Mt. Prairie community. The crib measured 14 feet 10 inches by 7 feet 5 inches and was constructed of rough-hewn logs joined by square notching. At a later date a small frame crib was joined to one of the shorter walls and a doorway was cut between the two cribs. Another bank of two cribs was constructed parallel to the first with a drive-through alley 8.6

feet wide between the two crib banks. The long crib and abutting frame crib were enclosed with vertically placed planking, while the other bank was enclosed with diagonally placed slats with 3 inch openings between slats. In final form the structure is reminiscent of English barns, though the drive-through is in the gable end.

Also located on the Scobee farmstead is another barn type unique in the project area, the banked barn. This particular example, which probably dates about 1849, was constructed of limestone slabs and heavy, hewn timbers. A sideslope of the terrace containing the farmstead was partially excavated, and courses of dressed limestone slabs were placed in the depression to a height equal to that of the terrace. The rear wall measured 40.5 feet long and stood approximately 6 feet high; the side walls were approximately 25 feet long. Two interior slab walls were added, creating a central vault with two small flanking vaults. Access to the vaults was from the base of the slope. The superstructure, which was entered from the terrace, had collapsed before field

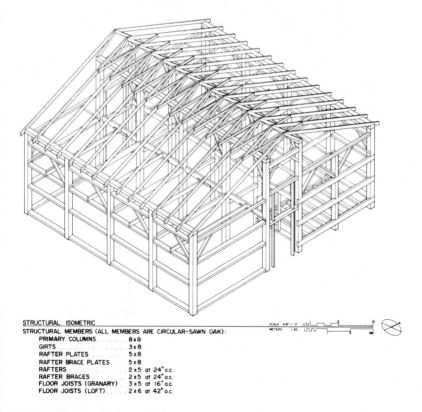

STRUCTURAL ISOMETRIC

STRUCTURAL MEMBERS (ALL MEMBERS ARE CIRCULAR-SAWN OAK):

PRIMARY COLUMNS . . . . 8 x 8
GIRTS . . . . 3 x 8
RAFTER PLATES . . . . 5 x 8
RAFTER BRACE PLATES . . . . 5 x 8
RAFTERS . . . . 2 x 5 at 24" o.c.
RAFTER BRACES . . . . . . 2 x 5 at 24" o.c.
FLOOR JOISTS (GRANARY) . . 3 x 5 at 16" o.c.
FLOOR JOISTS (LOFT) . . . . 2 x 6 at 42" o.c.

8.4. Isometric drawing of the Mitchell Meteer barn.

inspection. It had been constructed of large timbers, the dimensions of which ranged up to 9 inches by 13 inches. All observed timbers exhibited mortise-and-tenon joinery.

Residences

One result of archaeological survey and archival research was the identification of more than 350 pre-1920 residences, some of which consisted of foundations, piles of rubble, or known locations with no visible signs of a building. The goals of this survey included determining which structures/sites were eligible for inclusion on the National Register of Historic Places; dating main blocks of, and additions to, those structures; mapping those residences and related farmsteads (discussed previously); preparing architectural renderings of houses determined eligible; and examining functional and stylistic differences among the structures.

To adequately meet these goals, we needed a means of objectively measuring similarities and differences among structures—a need that was met by developing a classification system for rural residential architecture. As pointed out elsewhere (O'Brien et al. 1980), such as classification was used as an initial sorting procedure for determining the eligibility of a structure for inclusion on the National Register. Used in such a way, it can answer questions such as: Are there similar or identical structures present in a particular area, some of which may not need intensive study owing to duplication? Before introducing the classification system, we turn our attention in the following section[3] to architectural style and function, the two major components of our analysis of frontier houses.

STYLISTIC VERSUS FUNCTIONAL VARIABILITY

House form is conditioned by a host of factors that operate at several levels of specificity. We focus here on only two factors: style and function. *Style,* as used here, refers to architectural features that do not directly affect activities carried out by the group occupying the structure. Style is easily observable and serves as a basis for distinguishing one structure from another. *Function* refers to architectural attributes that aid, condition, or in some way relate to activities performed within or adjacent to a structure. House *form,* then, is a phenomenological entity (i.e., it exists, can be defined, etc.) that is composed in part of stylistic and functional components. Style and function, though treated here as mutually exclusive, are often difficult to separate analytically. For example, facade structure, especially the order of window and door placement, is usually considered part of architectural style.

3. The section is a revised version of O'Brien et al. (1980).

Yet entry placement conditions traffic flow, access, and ventilation, while window location and frequency affect available light, ventilation, and heat loss in the winter.

Similarly, a second story is treated as a stylistic element, yet its construction is conditioned to some degree by economic factors, family size, control of technology, and possibly kinship ties. Facade characteristics of second stories, though part of architectural style, thus are conditioned not only by factors that determine whether a second story will be built but also by previously noted functional considerations of light, ventilation, and heat loss. In making inferences about function, it is likely that the classification system described here will imply far more overt, conscious decisions about use of space and adaptation to the environment than were actually recognized by the early Euro-American inhabitants of the Salt River valley. Many of the attributes noted here as being functionally conceived might, in fact, be the product of random or somewhat arbitrary decisions, though repetitive patterns in functional groupings might argue against this interpretation.

The existing literature provides few guidelines for systematic classification of architecture. Treatments by architects, folklorists, and rural settlement geographers are almost exclusively descriptive in nature, while anthropological and archaeological works often place more emphasis on functional attributes. Kniffen (1965:552), a geographer, presents one interpretation of the architect's point of view: "Aside from a few architectural historians, the architect's interest is not in origins, diffusions, or alterations of folk types. It rather focuses on the 'architectural period' represented by the more pretentious structures." Kniffen's own view is that folk housing "reflects cultural heritage, current fashion, functional needs, and the positive and negative aspects of noncultural environment" (1965:549) and is observable through analysis of form, height, floor plan, roof pitch, and other features. Another geographer, Stone (1975:188), provides general guidelines for analysis of residences by listing the kinds of dimensions suitable for analysis, such as horizontal plan, shape, size, and use of space; vertical plan, shape, size, and use of space; type of roof; construction materials; and internal and external architectural detail.

Perhaps because of their affinity with archaeological remains, "where stone foundations or post-mold patterns are the only evidence" (Kniffen 1965:553), anthropologists have treated houses with more of a functional emphasis than is apparent in treatments by geographers. Perusing the anthropological literature on housing (e.g., Flannery 1972; Hunter-Anderson 1977; Robbins 1966; Whiting and Ayres 1968) illustrates the range of factors that seem to affect the built environment, including variation in the physical environment, level of technology, and the subsistence base. Hunter-Anderson approaches residence analysis through the logic of a functional model. To her, the form of residential activity is determined by the set of domestic activities composed of living elements (biological functions such as sleeping and eating) and role elements (each person's role in society). Residences are defined as domestically oriented constructs protecting occupants from the environment while allowing them to move within the structure and in relation to one another (Hunter-Anderson 1977:301–3). This approach emphasizes the kinds of activities to be carried out within a building in terms of the range of activities, their scheduling, group size associated with each activity, spatial requirements, frequency, and technological requirements. We can infer that such functional basics will be reflected to some degree in floor area, floor plan, number of rooms, and the frequency and placement of doors, windows, stairs, and porches. Specific attributes of these dimensions condition access, traffic flow, effective heat and light, or activity space, all important considerations relating to activity sets within a household. The functional import of such attributes, selected on logical, a priori grounds, does, in fact, have considerable support from three independent sources: nineteenth-century manuals on construction of farm buildings, ethnoarchaeological field observations, and historical excavation beneath structures.

Although summaries of "ideal" behavior were certainly not followed by all who built farmhouses, primers or construction guides do provide clues about "normative" rules taken into account when designing and building. Allen (1853), for example, stresses convenience, especially in terms of space for, and access to, household activities. Effective use of heat and light are especially important in the floor plans Allen illustrates. Activity-intensive areas such as the kitchen and family rooms all have two or three windows, whereas rooms with fewer activities (or those used at night, such as bedrooms), are illustrated as having single windows. Placing chimneys centrally in northern climates serves to warm lower and upper story rooms without fireplaces. Conversely, designs for southern climates usually place chimneys on end walls, if hearth activities are not carried out in separate buildings, to minimize heat during the summer.

Ekblaw's (1914) construction guide for farm structures emphasizes functional features. The kitchen, for example, requires good lighting and ventilation, adequate work space, and few doors to maximize wall space for storage. The importance of the living room, especially its multifunctional and multigroup dimensions, is represented in effective heating from a fireplace and abundant light from multiple windows. The multiple nature of activities in this room was stressed by noting "in olden times, there was perhaps greater attention given to the living room than any room in the house" (Ekblaw 1914:267).

Following similar lines of thought, archaeologists have long been concerned with activity structure, though often in an intuitive, implicit fashion.

Most discussions of activity, framed in terms of the poorly defined concepts of "tool kit" and "activity area," are based on distribution patterns of portable artifacts (Schiffer 1976; Struever 1968). Analysis of room functions or activities, where standing walls are available, has also emphasized portable artifacts, though structural elements such as hearths and benches have also been used (e.g., Healan 1974; Hill 1968; Schiffer 1976).

In an attempt to generate hypotheses about processes that condition activity patterns and subsequent patterns in archaeological material, archaeologists have undertaken ethnological fieldwork (e.g., Binford 1978*a,b*, 1980; Yellen 1977). Insights gained during such work can be framed as working hypotheses and evaluated against the architectural record. Mention has been made of variables such as floor area, spatial relations of chimneys, windows, and doors, traffic flow, and other factors that appear to condition activities. Although he is describing pattern in portable artifacts, Binford's remarks are applicable to the study of activity sets within structures:

Some activities interfere with others. Similarly, some activities require more or less space, more or less time to completion, and more or less participants. In addition, activities vary in the amount of debris or pollution (noise or oder) produced during the course of performance. They further vary in the relative degree to which the debris or pollution is noxious and this inhibits or disrupts the performance of other activities. [Binford 1978*b*:354]

Pattern in portable artifacts appears to be a function of such constraints, as Binford outlines. Formal properties of architecture should also reflect the activity sets likely to be carried out within a structure.

Given seasonal variability in temperature and precipitation, one of the most important constraining factors might be the winter interior activity set, where multiple activities, both domestic and other kinds, that ordinarily might take place outside or in dependency structures are forced inside a residence owing to inclement weather. It is thus useful to consider those domestic activities regularly performed, regardless of weather, as constituting the basic domestic activity set. Solutions to seasonal activity differences include scheduling activities in advance so they need not be carried out during times of inclement weather. Degree of technology conditions this somewhat, especially regarding storage capability. Repetitive maintenance and domestic tasks are difficult to reschedule and therefore must be accommodated within a single structure.

That multiple activities are carried out in different rooms and that some areas of houses are more activity-intensive than others is well documented by the differential distribution of portable artifacts found during archaeological excavations (chap. 9). Perhaps the best example of an overlapping activity area is the zone adjacent to a fireplace, where the availability of heat and light forces the concentration of activities ranging from cooking to manufacture of wooden implements. Using foundation outlines, we can plot distributions of portable artifacts against floor plans to relate activity structure more directly to areas of the house (chap. 9).

To summarize, while it is difficult to obtain a detailed list of architectural features suitable for analysis of rural houses, a general system can be created from architectural history, rural settlement geography, anthropology, and archaeology. Kinds of stylistic features are readily available in the architectural literature. Determining potentially useful functional attributes is more difficult, and results from functional analyses are more inferential. Nevertheless, studies emphasizing activity structure within rural households are vital for ecological studies of historical land use. With this in mind, we may now outline the classification system used in this analysis.

A CLASSIFICATION SYSTEM FOR FRONTIER HOUSES

The need to classify residences is not new to historical geography. For example, Kniffen saw a need to construct a typology that would categorize the wide assortment of forms he observed throughout the eastern and southeastern United States: "To make the most of the opportunity it was deemed necessary to set up concurrently a typology quantified as to numerical importance and qualified as to areal and temporal positions, and to seek out origins, routes of diffusion, adaptations, and other processes affecting change or stability" (Kniffen 1965:550).

Jakle's (1976) treatment of rural houses in a two-county area of Illinois is an example of a grouping system in which house characteristics were combined to identify structural types and then, with inclusion of architectural style, house types. Despite using such a system, Jakle apparently believes it leaves much to be desired. He notes that, though geographers have long been interested in identifying house types and tracing their diffusion, they have not used an objective classification scheme: "They have yet to agree as to which house characteristics are really significant and how these characteristics should be scaled" (Jakle 1976:31). Jakle also raises questions germane to the arguments presented here: Can structure and decoration be separated? If so, is style as significant to house appearance as structural forms? Do main house units deserve special emphasis, or should additions be included automatically in analysis? He also suggests that whatever cognitive dimensions Americans use in evaluating houses should be incorporated into comprehensive classification schemes.

The proposed classification system discussed below was designed to provide an extensive, systematic description of the architectural resources in the project area; provide the basis for preliminary analysis of function in terms of activity space within structures; and summarize general repetitive architectural styles. The classification is not limited to examples found in the Salt River valley but can be used or expanded for use in other geographic areas. Our rationale for developing such a system is twofold. First, the system identifies variation in stylistic and functional dimensions of architecture; second, it then allows us to focus on those dimensions that are important to solving specific problems. Thus, when we reduce the set of dimensions used in the initial classification, we can combine the remaining attributes into more manageable classes.

Ideally, a classification system focuses on a set of dimensions selected for their potential for solving specific, previously defined problems. As used here, *dimension* refers to a set of mutually exclusive, alternative features, each containing a virtually unlimited number of *attributes* (Dunnell 1971:71). As opposed to hierarchical systems, classification does not assume a single "natural" order inherent in a set of objects, but instead suggests that an infinite number of organizations can be created, depending on problem definition and criteria selection. *Paradigmatic classification* is characterized by exhaustive combination of unweighted attributes such that all attributes in a system are equally important and all classes have the same amount of information. Four main advantages accrue from a paradigmatic system: there is absolute consistency in comparison of classes; there are few assumptions as to the importance of various dimensions of phenomena; attribute states within dimensions are infinitely expandable during analysis; and attribute states can be evaluated case by case.

In terms of actual application, the classification system operates as follows: each dimension is evaluated in terms of its attribute state, dimension by dimension; each attribute state of each dimension is assigned a number; classes are defined in terms of a number string representing attributes across all dimensions; and class definitions are sorted in ascending order to determine which classes have real objects in any given field. By way of example, if we are interested in only two dimensions—number of stories and number of rooms—then:

Dimension 1: Number of stories
    Attribute states: 1. One story
                    2. Two stories
                    3. Three stories, etc.
Dimension 2: Number of rooms
    Attribute states: 1. One room
                    2. Two rooms
                    3. Three rooms, etc.

The class definition of a two-story, two-room house then would be 2-2, or in our notation, 02-02.

While this example admittedly is simplistic, two advantages are readily apparent: the system can be applied rapidly, with consistency and a minimum of decisions about combinations of attributes, and it is amenable to direct computer entry. This latter feature saves considerable analysis time, since a simple program can sort through all possible combinations to determine which classes have members, tabulate the number of occurrences of each class, and sort the sample in ascending numerical order by definition criteria and list the total number of class members. Each dimension can be analyzed separately or in concert with different combinations of other dimensions to determine the most useful combination for any specific set of objects. Decisions about the relative importance of various attributes or dimensions can be based on inspection of the frequency of each attribute or various combinations of attributes rather than on preliminary inspection of the sample. Nonexistent classes can be discarded easily. For example, there usually will not be any three-story residences that contain only one room.

The classification system employs a set of n attributes arranged under thirty-one dimensions. These dimensions and a few of the accompanying attributes are presented below:

Dimension 1: Construction material
  1. Log
  2. Heavy timber
  3. Light frame
  4. Heavy frame
  5. Log and light frame
  6. Heavy timber and light frame

Dimension 2: Number of stories
  1. One
  2. One and a loft
  3. One and a half
  4. Two

Dimension 3: Roof type
  1. Gable
  2. Gable and shed extension
  3. Gable and one cross gable
  4. Gable and two cross gables

Dimension 4: Shape of house
  1. Square
  2. Rectangular
  3. L-shaped
  4. T-shaped

Dimension 5: Maximum depth of floor plan of lower story
  1. One room
  2. Two rooms

Dimension 6: Maximum width of floor plan at lower story
  1. One room
  2. Two rooms

Dimension 7: Number of rooms of lower story
  1. One room
  2. Two rooms

Dimension 8: Number of rooms of upper story
  1. One room
  2. Two rooms

Dimension 9: Number and
placement of chimneys
1. None
2. One on dividing wall, one
   fireplace/flue
3. One on dividing wall, two
   fireplaces/flues
4. One on left end wall,
   interior
5. One on left end wall,
   exterior
6. One on right end wall,
   interior
7. One on right end wall,
   exterior
8. One on rear wall, right of
   midline
9. One on rear wall, on
   midline
10. Two, one on each
    end wall, interior
11. Two, one on each end
    wall, exterior
12. Two, one on a dividing
    wall, one on a rear wall
    of another room
13. Two, on two interior walls
14. Three, one on each end
    wall, interior, one on rear
    wall of another room

Dimension 10: Number and
placement of interior stairways
1. None
2. One, ascending from
   corner of room
3. One, ascending along
   middle of room wall
4. One, ascending along hall
   wall

Dimension 11: Shape of stairway
1. Not applicable
2. One, open
3. One, enclosed

Dimension 12: Number of front
entrances
1. One
2. Two

Dimension 13: Number of rear
entrances
1. None
2. One
3. Two

Dimension 14: Number of left
side entrances
1. None
2. One
3. Two

Dimension 15: Number of right side entrances
1. None
2. One
3. Two

Dimension 16: Number and placement of porches
1. None
2. One, front

Dimension 17: Facade location
1. In gable end
2. Perpendicular to gable

Dimensions 18–24: Structure of lower-story facade
18. L_2 19. L_Q 20. L_1 21. M   22. R_1 23. R_Q 24. R_2

Dimensions 25–31: Structure of upper-story facade
25. L_2 26. L_Q 27. L_1 28. M   29. R_1 30. R_Q 31. R_2
1. Not applicable
2. Not occupied
3. Single door
4. Large window
5. Small window
6. Dormer

Included are only those attributes used to classify early structures (for a full listing of attributes, see O'Brien et al. 1980). As shown above, the number of attributes under each dimension varies considerably. Since two columns in the coding format are used for each dimension, there is room to expand the number of attributes (the number 99 is used to denote an indeterminate attribute state). The system is structured so that the classifier can deal first with an original house block as a single unit and then with the original block along with subsequent additions. Each addition changes the form of the house so that a new class is created.

The most variable dimensions in the classification scheme are the number and placement of chimneys and the facade arrangement. To systematize the classification of facade arrangements, we created several dimensions (18–31 above). The facade is subdivided both vertically and horizontally—the latter applying only if the house being classified contains more than one story. Each horizontal unit is divided into four equal segments (fig. 8.5): the *midline* bisects the unit into two halves, which are then split by *quarter lines*. The resulting four units are labeled right and left *end sections* and right and left *middle sections*. Each dividing line and section is a separate dimension, making a total of seven facade dimensions for each story. Possible attributes of these dimensions include several combinations of doors. An attribute either occurs under a facade dimension (i.e., occupies one of seven spaces on the facade) or does not. For example, a facade unit that has a single door in the center and two large, flanking windows, each spaced evenly between the door and the corner of the structure, would be coded 02-04-02-03-02-04-02 (see above for attribute states). One advantage of this system is that one knows immediately upon inspection of the number string that the facade unit arrangement is symmetrical and is composed of a door with large windows on the quarter lines. No additional information is necessary to describe the door and window placement, and the placement can be compared objectively with other facade arrangements.

The rationale behind creating a systematic classification for facade arrangement is to sort out considerable variation that exists in the sample—variation that may have had important functional implications. Because of the inferred functional significance of the facade arrangement of a house, its pertinent dimensions, along with chimney number and placement and floor plan dimensions, were used to create the various classes discussed below. Other dimensions of individual classes are discussed in O'Brien et al. (1980). To streamline discussion, we have combined classes into the following groups: one-story, single-pen houses; story-and-a-half, single-pen houses; one-story, double-pen houses; story-and-a-half, double-pen houses; and two-story, double-pen houses. Within each group class definitions are presented.

One-Story, Single-Pen Houses. In this discussion we make no distinction between true one-story houses (cabins) and those that have a low loft tucked between the ceiling and the roof. In all examples that contain lofts (nine of ten structures), close inspection of construction detail suggested that the lofts were added after the original cabins were built, either by laying floor joists in from the eave line or, in most cases, by raising the walls about 2 feet, laying floor joists to support the loft, and then replacing the roof. The most plausible

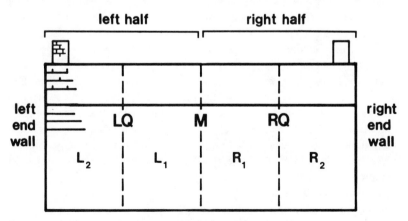

8.5. Location of facade dimensions used in the house classification system.

Table 8.1. Summary Data on One-Story, Single-Pen Houses

Class	Name	Construction Date	Dimensions (feet)
1a	Mappin, J.	ca. 1830	?
1b	Bannister	ca. 1835	15.5 × 15.5
2	Jordan	ca. 1835	18.5 × 17
2	Lutz	ca. 1840	17 × 15.5
3	Eakin	ca. 1840	21 × 17
4	Long, E.	ca. 1845	13.5 × 12.5
5	Dill	1840?	?
6	Fleming	ca. 1840	17.5 × 16
7	Dowell	ca. 1835	17 × 15.5
9	Hood	ca. 1845	14 × 13.5
10	Irvine	ca. 1835	21.5 × 18.5

explanation for adding a loft is an increase in family size. Raising the height of the original walls was not difficult and probably represented the first stage of cabin expansion.

Dimensions and estimated construction dates of the ten examples are listed in table 8.1. All houses but one are rectangular, following the trend established in the Bluegrass region and transported to Missouri (Marshall 1981:39). All were constructed of hand-hewn logs joined by V- or half-dovetail notching, and most if not all were at one time covered with horizontal lapped weatherboarding. In most cases the logs were well hewn and closely fitted, but in all cases some chinking was used—either small limestone slabs and wood chunks or plaster with horsehair added as a binding agent. Eight of the ten structures have entries perpendicular to the gable ends (fig. 8.6); all structures have gable-end brick chimneys—five are located on the interior and five on the exterior. Where stairways or ''ghosts'' of stairways could be located, they were found in the corners of the rooms.

The facades of these structures vary considerably across the sample (fig. 8.6), and the accompanying dimensions of facade arrangement are significant criteria for class definitions. Facades range from a door and window, each on quarter lines (class 1); to a door on the midline flanked by one window (classes 2 and 3) or two windows (class 7) on the quarter line(s); to a window on the midline flanked by a door (class 4); to a door and window to one side of the midline (class 5). One gable-entry cabin (class 6) contains only a door in the facade, while another gable-entry structure (class 9) contains a door and window separated by the midline.

In all but one example, the placement of windows appears to have been conditioned by chimney location. In five cabins that have non-gable-end entries and single facade windows, the latter are on the chimney side of the midline. Two of these (both in class 2) have an additional window just to one side of the chimney. A sixth cabin (class 4) has its window on the midline and the door on the chimney side; it also has an additional window next to the chimney. Another example (class 7) has two facade windows flanking the midline door and a third window on the opposing wall, between a second door and the chimney. Two other examples in this group, the gable-entry structures, have windows on both side walls, midway between the ends of the structure. If we are correct in assuming that the hearth area was the "central place" for household activities, all but one facade arrangement (class 5) would have yielded considerable light for that area during daytime hours.

In summary, early one-room log houses in the project area, many of which were later expanded into sizable dwellings, were well thought out, designed and constructed to serve as efficient centers of the colonial farmstead. Space was at a premium, and apparently every effort was made to maximize its use. Marshall's (1981:44) assessment of these structures is accurate: "It is clear that the humble 'log cabins' of the first settlers were stout and durable and designed to be maintained and added to as time, resources, and a growing family permitted. They were certainly not rude, temporary shelters, as many writers want us to believe."

Story-and-a-Half, Single-Pen Houses. The single example of this type of house that predates 1850 is a log structure (class 10) that was built as a story-and-a-half rather than being modified from an original one-story cabin (fig. 8.6). The cabin was constructed about 1840 of hand-hewn logs and subsequently was covered with 4 foot lengths of clapboard. An interior brick chimney was constructed in one gable end, and a small window was cut into the opposing wall. The facade consisted of a midline door flanked by two large windows on the lower story and a small midline window on the upper story. A loft was built over the lower story by placing notched joists into the side walls; a narrow corner stairway ascended to the loft.

One-Story, Double-Pen Houses. This group was once widespread across Little Dixie (Marshall 1981) as well as across the Bluegrass region (Montell and Morse 1976). Houses in this group consist of two structural units of roughly similar size, arranged laterally. One or both rooms may contain a loft. Two basic types exist in the project area—those constructed as one unit and those that grew through the addition of a frame or log pen to an existing log pen (fig. 8.7). Considerable variation exists in double-pen structures, as it does in the nomenclature folklorists use to describe them (e.g., saddlebag, tenant house, hall-and-parlor, "essential" double-pen).

The three dimensions used here to subdivide double-pen houses are floor plan, chimney number and placement, and facade arrangement. The variability exhibited by these dimensions as they apply to fifteen structures in the project area is shown in figure 8.8. Summary data on the structures are

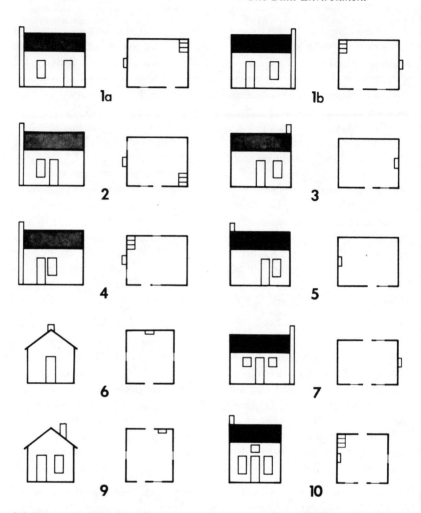

8.6. Facades and floor plans of one-story, single-pen houses and story-and-a-half, single-pen houses, by class and subclass (after O'Brien et al. 1980).

presented in table 8.2. The most common facade arrangement (class 11, seven examples) is two doors, one on either side of the midline, each flanked by a large window. The facade is mirrored on the rear of the house. Two floor plans exist, depending on the chimney placement: a wall divides the house into two equal-sized rooms with either a front passage between rooms or a door in the center of the dividing wall. Several types of chimney arrangement define subclasses: subclass 11*a*—a single chimney on the dividing wall, two fireplaces; subclass 11*b*—a single interior chimney on the left end wall; subclass 11*c*—two interior chimneys, one on each end wall; and subclass 11*d*—two exterior chimneys, one on each end wall.

Another common facade has a wider spacing between doors and a closer spacing between each door and its flanking window (fig. 8.8). In the five houses that fall in this class (class 12), doors are aligned on the quarter line, and windows are separated from the doors by about a foot. The floor plans are identical to those in class 11. Subclasses are: subclass 12*a*—a single exterior chimney on the left end wall; subclass 12*b*—a single exterior chimney on the right end wall; subclass 12*c*—a single chimney on the dividing wall, one

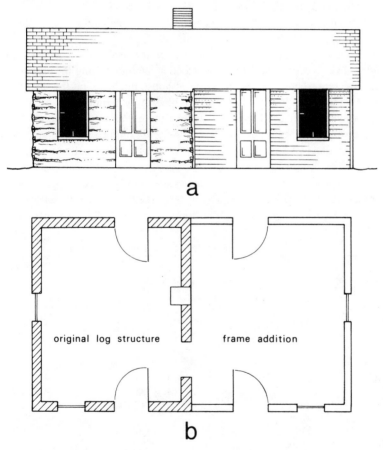

a

b

8.7. (*a*) Facade and (*b*) floor plan of mirror-image log-frame structure and addition (from O'Brien et al. 1980).

fireplace; subclass 12*d*—a single chimney on the dividing wall, two fireplaces; and subclass 12*e*—two interior chimneys, one on each end wall.

The probable pre-1850 examples of what commonly are referred to as hall-and-parlor houses were found in the project area. The distinctive features of this type of house are the single front door and unequal-sized rooms (Marshall 1981:48) separated by a frame partition. The type is widespread, occurring in the Tidewater and Carolina Piedmont areas east of the Appalachians and in central Kentucky (ibid.). The two examples from the project area have dissimilar chimney arrangements—one has two interior brick chimneys, one on either end (subclass 13*a*), and one has a single chimney with two fireplaces on the dividing wall (subclass 13*b*).

Another class in this group is class 14, which has a facade like that of class 11, minus the windows. The single example in this class has a single-chimney double fireplace on the dividing wall (fig. 8.8).

Functionally, a double-pen house doubles the available floor space of a single-block structure, and for many frontier families adding the second pen may have represented the second stage of house modification (the first being the addition of a loft in the original block). Although data to test the proposition are not available, we suspect there was an upper limit to the number of people that could be accommodated comfortably in a single-pen house, and that as families grew and that limit was reached, the next step was to expand the house laterally.

Several aspects of double-pen, single-story houses in the project area may be functional as well as stylistic. One is the placement of rear doors, which in most examples mirrors that of front doors. Several "folk" explanations are

Table 8.2. Summary Data on One-Story, Double-Pen Houses

Class	Name	Construction Date	Dimensions (feet)		
11*a*	Dooley	?	33.5	×	17.5
11*a*	Johnson	ca. 1850	36	×	19
11*a*	McGee	?	34	×	18
11*a*	Key	ca. 1850		?	
11*b*	McQueery	?		?	
11*c*	Greeves	?		?	
11*d*	Mappin, M.	ca. 1828	34	×	20
12*a*	Crow	ca. 1835	34.5	×	17.5
12*b*	Johnson	ca. 1840	35	×	17.5
12*c*	Allen	?		?	
12*d*	Dill	1850?		?	
12*e*	Orton	?		?	
13*a*	Long, H.	?	35	×	17
13*b*	Edwards	?		?	
14	Gibbons	?		?	

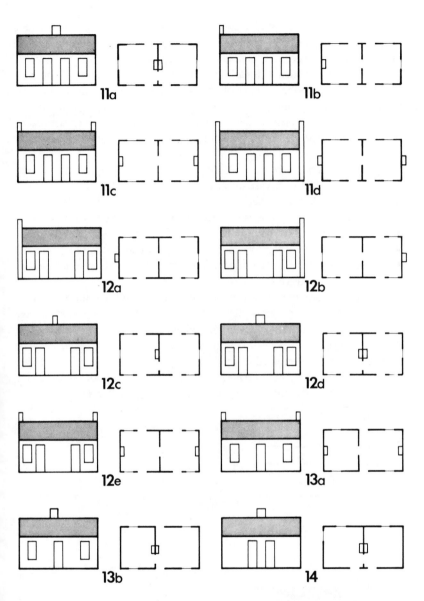

8.8. Facades and floor plans of one-story, double-pen houses, by class and subclass (from O'Brien et al. 1980).

given for the occurrence of four doors, all of which seem logical: to cool the house during summer by creating cross-drafts; to aid in escape from fire; and to provide separate access to the outside for persons in one room so as not to disturb those in the other (Montell and Morse 1976:28). Another functional aspect appears to be the number of chimneys and their placement. In some examples a single chimney on the dividing wall sufficed to heat the house; often this was the chimney connected to the original block. When the second pen was constructed, it was built abutting the original chimney, obviating the need for a second one.

A third functional aspect of double-pen houses is evident in the spacing between pens. While the vast majority of double-pen structures were built with the pens abutting, there is a significant class (class 36) that is characterized by a wide passage between pens, the entire structure being covered by a single roof. With the exception of having dual chimneys and wooden floors, these "dogtrot" houses are almost identical to double-crib barns, illustrating how early builders drew upon the single pen as a design element (Montell and Morse 1976:21).

There is considerable debate on whether dogtrot houses normally were built as single units or grew out of the later addition of a second pen. Regarding dogtrots in central Kentucky, Montell and Morse (1976:21) state, "Although possible, it is not likely that the dogtrot house resulted when an additional room was erected a few feet away from the additional cabin. Theoretically that is the way it happened, but . . . research indicates that both rooms . . . were generally built at the same time." Kniffen (1965:561), on

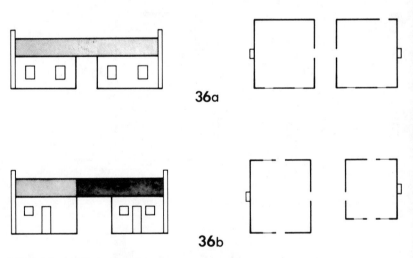

8.9. Facades and floor plans of dogtrot houses, by subclass.

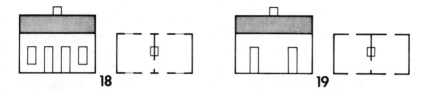

8.10. Facades and floor plans of story-and-a-half, double-pen houses, by class (from O'Brien et al. 1980).

the other hand, states that "the most familiar solution to adding to a log house is the 'dogtrot.'. . . Facing gable toward gable, then roofing over the intervening space is so obvious a solution to the problem that it was surely hit upon many times."

Of the three log dogtrots in the project area, two apparently were constructed as single units (subclass 36*a*), while the other was built in two stages (fig. 8.9). Unlike most dogtrot houses, the latter example (subclass 36*b*) contained pens of unequal size (15 feet by 16 feet and 17 feet by 21 feet); the breezeway between pens was 8 feet wide. The breezeways on the two houses with equal-sized pens eventually were covered over with clapboards on light stud framing, but the central passage on the third house never was enclosed. All three houses had brick exterior chimneys on each end.

One major advantage of the dogtrot is in providing a shady, airy place to carry out activities under a roof. During the hot months, cooking and other domestic activities requiring a low fire could be done within the breezeway, keeping the heat out of the living area. In addition, the breezeway could be a spot to stable livestock at night.

Story-and-a-Half, Double-Pen Houses. Three examples of story-and-a-half, double-pen houses that predate 1850 were found in the project area. We differentiate between these houses and single-story, double-pen houses by the greater height of the wall between loft floor and eave line (usually about 4 feet). Two separate classes were created based on facade characteristics and chimney placement. The structure in class 18 has a facade containing two doors, one on either side of the midline, each flanked by a large window. The chimney is on the dividing wall, with one fireplace in each room (fig. 8.10). The house, built by James Mappin, was originally a one-room log structure (subclass 1*b*) when it was erected about 1827. About 1835, Mappin modified the house by reversing the door and window on the facade, constructing another log pen against the chimney of the original structure, and adding a second fireplace.

Class 19 contains two log houses that were constructed as single units. The facades consist of two doors, one on each quarter line, and no windows (fig. 8.10). Single chimneys constructed of massive limestone slabs, with fire-places that open into opposing rooms, are on the dividing walls. Back doors oppose those on the facade. Small gable-end windows in the center of the wall or slightly off center are the only other first-floor openings. These two log structures, with their enormous chimneys and fireplaces, are the classic "saddlebag" houses that occur in many regions of the South.

Two-Story, Double-Pen Houses. The most variability in structural form occurs in two-story, double-pen houses, to which several terms have been applied, including the widely used "I-house." Construction techniques used to create the final form include "building from scratch" and adding to single pens and double pens (including dogtrots). There are examples in the project area that show a definite evolution from single pen to story-and-a-half, double-pen to full two-story, double-pen.

Three basic floor plans that date to the pre-1850 period were noted in our series of standing houses: two equal-sized rooms divided by a partition that meets the front wall at the midpoint, with a large chimney centered in the partition; two unequal-sized rooms divided by a partition that meets the front wall just to the left of the single front entry; and two equal-sized rooms downstairs and two unequal-sized rooms upstairs. This is by no means the limit to the range in variation in I-houses in the project area. However, we are hampered in our attempt to describe these early structures because of their deteriorated condition when recorded (most were collapsed) and our lack of knowledge about when they were constructed. Most of the structures postdate our period of interest, but others could well predate 1850. Our discussion is limited to four structures, two of which were studied intensively.

Class 19. The plans of the two houses in this class consist of two floors of equal-sized rooms separated by a dividing wall containing a large limestone-slab chimney with fireplaces in both lower rooms. Opposing front and back doors are centered in the walls of each lower room, and windows are in the gable ends. The original facades contained two doors, one on each quarter line, with large windows directly above them.

The Vandeventer house, situated 1.6 miles southeast of Florida, was constructed about 1840 by Hugh Hickman, who operated a mill near Florida. As Marshall (1981:65) notes, the house originally was a story-and-a-half log structure (class 19) that was modified to its existing form. Each pen exhibits a different style of corner notching—half-dovetail versus V—and each has a boxed-in stairway to the upper story. Hand-riven lath covers the walls in both stairways. The second story was constructed by placing heavy timbers vertically upon the original log walls, three logs above the ceiling joists of the first floor. Brick nogging then was placed between the timber wall studs. A subsequent modification to the facade was made by cutting out a window next to the left door.

The Simon house, 2.5 miles southeast of Paris, was constructed as a single unit about 1830 by Green Caldwell. Structural members are of heavy timber with considerable cross- and knee-bracing. Unlike the central placement of the gable-end windows in the Vandeventer house, lower-story windows in the Simon house are considerably off center. Also, unlike the dual access to the upper story in the Vandeventer house, there is a single boxed-in stairway.

Class 20. The single house in this class was built shortly after 1830 by Samuel H. Smith (chap. 7). The massive log structure abutted an earlier single-pen house that later was razed (except for the log joists and sills), with a frame addition erected in its place. The lower floor plan consisted of two rooms of unequal size separated by a frame partition, single front and rear doors, and a limestone gable-end, exterior fireplace-chimney that also heated the larger upper room (fig. 8.11). The facade contained the central door, which was flanked by large windows on the quarter lines. Two smaller windows sat directly above the ones on the lower story.

The three-bay house was made of oak logs (up to 17 inches in diameter), hewn to approximately 7 inches in thickness and joined at the corners by half-dovetail notching. The logs apparently were covered immediately with walnut weatherboarding, since their exteriors were unweathered beneath the boards. The long walls were topped by massive hand-hewn oak plates, 15.5 inches by 18 inches, which projected as cornices from the faces of the walls (fig. 8.11). The gables were framed by studs (2 inches by 4 inches, 24 inches on center). The roof consisted of rough-hewn oak rafters 4 inches square,

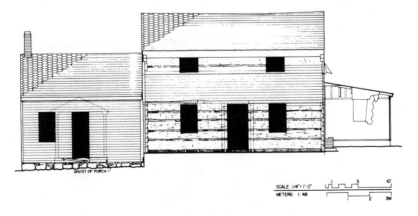

8.11. Facade of the Samuel H. Smith house, showing second log structure (center) and frame addition (left) built by Smith, and twentieth-century frame room (right).

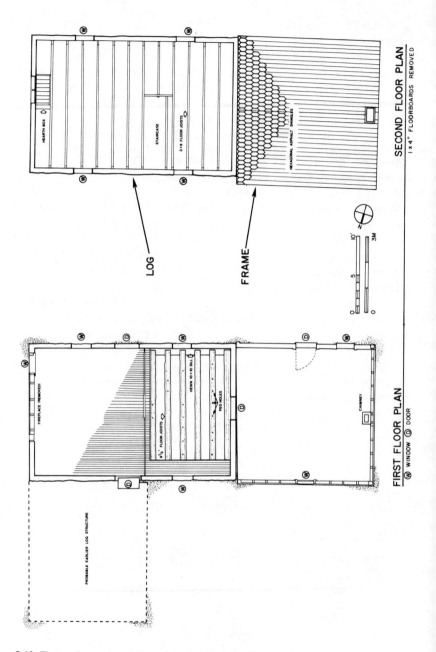

8.12. First- and second-story floor plans of the Samuel H. Smith house (twentieth-century additions not shown).

lapped and pegged at the ridge. Second-story floor joists (2.5 inch by 9 inch vertically sawn walnut, 24 inches on center) penetrated the exterior walls through notches cut in the logs and were cut flush with the outside surface of the logs. Original first-floor joists were 10 inch diameter logs, 24 inches on center, which rested on 9 inch by 18 inch hewn oak sills at the outer walls and spanned the width of the house without intermediate support (fig. 8.12). The top half of each log was hewn into a trapezoidal section; the bottom half was left rounded and scraped of its bark.

Finishing touches included laying milled 1 inch by 6.5 inch walnut tongue-and-groove floorboards over the joists on both floors; whitewashing the walls and exposed undersides of second-story floor joists; and building a stairway along the partition.

Smith carried out several alterations to the house about 1850. He plastered the walls and ceilings and made an addition to the gable end opposite the chimney (fig. 8.12), a one-story framed room resting on heavy oak sills (hewn timbers 7 inches square) and 8 inch diameter oak logs hewn in the same manner as those in the original block. The addition contained considerable mortise-and-tenon joinery and was pegged into the original structure with large wooden dowels. As noted earlier in this chapter, by 1850 Smith certainly had one of the most impressive residences in the region. After this date he continually added onto the structure until his death in 1872.

Class 24. The single example in this class is a house constructed about 1840 by Matthew Mappin about 1.4 miles northwest of the confluence of the Middle and Elk forks of the Salt River. The Mappin house began as a two-room log structure (subclass 11*d*) constructed shortly before 1830. Within a decade Mappin had six children and had achieved prominence in local county government. To accommodate the increase in his status and family size, he built a two-story house—with some Greek Revival stylistic references—at one end of the original log house, which was left to serve as a rear service wing.

The house (fig. 8.13) was built of heavy frame members with mortise-and-tenon construction. Framing members were fitted together and marked with roman numerals before the structure was raised into place. To make way, a gable-end chimney on the original cabin was removed, and a corbeled brick stove flue was installed at the center of the cabin. The new house was painted white with brown trim.

The overall dimensions of the large I-house were 32 feet 11 inches by 18 feet 4 inches. The two first-floor rooms were approximately equal in size, and originally each had a large fireplace on the end wall (fig. 8.14). The stairway to the second floor was in the southwestern corner of the northern room. On the second floor, two rooms of unequal size flanked an off-center stair hall.

8.13. Facade of the Matthew Mappin house.

The room to the left was the same size as the room below; the room to the right was narrowed by the 5.5 foot width of the stair hall (fig. 8.14).

As noted, the structural system was predominately heavy timber, using a combination of hewn and milled members, with lighter studs between. The walls rested on white oak sills, hewn to a 7 inch square section. Into the sills were mortised the first-floor joists—oak logs that spanned the depth of the building without intermediate support. The top half of each 10 inch diameter log was hewn into a trapezoidal section; the bottom half was left rounded and scraped of its bark. At the building corners were massive white oak corner posts, braced in both directions by milled oak knee braces. Lighter milled oak studs spaced 24 inches on center lined the walls. To these were nailed narrow strips of wood that held the catted clay nogging (dried clay with straw as a binder) in place. The second-floor ceiling joists were 8 inch diameter logs placed 24 inches on center, hewn on the bottom edges with the bark left on the sides and tops. Both the rafters and second-floor joists were made of milled oak lumber, the rafters 2 inches by 4 inches, 24 inches on center, and the joists 3 inches by 8.5 inches, 24 inches on center.

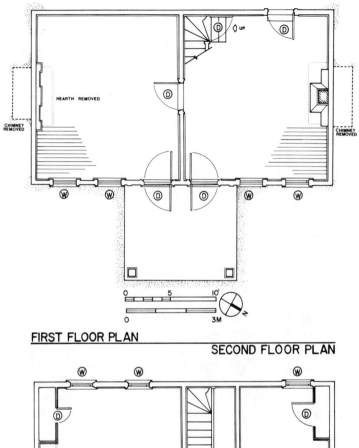

FIRST FLOOR PLAN

SECOND FLOOR PLAN

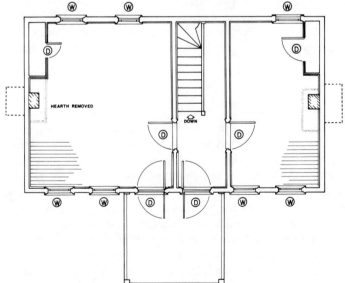

8.14. First- and second-story floor plans of the Matthew Mappin house (earlier cabin and later modifications not shown).

A large two-story portico was centered on the front of the house, indicating a Greek Revival influence. It had a steep, pedimented gable roof, its cornice on the same level as the cornice of the main roof. Two plain boxed pillars on each story supported the roof at the front edge. Against the face of the house on both stories were two thin pilasters with molded capitals. A plain wooden railing surrounded the second story of the porch. Originally two large brick exterior end chimneys flanked the house, with fireplaces that served both upper and lower rooms.

The facade arrangement was the same for both stories, consisting of two doors, one on either side of the midline, each flanked by two large windows on either side of the quarter lines. On the rear of the house three large windows were placed into the second-story wall, one in the smaller room and two in the larger room.

The Mappin house was one of many examples in the project area in which a later structure did not replace an earlier residence but supplemented it. From 1840 until 1893, well after Matthew Mappin's death, the original two-room cabin served as a kitchen and as a center of other household activities. This is supported both by conversations with people who lived in the house as children and by archaeological excavation (chap. 9). At least in Mappin's case, an additional set of rooms probably was necessitated by a growing family. His construction of what is still known locally as a "southern mansion," however, was due not to family size but to the more intangible conditions of upper South culture, namely the desire to rise above the ranks of the common small agriculturist to a position of preeminence in society. Based on our field observations, no contemporary house in the project area could rival Mappin's effort.

Summary

Analysis has shown that, despite the poor state of preservation of many of the standing structures in the project area, considerable variability in style and function can be documented in the components of rural farmsteads. Residences exhibit the most variation, in part owing to their predominance in the architectural sample, but also owing to the rapid changes many nineteenth-century houses went through. Factors that led to changes in these structures probably included an increase in family size, an accumulation of wealth, and a concomitant desire for greater prestige in the community.

To organize the analysis of variability within the sample of houses, we devised a paradigmatic classification scheme composed of formal dimensions, each of which contains a series of mutually exclusive attribute states. The precise combination of attributes defines a particular class of residence. Dimensions that appear most helpful in establishing "house types"—which are formed by reducing the number of dimensions used—are floor plan and facade arrangement.

Despite the small sample of standing structures and the lack of data regarding when certain structures were built, it is clear that the roots of much of the early architecture in the project area—including both barns and houses—can be traced to other upper South regions such as the Bluegrass. Instead of developing new architectural styles in the frontier area, immigrants transported existing styles to the new region. Although the built environment is only one aspect of transplanted upper South culture in the project area, it is intricately tied to other segments of that culture—segments we investigate in the following chapter.

9

The Frontier Household

William M. Selby,
Michael J. O'Brien,
and Lynn M. Snyder

In the previous chapter we emphasized the physical nature of the frontier farmstead and focused on features of the built environment, specifically the form and spatial organization of individual farmstead components. In this chapter we discuss the nonphysical nature of the farmstead and narrow our focus to the social and economic organization of frontier households.

Analysis at the household level presents an opportunity to study the development of the frontier from a seldom-seen perspective—to look at the frontier from the bottom up. As we have emphasized throughout, the household is the basic unit in our analysis of frontier settlement, which begins at the regional level, narrows to the community level, and narrows again to the farmstead and household levels. Because of the interconnected nature of the last two levels—the farmstead and the household—we discuss them together. It is important to note that while rural frontier farmsteads and households represent independent spheres for analysis in their own right, we obtain a much broader understanding of the function of these units when we incorporate the results of such analyses into a regional study of frontier settlement.

It is beyond the scope of this chapter to present an in-depth analysis of all aspects of frontier society evident at the household level. Rather, we summarize selected topics relative to household composition, subsistence, and economic development. We often use examples to illustrate points being made and, where possible, relate the examples to larger regional samples. Several topics discussed here are treated by Mason (1983) on a regional scale, and where appropriate his results are discussed. The analysis reported here differs from his in scale. Whereas he was concerned with regional trends in the development of an upper South agricultural society, we analyze actual case studies from the sample in order to isolate variables that acted to effect the patterns noted. Specific topics covered in our discussion include changes in the size of families through time, the distribution of wealth among agricultural households, the types of agriculture practiced, the material components of a frontier household, and the nature of nonagricultural subsistence pursuits.

The Concept of Household

We distinguish two kinds of households—the *ethnographic household* and the *archaeological household*. The former is defined as a group of people who cooperate in performing a wide range of domestic activities, from obtaining and preparing food to "maintaining a house and other facilities that serve as the spatial focus of the group" (Winter 1974:981). An *archaeological household* is one that is inferred through analysis of the archaeological record. Implicit in the latter definition is an emphasis on the material remains of culture. As with other aspects of the archaeological record, we are dealing with *remnants* of past activities, not with all their products and by-products. The importance of the distinction between the two types of households is heightened with regard to the condition of the historical archaeological record encountered in the project area, a point we will return to shortly.

South (1977*a*:86) states that a household represents a system within a system; thus the society of which a particular household is a part imposes a certain degree of consistency in the relation among its parts. By examining patterns resulting from the uniform nature of these relations, we can begin to construct a model of household structure, how it changed, and, finally, what the role of the household was in the larger, regional settlement and economic scheme. In South's view, the consistency that the larger system imposes on the household is revealed in the patterning of various classes of portable and nonportable artifacts:

The quantity of remains resulting from any behavioral activity would not necessarily parallel the importance placed on the activity within the cultural system but would have a definite relationship to the remains of other activities. It is these relationships among the by-products of human behavior that might be expected to reveal regularity when compared on an intersite basis. [South 1977*a*:86]

Thus his view of the household is focused on what we have termed the archaeological household. While such a focus is appropriate for the study of frontier households, there are many aspects that are not observed directly in the archaeological record. This point is discussed further below.

Sources of Data

One great advantage that historical-period settlement studies have is that often both archaeological and archival materials can be used to answer questions regarding specifics of the development of a region. This is especially true of analysis at the household level. In theory each source of data complements the other, as Saunders and Mason (1979) note when describing the role of documentary research in the Cannon Project:

Although analysis of written sources rather than artifacts is employed . . . the goals are similar to those of archeological settlement and community pattern studies. Emphasis is placed on determining factors which conditioned rural pioneer settlement. . . . Thus, archeological and geographical techniques which emphasize spatial relationships are utilized, allowing analysis on a regional scale.

Each data set—documentary versus archaeological—is discussed briefly below, accompanied by an assessment of possible random or directional biases present in the data.

Documentary Sources

Although we used historical records at all levels of analysis during the study, several classes of documents were particularly useful at the household level, including population and agricultural census schedules, wills, and probate inventories. Microfilm copies of the forms completed by federal census takers are in the State Historical Society of Missouri in Columbia. The census schedules cover the years 1830, 1840, and 1850. The amount of information they contain increases for each census. The 1830 census schedules record the head of a household, the number of household members by sex and age groups, and the number of slaves by sex and age groups. The 1840 census schedules contain similar information, plus listing the number of persons engaged in agriculture, commerce, or manufacturing, the number of "learned persons" in each household, and the number of slaves. By 1850 the names of all household members were recorded along with exact age, occupation, state of birth, and value of real estate owned.

In 1850 there also were separate schedules for slaves, products of agriculture, and products of industry. Included on the products of agriculture schedule was the value of farms, number of improved and unimproved acres, and livestock and crop yields for each farm that had produced over $100 worth of commodities during the previous year.

Possible sources of bias in these records include the deletion of persons and perhaps entire households from the census schedules and the lack of accuracy on the part of the farmer or enumerator in estimating agricultural yields. In almost all cases each census—population as well as agricultural—appears to have been undertaken by a single census taker who worked an entire county. Hence we expect that there is a fairly high degree of consistency in the records kept. While some errors have been noted in the census schedules, these are for the most part errors in spelling names, especially surnames. In the great majority of cases the census information can be corroborated by independent data.

Archaeological Data

As we explained in chapter 1, the information generated through the analysis of materials recovered from the archaeological excavations represents an independent data set relative to the conditions under which nineteenth-century farmsteads and households operated. In situations where these data are the *only* ones available, it might make sense to force them to the limit in order to answer questions about household organization, subsistence, and so forth. In our analysis, however, given the vast amount of documentary information that exists, the archaeological remains can best be used to supplement these data.

We have discussed elsewhere (O'Brien, Mason, and Saunders 1982) the distribution of material classes at several farmstead sites excavated during the course of the project. In analyzing these data our basic postulate followed that made by South (1977a:87), that there was a pattern to the discard of by-products of human behavior around a site that "might be viewed as a per capita, per year contribution to the archaeological record." For several reasons, the results of analysis were not entirely satisfying. Because of the extended, continuous occupation of most historical-period sites in the project area, deposits that resulted from the occupations are for the most part mixed beyond the point of being separable by time period. Deposits are mostly shallow (5–10 inches) and usually contain more than a century's worth of material. In a few instances, building additions of known date have sealed intact earlier deposits, which can be used as small control samples, but these instances are rare and the assemblages of material small.

Another possible bias that may have affected any interpretation of the archaeological data is the limited area of excavation at each site. The Corps of Engineers was quite specific as to what portions of sites could be excavated. Excavation was for the most part limited to areas within or immediately adjacent to houses. This contract stipulation precluded, in most cases, our sampling areas of farmsteads out from the main residence. Thus, a significant number of artifact classes may be absent or at least underrepresented in the recovered assemblages.

Despite these problems, the archaeological data base does provide information that otherwise would be absent from the study. One large gap it has filled is our knowledge of the subsistence base. Faunal material recovered from the sites has allowed us to identify an important component of the frontier household—what native and domestic animals were being used for food and in what quantities. Despite the frequent lack of temporal control over segments of the deposits, we can at least gain a quantified composite picture of this facet of the frontier diet.

Given the amount of time in which excavations were to be completed and the amount of money budgeted for them, site selection became important. To ensure effective use of available resources, the selection was based on several criteria. First, we assessed the condition of each site to determine the amount of postdepositional disturbance from farming or reservoir clearing. Second, we noted the existence of standing architecture to guide excavation. Third, and most important, we determined whether the site could be tied to documentary sources such as land purchase records, census data, and genealogies. If a site met the last two criteria and was judged not to have been greatly disturbed by postdepositional factors, it was considered as a possibility for more intensive study (O'Brien, Mason, and Saunders 1982:301).

Thirty-four sites met these minimal criteria, and we submitted eligibility forms on them to the National Register of Historic Places. From this sample we drew a subsample of twenty-one sites on which the documentary data were judged the most complete. Because of dwindling time and money, only seven of twenty-one sites were excavated extensively. The other farmsteads were mapped, surface collected where possible, and photographed. Importantly, five of the seven sites excavated were in the Smith settlement (chaps. 6 and 7). In this case we decided to bypass a regional sample and concentrate our efforts in the area where we had the best control over chronology and archival data. As we have pointed out elsewhere (O'Brien, Mason, and Saunders 1982), we believe that understanding the development of a single community in greater detail is more important than knowing a little about several unrelated sites. In retrospect we view this decision as a good one, considering the problems encountered in sorting the deposits temporally.

Of the seven sites excavated, two—the Matthew Mappin house site and the Samuel H. Smith house site—yielded the most information pertinent to discussion here. We also have the most complete documentary information on the occupants of these sites. We hasten to point out that analysis of some archaeological materials is still ongoing, including crockery, to distinguish patterns of flow of locally produced goods, and ceramics, to attempt to provide more precise dating of archaeological deposits and to create a paradigmatic classification of historical-period ceramics. We view the material remains as part of a frontier system that we elsewhere have referred to as the *upper South* pattern. In the following section we outline the characteristics of such a system, building upon the discussion presented in chapter 3.

The Upper South Pattern

As we noted in chapter 3, most settlers of the project area emigrated from the east-central region of Kentucky, where they had participated in an evolving social as well as economic and agricultural pattern termed by various authors (cf. Mitchell 1972, 1978) upper South culture. Several points regarding this cultural system have been made throughout this book and are summarized here. First, the cultural system can be viewed as encompassing the interactions between two groups of agriculturists: "yeoman farmers" with small tracts of land, and a class of "small planters" possessing from two to ten slaves and larger amounts of land (Mitchell 1978). Second, based on data from the Bluegrass region of Kentucky, as regions became more densely populated, class distinctions and differences based on wealth and landholding became more and more apparent (Byrd 1951). Third, colonists immigrated not as independent individuals, but rather as interdependent units (chap. 7). In opposition to the suggestions by several analysts that the agricultural frontier was composed of a disproportionately large number of single males, demographic analyses of several frontier areas (Eblen 1965)—including the Salt Valley (Mason 1983)—have shown that single young men played lesser roles in settling the frontier than commonly believed. Rather, large groups of interrelated families were the basic economic as well as social units.

In the following sections we deal with the upper South system in two parts: the agricultural pattern and the social pattern. As we hope to demonstrate, neither can be entirely separated from the other; we approach them separately for ease in presentation. After introducing the various components of the two patterns, we discuss case examples from the project area in an attempt to integrate the components into a single system.

The Agricultural Pattern

Originating in western Virginia and spreading later to central Kentucky and central Tennessee, upper South culture began as a fusion of elements from the southeastern Pennsylvania "hearth area"—such as corn, wheat, hogs, and beef cattle—with elements from the Chesapeake "hearth" —such as tobacco, hemp, and slavery (Mitchell 1972:741, 1978:81–82). Mixed farming and the production of tobacco and hemp with slave labor distinguishes the upper South agricultural region from the North, where slaves were not used and wheat rather than corn was the primary grain. The ratio of nonfood cash crops to food crops and the number of slaves differentiates the upper South from the lower South, which developed a plantation economy characterized by the production of cotton through intensive use of slave labor (Owsley 1949).

Table 9.1. Production Statistics for 681 Project Area Farms in 1850

Product	Number[a]	Percentage[b]	Mean[c]	S.D.[d]	Maximum[e]
Horses	679	99.7	5.0	2.9	25
Oxen	211	31.0	3.4	1.9	10
Mules and asses	96	14.1	8.9	15.8	103
Swine	670	98.4	30.6	22.0	175
Cattle	610	89.6	13.9	19.6	200
Sheep	595	87.4	26.0	17.7	170
Wool (lbs.)	575	84.4	57.2	39.9	300
Milk cows	674	99.9	4.5	2.9	30
Butter (lbs.)	662	97.2	153.5	102.1	1,000
Cheese (lbs.)	62	9.1	45.5	40.0	200
Corn (bu.)	680	99.9	832.1	608.1	5,000
Wheat (bu.)	466	68.4	82.2	85.1	700
Rye (bu.)	30	4.4	27.3	14.2	60
Oats (bu.)	562	82.5	181.3	202.7	1,500
Barley (bu.)	5	0.7	16.6	10.4	30
Buckwheat (bu.)	30	4.4	24.6	27.5	150
Hay (tons)	465	68.3	6.2	6.8	60
Clover seed (bu.)	4	0.6	1.2	0.5	2
Grass seed (bu.)	21	3.1	6.0	8.0	35
Peas and beans (bu.)	24	3.5	17.2	22.0	90
Irish potatoes (bu.)	520	76.4	17.8	14.8	160
Sweet potatoes (bu.)	259	38.0	15.5	14.3	100
Garden products ($)	323	47.4	13.7	18.5	150
Orchard products ($)	315	46.2	25.8	27.8	250
Maple sugar (lbs.)	53	7.8	126.2	142.7	800
Molasses (gals.)	41	6.0	10.9	30.6	200
Honey (lbs.)	125	18.4	41.6	32.2	200
Tobacco (lbs.)	75	11.0	2,898.7	3,210.6	17,000
Hemp (tons)	14	2.0	1.2	0.6	3
Flax (lbs.)	169	24.8	82.6	86.2	500
Flaxseed (bu.)	118	17.3	3.6	3.3	22
Hops (lbs.)	10	1.5	7.0	6.6	20

Source: Mason (1983).
Data compiled from the 1850 agricultural census.
[a]Number of farms raising or producing the commodity.
[b]Percentage of farms raising or producing the commodity.
[c]Mean number of units of the commodity per producing farm.
[d]Standard deviation.
[e]Maximum value for the commodity.

Farmers in the central Salt River valley produced a broad range of crops and livestock characteristic of upper South agriculture. Corn was the principal crop throughout the region, and nearly every farmer grew some. An important food source, it was used in making corn bread and cornmeal as well as providing the basic feed for cattle, hogs, and chickens. Bremer (1975) remarks that, as the fattening of animals for slaughter became important in the pre–Civil War years, corn production took on increasingly commercialized aspects, as evidenced by the rise in sales of the crop among local farmers. In addition to its value as a food crop, other parts of the plant were used for a variety of purposes: husks were used in horse collars, chair bottoms, bedding, and brooms, while cobs provided fuel, toys, and pipes.

Table 9.1 summarizes data on the number of farms in 1850 raising products discussed in this section. It also presents the average amount of agricultural products being raised, along with the standard deviations and the maximum production figures noted in the agricultural census. These figures can be compared with those in table 5.6, which lists the minimum production figures used here to identify market producers. The high standard deviations are a result of the considerable variation in amounts produced for each category. Under the category *corn*, for example, we note that, by 1850, 99.9% (680 of 681) of the farms in the project area were raising at least some of the commodity. The average production figure was 832 bushels, but some farms were producing up to 5,000 bushels.

Production figures from the 1840 census (grouped by county only) show that farms in Ralls County produced an average of 345 bushels of corn and Monroe County farms produced about 331 bushels each (Mason 1983). By 1850 the average corn yield had more than doubled. Oats was another grain produced in the region, perhaps primarily as feed for horses and mules. Census schedules indicate that during the 1830s an average oats crop consisted of fewer than 100 bushels. In 1850 an average of 181 bushels of oats was produced by roughly 82% of project area farmers (table 9.1). By 1860 this production figure was down by two-thirds, and by the mid-1860s only one-fourth of the farmers in the region produced any oats (Mason 1983).

Wheat was grown in small quantities by many farmers in the area (table 9.1) and used in making bread for home consumption. As commercial flour became more widely available wheat production became less common, and by 1860 fewer than one-fourth of the local farmers raised their own wheat (Mason 1983). Some farmers also gathered honey and produced maple sugar, using them at home and selling the surplus. In the early years of settlement these activities were particularly attractive owing to the abundance of both wild bees and sugar maples. When shipped to market both commodities brought a high price, which is the reason that as late as 1850 over 18% of area farmers still gathered honey or kept bees (table 9.1).

Raising livestock for domestic use (as well as for market production, which we discuss below) was an important facet of upper South agriculture. Hogs were the primary animals raised in the region (98% of households), providing an important food source and a valuable commodity. Early colonists of the region probably followed simple stock-raising techniques: hogs were allowed to run free in wooded areas during the summer, feeding on mast and other vegetation until, as winter approached, they began returning to the farm, where they were fed corn (cf. Price and Price 1978). Before slaughter or transport to market, hogs could have been rounded up and herded back to the farm to be fattened with corn. As crop and livestock production increased in the region, this system of stock management would have been curtailed with the fencing of fields and the clearing of timber.

Beef and dairy cattle were raised throughout the area. Because everyone raised dairy cattle, it is likely the local market for dairy products remained small. Beef cattle probably were allowed to range free much the same as hogs, feeding on grass during the warmer months and on corn and cornstalk fodder during fall and winter.

DEVELOPMENT OF A MARKET ECONOMY

Crop production in the Salt River valley was not limited to food intended primarily for household or livestock consumption. By the end of the frontier period, a large part of a farmer's efforts went into growing market commodities, including tobacco and hemp. This appears to have been true of at least 45% of area farmers, who were raising at least one market commodity (defined as producing at least the mean plus one standard deviation). Tobacco had arrived with the earliest settlers from Kentucky, and beyond a small role in home consumption it offered an attractive source of cash. Hemp was used in naval and commercial shipping, especially for making twine and bagging for baling and shipping cotton. By the 1830s area farmers were producing significant amounts of hemp for market. Demand continued to increase in the 1840s, resulting in still greater production. Unfavorable conditions in the market and increasing competition from hemp producers in other parts of the state brought about a decline in local production, and by 1850 farmers began shifting to tobacco production (Bremer 1975).

Some livestock was raised for market as well as domestic use. Horses and mules were work animals on most farms but were also raised commercially and for show. Mules, always in demand in the lower South, constituted a steady market for Missouri producers. Sheep, kept by most farmers in the area, provided wool—easily transported and the material for most handmade clothing. Chickens were a popular source of meat and eggs for both domestic use and market, as was other poultry such as turkeys, geese, and ducks.

Most farmers producing for market raised a combination of crops and livestock suited to their economic position, technological capabilities, and immediate need. Their objective was to strike a balance between providing for themselves and generating profit through marketable surpluses and com- modities. Mason (1983) points out that by 1850 livestock and tobacco had become the two major market commodities in the project area. According to the 1850 agricultural census, 21% of area farmers produced more than one market commodity. If only one was produced, tobacco apparently was preferred. Farmers who produced tobacco usually had this crop as their only market commodity, while livestock producers usually raised several kinds of livestock plus grain to feed them. There were seventeen farmers in the project area who produced market quantities of livestock, grain, and tobacco (Mason 1983).

Although some corn was used to manufacture whiskey, Bremer (1975) explains that poor conditions and the high cost of transportation made it more advantageous to use grain as feed for hogs and cattle headed for market than to try to sell the crop for cash:

roads remained of relatively limited utility for shipping out grain crops, given the high transport costs involved. Consequently the area failed to develop any extensive cash crop activity comparable to that of northern areas with ready access to river or lake transportation facilities. Products shipped out of the area either traveled under their own power as in the case of livestock, or took the form of goods with a higher value per unit produced—such as hemp, tobacco, whiskey or wool. [p. 46]

By 1850 livestock-grain producers were among the wealthiest members of the region, while those growing marketable quantities of tobacco could be found at all levels of wealth, primarily in the middle class. In addition, by 1850, 83% of livestock-grain producers were slave owners, while only 40% of tobacco growers and 36% of those who produced only tobacco owned slaves (Mason 1983). The net effect of producing surplus agricultural products— itself a correlate of amount of land and numbers of slaves owned—was a disparity in wealth among landholders in the region. Having presented a summary of the agricultural pattern in place by 1850, we now turn to a discussion of the development of the upper South social pattern.

The Social Pattern

Based on our assessments of several trends observed in records from the project area, we share Voss's (1969–70) view that the goal of most upper South immigrants was to become members of the planter class, or landed gentry, and to found prominent families on large tracts of land. In regions such as the Kentucky Bluegrass, the socially and politically dominant planter class established small estates, at the center of which were two-story "mansions," developed along the lines of southern plantation houses (chap. 8). Although wealth was based in part on monetary return from the sale of agricultural products, the heart of wealth was in landholdings.

One seemingly important question to be asked at this point concerns the length of time it took for this socially and politically active group to evolve. Was such a class apparent from the moment of colonization, or did it take several years to appear? Can the appearance of such a class be linked directly to surplus production? As Mason (1983) points out, for colonial America Main (1965) found that as production shifted from subsistence farming to commercial farming social stratification increased, as reflected in the proportion of taxes paid by individuals. Lemon and Nash (1968), however, disagree with Main's use of frontier, subsistence, and commercial farming and point out that in portions of colonial Pennsylvania farmers were exporting agricultural products within two years of settlement.

Tax records have been used in several studies of frontier areas to order households by wealth. Although this method has been questioned by some historians and geographers (e.g., Lemon and Nash 1968) because of its bias against small landowners, it does provide a rough approximation of wealth. Using the method, Lemon and Nash (1968) found that in a portion of colonial Pennsylvania there was an increase in wealth differentiation through time, with the wealthiest 10% of the sample households controlling 38% of the taxable wealth by 1800. Similar findings were made by Mitchell (1977) in the Shenandoah Valley.

To avoid the problems in using tax lists, we based wealth rankings for households in the Salt River valley strictly on ownership of land and slaves. While these two categories emphasize real property as opposed to personal property, the data are easily generated from census schedules and land records. Based on our analysis, the reverse of the findings discussed above holds: there was a decrease through time in the amount of wealth held by the wealthiest households in the upper decile. The greatest differentiation appeared in 1830 (the wealthiest 10% controlled 47% of the wealth) and the least in 1850 (the wealthiest 10% controlled 40% of the wealth). Despite these figures, Mason (1983) points out that the *range* in wealth—the difference between the richest and poorest—was much greater in 1850 than in 1830.

Mason also points out that the most significant conclusion reached from this study is that obvious differences in wealth were present from the period of initial colonization. He believes the greater concentration of wealth among the richest members of the population in 1830 compared with 1850 is due in part to the large number of landless households in 1830. This appears logical, since in 1830 all of the poorest decile and part of the next decile consisted of households with zero wealth. Since all households in the 1830 wealth ranking eventually became land entrants, the subsequent entry of land by households with no land in 1830 gradually reduced the concentration of wealth.

Thus it appears that households with greatly varying degrees of wealth immigrated to the Salt Valley. Once in the frontier area, the effects of relatively inexpensive land on the net wealth of households were twofold. First, it allowed the landless to become landowners, creating a substantial middle class. Second, it allowed the wealthy to become wealthier. By 1850,

92.7% of all resident households that eventually would enter land had done so, an increase of roughly 3% over the percentage of households in residence in 1830. Of the entrants present in 1830, 75% increased their landholdings by 1850, and the percentage of households with at least one slave increased from 27% in 1830 to 40% in 1850.

In summary, the high degree of wealth concentration in 1830 (47% of the wealth held by the upper decile of households)—twelve years after initial colonization (Mason 1983 suggests that probably 75% of the settlers in 1830 had been in residence less than three years)—demonstrates that the upper South social stratification system evident in the Bluegrass region of Kentucky (chap. 3) was reproduced immediately upon the arrival of colonists in the Salt River valley. In the following two sections we briefly discuss trends observed in the data on general settlement relative to changes in the basic elements of wealth discussed above—land and slaves. These elements will be examined in more detail in a later section, where we discuss case examples from several locales in the project area.

LAND

As we have noted throughout the book, the availability of relatively inexpensive land in Missouri was one important factor that led to emigration from the trans-Appalachian East during the early nineteenth century. Mason's (1983) analysis of the region encompassing the project area shows that the average amount of land residents entered between 1818 and 1835 was about 170 acres.[1] For the entire sales period 1818–58 the average purchase size by residents was about 189 acres. Of particular interest is that, between 1818 and 1835, 70.5% of all resident entrants purchased 160 acres or less. By far the most common entry was 80 acres (30.2%), followed by 160 acres (14.4%). Before 1836, only 6% of all residents entered more than 400 acres, with a maximum of 1,560 acres. Between 1818 and 1858, only 10% of all residents entered more than 400 acres, with a maximum of 2,160 acres. Based on land entry data, then, there was an emerging middle class of landowners with rather modest holdings and a minor class (approximately 10%) of "estate" owners.

Table 9.2 gives the frequency distribution of number of acres of land per farm, as listed in the 1850 agricultural census. The average farm size of 264 acres exceeds that noted for the period 1818–58 (189), while the number of farms listed (681) is a bit more than half the total number of entrants who purchased land between 1818 and 1858 (1,164). As Mason (1983) points out, this may be due to consolidation of smaller holdings into larger farms.

1. The acreage figures are weighted somewhat toward the upper end of the scale because of various land laws requiring the purchase of minimum-sized units (see chaps. 3 and 5).

Table 9.2. Frequency Distribution of Number of Acres of Land per Farm for the Households Listed in the 1850 Agricultural Census

Acres[a]	Farms	Percentage	Cumulative Percentage
1–99	106	15.6	15.6
100–199	213	31.3	46.9
200–299	160	23.5	70.4
300–399	91	13.4	83.8
400–499	36	5.3	89.1
500–599	25	3.7	92.8
600–699	20	2.9	95.7
700–799	5	0.7	96.4
800–899	8	1.2	97.6
900–999	1	0.1	97.7
1,000–1,099	3	0.4	98.1
1,100–1,199	5	0.7	98.8
1,200–1,299	0	0.0	
1,300–1,399	1	0.1	98.9
1,400–1,499	1	0.1	99.0
1,500–1,599	0	0.0	
1,600–1,699	2	0.3	99.3
1,700–1,799	1	0.1	99.4
1,800–1,899	1	0.1	99.5
1,900–2,000	2	0.3	99.8
Total	681		

Source: Mason (1983)
[a]$\bar{X} = 264$.

Although 20% of all entries made by residents between 1818 and 1858 were quarter section units, only 7% of the 681 farms listed in the 1850 agricultural census were less than 80 acres. Based on these data, we suspect that 40 acres was below the amount necessary to remain economically sound. Thus by 1850 it appears that the third stage of the model discussed in chapter 2—what Hudson (1969) refers to as the competition phase—was already in operation, only twenty years after the period of initial settlement (Mason 1983; Warren, O'Brien, and Mason 1981).

SLAVES

As we mentioned in chapter 3, the importance of slaves in the upper South socioeconomic system has been called into question by some historians (e.g., Trexler 1914; Viles 1920), who have emphasized the prestige value of slaves rather than their economic importance. Given the shift toward hemp and tobacco production in sections of the Bluegrass during the early nineteenth century, however, we doubt their emphasis applies to that region. Likewise, we doubt it applies directly to the Salt River valley. We do not mean that no prestige was attached to owning slaves; Mason (1983), Trexler (1914), and Viles (1920) offer ample documentation that slave ownership was an integral part of social position. As we will show, however, there was a fairly definite economic side to the practice of slavery in the upper South.

Upper South slavery developed in a different manner from the lower South tradition of using slaves in large-scale production of cotton and tobacco. Although slaves were used in cultivating and harvesting tobacco, hemp, and corn in the upper South, their role was limited to that of "farmhand" or domestic laborer, working in the fields alongside the landowner. The importance—economic as well as social—of slaves in the trans-Appalachian East can be seen in the percentage of households in the Bluegrass region that owned slaves. In 1792, 23% of Kentucky households owned slaves, with an average slaveholding of about 4.3 (chap. 3). In Woodford County the rate was 35.3% (Coward 1979).

In the central Salt River valley, similar percentages are evident for the first half of the nineteenth century (Mason 1983). According to data from the population census schedules for 1830, 1840, and 1850, 30–40% of all heads of rural households owned slaves. For each census the average number of slaves per entrant household that owned slaves rose, from 3.1 in 1830, to 4.0 in 1840, to 4.8 in 1850 (the averages for nonentrant households were slightly lower). Also, for each census the number of slave-owning households containing more than 5 slaves never rose above 25%. However, the number of slaves owned by the upper decile of slaveholders increased dramatically from one census to the next. The minimum and maximum for this group rose from 8 and 11 in 1830, to 9 and 28 in 1840, to 10 and 35 in 1850. These increases undoubtedly inflated the averages per household noted above.

These figures on slaveholding can be compared with those from other areas in Missouri. Based on the 1850 census for all households (including nonentrants) in the Boonslick region, Trexler (1914) calculated an average of 4.7 slaves per household. This compares with 4.6 per household for the state of Missouri (Trexler 1914) and 4.3 per household for the central Salt Valley. Calculating the percentage of slaves in the overall population of the project area, we note an increase from 13.3% in 1830, to 18.4% in 1840, to 21.2% in 1850. In the state as a whole, however, the percentage dropped from 17.8% to 15.2%, to 12.8% over the same period (Trexler 1914).

Two examples of slaveholdings from the project area provided by Mason (1983) are excellent case studies of the activities of agriculturists with many slaves. The first, Edward Shropshire, was listed in the 1840 census as owning 28 slaves. Beginning in 1831, he entered 400 acres near Crooked Creek, in section 3, T55N, R10W and, according to his will filed in 1843, was growing tobacco. Shropshire was unmarried, and his entire labor force consisted of slaves. Nineteen of his 28 slaves were listed in the 1840 census as being over the age of ten, and all were listed as being engaged in agriculture. Based on the amount of land and number of slaves owned, Shropshire was by far the wealthiest man in the project area in 1840.

The second wealthiest person in 1840 was William Huston, who owned 21 slaves and 760 acres, most of which was a few miles southeast of Florida. Only 8 of his 21 slaves were over ten years old in 1840, and in 1850, only 11 of 35 slaves were older than ten years of age. In 1850 Huston was engaged in general farming and was producing some flax (400 pounds). Mason (1983) suggests that the large number of children among Huston's slaves may indicate that he was raising slaves for sale.

Examples of the Upper South Pattern

The case examples used to examine the various components of the upper South cultural pattern are taken from the three communities discussed in detail in chapter 6: the Smith settlement, the McGee settlement, and the Poage settlement. By way of summary, the Smith settlement was formed by an extended family from Bath County, Kentucky, who immigrated in 1819 to an area just north of the Middle Fork, in T54–55N, R9W (fig. 7.1). Throughout the 1820s family offspring entered tracts of land in close proximity to one another, so that by 1830 a compact, interrelated settlement cluster dominated that portion of the region. The McGee settlement, situated south of the Smith settlement between the Middle and Elk forks and south of Elk Fork (fig. 7.2), was composed of several families interrelated through marriages in Kentucky. Land entries began as early as 1823 with the arrival of colonists from Mercer County, Kentucky, and increased dramatically throughout the 1820s and early 1830s. The Poage settlement, between the Middle and North forks (fig. 7.7), was composed of members of a single family and a related family, all of whom came from Greenup County, Kentucky. Settlement began in 1830, and within a few years colonization of the area by the related families was complete. Expansion of early holdings continued throughout the decade.

These three settlement clusters, or communities, were selected for treatment here because of our interest in the effects of social relations on farmstead and household composition and organization. In short, we have already demonstrated in chapter 7 some of the effects of kinship and intermarriage on the pattern of settlement in the three locales, supporting the proposition made in chapter 2 that proximity to family and kin was an important consideration during the colonization phase of settlement. The process that effected proximal settlement was termed *interdependent immigration,* as exemplified by the founders of what we have referred to as the McGee and Poage settlements. Also supported was the proposition that during the spread phase, *proximal budding* gave rise to clustered settlement distribution, as exemplified by land-entry locations of certain members. Given these findings, we can now examine individual households in terms of their size, wealth, agricultural practices, material goods, subsistence strategies, and changes in each of these categories through time.

Household Composition and Size

The basic structural unit of groups immigrating to the Salt River valley was the family, which was in some cases a simple nuclear family and in others a complex extended family. In this section we examine the size and composition of households in the project area to gain some appreciation for the variation in these dimensions over time. Our treatment of the topic is brief, since Mason (1983) presents an in-depth analysis of the subject. The following discussion of data relative to the project area at large is synthesized from his report.

Using data from the population census schedules, frequency distributions of numbers of persons per household (table 9.3) indicate that most immigrant families were quite large upon arrival in the mid to late 1820s (averaging 5.6 persons) and that the trend toward large family size continued throughout the 1830s (6.4 persons per household) and 1840s (6.6 persons per household). Although the 1830 and 1840 schedules do not list names of individual members (other than the head of the household) and do not indicate how members are related, age and sex distributions do suggest that most households were composed of families. Most were probably nuclear families, but many were more complex, apparently containing unmarried adult siblings of the head of the household and some older adults. In some cases the household was composed of a joint family, often composed of two generations of the original nuclear family plus the family of a married daughter or son. Better data exist for 1850, since names of all household members were taken. Roughly 30% of households in the project area contained persons with surnames different from that of the head of the household, though it is impossible in most cases to establish relationships.

Two families from the Smith settlement can be used to examine changes in the size of households from the 1820s on. Both are fairly typical of other households in the census, and we use the examples in an attempt to relate family size to other data over which we have fairly precise control.

The first household is that of Matthew Mappin, a native of Bath County, Kentucky, who immigrated with his brother to the Salt River frontier during the mid-1820s. He married Eliza McGee in 1826 and first entered land in the project area in 1828. His first house, a two-room cabin, was built about this time. By 1834 the Mappins had four daughters, and by 1838 they had added

Table 9.3. Persons per Household in the Project Area in 1830, 1840, and 1850

Person per Household[a]	1830		1840[b]		1850	
	Number of Households	Percentage	Number of Households	Percentage	Number of Households	Percentage
1	5	2.4	14	1.3	6	0.7
2	17	8.2	70	6.7	57	6.9
3	24	11.6	93	8.9	64	7.7
4	28	13.5	123	11.7	102	12.3
5	30	14.5	136	13.0	83	10.0
6	22	10.6	133	12.7	108	13.0
7	26	12.6	102	9.7	100	12.0
8	26	12.6	111	10.6	93	11.2
9	10	4.8	92	8.8	79	9.5
10	12	5.8	83	7.9	48	5.8
11	3	1.4	45	4.3	42	5.1
12	2	1.0	22	2.1	16	1.9
13	1	0.5	14	1.3	9	1.1
14	1	0.5	6	0.6	11	1.3
15	0	0.0	4	0.4	3	0.4
16	0	0.0	0	0.0	5	0.6
17	0	0.0	0	0.0	2	0.2
18	0	0.0	1	0.1	0	0.0
Households	207		1,049		830	
Population	1,192		6,766		5,502	
Mean number of persons per household	5.6		6.4		6.6	

Source: Mason (1983).

[a]Not including slaves and residents of towns.
[b]Including residents outside the project area.

Table 9.4. Vital Statistics on Nine Children of Matthew and Eliza Mappin

Name	Year of Birth	Year of Marriage	Year of Death
Mary Jane	1827	1846	1908
Catherine	1829	1852, 186?	1901
Evaline	1832	1853	1905
Eliza	1834	1853, 1866, 1870	1893
James	1836	—	1842
John	1838	—	1861
Susan	1841	1857	1914
Unnamed male	1844	—	1844
Mary Thomas	1846	1868	1879

two sons. About 1840, to accommodate his growing family, Mappin decided to expand his house, adding the massive Greek Revival block shown in figure 8.13 to the east wall of the cabin. Three more children were born in the 1840s—two daughters and a son—though the infant son died (in 1844), as did an older son (in 1842). Just before Mappin's death in January 1849 at the age of fifty-four, his household consisted of two adults and seven children.

Typical of project area families is the spacing between children, which in the case of the Mappins was no more than three years (table 9.4). Also typical is the age at which girls married, which ranged from sixteen to twenty-three for the Mappin offspring (table 9.4). Based on a sample from the project area that includes all persons whose age at marriage is known (104 cases), the average age at marriage was nineteen for females and twenty-four for males.

The second example is the household of Samuel H. Smith, who with his father, brothers, sisters, and brothers-in-law immigrated to Missouri from Bath County, Kentucky, about 1819. Born in 1806, Smith married Martha Yates (the daughter of a nearby family) in 1828 and entered a quarter section of land that same year. We surmise that an early cabin, which later grew into a massive log house (fig. 8.11), was erected about this date. Beginning in 1831 the Smith family grew at the rate of one child every two years for eighteen years. The remarkable feature of this growth is that children were spaced *exactly* two years apart until the Smiths had produced four daughters and five sons. At that point, unless a child we are unaware of died, the Smiths waited four years before adding another daughter to their family.

Both examples presented above suggest a pattern among households in the project area of maintaining large family sizes. Immigrating families tended to be large upon arrival in the Salt River valley, and couples that married after immigration likewise continued the trend of having large families, with a new child every two to three years. The existence of large family units suggests the influence of the upper South social pattern, with its emphasis on large, established families. More family members also provided the labor necessary for the growth and economic success of the family farm.

Household Wealth

Wealth of project area residents is measured by ownership of land and slaves. Several sources of data on these variables are available. First, the number of slaves per owner can be obtained from population census schedules. Second, landownership data are contained in the land entry records and in the agricultural census schedules for 1850. We pointed out in chapter 5 that our analysis of settlement patterns through time is based solely on land purchased directly from the federal government and does not take into account private transactions among individuals. This obviously creates a nonsystematic bias that impairs attempts to calculate aggregate landholdings of any single individual at any given time. We can, however, control for some of this bias by using the 1850 agricultural census, which lists the number of improved and unimproved acres and the value of all land owned by each household that produced $100 worth of commodities (Wright and Hunt 1900).

A survey of the relation between the amount of acreage owned and its value as listed in the census schedules shows no direct correlation. Thus it appears that the census enumerator made a judgment as to the productivity of the land and figured land values accordingly. On the average, land values fluctuated between $5 and $5.50 an acre. Our independent estimates of the mean value support Mason's (1983) use of $5.24 an acre.

Table 9.5 lists data from the 1850 agricultural census schedule relative to fourteen families—five from the Smith settlement, five from the McGee settlement, and four from the Poage settlement.[2] The table shows considerable variation in both the amount of acreage owned and the value placed on it.

Table 9.6 lists land value, number and value of slaves, and total wealth for each household, along with the rank of each household (by decile) relative to 681 project area farms listed in the agricultural census. As with the acreage and land value, there is considerable variation among households in number of slaves owned, from zero to twelve. As a group, sample households in the Poage settlement were the wealthiest, with all falling in the three upper deciles of wealth.[3] Richard D. Powers, with twelve slaves and 890 acres (valued at

2. Apparently other original families from the Smith, McGee, and Poage settlements emigrated from the region, or else the head of the household died and his widow remarried, thus not appearing in the census.

3. The upper and lower limits for each decile are as follows (in dollars): (1) 34,000–5,801,

$4,000),[4] fell well within the upper decile. His improved acreage (490 acres) was more than double that of any household in the sample, and his slaveholdings were exactly double those of his nearest competitor. The three other sample households in the settlement owned between 270 and 800 acres and from four to six slaves.

Households in the Smith settlement, on the average, did not rival those mentioned above in wealth. Only one of the five households reached the third decile (that of John B. Smith), and the others were in either the fourth or the fifth rank. John B. Smith had nearly double the amount of improved acreage owned by each of the other four and also owned twice as many slaves as anyone else. Otho Adams actually owned 210 acres more than Smith but received a lower valuation of his property.

The least wealthy group consisted of households from the McGee settlement. All five fell in the lower five wealth deciles, with one in the ninth decile (John S. McGee) and one in the tenth (Robert McGee). Only two households owned slaves, each with one. Although two residents of the McGee settlement (John Curry and Walker Simpson) owned more land than did the least landed resident of the Smith settlement, their land valuations never surpassed those from the latter locale (table 9.5).

Changes through time in the amount of wealth held by a household are difficult to document because of the aforementioned problems of demonstrating contemporaneity of landholdings for periods before 1850. To reduce the effects of this bias, we use only landholdings as they existed by 1830 for comparison with the 1850 data presented above. Our assumption is that few private transactions occurred before this date; thus the sum of land entries made before that year should be a fairly accurate assessment of the acreage a household held in 1830. Table 9.7 lists the amount and value of the acreage ($1.25 an acre), the number of slaves (listed in the 1830 population census) and their value ($200 each), and the total wealth for sample households in the Smith and McGee settlements. Since the Poage settlement was not formed until 1830, households from that locale cannot be used. However, the samples from the other two settlements are larger than those used previously, owing to

---

(2) 5,800–3,601, (3) 3,600–2,601, (4) 2,600–2,001, (5) 2,000–1,501, (6) 1,500–1,001, (7) 1,000–801, (8) 800–601, (9) 600–401, (10) 400–0 (Mason 1983).

4. As discussed earlier, there is no simple formula to calculate the valuation. In addition, there appears to have been no objective weighting of value between improved and unimproved land, as evidenced by the case of Eliza Mappin versus that of Otho Adams. Mappin owned 280 unimproved and 60 improved acres and received a valuation of $2,000. Adams owned 400 unimproved and 80 improved acres but received a valuation of only $1,400 (see table 9.3).

Table 9.5. Agricultural Census Data on a Sample of Fourteen Farmsteads

Census Category[a]	Eliza Mappin[b]	Samuel Smith	Joseph Smith	John Smith	Otho Adams	John Curry	Robert McGee
Improved land (acres)	60	60	80	150	80	80	30
Unimproved land (acres)	280	300	120	120	400	160	50
Value of land (dollars)	2,000	2,000	1,000	1,600	1,400	1,000	300
Value of farm implements (dollars)	5	75	130	100	150	100	25
Value of home manufacture (dollars)	50	50	—	20	—	40	30
Horses	4	8	4	3	5	5	6
Mules	—	—	—	—	—	—	—
Milk cows	2	1	3	—	5	4	5
Oxen	—	—	—	—	—	—	—
Cattle	1	10	5	—	10	10	3
Sheep	30	30	—	31	40	30	23
Swine	8	30	100	28	14	25	15
Value of animals (dollars)	180	360	335	265	350	275	200
Wheat (bu.)	—	52	85	100	100	—	36
Rye (bu.)	—	—	—	—	—	—	—
Corn (bu.)	250	500	750	1,000	500	250	600
Oats (bu.)	30	200	100	100	60	50	100
Wool (lbs.)	80	80	—	75	—	60	60
Hay (tons)	2	2	—	10	20	1	40
Flax (lbs.)	100	100	—	—	—	—	500
Flaxseed (bu.)	—	—	—	—	—	—	—
Maple sugar (lbs.)	70	500	—	—	—	—	—
Molasses (gals.)	3	4	—	—	—	—	—
Honey and beeswax (lbs.)	25	—	—	—	—	—	—

[a]Not all categories appearing in the census are listed.
[b]Widow of Matthew Mappin.

the appearance in the 1830 census of individuals who died or moved away before 1850.

The distribution of wealth within the Smith settlement is remarkably consistent. Six households owned 160 acres, two owned 80 acres, and one owned 240 acres. None owned slaves. Within the McGee settlement, the distribution of wealth is more uneven. John McKamey, who in 1830 ranked third in the project area in terms of total wealth (Mason 1983), owned 1,600 acres and five slaves, placing him in a category of his own. Only two other households owned slaves.

Table 9.5. *Continued.*

	Farmstead Owner						
Census Category[a]	John S. McGee	Robert Simpson	Walker Simpson	James Poage	Thomas Poage	Richard Powers	John Stewart
Improved land (acres)	36	50	60	200	220	490	125
Unimproved land (acres)	124	110	240	115	580	400	145
Value of land (dollars)	500	1,000	1,000	2,500	3,000	4,000	1,200
Value of farm implements (dollars)	160	85	25	80	200	200	100
Value of home manufacture (dollars)	10	—	15	60	75	175	50
Horses	8	5	6	6	8	12	6
Mules	—	—	—	11	—	63	—
Milk cows	6	3	4	9	8	17	6
Oxen	—	—	—	2	6	6	—
Cattle	5	7	6	9	45	3	60
Sheep	30	14	12	62	75	75	30
Swine	40	50	30	30	50	25	15
Value of animals (dollars)	445	274	350	700	800	3,340	600
Wheat (bu.)	15	30	40	50	200	200	30
Rye (bu.)	—	—	—	—	—	—	—
Corn (bu.)	500	350	400	1,500	1,000	1,250	1,000
Oats (bu.)	30	100	200	700	600	500	300
Wool (lbs.)	35	35	20	100	130	180	80
Hay (tons)	5	4	2	4	20	20	10
Flax (lbs.)	—	—	—	—	—	400	—
Flaxseed (bu.)	50	—	—	—	—	21	—
Maple sugar (lbs.)	—	—	50	—	—	—	—
Molasses (gals.)	4	—	—	—	—	—	—
Honey and beeswax (lbs.)	—	—	—	—	—	—	—

Although the sample is small, a comparison of slave- and landholdings for households in 1830 and 1850 indicates that, of the households appearing in both censuses, there was a strong tendency to increase holdings of both through time (table 9.8). All five households in the Smith settlement increased their landholdings by an average of 190 acres. Two households owned slaves by 1850, compared with one in 1830. Of the five households in the McGee settlement, only two increased their holdings (by 80 acres and 140 acres); the other three decreased their holdings by an average of 120 acres. Slaveholdings remained constant between years, with the exception of one household that added a slave.

While certainly not conclusive, the data presented thus far support the

Table 9.6. Value of Land and Slaves, Wealth, and Wealth Rank for a Sample of Fourteen Households in 1850 (in dollars)

Household	Land Value	Slave Value[a]	Wealth	Wealth Rank
Smith settlement				
Eliza Mappin	2,000		2,000	4th/5th
Samuel Smith	2,000		2,000	4th/5th
Joseph Smith	1,000	800 (2)[b]	1,800	5th
John Smith	1,600	1,600 (4)	3,200	3d
Otho Adams	1,400	400 (1)	1,800	5th
McGee settlement				
John Curry	1,000	400 (1)	1,400	6th
Robert McGee	300		300	10th
John S. McGee	500		500	9th
Robert Simpson	1,000	400 (1)	1,400	6th
Walker Simpson	1,000		1,000	7th
Poage settlement				
James Poage	2,500	1,600 (4)	4,100	2d
Thomas Poage	3,000	2,400 (6)	5,400	2d
Richard Powers	4,000	4,800 (12)	8,800	1st
John Stewart	1,200	2,000 (5)	3,200	3d

[a]The value of each slave is figured at $400 (Trexler 1914).
[b]Number of slaves in parentheses.

assumption that obvious differences in wealth existed from the period of initial colonization. The differences in wealth exhibited by households in the McGee and Smith settlements, compared with those in the Poage settlement, are not attributable totally to success in the frontier region. Thus, well-to-do colonists were able to take advantage of inexpensive land in the frontier at a faster rate than were colonists of moderate means.

The data also indicate that there was great similarity in wealth among interdependent family groups. For example, in 1850 all four sample households in the Poage settlement were in the upper 30% of the wealth ranks, while the five households in the McGee settlement were in the lower 50%. Of the five sons and sons-in-law of Joseph H. Smith, Sr., who entered land during the latter half of the 1820s,[5] four entered quarter section units (James C. Fox was the exception).[6] By 1850 the four were in the third, fourth, or fifth wealth ranks, with total wealth accumulations of between $1,800 and $3,200 (table 9.6).

5. Alexander Smith, probably the eldest son, entered land in 1819, upon arrival in the project area (chaps. 5 and 7).

6. As we mentioned in chapter 5, Fox apparently had little interest in agriculture, preferring to spend his time in politics. He was also a lawyer and made several trips to Kentucky to settle legal affairs there.

In summary, the data indicate that within our sample we are dealing with at least two social divisions—an upper class, characterized by large landholdings and numerous slaves, and a middle class, characterized by smaller landholdings and one slave or none. As we noted previously, this is a significant dimension of the upper South system. In the following section we add another dimension to the analysis to determine how it affects the model of two divisions within the system.

Agricultural Production

As we stated earlier, mixed farming—and in some areas the production of tobacco and hemp with slave labor—is the hallmark of the upper South agricultural pattern. Based on the data presented thus far, we find wide support for the notion that frontier agriculturists in the central Salt River valley were very much a part of the system that created this pattern. One aspect of the upper South agricultural pattern that is of particular interest here is the ratio between the amounts of food crops and nonfood crops produced. In other words, how much of a household's effort and time was put into raising hemp and tobacco—and possibly flax—as opposed to growing corn and other comestibles? Also, how much of an investment was tied up in livestock

Table 9.7. Amount and Value of Acreage, Number and Value of Slaves, and Wealth Held by Seventeen Households in the Smith and McGee Settlements in 1830

Household	Acreage	Value (dollars)	Number of Slaves	Value (dollars)	Wealth (dollars)
Smith settlement					
James Mappin	160	200			200
Matthew Mappin[a]	160	200			200
Samuel Smith[a]	160	200			200
Joseph Smith[a]	160	200			200
John Smith[a]	160	200			200
Alexander Smith	240	300			300
Otho Adams[a]	160	200			200
Ovid Adams	80	100			100
James C. Fox	80	100			100
McGee settlement					
John McKamey	1,280	1,600	5	1,000	2,600
John Curry[a]	160	200	1	200	400
John Simpson	160	200			200
Robert Simpson[a]	400	500			500
Walker Simpson[a]	160	200			200
Robert McGee[a]	160	200			200
Jane McGee	240	300	1	200	500
John S. McGee[a]	200	250			250

[a] Also appears in the 1850 census.

Table 9.8. Percentage Change between 1830 and 1850 in Amount of Acreage, Number of Slaves, and Wealth Held by Ten Households in the Smith and McGee Settlements

Household	Acreage		Number of Slaves		Wealth (dollars)	
	1830	1850	1830	1850	1830	1850
Smith settlement						
Matthew Mappin	160	340			200	2,000
Samuel Smith	160	360			200	2,000
Joseph Smith	160	200		2	200	1,800
John Smith	160	270		4	200	3,200
Otho Adams	160	480		1	200	1,800
McGee settlement						
John Curry	160	240	1	1	400	1,400
Robert Simpson	400	160		1	500	1,400
Walker Simpson	160	300			200	1,000
Robert McGee	160	80			200	300
John S. McGee	200	160			250	500

production? To answer these questions we turn to the statistics presented in the 1850 agricultural census (table 9.1),[7] both to summarize the region as a whole and to extract data relative to the households in the three-settlement sample.

Corn, as we noted, was grown by 680 of the 681 households appearing in the census. Although the average amount of corn raised per household was 832 bushels, the mean is highly inflated by a few households that raised 2,000–5,000 bushels. When the production figures for the upper 10% of corn producers are removed, the average yield drops to 693 bushels. Table 9.5 lists the corn yields for our sample of households in 1850. Estimated yields range from 250 to 1,500 bushels, with a fairly low correlation between acreage and yield. Using the criterion for identifying major producers of "market commodities" (the mean plus one standard deviation), only one farmer (James Poage) raised at least the minimum amount (1,440 bushels) necessary for consideration.

When figures for wheat, and especially for oats, are added to those for corn, the correlation between acreage owned and total grain production is significant. For example, households in the Poage settlement—the largest landowners in the sample—raised between 1,330 and 2,250 bushels of grain, considerably more than the other ten sample households. Only two households—those of Thomas Poage and Richard D. Powers—meet the criterion for major producers of wheat (167 bushels); and three meet those for producers of

7. Based on the fact that all yield figures are divisible by fifty, we can safely assume that the figures are only rough estimates.

oats—the two above plus James Poage (table 9.5). Wheat certainly was produced for consumption by humans, and ten households in the project area produced enough (167 bushels) to be considered major producers. Oats, however, probably were grown for livestock feed, as shown by the correlation between households with large numbers of mules and horses and high productivity of oats (discussed below).

Livestock production figures for the sample households show that all fifteen households raised horses and pigs and that fourteen also kept dairy cows and nondairy cattle. The one household with no cattle or dairy cows raised sheep, as did thirteen other households. Only two households raised mules, and only three kept oxen. These figures are consistent with the overall trends in the project area (table 9.1).

The dominance of sheep over the other types of livestock raised is somewhat surprising since, as Mason (1983) points out, sheep are not mentioned as characteristic of upper South agriculture. The average number of sheep per household in the project area was twenty-six, and the average number of pounds of wool was about fifty-seven. These figures fit well with the averages from the sample households in the McGee and Smith settlements, although six of the nine households with sheep owned slightly more than the average number. For three households in the Poage settlement, however, the number of animals was much higher, as was the amount of wool on hand (table 9.5). Quite likely these households were exporting wool to external markets.

The one farmer who raised no sheep, Joseph H. Smith, Jr., appears to have been a major producer of swine, producing almost double the number of animals needed to meet our criterion. Hence, he was one of only eighteen major swine producers in the region and one of few major producers of any commodity in our sample of households in the Smith and McGee settlements.

Among the four households in the Poage settlement, we find that for classes of livestock other than swine, at least one household—and usually two—has production figures well above the mean plus one standard deviation. In some cases the figures are so high that there is little doubt that the households were producing for external markets. For example, Thomas Poage and John Stewart had over four and six times the number of cattle listed for the other thirteen households—figures that put them well into the class of major producers. Their relatives—James Poage and Richard D. Powers—rather than raising cattle, were major producers of mules. In fact Powers was the second largest producer of mules in the project area. Because of their hardiness mules were favored over horses for agricultural work (Gray 1958). Mule raising in Missouri began during the 1820s, when Mexican donkeys were transported along the Santa Fe trail and bred to Kentucky horses (Ashton 1924). Although their popularity extended to the lower South, mule production was not practiced widely there. Rather, mules were produced in the upper South and shipped to the lower South.

Powers also raised more horses and milk cows than others in the sample, and, like Thomas Poage, more oxen. Although the sample is small, there is a strong correlation between households with large acreage and those with oxen. Both Powers and Poage owned extremely large tracts of land (890 and 800 acres, respectively), considerable portions of which lay on the prairie. To bring this land into production, gangs of oxen often were used to break the tough prairie sod. Thus these two agriculturists were able to use their wealth to obtain the animals needed to expand the realized niche through cultivation of the prairie.

Commodities other than grain and livestock were not produced widely among households in the sample. Tobacco and hemp, for example, grown by 11% and 2% of the households in the project area, do not appear at all. Flax, grown by 25% of all households, shows up in about that percentage of sample households. In two households—those of Robert McGee and Richard Powers—the amount of flax listed in the census (500 pounds and 400 pounds, respectively) places them at the top of the list of all flax producers in the project area. Interestingly, McGee owned only 80 acres, most of which must have been taken up by flax production.

One other major producer was Samuel H. Smith, who was credited in the agricultural census with 500 pounds of maple sugar. Slightly fewer than 8% of the 681 households produced maple sugar in 1850, and Smith was near the top in production.

In summary, our analysis of agricultural production figures for the sample households, both in terms of variability within the sample and relative to the project area as a whole, further emphasizes the differences in wealth between the middle class and upper class in upper South society. Without much doubt, our sample of fifteen households can now be divided into two groups: the upper-class Poage settlement families and the middle-class Smith and McGee settlement families. Households in the former settlement dominate almost all grain and livestock production categories, often by a margin that implies they were producing for export. Comparing production figures for those households with figures from the project area supports the conclusion.

Even within the middle class, households can be identified as major producers, as exemplified by Samuel Smith (maple sugar), Robert McGee (flax), and Joseph H. Smith, Jr. (swine). Based on the sample, however, major producers in the middle class produced *only* one commodity, as opposed to the multiple commodities often produced by upper-class households.

The frequency of slaves within the sample dispels the notion that slaves were used mainly for tobacco and hemp production, since no households discussed here raised either product. Mason's analysis also disputes the notion that wealth—of which slaves were a part—went hand in hand with tobacco production. He demonstrates that major livestock-grain producers (who also may have raised some tobacco) were among the wealthiest members of the project area, while producers of tobacco only were concentrated in the middle wealth ranks. While 83% of the livestock-grain producers owned slaves, only 40% of tobacco producers, whether or not they produced another commodity, did so. We conclude from this that instead of the wealthy, slave-owning "planter class" that Mitchell (1978) and others state was characteristic of the Bluegrass region and the upper South in general (chap. 3), there was by 1850 an emerging class of slave-owning stockmen (cf. Mason 1983) that would begin to dominate the upper class.

Material Goods

Data on the material goods owned by individual households were generated through the analysis of both archaeological materials and probate records. The archaeological household, the data base for which is the archaeological record, represents an incomplete reflection of the ethnographic household. Many items never enter the archaeological record, while a portion of the material remains that do enter it are lost or altered by postdepositional processes. We have attempted to overcome these problems by using probate records as a supplemental source of data. Probate records include inventories, which itemize crops, livestock, and other material goods; appraisals, which list the probable value of land, animals, and goods on hand; notes, which are bills accrued by the estate; and sales records, which list items sold by estates, their selling prices, and the buyers to whom the items were sold at the official estate auction. We focus primarily on probate inventories, which were taken by two or more court-appointed, bonded agents. Careful inspection of several sets of probate records from the project area showed that inventories are the most complete records taken during the probate period, duplicating the other records and surpassing them in detail.

The following discussion is limited to three households—those of Samuel H. Smith, Matthew Mappin, and John S. McGee. The areas in and around the Smith and Mappin residences were excavated extensively and produced considerable archaeological material. Also, the probate inventories of both households, especially the Smith household, appear quite thorough. Although the house site of the McGee family was not located during survey, we briefly discuss the probate inventory of the household for comparative purposes.

Our treatment of archaeological data from the two excavated sites varies considerably. Data from both sites are used to discuss spatial distributions of artifact classes, in which we focus on patterns of discard of material goods. Because of the advanced stages of analysis of the material from the Mappin site, we are able to discuss complete household items instead of simply listing fragments of items in various material classes. Material from the Smith house is not at a similar stage and is not used in the discussion of specific items. Before turning to the discussion of household items, we summarize information presented previously on the three households analyzed here.

Samuel Smith purchased 160 acres along the north bank of the Middle Fork in 1828. He apparently constructed a one-room log house on the site shortly after his purchase and later expanded his dwelling by adding a massive log structure on one end of the earlier house (figs. 8.11 and 8.12). The dwelling was again enlarged by a frame section added onto one end of the second log structure. This was the last addition built by Smith, who died in 1872.

In 1829 Matthew Mappin entered 160 acres of land that straddled both sides of the Middle Fork, approximately 1.5 miles southwest of Samuel Smith's farmstead. A two-room log house was erected about that year, and about ten years later the dwelling was enlarged substantially by a large, heavy-timber block added to one end of the log structure (figs. 8.13 and 8.14).[8] Mappin died in 1849.

In 1827 John S. McGee entered 200 acres of land on the south side of the Middle Fork, along the northwestern margin of what we have termed the McGee settlement. No house site can be linked to McGee, who died in 1851.

Technical Procedures

Excavation of the archaeological deposits at the Mappin and Smith sites was in 1 square meter units placed in and around the various construction stages of the houses; floorboards were removed to facilitate the excavation of units under the structures. The excavated areas ranged from 152 square meters at the Mappin site (fig. 9.1) to 162 square meters at the Smith site (fig. 9.2). While the entire log structure at the Mappin site was outlined and the interior excavated, only a portion of the interior of the Smith house was excavated. Sizable areas around the perimeters of both houses were also tested. All fill removed by excavation was water screened through quarter-inch hardware cloth.

Recovered materials from each unit were sorted into like groups, then counted or weighed or both. These materials can be placed into four broad, functional classes: kitchen, architectural, nonkitchen-household, and farmstead. Kitchen-related classes include most ceramics, nonwindow glass,

---

8. The log structure was razed in 1893 and replaced by a large balloon-frame Victorian addition. This activity undoubtedly affected the distribution of material, including bone (see O'Brien, Mason, and Saunders 1982).

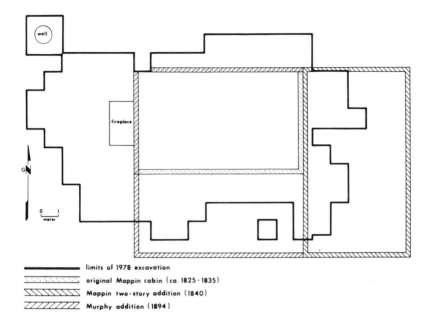

limits of 1978 excavation

original Mappin cabin (ca. 1825 - 1835)

Mappin two-story addition (1840)

Murphy addition (1894)

9.1. Excavation outline and construction phases at the Matthew Mappin house site (from Saunders 1979).

crockery, shell, and bone. Architectural classes include limestone, brick, plaster chinking, nails, window glass, and metal used in construction. Nonkitchen-household classes include such items as coins, toys, furniture parts, firearms, and personal items (pipes, jewelry, etc.). Farmstead-related classes include pieces of farm implements, tools, wire, and animal harnesses. These classes are similar to those developed by South (1977a) in his analysis of material patterns in the colonial East. Because we are interested only in material goods used by the households, architectural classes are not discussed here (see O'Brien, Mason, and Saunders 1982 for an extended treatment of architectural class distributions at the Mappin site). Vertebrate faunal remains, which are significant indicators of the frontier diet, are discussed in detail in the following section of this chapter.

Patterns of Discard

Analysis of the distributions of nonarchitectural classes at both sites revealed that considerable amounts of debris were deposited around the perimeters of the structures, with significant portions of the assemblages ending up under the buildings, despite the continuous stone foundations.

limits of excavation
original Smith cabin (ca. 1830)
first addition (log)
second addition (frame)

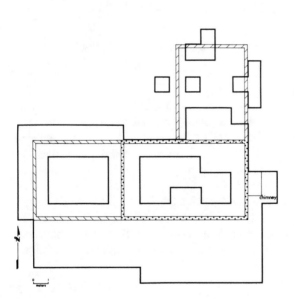

9.2. Excavation outline and construction phases at the Samuel H. Smith house site.

a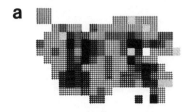

b

c

d

9.3. Distribution of (*a*) nonwindow glass, (*b*) ceramics, (*c*) crockery, and (*d*) metal, by weight, at the Matthew Mappin house site (solid shading indicates units that together contain the highest 10% of material, heavy hatching the next 15%, medium hatching the next 25%, light hatching the next 50%, and stipling 0%).

Importantly, items within several classes—especially kitchen-related classes—were not distributed evenly across excavated areas.

At the Mappin site, the highest-density units for most classes occurred outside or under the west end of the original log house. In a few cases, especially that of nonwindow glass, high-density units were under or to the east of the log structure—in the latter case below the heavy-timber addition erected about 1840. The distributions of weights of material in four classes—nonwindow glass, ceramics, crockery, and nonarchitectural metal are shown in figure 9.3. Crockery exhibits the most uneven distribution, being absent over large contiguous areas under the eastern half of the original structure. The presence of crockery under the timber addition, unless it is intrusive, suggests that crockery vessels were available, or at least were being used, in the project area before about 1840.

The largest concentration of glassware was inside the west wall of the log structure (fig. 9.3). Within the concentration were the remains of at least a dozen bitters and medicine bottles of varying sizes. Concentrations along the northern wall and in the southeast corner of the structure indicate that glass debris was being thrown or swept under the house.

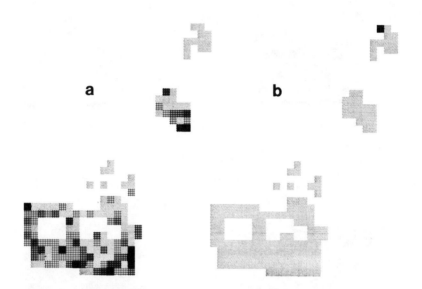

9.4. Distribution of (*a*) nonwindow glass and (*b*) ceramics, by weight, at the Samuel H. Smith house site (solid shading indicates units that together contain the highest 10% of material, heavy hatching the next 15%, medium hatching the next 25%, light hatching the next 50%, and stipling 0%).

The heaviest concentration of ceramic material (fig. 9.3) was under the west room of the log structure, directly beneath the hearth and kitchen area. Although our ability to firmly date much of the ceramic assemblage is limited, owing to the virtual absence of comparable material from the Midwest that has been firmly dated, we can recognize certain ceramic types that date to the period 1820–40. Thus we tentatively suggest that at least some of the deposit in this area of the site dates to the occupation of the log structure. A seriation study currently under way on ceramic material should aid in future attempts to chronologically order this and other assemblages.

A variety of metal artifacts—mostly fragments—were recovered, including tableware, hairpins, stove parts, razors, and a few pieces of agricultural implements. The largest concentrations of material occurred along portions of the north and south walls and outside the west wall.

At the Smith site, 162 1 square meter units were excavated, including 32 units placed to the northwest of the house (fig. 9.2). This was one of the few instances where areas away from a residence were excavated. Given the distributions presented below, data from these areas are invaluable for interpreting the spatial structure of discarded materials.

Only 7 grams of glassware were recovered from the site; all pieces were found along perimeter walls (fig. 9.4). These few grams compare with 13,000

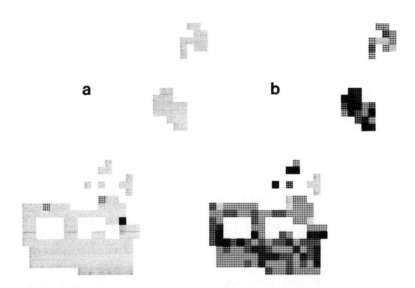

9.5. Distribution of (*a*) crockery and (*b*) metal, by weight, at the Samuel H. Smith house site (solid shading indicates units that together contain the highest 10% of material, heavy hatching the next 15%, medium hatching the next 25%, light hatching the next 50%, and stipling 0%).

grams from the Mappin site. At present we can only speculate that removal from the area of glass fragments larger than quarter inch square was both deliberate and systematic. Perhaps a specific dumping area for glass existed somewhere on the property.

The distribution of crockery is fairly even over the excavated areas, with a few notable exceptions (fig. 9.5). For example, crockery sherds are absent in the 12-square-meter area to the north of the house and occur only sporadically in units in and around the earliest structure. Major concentrations occur to the south and east of the log addition and in the block of units just to the northwest of the earliest structure.

Ceramic material occurred in almost all excavated units, with concentrations around perimeter walls of the log and frame additions and in the 20-square-meter area northwest of the earliest structure (fig. 9.4). This latter concentration, along with the concentration of crockery in the same units, suggests that the area was either a dump or the location of a specialized structure such as a summer kitchen.

Metal, other than nails, was virtually nonexistent at the Smith site (fig. 9.5). One piece of iron—possibly a broken plowshare—was found in the northernmost excavation unit. At present we cannot explain this unexpected phenomenon; perhaps, like the broken glassware, metal was deposited in a specific area of the site.

Table 9.9. Frequencies and Weights of Six Artifact Groups from the Matthew Mappin and Samuel H. Smith House Sites

Artifact Group	Smith	Mappin
Nonwindow glass (grams)	7	12,935
Ceramics (grams)	5,839	4,668
Ceramics (number)	2,183	2,000
Crockery (grams)	3,017	3,501
Crockery (number)	291	504
Buttons (number)	270	218
Toys (number)	25	26
Metal (grams)	120	31,017

Interassemblage Comparisons

Table 9.9 lists counts and weights of material classes in the two excavated assemblages. Except for the extremely low occurrences of nonwindow glass and nonarchitectural metal at Smith, frequencies and weights of most classes at each site are similar. The similarities in weight and frequencies of ceramics and crockery between sites suggest that households of similar status contained roughly the same proportions of some goods. For a better understanding of the composition of the archaeological assemblages—that is, to convert fragments of items to whole units, we now examine a partial reconstruction of the Mappin site archaeological assemblage.

Table 9.10 lists the minimum number of certain glass, ceramic, and crockery items recovered by excavation. Our estimates are extremely conservative; we tabulated as single units only those items that were without doubt not part of other tabulated items. As shown, the group containing the most members is ceramic tableware (170 individual vessels), followed by glass bottles (85) and utilitarian crockery vessels (33). Nonkitchen household glass (lighting implements, thermometers, etc.) is the least represented group.

Although supporting data are lacking at this point, we tentatively suggest that the percentages of occurrence of each form group, relative to the total number of individually tabulated items in the Mappin assemblage, typify archaeological assemblages from upper South sites that were continuously occupied since the frontier period. For example, ceramic tableware, with 170 vessels, constitutes approximately 52% of the tabulated units. The 85 glass bottles constitute 26% of the tabulated units. Another possible line of investigation for patterning would involve tabulating the total frequencies (or weights) of items in each of the overall classes—kitchen, household, and agricultural—and dividing the resulting totals by the grand total of all classes combined. This is similar to South's (1977a,b) approach to analyzing colonial structures in the Carolinas, though he also includes architectural classes in his analysis. We hope that this and other lines of investigation—coupled with the ceramic seriation program currently under way—will allow us to define an upper South material culture pattern. To lay the foundation for such work we examine below the probate records of the Smith, Mappin, and John S. McGee estates and compare the inventories of each. For Mappin we also briefly compare the inventory with the material recovered from excavation.

Probate Inventories

Analysis of the probate inventories yielded some interesting results, not only regarding the households under investigation, but also relative to the use of the documents. In some cases probate inventories can be used to check the accuracy of related information or to supplement that information. For

Table 9.10. Minimum Number of Glass, Crockery, and Ceramic Items from the Matthew Mappin House Site

Vessel Type	Number
Glass	
Household	
Lamp chimney	3
Globe	1
Lightbulb	1
Eyeglass lens	1
Thermometer	4
Eyedropper	2
Mirror	1
Waterer	1
Kitchen	
Tumblers	15
Goblet	1
Bowl	3
Canning jars	5
Bottles	85
Ceramics	
Kitchen	
Plates	52
Cups and saucers	50
Bowls	12
Unknown form	56
Crockery	
Kitchen	
Bowls	6
Jug	1
Butter pots	5
Pots	4
Storage jars	10
Unknown form	7

example, the inventory of the Mappin farmstead and household, taken in 1849, lists significantly higher amounts of agricultural products and more livestock than is shown in the 1850 agricultural census under the entry of Mappin's widow, Eliza Mappin. Records of the estate sale show that some of the animals and products—including tobacco—were purchased during the sale. That in 1849 Mappin had tobacco on hand, along with significantly more hogs, forces us to modify our previous discussion of his activities and to place him in the ranks of major producers.

While inventories are the most useful of the various probate records for studying the material aspects of the household, it is evident that there are certain biases in the documents. One apparent bias is that not all goods were listed when an inventory was taken. More specifically, whether certain classes of items were listed apparently was left to the discretion of the persons taking the inventory. For example, few household items were listed in the Mappin inventory after Matthew Mappin's death in 1849, and even fewer household items were listed in the John S. McGee inventory. Based on similar findings in other probate inventory records, we assume that, because of their higher value, agriculturally related items, along with bulk produce and livestock, were given priority over household items and were enumerated rather carefully. Thus inventory data on nonhousehold goods may be quite reliable guides to actual items on hand.

Presented below are the inventories for the three households/farmsteads. The items listed were copied in order from the originals, though spellings have been corrected. Question marks note an illegible word on the inventory sheet.

Samuel H. Smith

broadax, hoes, & shovel
1 pot rack
4 hayforks
1 grubbing hoe
1 old ax & spade
1 chopping ax
1 shovel plow
1 horse plow
1 two-horse plow
1 two-horse plow
1 one-horse plow
4 augers
1 drawing knife, chisel & square
1 iron wedge and froe

2 bread trays & sifter
2 andirons
2 jugs, washpan, tin bucket, cup
1 cook table
1 tin lard can with lard
1 lard stand with lard
lot tallow
1 pair sheep shears & branding iron
1 brass kettle
1 cooking stove & vessels
1 shovel & tongs
candle molds & funnels

2 pair saddlebags
1 clothes chest
3 bedsteads
1 wheel & reel
4 barrels
1 lot flour
1 lot meal
1 hackle
1 carpet
1 set wagon harness
4 pair plow gear
2 horse collars
2 pair hames
3 work bridles, halters & ropes
1 scoop shovel

1 hand saw
ropes
1 cutting box
1 harrow
1 box old [?]
1 pair singletrees &
  doubletree
stretchers & [?]
3 scythes
1 brier scythe
1 bell and tar can
1 grindstone
3 water barrels
3 salt barrels
1 fish gig
1 sheet iron box
4 iron kettles
2 baskets
1 barrel & molasses
1 barrel & keg
1 lard stand
1 barrel & soap grease
500 lbs. pork
1 meat box
1 washtub & board
1 skillet & lid, old
  bucket of lime
1 spinning wheel
1 soap cag
1 breakfast table
lot meal & flour
  barrels
1 pt. barrel salt
1 keg, boxes & nails

1 water bucket, tin
  bucket & dipper
1 dishpan & coffee
  mill
1 cook press
2 churns
14 chairs
1 dining table
1 heating stove
1 clock
2 lamps & candle stick
1 press
1 lot of Queensware
2 crocks & jar
1 monkeywrench
5 quindets [?] & horse
  fleures
2 looking glasses
2 pair scissors
1 sugar chest
1 bureau
1 double shotgun
1 pair steelyards
1 half bushel
1 bureau
1 lot books
1 stand table
1 heating stove
1 fly brush
2 pair window curtains
1 carpet
1 sausage grinder

2 hogsheads
1 man's saddle &
  bridle
50 bushels wheat
1 two-horse wagon
1 wheat fan
50 barrels corn
12 turkeys
8 meal sacks
2 dozen chickens
40 hogs
1 pale red cow
1 white cow
1 roan cow
1 two-year-old heifer
1 [?] red heifer
1 bull
1 mule colt
1 mule colt
1 black colt
1 two-year-old black
  colt
1 two-year-old bay filly
1 black mare
1 bay mare
1 roan horse
1 old black mare
1 bed & bedding
1 bed & bedding
1 bed & bedding
1 bed & bedding
1 bedstead & cosd [?]
1 bedstead & cosd [?]
1 bedstead & cosd [?]
6 bed blankets
3 quilts & 3 sheets
8 pillows

Matthew Mappin

1 stretcher
1 grubbing hoe
1 stove hammer

1 rifle gun, pouch &
  horn
1 grindstone

1 stock of hay
5 barrels of corn
5 barrels of corn

1 spade
1 hand saw
1 one-inch auger
1 half-inch auger
19 pounds of nails
1 reap hook
1 square, hinges & chisel
1 razor strap
tar buckets
1 sheep shears
1 hone
1 scythe blade
1 mowing blade
1 froe
1 singletree
1 steeple & ring for ox yoke
1 ox yoke ring & steeple
1 jug
stretcher chains & hook
1 blind bridle
1 hammer, gear & collar
1 Carey plow

1 sorrel horse
1 black horse
1 gray horse
2 bay mares
2 steers
6 cows
55 sheep
1 four-horse wagon
1 pair of stretchers
2 grubbing hoes
1 wheat fan
4 diamond plows
2 pair of doubletrees
5 [?]

1 ox sled
log chains
1 diamond plow & stock
1 Carey plow
1 bare share plow
1 bare share plow
1 lot of old harness
1 wheat fan
window blinds & sash
1 large gun
1 large gun
1 large gun
10 first-choice hogs
10 fifth-choice hogs
10 second-choice hogs
10 third-choice hogs
10 sixth-choice hogs
6 hogs eighth lot
1 cow
3 yearling calves
1 yoke of oxen
1 bay filly
1 sorrel mare
1 brown horse

John S. McGee

4 pairs of wagon [?]
4 collars & pair blind bridles
2 weeding hoes
3 axes
1 iron wedge
2 calves
1 pair of steelyards
1 spade
6 beehives
1 grindstone
1 scythe & cradle
1 set of turning tools
1 scythe & [?]

5 barrels of corn
5 barrels of corn
1 lot of tobacco
1 harrow
1 lot of plank
1 dry hide
1 trough & kettle
10 head of sheep
9 head of sheep
37 geese
1 bed & bedding
1 small table
1 large gun
1 beehive
1 black mare
1 bell cow & bell
1 brindle & white cow
1 red cow
1 ax
1 draw knife
11 chains
1 tong & shovels
1 sugar chest
1 press & bookcase
andirons
1 dining table
1 clock

1 rifle gun & powderhorn
1 hand saw & square
3 halter chains
1 brass clock
2 beds & bedding
1 set of planes
2 men's saddles
1 [?] scythe
11 head of hogs
6 head of steers
6 head of heifers
2 bedsteads
1 press
1 dining table

Excluding livestock and agricultural products, the Mappin inventory contains 43 separate entries for items connected with maintenance of the farmstead (nails, hammers, tar buckets, etc.) or agriculture (plows, harnesses, wheat fans, etc.); fourteen entries for household items (guns, a clock, a dining table, bedding, etc.); and a single entry for kitchen items (a sugar chest). The McGee inventory contains twenty-two entries for items connected with farmstead maintenance and agriculture, six entries for household items, and no entries for kitchen items. The Smith inventory contains thirty-eight entries that are assignable to the farmstead class, fifty-one that fall in the household class, and eighteen that can be placed in the kitchen class. Several entries (lard, tallow, and other perishable household products) were deleted from consideration.

Based on frequency of occurrence, it is obvious that the inventory takers who itemized the Smith estate were the most thorough, listing more in the way of household goods than those conducting the other two inventories. Given that the Smith estate was inventoried in 1872—over twenty years after the other two inventories presented here were taken—and that the estate was appraised (total value of goods listed, including livestock and agricultural products, was $1,091.65), there may have been significant reasons for the thorough inventory. One reason may have been that there was a change in the law regarding how inventories were to be taken, or, alternatively, the thoroughness may be attributable simply to the inclinations of the inventory takers.

Assuming that there was comparability in the inventorying of agricultural-farmstead equipment, the three inventories can be compared to determine similarities and differences that might correlate with the amount of land owned, crops produced, or wealth in general. Fortunately, the dates of the Mappin and McGee inventories (1849 and 1851, respectively) fell just before and after the 1850 agricultural census, allowing us to compare the three data sets. The data from the Smith inventory can be used as a measure of change over time in the composition of the agricultural-farmstead class of materials.

In our previous discussions of wealth and agricultural productivity, we noted that based on slave- and landholdings the Mappin household was on the border of the fourth and fifth wealth deciles relative to all households appearing in the 1850 agricultural census. According to information from the estate inventory, Matthew Mappin had considerably more livestock and agricultural products on hand when he died in 1849 than what is listed in the next year's census. Based on the criteria above, the McGee household was in the ninth wealth decile. By comparing the census data with the inventory, we note that McGee had three fewer horses in 1851, three more head of cattle, the same number of milk cows, six heifers compared with none in 1850, twenty-five more sheep, and twenty-nine fewer hogs. If the data are accurate, this comparison presents an insight into the annual fluctuations in the sizes of frontier livestock holdings.

The numbers and kinds of large farm implements owned by the two farmers are fairly even. McGee owned four plows and Mappin owned five; in addition, each owned a wagon. However, Mappin also owned a harrow and a team of oxen, neither of which is listed in the McGee inventory. Almost all of Mappin's equipment was sold at the estate auction in 1849, resulting in a valuation on farm machinery of only $5.00 in the census (table 9.5). Frequencies of other farmstead-related items are fairly equally distributed between the two households. Each owned a variety of wood-cutting and agricultural tools (axes, wedges, spades, scythes, etc.) and several livestock-related items (bridles, collars, etc.). Although carpentry tools are listed in both inventories, there appears to be an underrepresentation of these items in the McGee inventory.

According to the 1850 agricultural census, Samuel Smith owned $75 worth of farm machinery, the second lowest valuation listed for the five farmsteads in our sample from the Smith settlement. By 1872 he owned six plows, one wagon, and one harrow. The list of other farmstead-related items is extensive and includes various carpentry tools, agricultural tools, and livestock-related gear. Given the larger machinery holdings listed in the Smith inventory than in the McGee inventory, and the lower valuation placed on Smith's machinery in 1850 ($75) than on McGee's machinery ($160), it is conceivable that Smith added significantly to his holdings between 1850 and 1872. Or, alternatively, in 1850 his machinery may simply have been worth less than McGee's.

Household articles listed in the Smith inventory include bedding (sheets, blankets, quilts, and pillows), curtains, carpet, lamps, guns, books, two heating stoves, a spinning wheel, and several pieces of furniture (beds, tables, a bureau, a clothes chest, and fourteen chairs). Kitchen-related items include a cooking stove, a meat box, a sugar chest, cooking utensils (pots, skillets, kettles, etc.), a coffee mill, a sausage grinder, and an assortment of ceramic, crockery, and glass vessels. Included in this latter group are ''2 crocks & jar'' and ''1 lot of Queensware.''

In summary, probate inventories contain a wealth of information on early households and farmsteads. Like other types of documents, they contain certain biases and must be used with caution. However, when they are used with other sources of data these biases can be assessed and often corrected. It should be evident from our discussion that probate inventories contain information that cannot be generated from analysis of the archaeological record. The opposite also is often true—the archaeological record may contain data not present in inventories. For example, the incomplete inventory of the Mappin estate, especially with regard to kitchen-related items, can be supplemented by excavation. Another area in which excavation is indispensable is in providing data on the subsistence practices of frontier households, which we examine in the following section.

Faunal Remains

In this section we examine the subsistence practices of frontier agriculturists as reflected in the assemblages of vertebrate remains excavated from beneath and adjacent to the Smith and Mappin residences. The identification and analysis of vertebrate remains was one important aspect of the work performed during the course of the Cannon Project. Research topics developed in conjunction with this work included taxonomically identifying recovered remains, identifying the origins (cultural versus noncultural deposition) of the remains, examining the exploitation of native taxa by individual households, and studying the use of domestic taxa by households.

A much broader treatment of the vertebrate assemblage than that presented here can be found in Snyder (1982). Our goal is to summarize data from the two sites and apply the results of analysis of these assemblages to the topics listed above. Based on Snyder's analysis, the two assemblages discussed here are representative of the other assemblages, though minor variations exist in the taxa present and the frequency of their occurrence.

Again, we point out various biases that may exist in the sample. First, excavations were restricted to areas beneath and adjacent to the residences. While these structures shielded the assemblages from the weather, allowing us to excavate intact faunal elements instead of badly deteriorated scraps, materials that might have been stored or discarded in other portions of a site are missing from the sample. Second, the activity of small carnivores may have biased the assemblages. Rodent gnawing and pitting, puncturing, and other marks produced by gnawing carnivores were noted on remains of a number of native and domestic taxa. This observation, coupled with the consistent occurrence of rat and domestic cat remains at the sites, suggests that both taxa may have been active agents in distributing and redistributing portions of the vertebrate assemblage.

Based on the considerations above, we recognized three general groupings of vertebrate fauna. Domestic food animals (pigs, sheep, cattle, goats, chickens, and turkeys) constitute the bulk of the assemblages. Although they are not considered here as a food source, horses and mules are included with the domestic fauna. A number of potential native food sources make up a second division. These include fish, ducks, game birds, white-tailed deer, cottontail rabbits, and tree squirrels. Fur bearers, which might also have been trapped for their pelts, are included in this category. The third division is composed of nonsubsistence-related or site-intrusive taxa, including cats, reptiles and amphibians, small birds and raptors, rodents and insectivores, and

Table 9.11. Summary of Identified Vertebrate Remains from the Matthew Mappin and Samuel H. Smith House Sites, Organized by Taxa

Taxon	Number of Specimens Mappin	Smith
Fish		
Sucker (Catostomidae)	11	1
Buffalo fish/carpsucker *(Ictiobus/Carpiodes)*	2	—
Carpsucker *(Carpiodes* sp.)	5	—
Redhorse *(Moxostoma* sp.)	13	3
River redhorse *(Moxostoma carniatum)*	—	3
Catfish (Ictaluridae)	78	5
Bullhead/channel catfish *(Ictalurus* spp.)	57	8
Black/yellow bullhead (*Ictalurus* cf. *melas/ natalis)*	5	3
Black bullhead *(Ictalurus* cf. *melas)*	5	—
Channel catfish *(Ictalurus* cf. *punctatus)*	23	23
Flathead catfish *(Pylodictis olivaris)*	1	—
Sunfish/bass (Centrarchidae)	21	4
Bass *(Micropterus* sp.)	36	4
Sunfish/bluegill *(Lepomis* sp.)	11	3
Crappie *(Pomoxis* sp.)	15	—
Walleye *(Stizostedion* cf. *vitreum)*	6	—
Freshwater drum *(Aplodinotus grunniens)*	34	1
Amphibian		
Toad (Bufonidae)	86	30
Reptile		
Turtle (Testudines)	5	—
Nonvenomous snake (Colubridae)	6	—
Avian		
Mallard, gadwall, pintail *(Anas* sp.)	1	—
Diving duck (Aythyinae)	1	—
Hawk, eagle (Accipitridae)	1	—
Marsh hawk (Accipitridae [cf. *Circus cyaneus]*)	—	1
Sharp-shinned hawk *(Accipiter* cf. *striatus)*	2	—
Sparrow hawk *(Falco sparverius)*	2	—
Cf. ruffled/sharp-tailed grouse (Tetraonidae)	1	—
Domestic chicken *(Gallus gallus)*	270	143
Bobwhite quail *(Colinus virginianus)*	9	4

other small mammals such as bats, skunks, and woodchucks. Taxa in this grouping contribute significantly to the size of site assemblages, and most if not all are at least indirectly related to human occupation of the site. We presume, however, that they were not exploited for subsistence or commercial purposes. Thus they are included in tabulations of taxa from each site but are excluded from further analysis. A summary of identified vertebrate remains from the two sites, organized by taxa, is presented in table 9.11.

Table 9.11. *Continued.*

Taxon	Number of Specimens	
	Mappin	Smith
Turkey *(Meleagris gallopavo)*	100	19
Great horned owl *(Bubo virginianus)*	1	—
Woodpecker (Picidae)	1	—
American crow *(Corvus brachyrhynchos)*	3	—
Thick-billed parrot (Psittacidae		
[cf. *Rhynchopsitta pachyrhyncha]*)	—	1
Perching birds (Passeriformes)	10	1
Mammal		
Opossum *(Didelphis virginiana)*	6	44
Short-tailed shrew *(Blarina brevicauda)*	1	1
Least shrew *(Cryptotis parva)*	3	—
Eastern mole *(Scalopus aquaticus)*	7	13
Bat *(Chiroptera* sp.)	—	2
Eastern cottontail *(Sylvilagus* cf. *floridanus)*	276	176
Woodchuck *(Marmota monax)*	3	3
Tree squirrel *(Sciurus* spp.)	180	191
Gray squirrel *(Sciurus carolinensis)*	5	2
Fox squirrel *(Sciurus niger)*	16	11
New World mice (Cricetidae)	1	—
New World mice/house mouse (Cricetidae/		
Muridae)	76	6
Vole (Microtinae)	44	3
Norway rat *(Rattus* cf. *norvegicus)*	493	53
House mouse *(Mus musculus)*	36	1
Raccoon *(Procyon lotor)*	1	15
Mink *(Mustela vision)*	6	1
Striped skunk (cf. *Mephitis mephitis)*	7	—
Domestic cat *(Felis catus)*	131	214
Horse (Equidae)	1	—
Domestic pig *(Sus scrofa)*	399	80
Cattle *(Bos taurus)*	12	11
Domestic sheep *(Ovis aries)*	—	10
Domestic sheep/domestic goat *(Ovis aries/*		
Capra hircus)	9	—

Mappin Site Assemblage

The Mappin site produced the largest bone assemblage (18,861 elements) of any site excavated, and the largest sample of identifiable elements (2,535). Fifty-four taxa are represented, including sixteen of fish, three of reptiles/amphibians, thirteen of birds, and twenty-two of mammals. Fish remains account for 12.7% of identifiable elements, reptile and amphibian remains for 0.4%, bird remains for 15.8%, and mammal remains for 68.4%.

Fish constitute a higher percentage of identified remains (12.7%) at the Mappin site than at any of the other sites excavated, with several species of catfish (*Ictalurus* spp.) composing over 50% of the class. Other taxa represented with some frequency are bass (*Micropterus* spp.) and freshwater drum (*Aplodinotus grunniens*).

Domestic chicken (*Gallus gallus*) is the predominant avian taxon; 270 elements compose 67.2% of the class. The remains of at least ten turkeys (*Meleagris gallopavo*) also were recovered. Although separating native and domestic turkey remains proved impossible, due to specimen breakage and damage by rodent or carnivore gnawing, the large number of elements recovered suggests a domestic, readily available source of meat. Native game birds and ducks such as bobwhite (*Colinus virginianus*) and teal (*Anas* spp.) also were present, although in low frequencies.

Both cottontail rabbits (*Sylvilagus* cf. *floridanus*) (276 elements) and tree squirrels (*Sciurus* spp.) (201 elements) were common, constituting 16.1% and 11.7% of the mammalian class, respectively. While some elements of these taxa undoubtedly are intrusive into the assemblages, cut marks observed on several specimens of both species indicate that inhabitants of the site exploited both taxa as native food sources. Unexpectedly, white-tailed deer (*Odocoileus virginiana*) are absent from the assemblages (only six elements were found in the combined assemblages from the six excavated sites). Perhaps the rarity of this popular game animal can best be explained by the drastic reduction of the North American deer herds by westward frontier expansion (Murphy 1970; Robb 1951).

Pork was the predominant domestic meat source, contributing 95% of identifiable domestic elements. All portions of the hog carcass are represented, and inferred ages range from less than twelve months to over thirty months.[9] Saw, cleaver, and/or ax marks, as well as cut marks, were noted on many specimens. Variation in the placement of cuts, such as for separating front hocks and feet from the shoulders, suggest home butchering rather than a standardized commercial operation. Other domestic taxa that butchering evidence implies contributed to human consumption were cattle and sheep.

Smith Site Assemblage

The relatively small assemblage from the Smith house site (837 identified elements from a total of 4,087 vertebrate specimens) contains thirty-seven taxonomic groupings: eleven of fish, one of amphibians, six of birds, and nineteen of mammals. Fish remains are, as at other sites,

---

9. Criteria used to age suid remains are the rate of epiphyseal fusion of select postcranial elements and dental eruption schedules for mandibular and maxillary elements.

predominantly of catfish. Domestic chicken remains constitute 84.6% of the avian elements and 13.1% of the total assemblage. Turkey remains constitute 11.2% of the identified bird elements and 1.7% of the assemblage. The remains of eastern cottontails and tree squirrels are plentiful, contributing 21.0% and 24.4% of their class, respectively. Specimens of both taxa exhibit cut marks.

Pig remains constitute 79.2% of domestic mammalian meat sources, cattle 10.9%, and sheep 9.9%. Specimens of all three taxa exhibit evidence of butchering, and both hindquarter and forequarter cuts are represented. All ages of hogs were noted, from younger than twelve months to older than thirty months.

Interassemblage Comparison

Although we discuss only two vertebrate faunal assemblages here, their similarities—both with each other and with the other four excavated assemblages—are striking. Regarding native taxa, each assemblage contains sizable frequencies of elements of tree squirrels and eastern cottontails in the mammalian class and of catfish in the fish class. White-tailed deer remains are absent from both assemblages. Of domestic taxa, chicken remains occur at both sites in about equal proportions to the entire assemblages (10.6% and 13.1%); the remains of sheep and cattle, however, are poorly represented (1.0% and .5% of the total assemblages for cattle). The underrepresentation of cattle bones might be due to postdepositional processes and to the ways certain domestic taxa were butchered. For example, the common whole bone cuts of pork (e.g., ham and picnic shoulder) are recognized more easily in the faunal assemblages than are smaller steak and roast round bone segments that result from beef butchering. In addition, the taxa represented by small butchered leg bone segments in the six assemblages often were not identifiable owing to extensive rodent gnawing. To attempt to overcome this bias, we calculated the minimum number of individuals for pig and cattle. The pig/cattle ratio is 6:1 for the Mappin site and 4:1 for the Smith site.

The high frequencies of pig remains allowed us to assess the parts of the animals recovered. At both sites, virtually all parts of the carcass are represented (table 9.12). The larger number of "low value" elements (i.e., cranial fragments, vertebrae, lower limbs, and foot bones) is probably a function of home processing and consumption of all edible portions of the carcass. An alternative explanation is that remains of butchering debris as well as of food processing and consumption are represented in the assemblages. Lyman (1977:69) suggests that distinguishing front from hind phalanges and metapodials might be useful in separating remains of food items from refuse resulting from butchering and carcass reduction. This is based on the

Table 9.12. Meat Cuts Represented by Pig Remains from the Matthew Mappin and Samuel H. Smith House Sites

Type of Cut and Associated Elements[a]	Number of Specimens	
	Mappin	Smith
Head cheese, stew meat, scrap		
Premaxilla/maxilla	15	
Maxilla		1
Malar		1
Mandible	12 (4)[b]	2
Miscellaneous fragments	7	
Neck bones, stew meat		
First cervical (atlas)	1 (1)	
Cervical vertebra		2
Thoracic vertebra	10 (3)	5
Lumbar vertebra	12 (8)	5
Ham hocks, pigs feet, stew meat		
Forelimb		
Humerus (distal)	6 (4)	
Radius (distal)	4	1 (1)
Ulna (distal)	3	1 (1)
Carpals	13 (2)	2
Metacarpals	25	4
Hind limb		
Tibia (distal)	11 (8)	
Fibula (diaphysis)	3	
Tarsals	34 (14)	8
Metatarsals	17	1
Phalanges		15
Roasts, chops		
Rib (proximal)	11 (5)	3

assumption that front feet rather than hind feet were preferred for pickling (Eakins 1924:311). The abundance of lower-limb elements in several assemblages indicates this might be a useful avenue for further analysis.

Although the frequency of cow remains is low at both sites, we note that both forequarter and hindquarter cuts of beef are represented in the assemblages as well as remains representing soup or stew meats and long-bone sections representing steak or roast cuts (table 9.13). Because of the biases noted earlier, steak, chop, and roast cuts probably are underrepresented in the sample.

Domestic sheep remains[10] also are relatively scarce; only seven elements were recovered from the Mappin site and nine from the Smith site. As we

10. In most cases elements could be identified positively as the remains of sheep. However, in a few instances it was not possible to distinguish between sheep and goats.

Table 9.12. *Continued.*

Taxon	Number of Specimens	
	Mappin	Smith
Shoulder/picnic ham		
Scapula (distal)	8 (5)	
Humerus (diaphysis)	5 (1)	7 (1)
Ulna (proximal/diaphysis)	10 (3)	
Ulna (proximal)		6
Radius (proximal/diaphysis)	12 (1)	
Radius (proximal)		8 (2)
Arm steak/roast		
Humerus (diaphysis section)		1 (1)
Ham/butt portion		
Innominate	1 (1)	
Ischium	3	
Ischium (anterior)		2 (1)
Ilium (posterior)	1 (1)	
Femur	2 (1)	
Tibia (diaphysis)		1
Tibia (proximal/diaphysis)	8 (4)	
Fibula (proximal)	2 (1)	
Ham/loin portion		
Ilium (anterior)	8 (4)	3 (1)
Ham/shank portion		
Femur (distal)	1 (1)	

[a]Principal meat cuts generalized from Eakins 1924; Levie 1967; U.S. Department of Agriculture 1903, 1978.
[b]Number of sawed/cut specimens in parentheses.

noted in an earlier section, sheep were common in the project area during the frontier period; figures from the 1850 agricultural census schedule show that sheep rank with hogs as the most commonly kept animals. Their apparent underrepresentation in the faunal assemblages is likely due to their function primarily as wool producers rather than as meat sources (cf. Bowen 1975). However, elements representing both forequarter and hindquarter cuts are present (table 9.14). Several elements show evidence of butchering, and we therefore assume that sheep contributed at least occasionally to the diet of the inhabitants.

Summary

In this chapter we have attempted to paint a broad picture of upper South households residing in the Salt River valley during the frontier period.

Settlers arrived in the Salt River region as participants in an economic and social system that in effect was transplanted from the region they had emigrated from. This system, termed upper South culture, determined in part how immigrants perceived the frontier environment and what economic and social adaptations were potentially most beneficial to them.

Several patterns of adaptation were examined in detail. Households in the project area tended to be large, and children usually were spaced two to four years apart. Based on our sample of households, wealth—as measured by land and slaves—was found to be spread evenly among interrelated families, so that "communities" were composed of families of roughly equivalent wealth. As we would expect, this wealth stratification was mirrored in other aspects of the households. For example, wealthier households on the average produced more grain, owned more livestock, and dominated the role of major producer.

Table 9.13. Meat Cuts Represented by Cow Remains from the Matthew Mappin and Samuel H. Smith House Sites

Type of Cut and Associated Elements[a]	Number of Specimens	
	Mappin	Smith
Soup/stew bones		
Cervical vertebra		1 (1)[b]
Chuck steak/roast		
Scapula (posterior)	1	
Arm pot roast		
Humerus		1 (1)
Beef shank		
Humerus (distal)	1	
Stew meat, foot bones		
Carpals	3	1
Metacarpal (distal)	1	
Loin/sirloin steak		
Ilium (left anterior)		1
Rump roast		
Femur (proximal)	2 (1)	
Hind shank		
Femur (distal)	1	
Tibia		1 (1)
Hock bones, stew/soup meat		
Calcaneum (distal)	1	
Rib roast, steak		
Rib section		3 (2)
Beef ribs		
Rib (shaft section)	2 (1)	

[a]Principal meat cuts generalized from Eakins 1924, Hamblin 1981, Levie 1967, U.S. Department of Agriculture 1903.
[b]Number of sawed/cut specimens in parentheses.

Table 9.14. Meat Cuts Represented by Sheep Remains from the Matthew Mappin and Samuel H. Smith House Sites

Type of Cut and Associated elements[a]	Number of Specimens	
	Mappin	Smith
Neck bones		
Cervical vertebra	2 (2)[b]	
Foreshank		
Humerus (distal)	1	1
Carpals		3
Arm roast		
Humerus (entire)	1	
Loin roast		
Acetabulum/ilium	1 (1)	
Leg of lamb		
Femur (distal)		1 (1)
Shank		
Tibia (diaphysis)	1	
Tibia (shaft section)		1
Tibia (distal)		1
Tibial tarsal	1	
Tarsal		1
Metatarsal (distal)		1

[a]Principal meat cuts from Eakins 1924, Hamblin 1981, Levie 1967, U.S. Department of Agriculture 1903.
[b]Number of sawed/cut specimens in parentheses.

The material goods of households included the essentials of feeding, clothing, and sheltering a family and operating a farm. The remains of food consumed by families indicate that, although the meat portion of the diet consisted in part of native taxa, domestic animals—especially pigs—contributed the largest percentage. Sheep, cattle, and chickens composed the remainder of the domestic animal contribution to the diet. In addition, the early appearance of wealth stratification, production of commodities, and similarities in subsistence crop production attest to the cultural homogeniety of the immigrants under the influence of upper South culture.

As the process of adaptation continued, however, residents began to break from established cultural patterns and to develop new perceptions, strategies, and goals. Several striking differences are noted. First, the wealth held by households in the Salt Valley was linked not to tobacco and hemp production, but rather to livestock and grain production. Second, slaves appear to have been important economically for large-scale livestock and grain production, but not for tobacco or hemp production. Third, inexpensive land allowed most immigrants to become landowners, leading to the development of a large middle class.

These changes occurred as a response to the unique combination of economic and social variables that formed the environment of the southern Prairie Peninsula during the first half of the nineteenth century. We have examined some of these variables, as well as the ways Euro-Americans adapted to them at the household-farmstead level. By integrating this level of analysis with that of the community and the region, we hope we can begin to understand the complexities of settlement and subsistence in frontier areas. The integration of these analytical levels is summarized in the following chapter.

10

Concluding Remarks

Michael J. O'Brien

Throughout this book we have attempted to demonstrate that the frontier settlement of the central Salt River valley of northeast Missouri was a dynamic process. Adaptations to this segment of the southern Prairie Peninsula—a broad, midcontinental mosaic of grassland and forest—changed constantly and rapidly throughout the first half of the nineteenth century as perceptions of these biomes shifted, technology reached the point where the realized niche began to expand, and exploitation of new areas became profitable. Previous chapters have addressed select aspects of the overall adaptation of nineteenth-century Euro-American agriculturists to a frontier environment. To organize discussion, components of the settlement system have been treated individually, including analysis of the regional settlement pattern and the physical and cultural factors that influenced the pattern; the development of communities and regional centers; and the social and economic organization of farmsteads and households. Observations made during analysis of these components have been compared with implications of the model of frontier adaptations presented in chapter 2. In this final chapter we summarize outcomes of this comparison and suggest ways the model can be revised and expanded.

The model is derived in part from ecological theory adapted by Hudson (1969) to explain the processes behind observable patterns of human settlement and in part from our views and those of others interested in the settlement of frontier areas by Euro-American colonists. Hudson's theory recognizes three processes of settlement; though they tend to overlap in time, they can be thought of as stages of frontier occupation.

During stage I, or the colonization phase of settlement, a population expands into a new area, which may be either a new environment, an unexploited portion of an old environment, or a new territory. There are several possible outcomes of this expansion, depending upon the fitness of the population. Settlement can expand along all preexisting vectors, along one or a few of them, or along entirely new vectors. Although agriculturists entering the Salt River valley in 1818 were preceded by French salt producers, thus making them users of unexploited portions of an old environment, it is more realistic to view them as entering a new territory. Dimensions of the physical environment of the frontier area, while in some respects similar to those of the source areas, were significantly different in other respects. The colonists had to decipher classes formed by various combinations of attributes of environmental dimensions and make decisions concerning settlement location. These decisions were made at two levels: the "macro" level, that is, in what part of the region to locate, and the "micro" level—which specific tracts of land to select.

The various context variables that entered these decisions can be placed into two classes: environmental and social. With respect to environmental variables, resources in the Salt River region were virtually untapped, and the model assumes that immigrants would attempt to maximize their access to important environmental characteristics. Since locational decisions may have been conditioned by individual or group perceptions of the economic potential of various environmental variables formulated in the source areas, the model proposes that the realized niche of colonists in the Salt River valley was similar to those of regions from which they emigrated. Analysis of settlement dimensions in other frontier regions of the midwestern and eastern United States suggests that included in a list of beneficial characteristics are good soils and proximity to the ecotone and to permanent sources of water.

Apparently as important as physical environmental characteristics in conditioning settlement were the social dimensions. The model suggests that locational decisions may have been influenced by group relationships established in the source areas. It further suggests that early locational strategies took into account the benefits of proximal settlement (e.g., cooperative labor and maintaining social ties) and that these strategies will be evident in the settlement pattern.

Taking into account these two sets of context variables—environmental and social—we proposed a compound settlement pattern: in some areas colonial settlement units were clustered owing to interdependent immigration, and in others they were random owing to independent immigration. The results of our analysis support this proposition. During the colonization phase there was, in effect, a two-tier settlement pattern. The upper tier, an aggregated settlement structure (Warren and O'Brien 1982), consisted of a series of settlement clusters spaced across the region. The common bonds within these clusters were based on kinship and intermarriage. The lower tier, a dispersed settlement structure (ibid.), varied from regular spacing of farmsteads along the ecotone to complex mosaics of landholdings.

The observed pattern of settlement within these tiers conforms fairly well to the predictions of the model. Given that environmental zonation in the region is composed of bands that parallel major streams, and that this zonation was important to frontier colonists, the model assumes that *in general* the realized niche of the colonists should be expressed as linear bands. General locations of land entries made before 1830 suggest that most were within one mile of a perennial stream; that nearly all were centered within forested areas, though many were near or on the prairie-timber ecotone; and that most appear to have centered on upland rims, gently sloping valley sides, or high bottomland terraces. Very few occurred on level uplands or low floodplains.

However, the model also recognizes the possible existence of environmental anomalies that may have crosscut the parallel zones—anomalies that may have been important to frontier agriculturists. One such anomaly is the occurrence of two areas of low forest density in the southwest portion of the project area. There the two low density areas crosscut the parallel zones, a phenomenon that appears to have attracted early settlement. Doubtless other physical anomalies that we are unaware of existed during the early colonial period.

In summary, two seemingly discrete sets of physical contexts account for most settlement during the colonization phase of settlement: forested upper valley sides near ecotonal boundaries and perennial streams, and forested rolling hills or bottomland terraces near major rivers. Significantly, the former association is more common and offers support for the proposition that forest-edge environments attracted frontier settlement because of access to fuel, building materials, pastures, and sparsely timbered soil that did not require a heavy investment of labor to clear.

The social dimensions of colonial settlement were treated in depth by examining three settlement clusters—the Smith settlement, the McGee settlement, and the Poage settlement. The first two originated during the second and third decades of the nineteenth century, and the Poage settlement originated between 1830 and 1833. All three settlement clusters were products of interdependent immigration, or the movement of interrelated families from a source area and the proximal settlement of the family units in the frontier. Analysis of interrelations among family units indicates that families immigrated simultaneously (as in the case of the Smith, Adams, and Johnson families) or in waves (as in the case of the Poage, Powers, and Stewart families and the McGee, McKamey, and other Mercer County, Kentucky, families).

During stage II, or the spread phase of settlement, the model recognizes two distinct processes: reproduction and immigration. The latter process includes persons not related to previous colonists and also those who had ties to established residents in the frontier region. Thus there is some overlap between this phase and the colonization phase. Although all new immigrants colonized previously unsettled areas of the biotope, for some the realized niche was essentially the same as that occupied by previous colonists. For others the realized niche expanded as they tapped new dimensions of the biotope.

In similar fashion, established residents expanded their landholdings either along previous trajectories or along new lines. The model suggests that colonial family units were composed of nearly mature offspring who began entering land of their own shortly after arriving on the frontier. Because of the many social advantages of settling near their kin, these offspring purchased land near that of their natal families. The effect of this process, termed budding, would have been the clustering of farmsteads.

The net effect of the processes of spread would be three distinct, though overlapping, settlement patterns: small settlement clusters within the niche space, larger settlement clusters within the niche space, and a random arrangement of farmsteads between the clusters. The first prediction is supported by data available from the Smith settlement. By 1830 all sons of Joseph H. Smith, Sr., entered land in the immediate vicinity of their father's holdings, and daughters married persons owning land in the same area. The second prediction—the existence of larger settlement clusters produced by continued interdependent immigration of families related to groups already residing in the frontier—is noted in both the Ely and the McGee settlements. In the latter, families from Mercer County, Kentucky, continued to arrive throughout the 1820s, settling near established families related to them by kinship or previous intermarriage. The third prediction—a random arrangement of farmsteads between clusters—is also supported, although the magnitude of independent immigration is difficult to assess at this point, given our incomplete knowledge of relations among family units other than those discussed here.

There also is considerable support for another settlement process that operated during the spread phase—the attraction of regional trade and service centers. The attraction of one center in particular caused a nonuniform pattern of growth across the region. After 1830 the region peripheral to Paris grew at a tremendous rate as residents and nonresidents alike entered land as close as possible to the center. This magnetlike attraction is not seen for other towns in the project area. Florida, for example, which was platted before Paris and for a time rivaled it in services and population, did not attract dense settlement. Thus the model should be adjusted to take into account the administrative services that a county seat offered and the attraction these services had for settlement.

The model also proposes that existing or planned roads were strong attractions for settlement. The location of pre-1826 settlement clusters along the few established roads through the southern and eastern portions of the project area indicates an early desire for proximity to transportation routes. In some instances later roads transected the realized niche (for example, the feeder routes through the Smith settlement), and new farmstead locations tended to parallel these routes.

During the spread phase, the realized niche expanded as a function of changes in the cultural system. Perceptions of the physical environment apparently shifted as a result of crowding—that is, as preferred niches filled up—and of the ability to bring the prairie biome into agricultural production. Expansion onto the prairie began in earnest about 1835, when large tracts of grassland were purchased by eastern speculators and residents began adding prairie to previous purchases. With changes in technology, such as the introduction of the steel plow and drainage tiles, agriculturists were able to reorder the economic importance of vectors within the biosphere. Although we have limited agricultural data before 1850, we suggest that this reordering of vectors effected sweeping changes in the agricultural structure of rural farmsteads. For example, fairly large enterprises that in the early 1830s were dedicated to livestock production and feed-grain cultivation would have been able to raise the capital necessary to significantly expand their landholdings onto the prairie, bring more land into production, and feed even more livestock. Smaller producers, who may not have had the requisite capital, would have been forced to remain at previous production levels and may eventually have been undercut by the larger, more economical enterprises.

In summary, the spread phase was a dynamic and very complex process that produced a series of overlapping settlement patterns in the Salt River valley and signaled the beginning of a host of significant changes in the frontier complexion of the region. Although we are able to identify the patterns—often through single examples—much more detailed analysis will have to be done before we can assess their overall spatial and temporal significance.

By the end of 1836 approximately 88% of the project area lands had been entered. Given the intense crowding that existed within preferred sections of the realized niche—despite the expansion of the niche as discussed above— we assume that this date roughly marks the beginning of stage III, or the competition phase of settlement. By 1850 the effects of competition on the settlement system become more clear. By that date the average size of the 681 farms listed in the agricultural census was 264 acres, compared with 189 acres for the period 1818–58. The number of farms listed in the census was 681, compared with a total of 1,164 entrants who entered land between 1818 and 1858. Thus these data suggest that smaller farms were being sold out to larger concerns. Also, only 7% of the 681 farms listed in the census were less than 80 acres, indicating that this acreage was about the minimum size for an economically sound farm.

The model predicts that competition among landholders reinforced the trend toward settlement regularity that first became evident during stage II. While available data support this assumption, more work needs to be done on this aspect of rural settlement. Since we assume that the competition phase lasted well past the terminal date of our discussion (1850), more modern sources of data may be appropriate analytical tools. These include late-nineteenth-century county atlases, which pinpoint farmstead and road locations and indicate community sizes and layouts, and United States Geological Survey topographic sheets, which show current locations of these same features. Together these sources, along with detailed analyses of land transactions between individuals, have tremendous potential for explaining settlement dynamics during the late nineteenth and twentieth centuries, and they should allow objective testing of the spatial implications of the competition process (Warren, O'Brien, and Mason 1981). For instance, preliminary analysis of modern farmstead locations suggests that the proposal of settlement regularity in space is generally correct. However, site densities clearly are biased toward level uplands and upper valley side locations and are relatively uncommon to rare in lower valley side and bottomland locations (Warren and O'Brien 1981). This indicates that the realized niche of agriculturists shifted toward extensive upland areas, probably early during stage III. However, detailed analysis of locational records will be necessary to quantify the extent of this shift and to evaluate the relative significance of causal factors.

Upper South Culture

Discussion throughout the book has referred to an economic and social system termed upper South culture. The model of this cultural system, derived from the work of Mitchell (1972, 1978) and others, involves the interactions between two agricultural groups—"yeoman farmers" and "small planters"—and their accompanying life-styles. Although the agricultural and social patterns of upper South culture can be separated for initial analytical purposes, the model implies that each pattern is tied intricately to the other, and in the final analysis they must be viewed together.

We examined several components of upper South culture, including the built environment and the economic and social structure of households. The analysis of structural attributes suggests that residence form often changed in predictable fashion and that house size was linked both to family size and to wealth. Based on our brief discussion of family size and composition, it appears that the average upper South family was large and that children were spaced out over a two to four year period. Analysis of vertebrate faunal remains indicated that, while a wide variety of native taxa were being consumed, the primary meat in the diet was the domesticated pig.

Perhaps the most significant contribution of the project relative to the study of upper South culture was the analysis of wealth and agricultural production. Based on the results of limited investigation, it appears that there are indeed two major socioeconomic divisions within the project area: an upper class with large slave- and landholdings and a middle class with small landholdings and one slave or none. The upper class was composed mainly of stockmen and grain producers, while middle-class landowners engaged in a variety of pursuits, including tobacco and hemp production. These findings necessitate substantial revision of the upper South model as it applies to the central Salt River valley.

For the Future

We hope that the work reported here has contributed in some significant way to the study of the American frontier and that it will encourage others to pick up where we leave off in an investigation of the processes that led to the development of the frontier. Although the study undoubtedly has value as a body of comparative material on the frontier, we believe its real value is in demonstrating the necessity for a formal theory of human settlement and for explicit models that account for those factors that contributed to the observed patterns of settlement.

As a burgeoning literature on the subject attests, the study of the frontier as a dynamic, often elusive state is becoming a fast-growing, cross-disciplinary field of endeavor. From our perspective, we hope some of this energy will be directed toward the analysis of settlement in the prairie and timber biomes of the Midwest. This geographic area has received considerable treatment in the past, but an almost endless number of avenues remain open for investigation. The ideas presented here can be tested with fresh sets of data from adjacent frontier areas, and new questions can be posed for future research. Only after this cycle has been repeated a number of times will we really begin to understand the complex relations in the frontier story of grassland, forest, and historical settlement.

References

Allen, L. F. 1853. *Rural architecture*. New York: Saxton.

Anderson, H. M. 1938. Missouri, 1804–1828: Peopling a frontier state. *Missouri Historical Review* 31:150–80.

Arensberg, C. M. 1961. The community as object and as sample. *American Anthropologist* 63:241–64.

Asch, N. B., R. I. Ford, and D. L. Asch. 1972. Paleoethnobotany of the Koster site: The Archaic horizons. *Illinois State Museum, Reports of Investigations* no. 24.

Ashton, J. 1924. History of jack stock and mules in Missouri. *Monthly Bulletin of the Missouri Board of Agriculture* 22(8).

Bakeless, J. 1939. *Daniel Boone*. New York: Morrow.

Baker, F. S. 1949. A revised tolerance table. *Journal of Forestry* 47:179–81.

Barlowe, R. 1978. *Land resource economics: The economics of real estate*. 3d ed. Englewood Cliffs, New Jersey: Prentice-Hall.

Barnes, H., and F. A. Stanbury. 1951. A statistical study of plant distribution during the colonization and early development of vegetation on china clay residues. *Journal of Ecology* 39:171–81.

Beck, L. C. 1823. *A gazetteer of the states of Illinois and Missouri*. Albany, New York: Webster.

Berkhofer, R. F., Jr. 1964. Space, time, culture and the new frontier. *Agricultural History* 38:21–30.

Bidwell, P. W., and J. I. Falconer. 1925. *History of agriculture in the northern United States, 1620–1860*. Washington, D.C.: Carnegie Institution.

Billington, R. A. 1966. *America's frontier heritage*. New York: Holt, Rinehart and Winston.

Binford, L. R. 1962. Archaeology as anthropology. *American Antiquity* 23:217–25.

——. 1978a. *Nunamiut ethnoarchaeology*. New York: Academic Press.

——. 1978b. Dimensional analysis of behavior and site structure: Learning from an Eskimo hunting stand. *American Antiquity* 43:330–61.

——. 1980. Willow smoke and dogs' tails: Hunter-gatherer settlement systems and archaeological site formation. *American Antiquity* 45:4–20.

Birch, B. P. 1971. The environment and settlement of the prairie–woodland transition belt—a case study of Edwards County, Illinois. *Southampton Research Series in Geography* 6:3–31.

——. 1974. Initial perception of prairie: An English settlement in Illinois. In

Frontier settlement, edited by R. G. Ironside, 178–94. Studies in Geography, Monograph no. 1. Edmonton: University of Alberta.

———. 1979. British evaluations of the forest openings and prairie edges of the north-central states, 1800–1850. In *The frontier*, vol. 1, edited by W. W. Savage, Jr., and S. I. Thompson, 167–92. Norman: University of Oklahoma Press.

Blalock, H. M., Jr. 1972. *Social statistics*. 2d ed. New York: McGraw-Hill.

Boggess, A. C. 1908. *The settlement of Illinois, 1778–1830*. Freeport, New York: Books for Libraries Press.

Bogue, A. G. 1960. Social theory and the pioneer. *Agricultural History* 34:21–34.

Bohland, J. R. 1972. Behavioural aspects of rural settlement. In *International geography*, vol. 2, edited by P. Adams and F. M. Helleiner, 704–6. Toronto: University of Toronto Press.

Bond, R. R. 1957. Ecological distribution of breeding birds in the upland forests of southern Wisconsin. *Ecological Monographs* 27:351–84.

Borchert, J. R. 1950. The climate of the central North American grassland. *Annals of the Association of American Geographers* 40:1–39.

Boughey, A. S. 1973. *Ecology of populations*. 2d ed. New York: Macmillan.

Bourdo, E. A., Jr. 1956. A review of the General Land Office survey and of its use in quantitative studies of former forests. *Ecology* 37:754–68.

Bowen, J. 1975. Probate inventories: An evaluation from the perspective of zoo-archaeology and agricultural history at Mott Farm. *Historical Archaeology* 9:11–25.

Bozell, J. R., and R. E. Warren. 1982. Analysis of vertebrate remains. In *The Cannon Reservoir Human Ecology Project: An archaeological study of cultural adaptations in the southern Prairie Peninsula*, edited by M. J. O'Brien, R. E. Warren, and D. E. Lewarch, 171–95. New York: Academic Press.

Bradbury, J. 1904. Travels in the interior of America. In *Early western travels*, vol. 5, edited by R. G. Thwaites. Cleveland: Clark.

Braithwaite, R. B. 1960. *Scientific explanation*. New York: Harper Torchbooks.

Braun, E. L. 1950. *Deciduous forests of eastern North America*. Philadelphia Blakiston.

Bray, J. R., and J. T. Curtis. 1957. An ordination of the upland forest communities of southern Wisconsin. *Ecological Monographs* 27:325–49.

Bremer, R. G. 1975. Cannon Reservoir area historical study. Technical Report no. 75-06. Lincoln: University of Nebraska, Department of Anthropology.

Brookfield, H. C. 1964. Questions on the human frontiers of geography. *Economic Geography* 40:283–303.

Brown, A. A., and K. P. Davis. 1973. *Forest fire: Control and use*. 2d ed. New York: McGraw-Hill.

Brown, J. H. 1981. Two decades of homage to Santa Rosalia: Toward a general theory of diversity. *American Zoologist* 21:877–88.

Bryant, W. S., M. E. Wharton, W. H. Martin, and J. B. Varner. 1980. The blue ash–oak savanna-woodland, a remnant of presettlement vegetation in the inner Bluegrass of Kentucky. *Castanea* 45:149–64.

Bryson, R. A. 1966. Airmasses, streamlines, and the boreal forest. *Geographical Bulletin* 8:228–69.

Bunting, T. E., and L. Guelke. 1979. Behavioral and perception geography: A critical appraisal. *Annals of the Association of American Geographers* 69:448–62.

Bylund, E. 1960. Theoretical considerations regarding the distribution of the settlement in inner north Sweden. *Geografisk Annaler* 42:225–31.

Byrd, P. 1951. The Kentucky frontier in 1792. Part 1. *Filson Club History Quarterly* 25:181–203.

Cable, J. R. 1923. *The bank of the state of Missouri.* Studies in History, Economics, and Public Law 102. New York: Columbia University.

Carter, C. E., ed. 1936. *The territorial papers of the United States.* Vol. 7. *The territory of Indiana, 1800–1810.* Washington, D.C.: U.S. Government Printing Office.

————. 1951. *The territorial papers of the United States.* Vol. 15. *The territory of Louisiana-Missouri, 1815–1821, continued.* Washington, D.C.: U.S. Government Printing Office.

Casagrande, J. B., S. I. Thompson, and P. D. Young. 1964. Colonization as a research frontier. In *Process and pattern in culture: Essays in honor of Julian H. Steward,* edited by R. A. Manners, 281–325. Chicago: Aldine.

Chang, K. C. 1962. A typology of settlement and community patterns in some circumpolar societies. *Arctic Anthropology* 1:28–41.

————. 1968. Toward a science of prehistoric society. In *Settlement archaeology,* edited by K. C. Chang, 1–9. Palo Alto, California: National Press Books.

Clark, T. 1979. *Historic maps of Kentucky.* Lexington: University Press of Kentucky.

Clarkson, J. D. 1970. Ecology and spatial analysis. *Annals of the Association of American Geographers* 60:700–16.

Connell, J. H., and E. Orias. 1964. The ecological regulation of species diversity. *American Naturalist* 98:399–414.

Conzen, M. P. 1971. *Frontier farming in an urban shadow: The influence of Madison's proximity on the agricultural development of Blooming Grove, Wisconsin.* Madison: State Historical Society of Wisconsin.

Cottam, G. 1949. The phytosociology of an oak woods in southwestern Wisconsin. *Ecology* 30:271–87.

Cottam, G., and J. T. Curtis. 1956. The use of distance measures in phytosociological sampling. *Ecology* 37:451–60.

Coward, J. W. 1979. *Kentucky in the new republic: The process of constitution making.* Lexington: University Press of Kentucky.

Curti, M. 1959. *The making of an American community: A case study of democracy in a frontier county.* Palo Alto, California: Stanford University Press.

Curtis, J. T. 1959. *The vegetation of Wisconsin.* Madison: University of Wisconsin Press.

Curtis, J. T., and R. P. McIntosh. 1951. An upland forest continuum in the prairie-forest border region of Wisconsin. *Ecology* 36:558–66.

Davidson, U. M. 1950. The original vegetation of Lexington, Kentucky, and vicinity. Master's thesis, Department of Botany, University of Kentucky.

Davis, A. M. 1977. The prairie-deciduous forest ecotone in the upper Middle West. *Annals of the Association of American Geographers* 67:204–13.

Davis, D. H. 1927. *The geography of the Blue Grass region of Kentucky.* Frankfort: Kentucky Geological Survey.

Dodds, J. S., J. P. McKean, L. O. Stewart, and G. F. Tigges. 1943. *Original instructions governing public land surveys of Iowa: A guide to their use in resurveys of public lands.* Ames: Iowa Engineering Society.

Dorsey, D. B. 1935. The Panic of 1819 in Missouri. *Missouri Historical Review* 29:79–91.

Dunnell, R. C. 1971. *Systematics in prehistory.* New York: Free Press.

Eakins, H. S. 1924. *Military meat and dairy hygiene.* Baltimore: Williams and Wilkins.

Eblen, J. E. 1965. An analysis of nineteenth century frontier populations. *Demography* 2:399–413.

Ekblaw, K. J. T. 1914. *Farm structures.* New York: Macmillan.

Elkins, S., and E. McKitrick. 1954. A new meaning for Turner's frontier. *Political Science Quarterly* 69:321–53, 565–602.

English, P. W., and R. C. Mayfield. 1972. The cultural landscape. In *Man, space, and environment: Concepts in contemporary human geography,* edited by P. W. English and R. C. Mayfield. New York: Oxford University Press.

Evans, P. A. 1974. Merchant gristmills and communities, 1820–1880. An economic relationship. *Missouri Historical Review* 68:317–26.

Filson, J. 1784. *The discovery, settlement and present site of Kentucke.* Wilmington: James Adams, Printer.

Finley, J. B. 1853. *Autobiography.* Cincinnati: Cranston and Curtis.

Flannery, K. V. 1972. The origins of the village as a settlement type in Mesoamerica and the Near East: A comparative study. In *Man, settlement and urbanism,* edited by P. J. Ucko, R. Tringham, and G. W. Dimbleby. London: Duckworth.

Flint, T. 1826. *Recollections of the last ten years.* Boston: Cummings, Hilliard.

———. 1828. *A condensed geography and history of the western states, or the Mississippi Valley.* Vol. 2. Cincinnati: Farnsworth.

Foley, W. E. 1967. Territorial politics in frontier Missouri: 1804–1820. Ph.D. dissertation, Department of History, University of Missouri.

Found, W. C. 1971. *A theoretical approach to rural land-use patterns.* London: Arnold.

Fowells, H. A. 1965. *Silvics of forest trees of the United States.* Agriculture Handbook no. 271. Washington, D.C.: U.S. Department of Agriculture.

Gates, P. 1960. *The farmer's age: Agriculture, 1815–1860.* New York: Holt, Rinehart and Winston.

Gates, P. W. 1942. The role of the land speculator in western development. *Pennsylvania Magazine of History and Biography* 66:314–33.

Gauch, H. G., Jr. 1982. *Multivariate analysis in community ecology.* Cambridge: Cambridge University Press.

Gilbert, M. L., and J. T. Curtis. 1953. Relation of the understory to the upland forest in the prairie-forest border region of Wisconsin. *Transactions of the Wisconsin Academy of Science, Arts and Letters* 42:183–95.

Gjerde, J. 1979. The effect of community on migration: Three Minnesota townships, 1885–1905. *Journal of Historical Geography* 5:403–22.

Gleason, H. A. 1926. The individualistic concept of the plant association. *Bulletin of the Torrey Botanical Club* 53:7–26.

Golley, F. B., ed. 1977. *Ecological succession. Benchmark Papers in Ecology, vol. 5.* Stroudsburg, Pennsylvania: Dowden, Hutchinson and Ross.

Gray, L. C. 1958. *History of agriculture in the southern United States.* Glouchester, Massachusetts: Peter Smith. (Reprint of 1933 Carnegie Institution edition.)

Greene, E. B., and V. D. Harrington. 1932. *American population before the federal census of 1790.* New York: Columbia University Press.

Gregory, R. 1965. *Mark Twain's first America: Florida, Missouri, 1835–1840.* Published by the author.

Greig-Smith, P. 1952. The use of random and contiguous quadrats in the study of the structure of plant communities. *Annals of Botany* 16:293–316.

———. 1961. Data on pattern within plant communities 1. the analysis of pattern. *Journal of Ecology* 49:695–702.

———. 1964. *Quantitative plant ecology.* 2d ed. London: Butterworth.

————. 1979. Pattern in vegetation. *Journal of Ecology* 67:755–79.

Gribbin, J. 1978. *Climatic change.* Cambridge: Cambridge University Press.

Grogger, H. E., and G. R. Landtiser. 1978. *Soil survey of Howard County, Missouri.* Washington, D.C.: U.S. Department of Agriculture, Soil Conservation Service.

Grossman, L. 1977. Man-environment relationships in anthropology and geography. *Annals of the Association of American Geographers* 67:126–44.

Haggett, P. 1965. *Locational analysis in human geography.* New York: St. Martin's Press.

Haggett, P., A. D. Cliff, and A. Frey. 1977. *Locational analysis in human geography.* 2d ed. New York: Wiley.

Haining, R. 1982. Describing and modeling rural settlement maps. *Annals of the Association of American Geographers* 72:211–23.

Hale, M. E. 1955. Phytosociology of corticolous cryptograms in the upland forests of southern Wisconsin. *Ecology* 36:45–63.

Hall, P., ed. 1966. *Von Thünen's isolated state.* New York: Pergamon.

Hamblin, N. 1981. Faunal analysis. In *The Lewis Weber site: A Tucson homestead.* Publications in Anthropology, no. 14. Tucson, Arizona: National Park Service Western Archaeological Center.

Hammon, N. O. 1972. The Fincastle surveyors in the Bluegrass, 1774. *Register of the Kentucky State Historical Society* 70:287–88.

Hardesty, D. L. 1975. The niche concept: Suggestions for its use in studies of human ecology. *Human Ecology* 3:71–85.

Harlow, W. M., and E. S. Harrar. 1969. *Textbook of dendrology.* New York: McGraw-Hill.

Harris, M. 1968. *The rise of anthropological theory: A History of theories of culture.* New York: Crowell.

Harvey, D. W. 1966. Theoretical concepts and the analysis of agricultural land-use patterns in geography. *Annals of the Association of American Geographers* 56:361–74.

Healan, D. M. 1974. Residential architecture and household patterning in ancient Tula. Ph.D. dissertation, Department of Anthropology, University of Missouri-Columbia.

Henlein, P. C. 1959. *Cattle kingdom in the Ohio Valley, 1783–1860.* Lexington: University of Kentucky Press.

Henning, E. C. n.d. Mappin: A Monroe County pioneer family. Manuscript in possession of author.

Hewes, L. 1950. Some features of early woodland and prairie settlement in a central Iowa county. *Annals of the Association of American Geographers* 40:40–57.

Hill, J. N. 1968. Broken K Pueblo: Patterns of form and function. In *New perspectives in archeology,* edited by S. R. Binford and L. R. Binford, 103–42, Chicago: Aldine.

Hodder, I. 1977. Some new directions in the spatial analysis of archaeological data at the regional scale (macro). In *Spatial archaeology,* edited by D. L. Clarke, 223–351. London: Academic Press.

Holcombe, R. I. 1884. *History of Marion County, Missouri.* St. Louis: Perkins.

Horsman, R. 1970. *The frontier in the formative years, 1783–1815.* New York: Holt, Rinehart and Winston.

————. 1978. Changing images of the public domain: Historians and the shaping of Midwest frontiers. In *This land of ours: The acquisition and disposition of the public domain,* 60–86. Indianapolis: Indiana Historical Society.

Houck, L. 1908. *History of Missouri,* vol. 3. Chicago: Donnelley.

Howell, D. L. 1955. Distribution and composition of primeval forests in three Missouri counties. Master's thesis, Department of Forestry, University of Missouri-Columbia.

Howell, D. L., and C. L. Kucera. 1956. Composition of pre-settlement forests in three counties of Missouri. *Torrey Botanical Club, Bulletin* 83:207–17.

Hudson, J. C. 1969. A location theory for rural settlement. *Annals of the Association of American Geographers* 59:365–81.

———. 1977. Theory and methodology in comparative frontier studies. In *The frontier*, edited by D. H. Miller and J. O. Steffen, 11–31. Norman: University of Oklahoma Press.

Hunter-Anderson, R. L. 1977. A theoretical approach to the study of house form. In *For theory building in archaeology*, edited by L. R. Binford, 287–315. New York: Academic Press.

Hutchinson, G. E. 1965. *The ecological theatre and the evolutionary play*. New Haven: Yale University Press.

Huxol, D. L. 1980. Quaternary terraces of the Salt River Basin, northeast Missouri. Master's thesis, Department of Geology, University of Missouri–Columbia.

International Geographical Union. 1975. *IGU Commission on Rural Settlements in Monsoon Lands (1972–76), News Letter,* 7–11. Varanasi, India: Banaras Hindu University, Department of Geography.

Jakle, J. A. 1976. *The testing of a house typing system in two middle western counties.* Occasional Papers no. 11. Urbana: University of Illinois, Department of Geography.

Jennrich, R., and P. Sampson. 1977. Stepwise discriminant analysis. In *BMDP-77: Biomedical computer programs, P-series,* edited by M. B. Brown, 711–33. Berkeley, University of California Press.

Jochim, M. A. 1976. *Hunter-gatherer subsistence and settlement: A predictive model.* New York: Academic Press.

Johnson, G. A. 1977. Aspects of regional analysis in archaeology. *Annual Review of Anthropology* 6:479–508.

Johnson, H. B. 1976. *Order upon the land: The U.S. rectangular land survey and the upper Mississippi country.* New York: Oxford University Press.

Jones, A. S., and E. G. Patton. 1966. Forest, "prairie," and soils in the Black Belt of Sumter County, Alabama, in 1832. *Ecology* 47:75–80.

Jones, G. N. 1963. Flora of Illinois. *American Midland Naturalist Monograph* no. 7.

Jones, R. L. 1956. Ohio agriculture in history. *Ohio Historical Quarterly* 65:229–58.

Jordan, T. G. 1964. Between the forest and the prairie. *Agricultural History* 38:205–16.

———. 1966. On the nature of settlement geography. *Professional Geographer* 18:26–28.

———. 1967. The imprint of the upper South on mid-nineteenth century Texas. *Annals of the Association of American Geographers* 57:667–90.

———. 1975. Vegetational perception and choice of settlement site in frontier Texas. In *Pattern and process research in historical geography,* edited by R. E. Ehrenberg, 224–57. Washington, D.C.: Howard University Press.

Kentucky Geological Survey. 1857. *Third report of the Geological Survey in Kentucky, made during the years 1856 and 1857,* assembled by D. D. Owen. Frankfort: Hodges.

Kershaw, K. A. 1963. Pattern in vegetation and its causality. *Ecology* 44:377–88.

King, F. B. 1978. Vegetational reconstruction and plant resource prediction. In

Holocene adaptations within the lower Pomme de Terre River Valley, Missouri, edited by M. Kay, 2 = 1–2 = 89. Report submitted to the U.S. Army Corps of Engineers, Kansas City District.

King, F. B., and R. W. Graham. 1981. Effects of ecological and paleoecological patterns of subsistence and paleoenvironmental reconstructions. *American Antiquity* 46:128–42.

Klippel, W. E., and J. Maddox. 1977. The Early Archaic of Willow Branch. *Midcontinental Journal of Archaeology* 2:99–130.

Kniffen, F. B. 1965. Folk housing: Key to diffusion. *Annals of the Association of American Geographers* 55:549–77.

Lemon, J. T. 1980. Early Americans and their social environment. *Journal of Historical Geography* 6:115–31.

Lemon, J. T., and G. B. Nash. 1968. The distribution of wealth in eighteenth century America: A century of change in Chester County, Pennsylvania, 1693–1802. *Journal of Social History* 2:1–24.

Levie, A. 1967. *The meat handbook.* 2nd ed. Westport, Connecticut: Avi.

Lewis, K. E. 1977. Sampling in the archaeological frontier: Regional models and component analysis. In *Research strategies in historical archaeology,* edited by S. South, 151–202. New York: Academic Press.

Leyburn, J. G. 1935. *Frontier folkways.* New Haven: Yale University Press.

Little, S. 1979. Fire and plant succession in the New Jersey Pine Barrens. In *Pine Barrens: Ecosystem and landscape,* edited by R. T. T. Forman, 297–314. New York: Academic Press.

Losch, A. 1954. *The economics of location,* translated by W. H. Woglom. New Haven: Yale University Press.

Loucks, O. L. 1970. Evolution of diversity, efficiency, and community stability. *American Zoologist* 10:17–25.

Loucks, O. L., and B. J. Schnur III. 1976. A gradient in understory composition in southern Wisconsin. In *Central Hardwood Forest Conference,* edited by J. S. Fralish, G. T. Weaver, and R. C. Schlesinger, 99–116. Carbondale: Southern Illinois University.

Lyman, R. L. 1977. Analysis of historic faunal remains. *Historical Archeology* 11:67–73.

McAfee, R. B. 1931. The history of the rise and progress of the first settlement on Salt River and establishment of the New Providence Church. *Register of the Kentucky State Historical Society* 29(87):117–32.

MacArthur, R. H. 1955. Fluctuations of animal populations, and a measure of community stability. *Ecology* 36:533–36.

————. 1972. *Geographical ecology: Patterns in the distribution of species.* New York: Harper and Row.

McGee, J. J. 1940. The McGee family. *Register of the Kentucky State Historical Society* 38:314–22.

McHargue, J. S. 1941. Canebrakes in prehistoric and pioneer times in Kentucky. *Annals of Kentucky Natural History* 1.

McManis, D. R. 1964. *The initial evaluation and utilization of the Illinois prairies.* Research Paper no. 94. Chicago: University of Chicago, Department of Geography.

Main, J. T. 1965. *The social structure of revolutionary America.* Princeton: Princeton University Press.

March, D. D. 1967. *The history of Missouri.* New York: Lewis.

Margalef, R. 1968. *Perspectives in ecological theory.* Chicago: University of Chicago Press.

Marshall, H. W. 1981. *Folk architecture in Little Dixie: A regional culture in Missouri.* Columbia: University of Missouri Press.

Mason, R. D. 1982. A regional chronology of the early historical period. In *The Cannon Reservoir Human Ecology Project: An archaeological study of cultural adaptations in the southern Prairie Peninsula,* edited by M. J. O'Brien, R. E. Warren, and D. E. Lewarch, 131–41. New York: Academic Press.

———. 1983. *Euro-American pioneer settlement systems in the Salt River region, northeast Missouri.* Monograph Series. Columbia: University of Missouri, American Archaeology Division.

Mason, R. D., R. E. Warren, and M. J. O'Brien. 1982. Historic settlement patterns. In *The Cannon Reservoir Human Ecology Project: An archaeological study of cultural adaptations in the southern Prairie Peninsula,* edited by M. J. O'Brien, R. E. Warren, and D. E. Lewarch, 369–88. New York: Academic Press.

Megown, J. 1878. History of Ralls County, Missouri. In *Illustrated historical atlas of Ralls County, Missouri,* 9–11. Philadelphia: Edwards Brothers of Missouri.

Michaux, F. A. 1904. Travels to the west of the Alleghany Mountains. In *Early western travels,* vol. 3, edited by R. G. Thwaites, 105–306. Cleveland: Clark.

Miller, A. M. 1919. Geology of Kentucky. *Kentucky Geological Survey,* Series 5, Bulletin 2.

Minot, G., ed. 1854. *The statutes at large and treaties of the United States of America,* vol. 9. Boston: Little and Brown.

———. 1866. *The statutes at large and treaties of the United States of America,* vol. 10. Boston: Little and Brown.

Missouri Botanical Garden. 1974. *Environmental assessment: Clarence Cannon Dam and Reservoir.* St. Louis.

Mitchell, R. D. 1972. Agricultural regionalization: Origins and diffusion in the upper South before 1860. In *International geography,* vol. 2, edited by W. P. Adams and F. M. Helleiner, 740–42. Toronto: University of Toronto Press.

———. 1977. *Commercialism and frontier: Perspectives on the early Shenandoah Valley.* Charlottesville: University Press of Virginia.

———. 1978. The formation of early American cultural regions: An interpretation. In *European settlement and development in North America: Essays on geographical change in honour and memory of Andrew Hill Clark,* edited by J. R. Gibson, 66–90. Toronto: University of Toronto Press.

Mohlenbrock, R. H. 1975. *Guide to the vascular flora of Illinois.* Carbondale: Southern Illinois University Press.

Montell, W. L., and M. L. Morse. 1976. *Kentucky folk architecture.* Lexington: University Press of Kentucky.

Morgan, W. B., and R. P. Moss. 1965. Geography and ecology: The concept of the community and its relationship to environment. *Annals of the Association of American Geographers* 55:339–50.

Murdock, G. P. 1949. *Social structure.* New York: Macmillan.

Murphy, D. A. 1970. White-tailed deer. In *Conservation contrasts,* edited by W. O. Nagel, 129–38. Jefferson City: Missouri Department of Conservation.

National Historical Company. 1883. *History of Howard and Cooper counties, Missouri.* St. Louis: National Historical Company.

———. 1884. *History of Monroe and Shelby counties, Missouri.* St. Louis: National Historical Company.

Netting, R. M. 1969. Ecosystems in process: A comparative study of change in two West African societies. In *Ecological essays,* edited by D. Damas, 102–12. Bulletin 230. Ottawa: National Museum of Canada.

O'Brien, M. J., and D. R. Henning. 1982. Introduction. In *The Cannon Reservoir Human Ecology Project: An archaeological study of cultural adaptations in the southern Prairie Peninsula,* edited by M. J. O'Brien, R. E. Warren, and D. E. Lewarch, 3–12. New York: Academic Press.

O'Brien, M.J., D. E. Lewarch, J. E. Saunders, and C. B. Fraser. 1980. *An analysis of historical structures in the Cannon Reservoir area, northeast Missouri.* Technical Report no. 80-17. Lincoln: University of Nebraska, Department of Anthropology.

O'Brien, M. J., R. D. Mason, and J. E. Saunders. 1982. The structure of historical communities. In *The Cannon Reservoir Human Ecology Project: An archaeological study of cultural adaptations in the southern Prairie Peninsula,* edited by M. J. O'Brien, R. E. Warren, and D. E. Lewarch, 301–35. New York: Academic Press.

O'Brien, M. J., J. E. Saunders, D. E. Lewarch, and R. D. Mason. 1978. *Cannon Reservoir Human Ecology Project report: Historic period research design.* Technical Report no. 80-17. Lincoln: University of Nebraska, Department of Anthropology.

O'Brien, M. J., and R. E. Warren. 1982. The approach. In *The Cannon Reservoir Human Ecology Project: An archaeological study of cultural adaptations in the southern Prairie Peninsula,* edited by M. J. O'Brien, R. E. Warren, and D. E. Lewarch, 13–27. New York: Academic Press.

O'Brien, M. J., R. E.Warren, and D. E. Lewarch, eds. 1982. *The Cannon Reservoir Human Ecology Project: An archaeological study of cultural adaptations in the southern Prairie Peninsula.* New York: Academic Press.

Olsson, H. 1979. Vegetation of the New Jersey Pine Barrens: A phytosociological classification. In *Pine Barrens: Ecosystem and landscape,* edited by R. T. T. Forman, 245–63. New York: Academic Press.

Owen, C. O., and Company. 1895. *Portrait and biographical record of Marion, Ralls, and Pike counties, Missouri.* Chicago: C. O. Owen.

Owsley, F. L. 1949. *Plain folk of the old South.* Baton Rouge: Louisiana State University Press.

Parsons, J. R. 1972. Archaeological settlement patterns. *Annual Review of Anthropology* 1:127–50.

Peet, R. K., and O. L. Loucks. 1977. A gradient analysis of southern Wisconsin forests. *Ecology* 58:485–99.

Perrin, W. H. 1882. *History of Bourbon, Scott, Harrison and Nicholas counties, Kentucky.* Chicago: Baskin.

Peters, B. C. 1970. Pioneer evaluation of the Kalamazoo County landscape. *Michigan Academician* 3:15–25.

———. 1973. Changing ideas about the use of vegetation as an indicator of soil quality: Example of New York and Michigan. *Journal of Geography* 72:18–28.

Peters, R., ed. 1845. *The statutes at large and treaties of the United States of America,* vol. 3. Boston: Little and Brown.

———. 1846. *The statutes at large and treaties of the United States of America,* vol. 4. Boston: Little and Brown.

Pianka, E. R. 1974. *Evolutionary ecology.* New York: Harper and Row.

———. 1978. *Evolutionary ecology.* 2d ed. New York: Harper and Row.

Pielou, E. C. 1960. A single mechanism to account for regular, random and < aggregated populations. *Journal of Ecology* 48:575–84.

————. 1977. *Mathematical ecology.* New York: Wiley.

Polk and Company. 1876. *Missouri state gazetteer and business directory for 1876–77.* St. Louis: Polk.

Pooley, W. V. 1908. The settlement of Illinois from 1830–1850. *Bulletin of the University of Wisconsin* 220, History Series 1:287–595.

Power, R. L. 1953. *Planting Corn Belt culture: The impress of the upland southerner and yankee in the Old Northwest.* Indianapolis: Indiana Historical Society.

Powers, R. D. 1931. Letter to James Powers, Greenup County, Ky., 1 January 1831. *Monroe County Appeal,* 13 August.

Price, J. E., and C. R. Price. 1978. An investigation of settlement patterns and subsistence on the Ozark Escarpment in southeast Missouri during the first half of the nineteenth century. Manuscript on file, Department of Anthropology, American Archaeology Division, University of Missouri-Columbia.

Reeder, R. L., E. E. Voigt, and M. J. O'Brien. 1983. Investigations in the lower Perche-Hinkson drainage. Publications in Archaeology No. 1. Columbia: University of Missouri-Columbia, American Archaeology Division, Department of Anthropology.

Richards, J. A. 1961. *An illustrated history of Bath County, Kentucky with historical and biographical sketches and notes and anecdotes of many years.* Yuma, Arizona: Southwest Printers.

Robb, D. 1951. *Missouri's deer herd.* Jefferson City: Missouri Game Commission.

Robbins, M. C. 1966. House types and settlement patterns: An application of ethnology to archaeological interpretation. *Minnesota Archaeologist* 28:3–26.

Rohrbough, M. J. 1968. *The land office business: The settlement and administration of American public lands, 1789–1837.* New York: Oxford University Press.

————. 1978. *The Trans-Appalachian frontier: People, societies and institutions, 1775–1850.* New York: Oxford University Press.

Ronnebaum, C. 1936. Population and settlement in Missouri, 1804–1820. Master's thesis, Department of History, University of Missouri-Columbia.

Rouse, I. 1972. Settlement patterns in archaeology. In *Man, settlement, and urbanism,* edited by P. J. Ucko, R. Tringham, and G. W. Dimbleby, 95–107. London: Duckworth.

Rowntree, L. B., and M. W. Conkey. 1980. Symbolism and the cultural landscape. *Annals of the Association of American Geographers* 70:459–74.

Saalberg, G. 1966. The status of New Madrid land claims in Howard County, Missouri. Manuscript on file, Department of Geography, University of Missouri-Columbia.

————. 1967. The New Madrid land claims in Howard County, Missouri. *Missouri Mineral Industry News* 7:67–79.

Sanders, W. T. 1971*a.* Settlement patterns in central Mexico. In *Handbook of Middle American Indians.* vol. 10. *Archaeology of northern Mesoamerica,* part 1, edited by G. Ekholm and I. Bernal, 3–44. Austin: University of Texas Press.

————. 1971*b.* Cultural ecology and settlement patterns of the Gulf Coast. In *Handbook of Middle American Indians,* vol. 2. *Archaeology of northern Mesoamerica,* part 2, edited by G. Ekholm and I. Bernal, 543–57. Austin: University of Texas Press.

Sauer, C. O. 1920. The geography of the Ozark Highland of Missouri. *Geographic Society of Chicago, Bulletin* 7.

————. 1927. Geography of the Pennyroyal. *Kentucky State Geological Survey,* Series 6, 25:134–35.

Saunders, J. E. 1979. Introduction to historical archeology in Cannon Reservoir: Preliminary analysis of two case examples. In *The Cannon Reservoir Human Ecology Project: Recent advances in the archaeology of northeast Missouri*, edited by M. J. O'Brien and D. E. Lewarch. Notebook no. 5. Lincoln: University of Nebraska, Department of Anthropology.

Saunders, J. E., and R. D. Mason. 1979. Historical archeology and documentary research. In *Cannon Reservoir Human Ecology Project: A regional approach to cultural continuity and change*, edited by M. J. O'Brien and R. E. Warren, 319–50. Technical Report no. 79–14. Lincoln: University of Nebraska, Department of Anthropology.

Schiffer, M. B. 1976. *Behavioral archeology*. New York: Academic Press.

Schiffer, M. B., A. P. Sullivan, and T. C. Klinger. 1978. The design of archaeological surveys. *World Archaeology* 10:1–28.

Schroeder, W. A. 1968. Spread of settlement in Howard County, Missouri, 1810–1859. *Missouri Historical Review* 63:1–37.

———. 1981. *Presettlement prairie of Missouri*. Natural History Series no. 2. Jefferson City: Missouri Department of Conservation.

Schwartz, C. W., and E. R. Schwartz. 1981. *The wild mammals of Missouri*. 2d ed. Columbia: University of Missouri Press.

Scrivner, C. L. 1961. Soils of Howard County. *University of Missouri Agricultural Experiment Station, Bulletin* 749.

Shelford, V. E. 1963. *The ecology of North America*. Urbana: University of Illinois Press.

Simmons, I. G. 1966. Ecology and land use. *Institute of British Geographers, Transactions* 38:59–72.

———. 1970. Land use ecology as a theme in biogeography. *Canadian Geographer* 14:309–22.

Sims, R. P., D. G. Preston, A. J. Richardson, J. H. Newton, and D. Isgrig. 1968. *Soil survey of Fayette County, Kentucky*. Washington, D.C.: U.S. Department of Agriculture, Soil Conservation Service.

Singh, N., and R. P. B. Singh. 1975. Some methodological components in rural settlement research. In *Readings in rural settlement geography*, edited by R. L. Singh and K. N. Singh, 26–40. Research Publication no. 14. Veranasi: National Geographical Society of India.

Singh, R. L. 1975. Meaning, objectives, and scope of settlement geography. In *Readings in rural settlement geography*, edited by R. L. Singh and K. N. Singh, 4–17. Research Publication no. 14. Veranasi: National Geographical Society of India.

Smith, B. D. 1975. *Middle Mississippi exploitation of animal populations*. Anthropological Papers no. 57. Ann Arbor: University of Michigan, Museum of Anthropology.

Snyder, L. M. 1982. *Unmodified vertebrate remains recovered from six Euroamerican sites, Monroe County, Missouri: A preliminary analysis*. Technical Report no. 82-01. Lincoln: University of Nebraska, Department of Anthropology.

South, S. 1977a. *Method and theory in historical archeology*. New York: Academic Press.

South, S., ed. 1977b. *Research strategies in historical archaeology*. New York: Academic Press.

Sprugel, D. G., and F. H. Bormann. 1981. Natural disturbance and the steady state in high-altitude balsam fir forests. *Science* 211:390–93.

Starker, T. J. 1934. Fire resistance in the forest. *Journal of Forestry* 32:462–67.

Stephens, H. A. 1969. *Trees, shrubs, and woody vines in Kansas.* Lawrence: University Press of Kansas.

Steward, J. H. 1955. *Theory of culture change.* Urbana: University of Illinois Press.

Steyermark, J. A. 1963. *Flora of Missouri.* Ames: Iowa State University Press.

Stone, K. H. 1965. The development of a focus for the geography of settlement. *Economic Geography* 41:346–55.

———. 1975. Multiple-scale classifications for rural settlement geography. In *Readings in rural settlement geography,* edited by R. L. Singh and K. N. Singh, 185–201. Research Publication no. 14. Veranasi: National Geographical Society of India.

Stottard, D. R. 1967. Organism and ecosystem as geographical models. In *Models in geography,* edited by R. J. Chorley and P. Haggett, 511–48. London: Methuen.

Strahler, A. N. 1957. Quantitative analysis of watershed geomorphology. *American Geophysical Union, Transactions* 38:913–20.

Struever, S. 1968. Woodland subsistence-settlement systems in the lower Illinois valley. In *New perspectives in archeology,* edited by S. R. Binford and L. R. Binford, 285–312. Chicago: Aldine.

———. 1971. Problems, methods, and organizations: A disposition in the growth of archaeology. In *Anthropological archaeology in the Americas,* edited by B. J. Meggers, 131–51. Washington, D.C.: Anthropological Society of Washington.

Styles, B. W. 1981. *Faunal exploitation and resource selection: Early Late Woodland subsistence in the lower Illinois valley.* Scientific Papers no. 3, Evanston, Illinois: Northwestern University Archeological Program.

Sutherland and McEvoy. 1860. *The Missouri state gazetteer and business directory.* St. Louis: Sutherland and McEvoy.

Swierenga, R. P. 1973. Towards the "new rural history": A review essay. *Historical Methods Newsletter* 6:111–22.

Taaffe, E. J. 1974. The spatial view in context. *Annals of the Association of American Geographers* 64:1–16.

Tiffin, E. 1815. *Instructions for deputy surveyors.* Washington, D.C.: U.S. Department of Interior, Bureau of Land Management.

Tomanek, G. W., and G. K. Hulett. 1970. Effects of historical droughts on grassland vegetation in the central Great Plains. In *Pleistocene and Recent Environments of the central Great Plains,* edited by W. Dort, Jr., and J. K. Jones, Jr., 203–10. Lawrence: University Press of Kansas.

Transeau, E. N. 1935. The Prairie Peninsula. *Ecology* 16:423–37.

Treat, P. J. 1910. *The national land system, 1785–1820.* New York: Treat.

Tresner, H. D., M. P. Backus, and J. T. Curtis. 1954. Soil microfungi in relation to the hardwood forest continuum in southern Wisconsin. *Mycologia* 46:314–33.

Trexler, H. A. 1914. *Slavery in Missouri.* Studies in History and Political Science 32–2. Baltimore: Johns Hopkins University.

Trigger, B. 1967. Settlement archaeology: Its goals and promise. *American Antiquity* 32:149–60.

———. 1968. The determinants of settlement patterns. In *Settlement archaeology,* edited by K. C. Chang, 53–78. Palo Alto, California: National Press.

Turner, F. J. 1893. The significance of the frontier in American history. *Annual Report of the American Historical Association,* 199–227.

U.S. Bureau of the Census. 1960. *Historical statistics of the United States, colonial times to 1957.* Washington, D.C.: Bureau of the Census.

U.S. Department of Agriculture. 1903. Meat on the farm: Butchering, curing, and keeping. *Farmers Bulletin,* no. 183.

――――. 1978. Pork slaughtering, cutting, preserving, and cooling on the farm. *Farmer's Bulletin,* no. 2265.

Vandermeer, J. H. 1972. Niche theory. *Annual Review of Ecology and Systematics* 3:107–32.

Vayda, A. P., and R. A. Rappaport. 1968. Ecology, cultural and noncultural. In *Introduction to cultural anthropology,* edited by J. A. Clifton, 476–97. Boston: Houghton Mifflin.

Viles, J. 1920. Missouri in 1820. *Missouri Historical Review* 15:36–52.

――――. 1923. Old Franklin: A frontier town of the twenties. *Mississippi Valley Historical Review* 9:276.

Voss, S. F. 1969–70. Town growth in central Missouri, 1815–1860: An urban chaparral. *Missouri Historical Review* 64:64–80, 197–217, 322–50.

Wade, R. C. 1959. *The urban frontier: The rise of western cities, 1790–1830.* Cambridge: Harvard University Press.

Walker, F. 1854. The first settlement of Kentucky. *De Bow's Review* 16:152.

Warren, R. E. 1976. Site survey and survey design. In *Cannon Reservoir Archaeological Project report* (Appendix 2), edited by D. R. Henning, 1–333. Technical Report no. 76-03. Lincoln: University of Nebraska, Department of Anthropology.

――――. 1979. Archeological site survey. In *Cannon Reservoir Human Ecology Project: A regional approach to cultural continuity and change,* edited by M. J. O'Brien and R. E. Warren, 71–100. Technical Report no. 79-14. Lincoln: University of Nebraska, Department of Anthropology.

――――. 1982. The historical setting. In *The Cannon Reservoir Human Ecology Project: An archaeological study of cultural adaptations in the southern Prairie Peninsula,* edited by M. J. O'Brien, R. E. Warren, and D. E. Lewarch, 29–70. New York: Academic Press.

Warren, R. E., C. K. McDaniel, and M. J. O'Brien. 1982. Soils and settlement in the southern Prairie Peninsula. *Contract Abstracts and CRM Archeology* 2(3):36–49.

Warren, R. E., and M. J. O'Brien. 1981. Regional sample stratification: The drainage class technique. *Plains Anthropologist* 26:213–27.

――――. 1982. Models of adaptation and change. In *The Cannon Reservoir Human Ecology Project: An archaeological study of cultural adaptations in the southern Prairie Peninsula,* edited by M. J. O'Brien, R. E. Warren and D. E. Lewarch, 85–100. New York: Academic Press.

Warren, R. E., M. J. O'Brien, and R. D. Mason. 1981. Settlement dynamics in the southern Prairie Peninsula: A regional model of frontier development. In *Current directions in midwestern archaeology: Selected papers from the Mankato Conference,* edited by S. Anfinson, 15–34. Occasional Publications in Minnesota Anthropology, no. 9. Minnesota Archaeological Society.

Watson, F. C. 1979. *Soil survey of Knox, Monroe, and Shelby counties, Missouri.* Washington, D.C.: U.S. Department of Agriculture, Soil Conservation Service.

Weisenberger, B. C., R. L. Blevins, and D. M. Hersh. 1963. *Soil survey of Bath County, Kentucky, Series 1959,* no. 30. Washington, D.C.: U.S. Department of Agriculture, Soil Conservation Service.

Wells, P. V. 1976. A climax index for broadleaf forest: An *n*-dimensional, ecomorphological model of succession. In *Central Hardwood Forest Conference,* edited by J. S. Fralish, G. T. Weaver, and R. C. Schlesinger, 131–75. Carbondale: Southern Illinois University.

Wetmore, A. 1837. *Gazetteer of the state of Missouri.* St. Louis: Keemle.

White, P. S. 1979. Pattern, process, and natural disturbance in vegetation. *Botanical Review* 45:229–99.

Whiting, J. W., and B. Ayres. 1968. Inferences from the shape of dwellings. In *Settlement archeology,* edited by K. C. Chang, 117–33. Palo Alto: National Press Books.

Whittaker, R. H. 1965. Dominance and diversity in land plant communities. *Science* 147:250–60.

———. 1967. Gradient analysis of vegetation. *Biological Reviews* 42:207–64.

———. 1972. Evolution and measurement of species diversity. *Taxon* 21:213–51.

———. 1975. *Communities and ecosystems.* 2d ed. New York: Macmillan.

———. 1979. Vegetational relationships of the Pine Barrens. In *Pine Barrens: Ecosystem and landscape,* edited by R. T. T. Forman, 315–31. New York: Academic Press.

Willey, G. R. 1953. *Prehistoric settlement patterns in the Viru Valley, Peru.* Bulletin no. 155. Washington, D.C.: Bureau of American Ethnology.

Winsor, R. A. 1975. Artificial drainage of east central Illinois. Ph.D. dissertation, Department of Geography, University of Illinois-Urbana.

Winter, M. C. 1974. Residential patterns at Monte Alban, Oaxaca, Mexico. *Science* 186:981–87.

Winters, H. D. 1967. *An archaeological survey of the Wabash valley in Illinois.* Reports of Investigations no. 10. Springfield: Illinois State Museum.

———. 1969. *The Riverton Culture: A second millennium occupation in the central Wabash valley.* Reports of Investigations no. 13. Springfield: Illinois State Museum.

Wood, W. R. 1976. Vegetational reconstruction and climatic episodes. *American Antiquity* 41:206–7.

Wright, C. D., and W. C. Hunt. 1900. *The history and growth of the United States census.* Washington, D.C.: U.S. Government Printing Office.

Wuenscher, J. E., and A. J. Valiunas. 1967. Presettlement forest composition of the River Hills region of Missouri. *American Midland Naturalist* 78:487–95.

Yellen, J. E. 1977. *Archeological approaches to the present: Models for reconstructing the past.* New York: Academic Press.

Zawacki, A. A., and G. Hausfater. 1969. *Early vegetation of the lower Illinois valley.* Reports of Investigations no. 17. Springfield: Illinois State Museum.

Index